RETHINKING
ADMINISTRATIVE THEORY

RETHINKING ADMINISTRATIVE THEORY

The Challenge of the New Century

Edited by Jong S. Jun

PRAEGER

Westport, Connecticut
London

Library of Congress Cataloging-in-Publication Data

Rethinking administrative theory: the challenge of the new century/ edited by Jong S. Jun.
    p. cm.
  Includes bibliographical references and index.
  ISBN 0–275–97248–8 (alk. paper)
  1. Public administration.   I. Jun, Jong S.
 JF1351.R4629   2002
 351'.01—dc21   00–052868

British Library Cataloguing in Publication Data is available.

Library of Congress Catalog Card Number: 00–052868
ISBN: 0–275–97248–8

First published in 2002

Praeger Publishers, 88 Post Road West, Westport, CT 06881
An imprint of Greenwood Publishing Group, Inc.
www.praeger.com

Printed in the United States of America

The paper used in this book complies with the
Permanent Paper Standard issued by the National
Information Standards Organization (Z39.48-1984).

10 9 8 7 6 5 4 3 2 1

Contents

Preface

This book brings to the field of public administration more than a series of related chapters. In attempting to rethink administrative theory, the contributors support the idea that thinking about theoretical perspectives is crucial for refocusing the study of public administration. The essays attempt to suggest new possibilities in improving administrative theory and public administration. The book has grown out of essays originally published in the journal of *Administrative Theory and Praxis* in December 1999. The contributors had the opportunity to revise and expand their arguments into full-length articles for this anthology. As with most anthologies, the chapters offer a wide range of styles and subjects, and yet the book as a whole provides a key to understanding the context of the essays that are contained within it.

The compilation of this book has given me the great pleasure of working with my colleagues who are closely associated with the Public Administration Theory Network (PAT-Net). I should like to express my appreciation to all contributors. They have helped me at every stage, keeping the futuristic theme(s) in their writing as well as meeting deadlines. I cannot take credit for their ideas expressed in this volume, but can for any flaws in compiling the book. I am particularly indebted to Lianne Campodonico for much needed encouragement and helpful criticisms, as well as her editorial support and patience. I also like to thank Richard Box, the editor of *Administrative Theory and Praxis*, for letting us develop the book based on the symposium issue.

Introduction: Administrative Theory in the New Century

Jong S. Jun

The twenty-first century lies ahead like a vast terrain, waiting to be explored with our imagination and our creativity. Much of the territory ahead is hidden, uncertain, and emerging as complex forces interact with one another. The challenge for administrators is not only to solve today's and tomorrow's institutional and societal problems, but, most important, to deal with ethical problems and understand complex human issues as well as to help improve peoples' ability to create changes in the future.

The new century presents the opportunity to ask difficult questions: Why do the structure and processes that we established in the past not work well? Why have public institutions not changed much while the world has changed dramatically? Why are the functions of centralized government and modernizing projects not appreciated by citizens as well as employees at the local level? Does the globalization movement contribute to human betterment and to the democratization of society? Can administrative theory offer new perspectives in understanding the complex and interactive world of the coming decades? Although we may not be able to find complete answers to these questions, they are important areas of concern to students of public administration and organization theory. These and other hard questions demand critical reflection upon our past, present, and future. As Robert Heilbroner points out in his book *Visions of the Future*, "Yesterday denotes an era in which we look to the future with confidence, because men and women believe that forces will be working there for their betterment, both as individuals and as a collectivity" (1995:11). He further provides a warning about this vision of the future: "To avoid the naiveté of Yesterday," critical examination of the past as well as "effective control over the future-shaping forces of Today" can serve as a guide for looking to the future. We cannot control the future, especially in dealing with unforeseeable external events, but we can query "the imaginable limits of our capacity to bring the future under our control" (ibid.:95-119).

In order to reduce uncertainty about the future, people attempt to forecast and introduce rational design when developing projects. But because this is necessarily done from the limited perspective of the present, the design is inadequate, because the future is unfathomable, evolving, and socially constructed. Although some of our anticipations may come to pass, the future depends most of all on our imagination, on our ingenuity, on our commitment, and on our compassion toward humanity today. As we begin the new millennium, we should reflect critically on the limits of the instrumental, technical, and rational characteristics of public administration and management of the twentieth century. Building on the lessons we learn from the past, we can experiment with new ideas to effect fundamental change in the future.

REFLECTION ON THE TWENTIETH CENTURY

The twentieth century may be characterized as a period of great transition between the industrial era and the postindustrial era, or between the modern period and the so-called postmodern period, with all that this implies for Western and some Asian countries which have achieved a postindustrialized state during this period. The transition from an agrarian period to an industrial state is still a struggle for most non-Western countries. Although the newly industrializing countries (NICs) in Asia seem to cope better with scientific and technological progress than less industrialized countries, people there are suffering from the crunch generated by rapid changes in consciousness, cultural norms, behaviors, expectations, activities, social realities, and a shift to electronic ways of doing things. Both industrial and postindustrial countries today attach value to rational, scientific, and technocratic activities because these have led to discoveries, increased production, profit, and a higher standard of living for an ever-increasing portion of the world's population. The emphasis on rationalism has inevitably conditioned our perceptions of the world. Now, the logic of science and technology is the dominant force in our lives. This way of thinking is so omnipresent that we fail to recognize that it permeates everything that we do: how we communicate; how we move about; the shape, style, and goals of our organizations; our aspirations; our perceptual processes; our worldviews; our reading habits; the television we watch; and even our human interactions. The very way that our minds work is affected by these values. Our contemporary civilization is so much the product of the technological revolution of the past century that we barely sense that any other possible perspectives or values exist—nor can we easily visualize life without the physical products of this technological revolution.

There have been, however, some challenges to this way of thinking. Marxists, of course, attacked the economic assumptions underlying the industrial era. The arguments set forth by social critics who recognized the inhumane characteristics of the industrial age are the most important. Among the authors of these arguments are Jacques Ellul, Eric Fromm, David Reisman, Rollo May, and the first generation of critical social theorists from the Frankfurt School of Social Research, such as Max Horkheimer, Thedore Adorno, and Herbert Marcuse, followed by Jürgen Habermas, and many other critical social theorists. The substance of their argument is that the industrial person has been socialized to react, rather like an automaton, to the stipulations associated with the need for order and predictability in industrial systems. This, as they argue from many perspectives, is antithetical to the basic qualities of human life. These thinkers challenge us to confront the effects of these values and behaviors on ourselves, and to take emancipatory action, creating a new culture, based on humanistic values, for the post-industrial world.

The twentieth century may well be characterized as an era of progress and of despair. Many industrialized countries have accumulated a great deal of material wealth through technological and economic development, and at the same time, have generated many undesirable consequences, such as a widening chasm between rich countries and poor countries, environmental degradation, moral decay, high material consumption, social injustices, worker dissatisfaction, the degradation of the quality of life, a loss of personal autonomy, and a loss of civic virtues. In the 1960s, Sir Julian Huxley cautioned us that the age of technology might come to exceed "man's ability to control it." Although technology helped to improve organizational efficiency, productivity, and competition throughout the twentieth century, it also was a factor in reducing individuals' autonomy and their potential for development.

With the new information technology, people have the opportunity to become more informed, learned, and connected; at the same time, their opportunities for face-to-face dialogue and shared understanding are reduced. Although the potential for future technology in organizations is great, it is important that we reemphasize our ability to control the use of technology rather than blindly commit ourselves to the trends in technological development and information (see Ralph Hummel in this volume). If science and technology are to be used to improve the quality of life (or working life) and are not to be detrimental to social justice or the environment, people need to be more critical of their implications. We should exercise more conscious influence over the governance of future organizations. We should, through reflexive analysis of our value systems, institutions, and communities, participate in the process of constructing the kind of organizational and global world that we want.

ADMINISTRATIVE THEORY OF THE TWENTIETH CENTURY

To keep pace with industrialization and the political and economic crises of the twentieth century, the field of public administration has focused much of its efforts in the development of management and professional capability, applying an organizational approach that emphasized efficiency and rationality. This organizational (or management) approach, however sincere, represented either the status quo, or only incremental changes in policies designed by policymakers and top administrators, which too often proved to be outmoded, unresponsive, and ineffective in resolving political or societal dilemmas. The intellectual efforts in the development of administrative theory were also skewed toward the adoption of scientific and technical methods as well as the structural-functional perspective. The practice of public administration in the twentieth century included at least five interacting perspectives that are largely opposed to democratic values and the democratic governance of public institutions: (1) centralized governing, (2) excessive dependence on instrumental and rational management, (3) influence of elite and professionals, (4) use and abuse of organizational knowledge, and (5) pluralistic politics in policy-making.

First, the strong emphasis on governing through national and subnational governments was beset with many perplexing questions that were related to democratic processes, goals, equity, equality, and participation. Although government and public institutions played an important role in promoting the values and needs of people, the excessive control by centralized government institutions often produced undesirable consequences, such as inefficiency, corruption, and people's dissatisfaction with programs. The ongoing struggles between national and local governments, organizations and individuals, and government agencies and citizens, pointed out the need for the improvement in interaction processes and discourse.

Second, the instrumental and rationalistic emphasis of management of the twentieth century worked to legitimize expanding administrative activities by establishing more rules and regulations, recruiting people to implement them, and adding layers of hierarchy to strengthen organizational control. Although bureaucratic procedures were necessary in order to operate large organizations, bureaucracy overextended itself by emphasizing technique and form. The expansion of organizational size certainly contributed to the bureaucratization of large public organizations, and, consequently, large organizations spent tremendous resources to develop an organizational capacity for information gathering. As organizations improved their intelligence capacity, they made the work environment more efficient, controlled, and coordinated. Organizational decision-making became more rational and analytical, using quantitative information to satisfy the information needs of the top administrators. It may be argued that the rational acts of administrators were based on good intentions: their wish was to accomplish organizational goals. With a rational-instrumental way of governing, however, the qualitative and ethical dimensions of human activity are grossly underestimated (Cantril 1967). U.S. Secretary of Defense Robert McNamara's role during the Vietnam conflict is a classic example. Nearly three decades later, he confessed that his leadership and policy-making role during the conflict was morally wrong. The Holocaust committed by Nazi Germany is an extreme example of the application of technical rationality that was blindly exercised by bureaucrats (Arendt 1958; Adams & Balfour 1998).

Third, the centralized governing and management emphasis was also based on the Platonic assumption that the professional people know what is best for the people, whether the context is the organization or a society. They were seen as experts with experience and formal training in specialized areas of work. They were loyal to the top administrators and also interested in promoting their vested interest. However, centralized government and management is important in a society that desperately needs to lift itself out of poverty, engage in short-term and long-term planning, and develop socioeconomic and administrative infrastructures. As was the case with foreign-aid assisting in developmental projects, the government played a significant role in mobilizing the people and resources (Esman 1991). Paradoxically, the continued emphasis on managerial responsibility (or the experts' responsibility) hampered the ability of nonexperts to learn to take responsibility for a project. After the departure of the experts and the discontinuance of support from the central bureaucrats, the community people were unable to govern themselves.

Fourth, the pursuit and use of organizational knowledge were, perhaps, based on good intentions: a desire to make organizations more efficient and responsive to people's needs. At the same time, however, knowledge gained by testing hypotheses and manipulating conditions was also intended to control human behavior. In fact, starting in the early twentieth century, many behavioral scientists and industrial psychologists believed that organizational knowledge could be used, through economic, social, structural, and technological means, to change people's behavior. Although the manipulative effects of managerial influence cannot perhaps be proven or eliminated, the issue is a serious ethical question regarding the right of people to participate in the organizational process. Many organizational development consultants using the behavioral science or systems approach attempted to change the motivational problems of workers as well as the leadership styles of managers. The irony is that although these manipulative and behavioral change techniques produced marginally positive effects, their lack of effectiveness did not prevent behavioral scientists (and organization development consultants) from continuing to sell their knowledge packages to client organizations as well as continuing to teach these techniques to their students.

Finally, pluralism, a highly visible development, particularly among democratic countries, was both an unanticipated consequence of historical evolution and the generator of a variety of unintended spin-offs. In either case, it had great significance for administrative theory and public administration. Pluralistic politics evolved in a natural way from circumstances prevailing in many countries during the formative years of representative democracy. In broad, societal terms, pluralism was very distinctly relevant to the concerns of public administration. To a large extent, pluralism simply refers to a governmental policymaking process wherein individuals or the representatives of interested groups may become directly involved in policy decisions. Where especially complex or important matters are concerned, dozens, even hundreds, of interests may interject themselves into the arena to try, through negotiation, manipulation, bargaining, bribes, expert witnesses, and so forth, to affect decisions in their favor. These lobbying interests may be gigantic or very small; ad hoc or long-term; loose confederations or highly organized structures; well financed or literally penniless—the system offers them a voice regardless. The growing criticism of pluralism raises a number of questions about how well pluralistic theory actually functions in the people's general interest.

Much of what pluralism represented was an unanticipated consequence of the movement from representative to pluralistic democracy. Included were threats to democratic government per se, risks to creative problemsolving, and other problems such as a lack of representation and public participation. Noteworthy too, was the fact, increasingly being brought to our attention, that public bureaucracy actually contemplated only certain kinds of problems in a serious way. Pluralism was worked well with problems that clearly related to a defined group. In such a situation, group attention was directed to alternatives and a position was normally adopted that was acceptable to the groups involved—or at least to a majority of them. A decision acceptable to society may not have been made; it may have been a decision acceptable to interest groups only. Furthermore, the mechanics of interest-group politics in many countries nurtured the weakness and corruption of government and public institutions. Theodore Lowi criticizes "interest-group liberalism," which is another name for *pluralism,* in his work *The End of Liberalism: Ideology, Policy, and the Crisis of Public Authority*. Lowi argues that there are high costs involved in interest-group politics. Most evident of these are the following: (1) the atrophy of institutions of popular control; (2) the maintenance of old and creation of new structures of privilege; and (3) conservatism, in several senses of the word (Lowi 1969). Pluralism has this effect: the bureaucracy and the political system resist change, are operated by an elite, and reduce public involvement. The sum effect is conservatism in the face of an increased need for flexibility and creativity, for innovation and change in government at all levels.

The implications of the preceding problems for public organizations are rather conspicuous as we begin the new century. The administrative theory of the past was predicated upon an instrumental rationality, which is a basic characteristic of the market system: it maximizes economic gains and lacks an understanding of human relationships (Ramos 1981). Reflexive, prudent practitioners know that the everyday world of administration is much more than the interests of influential groups and individuals or the implementation of programs designed by top managers and professionals. They know that they have to make an effort to involve the public so that they can learn how policies and programs are affecting their clientele. They also need to understand the evolving political context and facilitate the processes of creating various public spheres for discourse. Their administrative practice can be improved not only by applying scientific and technical methods, but also by gaining knowledge through nonscientific and qualitative methods. Thus, the challenge for future administrators is to realize the importance of the critical use of both scientific and nonscientific knowledge, and to consider the technical context as well as the broader human experiential context. Understanding the human context would allow practitioners to understand

and interpret local knowledge which entails human experience that is often hidden (Geertz 1983). In the future, the academics and practitioners will be responsible for the critical use of human knowledge that produces positive alternatives to negative consequences for people and for society as a whole. It behooves us, therefore, to be critically concerned with the activities that we are pursuing and the change processes to which we are contributing.

Furthermore, the strong management emphasis of the twentieth century assigned more responsibility to the top echelon of complex organizations, which ensured institutional domination over the people below. The management-driven changes of today focus on various "reinventing" projects such as organizational engineering to promote efficiency and productivity, building entrepreneurship, privatization, benchmarking, performance measurement, and evaluation. The new technological and rational approaches to the management of organizations have made the workplace somewhat more efficient and friendly, but they have ignored the broader human context of the society (or the community) as a whole. The question may be raised, to what extent is the philosophy of today's public institutions really different from the philosophy held at the beginning of the twentieth century? Although highly industrialized countries do better in terms of empowering people to develop certain skills, in many of these countries people lack the opportunity to expand their critical consciousness and their potential. In most cases, organizational change projects and community development projects are top-down, conventionalizing, and manipulative, with the people below having little to say about their design or implementation.

Since the 1960s, the literature on public administration and organization theory has reflected managerial attempts to integrate individual needs and organizational goals. These integrative efforts, however, have been carried out using a framework that retains the privilege of management. In the coming years, in order to achieve a greater integration, organizations need to place more emphasis on the fulfillment of individual needs and the recognition of people as unique individuals. Without developing the spirit of individuals, the extent and implications of organizational, societal, and ecological problems will remain mostly unappreciated. Furthermore, in this postmodern age of chaos and complexity, some authors stress that the changing concept of the individual self (see Michael Diamond in this volume), as well as a new consciousness of the self (see O. C. McSwite in this volume), is essential for understanding relationships among individuals, groups, and organizations.

THE CHALLENGES OF THE TWENTY-FIRST CENTURY IN A SOCIETAL AND WORLD CONTEXT

Since the early 1960s, postindustrialized countries have been experiencing an information revolution. It is changing our lives immeasurably, but we are inevitably inclined to view the impacts of information technology—and adopt it in order to improve organizational performance—in ways that we inherited from an earlier time. At the same time, information technology offers possibilities for promoting better human interactions. Technology (and information technology) can create new ways in which organizations can be decentralized and connected to promote better collaboration and understanding among people. It also helps people to become informed about, and involved in, networking and participation. However, we have to be more critical of the application of technology rather than passive users of it. Technology can be a positive force in improving work processes and policymaking, not just a rational means to enrich instrumental ways of managing organizations and society.

Clearly, the postindustrial, or postmodern, era is different in substantial ways from the world of the past. Information and knowledge are readily available, even to people in remote parts of the world, through telecommunication and Internet systems. This new technology not only helps people understand the external world, but also connects them with each other socially, culturally, economically, and politically. Interactions have moved from the global level to the local level, and vice versa. As a result of global interactions, countries are becoming much more multicultural and fragmented, particularly in the West. Profound changes and developments are occurring throughout the world, offering a broad range of implications for public administration.

Since the early 1990s, advances in technology, telecommunication, and transportation have accelerated the process of globalization in terms of exchanges of people, products, services, culture, information, knowledge, and ideas across international borders. Economic globalization has particularly suceeded in building the global market and helping both multinational corporations and consumers in the industrialized societies. However, it has created problems, such as unequal access to technology, wage inequality, environmental degradation, decay in local economy, and resource exploitation. To counter these disturbing trends, we need a different perspective on globalization, one that involves social movements such as people's involvement in transcending the consciousness of economic globalization, democratization, and sustainable development. Social forces could transform the old politics and administrative processes into emerging patterns of social interactions and interdependence. To understand new international transformation, we need to transcend conceptual orientations of state-driven global policy, rationalism, positivism, scientific research, and management because they are limited in reflecting changes that occur locally. By shifting our perspective to ways of understanding local conditions and social interactions, we could be able to develop deeper sensitivity to the potential for global, national, and local changes as well as conceptualize our learning in a new and different way.

With the continuation of globalization, our approach to coping with socioeconomic and political changes, as well as solving contemporary problems must go beyond the use of rational and technical analysis. Many problems will also have to be approached in the future through means that are less rational and more ethical and value-oriented (see O.C. McSwite, Louis Gawthrop, Hendrick Wagenaar,

Dvora Yanow, and Hugh Willmott in this volume). For the past four decades in American public administration, as illustrated by Dwight Waldo, numerous attempts have been made to apply structural and technical approaches to public problem-solving that involved distinctly nontechnical political and ethical issues (Waldo 1968). The U.S. models have also had both positive and negative consequences on other countries, particularly non-Western countries, in their efforts to introduce administrative reform (see David Rosenbloom in this volume).

Other theoretical perspectives are thoughtfully argued by the contributors to this book, revealing other ways of improving the organizational innovation, change, and knowledge offered by technical and functional solutions (see Michael Diamond, Thomas Clarke and Stewart Clegg, and Ralph Hummel in this volume). These perspectives require a better understanding of individuals in organizations and their relationships to a changing world. In the future, we may serve the public good most through the ways in which we work; through personal autonomy, growth, renewal, and the development of processes to enhance collaboration and participation.

Indeed, in a time of rapid change, unanticipated dysfunctional consequences are likely due to management-driven change projects and rigid adherence to goals. We are likely to derive great advantages from liberating ourselves of organizational goal commitments. Instead, we can develop more open and democratic possibilities, understand problems collectively, and develop future plans through democratic discourse and dialogue (see John Forester, David Farmer, and Jong Jun in this volume). Institutions need to protect individual autonomy and, at the same time, find ways of encouraging people to participate in the collaborative process. It will also be the responsibility of future administrators to facilitate all forms of public discourse so that citizens can engage in their own self-governance, and government agencies can provide support resources for citizens and group actions. In such a context, the process we employ may be positive and developmental; it may make a visible, felt impact on the networking activities of society and the world. It may prove to be the proper route to an effective and continuously emerging human experience.

In the context of an interactive and democratic process, participants are not asked to "sacrifice themselves," "join in the crusade," "pitch in and help out," or in other words, to achieve in the way traditional communitarianism espouses. Instead, they are offered an equal opportunity for personal autonomy and growth, as well as a chance to make a socially significant contribution (Jun 1998). But their own development is perceived as no less socially relevant than the seemingly larger, but intersubjectively rational and ephemeral, objectives of the collective project itself. These objectives are a guide for communicative rational action and an opportunity for ethical action (Jürgen Habermas 1984; 1996). Current trends in social sciences reflect some of the values I have discussed thus far. The problem is that democratic alternatives do not appear possible within the value framework that currently enshrouds the field of public administration and management-oriented organization theory.

THE THEORETICAL CHALLENGES OF THE TWENTY-FIRST CENTURY

As we begin the twenty-first century, we are groping for new theoretical perspectives that will help us to make radical departures from the management-driven approach that emphasizes the strong administrative state. Thus, we need to recapitulate and rethink some of the fundamental beliefs and management orientations that I have implicitly or explicitly addressed in the preceding pages. Whether or not the promotion of democratic governance and values possesses a philosophy that is sufficient to meet the challenges of the new century is a fair question. I like to think that the democracy movement, especially its focus on putting public administration and management in the broader context of society and the world, provides that philosophical perspective. As public administration in the twentieth century promoted the administrative state with a strong emphasis on the role of government and professionals, this new century may well be called "the democratic century," in which democracy, administration, and civil society work together in a triangle relationship.

For most of the twentieth century, the influential people in the top echelons of institutions the world over rarely gave much thought to consistency, adequacy, equality, or equity in governing and managing society and institutions. Managers and academics in public administration did not critically reflect on the reasons for rational-instrumental solutions and the implications of these solutions. We were too confident in our convictions, too sure of our inevitable economic and technological progress, and too convinced that we understood how to run large organizations in the most efficient way possible. Today we have emerged into an uncertain interlude of economic prosperity, technological development, and instability in industrialized countries. Progress has inspired our feelings of material satisfaction, rationalism, and psychological security.

But the administrative theories that we practice today will not be adequate to meet the challenges of the coming decades as we deal with democratic agendas. In order to make public institutions more effective in democratic governance, new theoretical perspectives are needed so that old concepts can be critically reevaluated and, if necessary, discarded in order to create profound change based on new ideas and new perspectives. This endeavor, of course, requires our commitment to developing a socially grounded and value-oriented administrative theory that is not blindly led by technologically or management-driven organizational change. This work also requires that we confront future organizations with open minds in relation to the environment, people, and networking possibilities.

In the twentieth century, public administration theories focused on the improvement of internal management: structural and functional coordination as well as organizational performance. This focus represented a heavy commitment to the highly rationalized, positivistic, bureaucratic organizational model so precisely cultivated during the waning decades of the industrial era. It was yet another form of technocratic ideology. Our continued use of this approach means that we are attempting to solve the problems of today and confront those of tomorrow with a perilously outmoded organizational model and theoretical perspective.

The management approach to governing and change is premised on the notion that bureaucracies—their rules and regulations, roles and positions, and functional relationships—set the boundaries of social reality within which change and coordination must occur. For example, government reforms are essentially rearrangements of power, structure, and functions to achieve the agency goals. In most cases of reform, reformers assume that the management's approach to change will solve immediate organizational and functional concerns. The desires and concerns of workers and citizens are not adequately addressed. When change is implemented in the public arena, governmental reform frequently faces resistance because people see the problem differently and argue that the approach designed by management is not the only one available.

Critics of the public management approach argue that public employees are working for management and not the public, implementing organizational rules and regulations, providing executives and managers with information, and measuring the progress made toward accomplishing goals. In the past three decades, management has become more aware of strategies for making organizational work efficient, and has implemented methods aimed at improving workers' behavior. In the 1990s, borrowing ideas from the private sector, public administration has become more aware of the needs for "reengineering" (or "reinventing") government, client (or customer) services, and performance measurement (see Yiannis Gabriel, Francesco Cerase, Thomas Clarke and Stewart Clegg in this volume). Management techniques provide employees with some sense of participation and involvement: they are given some limited opportunities to make choices, and thus find some meaning in their jobs. Management of efficiency and productivity is widely seen as legitimate, because no reasonable person would disagree with the importance of improving public services. However, the responsibility of public organizations goes beyond how well they are managed internally. And because internal changes are also affected by external forces, public organizations cannot be passive toward citizens and view them as customers of their services. It is more appropriate to see citizens as advocates. They demand not only a change in the behavior and conduct of public administrators, but also in the processes of governance; in many circumstances, they perceive themselves as the owners of the government, because they pay for its services.

In this context, change is paradoxical in the sense that we cannot find a systematic path to organizational change or community planning. In the practice of planning, at least in the United States, alternatives are developed through continuous discourse and dialogue among the stakeholders by engaging in the deliberative and open-ended process of agreement and disagreement. It is also paradoxical because change requires changes in the consciousness of both public administrators and people outside government institutions. Democratic deliberation in the public sphere offers no guarantee of success. But neither do the deliberations of organizations and managerial leadership. What democratic participation and deliberation offer is a creative process for energizing people. Through the participatory nature of rational discourse and mutual understanding, people may be able to develop a better sense of ethics and consensual values (see Louis Gawthrop, Curtis Ventriss, Hendrik Wagenaar, and Dvora Yanow and Hugh Willmott in this volume).

Scholars and practitioners of public administration today find themselves in transition: they are changing their perspective from one that focuses on knowledge about governing and managing organizations, to one that looks at new ways of collaborating with people as well as facilitating processes of innovation. This transformation of orientation inevitably puts more emphasis on the critical examination of hierarchical relationships and vertical communication, pointing out the change in consciousness of top administrators and managers that is required for them to see the value of less hierarchical, horizontal relationships and democratic discourse. When organizational and public space is created that is less threatening to people, more meaningful participation of people will occur in political and organizational processes.

In the future, there will most likely be continuing attempts to promote rational approaches to complex problems, such as rational choice theory, comprehensive planning, cyber governance, and computer simulations; but these rational approaches can never fully provide satisfactory explanations of hidden human problems or the symbolic aspects of institutions and politics. Managers in rationally and centrally governed societies may try to develop grand schemes for rearranging the social world, but they cannot take the place of the humanistic and value-oriented community in designing the future workplace. First, human problems require reflexive interpretation, discourse, dialogue, people relations, and democratic process. After that, rational design and problem solving may occur. Although we may not be able to resist the technological influence in some areas, we need to seek, with our imaginations, democratic possibilities. The impetus toward rational and technical solutions today is utterly hostile to democratic governance as well as the empowerment of citizens and groups because of the power and influence vested in science and technology, rational policy analysts, and professional public servants. It is urgently necessary that administrators and managers of tomorrow's institutions become aware of democratic possibilities for enhancing individual autonomy and collective action: this will enhance people's trust, care, and ability to self-govern.

THE PURPOSE OF THE BOOK

The purpose of this book is suggested by its title: *Rethinking Administrative Theory: The Challenge of the New Century.* Ideas discussed by the authors contributing to this book can help us understand human and organizational issues as the coming decades unfold. The book does not express all of our ideas and theoretical arguments: no single volume could. But this book, I believe, shows the authors' seriousness about changing our approaches to the study of public administration and organization theory. Although the most conspicuous development in public administration in the twentieth century was the growth of bureaucracy and the professionalization of the public service, the major theme of this book is that the new century requires democratic governance, which is characterized by a broader public concept of public administration, beyond consumerism and management, beyond the rational-instrumental justification of administrative legitimacy. Democratic government entails democratic ethics and virtues, value-pluralism, relationships and networking, participation, and public discourse to promote public deliberation.

The essays in this book encourage the development of diverse perspectives that will lead to a more unrestrained engagement in the search for theoretical approaches to understanding complex phenomena. Thus we may rethink or alter the paradigms, frames, or perspectives within which we now labor, too often fruitlessly, in an attempt to achieve an adequate balance between organizational goals and individual needs, as well as between individual autonomy and the public good. The contributors are concerned with a broader understanding of public administration, particularly the responsibility of public administrators to be relevant to the needs of the world: those of society, institutions, and citizens.

Theoretical arguments made by the contributors assume that it is impossible to genuinely understand new problems with old theories. And although many old problems still remain with us, they should be critically examined from new perspectives because of the changing context of society and the world. Are the theoretical ideas presented in this book completely new? Most are not really new, but they touch on significant issues of contemporary organizations. As Martin Parker points out, perhaps "This text as already been written by someone else," at least some part of it. Some of the contributors to this book advocate adopting a new paradigm perspective (see Thomas Clarke and Stewart Clegg). Shifting from an established frame to a new one requires critical reflexivity on the part of the practitioner. As a scholar searching for dialectical, social, and democratic possibilities, I am aware that scholars often advance theoretical metamorphoses without giving critical attention to current traditions, institutional history, or administrative culture. Because of the fragmentation, diversity, and complexity of the social world, it is hard to know what concepts and ideas will be most relevant to the challenges of the future. Some important ideas that scholars advance, whether late modernist, critical modernist, or postmodernist, introduce the importance of relationships and interconnectedness, discourse and dialogue, ethical responsibility, compassion toward other human beings, trust building, and value-oriented administration. These features are highly qualitative aspects of effective organizations and democratic governance. They cannot be reduced to rational, instrumental, or technical explanations.

In this book, the contributors present their theoretical perspectives reflecting on the development of administrative and management theory in the late twentieth century, and make some normative assertions about theoretical directions in the coming decades as opposed to an empirical analysis of trend indicators. The content of the book encompasses not only the administrative and management issues of large organizations, but also a reexamination of the purpose and the *publicness* of public administration (see Curtis Ventriss, Yiannis Gabriel, and Francesco Cerase in this volume). Some authors stress unrestricted discourse and imagination (David Farmer and O.C. McSwite in this volume): others see the need for a dialectical process in which alternative ideas may be explored through social interactions, as well as a critical reflection on the past, the present, and the future (see Michael Diamond, M. Shamsul Haque, John Forester, and Jong Jun). The Bogason essay presents a critical assessment of the literature on postmodern conditions and its implications for research activity in public administration. Ideas presented in this book do not, of course, represent all current democratically oriented theoretical perspectives on public administration. This book does, however, represent a broad sampling of humane, inclusive approaches to public administration

REFERENCES

Adams, G. B., and Balfour, D. L. 1998. *Unmasking Administrative Evil.* Thousand Oaks, CA: Sage Publications.

Arendt, H. 1958. *The Human Condition.* Chicago: The University of Chicago Press.

Cantril, H. 1967. *The Human Dimensions: Experiences in Policy Research.* New Brunswick, NJ: Rutgers University Press.

Esman, M. 1991. *Management Dimensions of Development: Perspectives and Strategies.* West Hartford, CT: Kumarian Press.

Geertz, C. 1983. *Local Knowledge.* New York: Basic Books.

Habermas, J. 1996. *Between Facts and Norms,* Translated by W. Rehg. Cambridge, MA: The MIT Press.

————.1984. *The Theory of Communicative Action*, Translated by. T. McCarthy, Boston, MA: Beacon Press. Vol. 1.

Heilbroner, R. 1995. *Visions of the Future.* New York: Oxford University Press.

Jun, J. S. 1998. The Need for Autonomy and Virtues: Civic-Minded Administrators in a Civil Society. *Administrative Theory and Praxis.* 21(2):218-26.

Lowi, T. J. 1969. *The End of Liberalism: Ideology, Policy, and the Crisis of Public Authority.* New York: Norton.

Ramos, A. G. 1981. *The New Science of Organizations: A Reconceptualization of the Wealth of Nations.* Toronto: University of Toronto Press.

Waldo, D. 1968. Public Administration in a Time of Revolution. *Public Administration Review.* (January-February), 28(1):362-68.

PART ONE

The Need For Rethinking

INTRODUCTION

Because of the inadequacy of current administrative theory, as well as the need for improving administrative praxis, the search for new theoretical perspective is an ongoing concern of academics and practitioners. To explore alternative approaches, we need to begin with the task of critically reflecting on current thinking of administrative theory. In attempting to rethink administrative theory, the authors believe that thinking about theoretical implications in the broader context is critical for exploring future possibilities.

The article by O.C. McSwite argues that the debate between capitalist (open) systems and socialist (planned) systems has become moot, just as in the field of leadership theory when leadership moved from a unidimensional democratic-authoritarian model to a two dimensional framework. The legitimacy issue, and the "Man of Reason" form of administrative governance it legitimated, is over. In the same vein, the spread of market psychology has moved social thought from an ontology of individualism to one that sees human beings as socially situated and produced. The principal-agent model of administrative responsibility is thus an anachronism. The pathologies of the modernist episode are becoming manifest and broadly evident in post-modernism. Such changes open new possibilities for an epistemology that resolves the differences between structuralist and post-structuralist perspectives, and for an ontology that shows the human being as more than an ego. According to McSwite, the implication for public administration is that it can drop the debate over legitimacy, see administrative responsibility as a matter of cooperation, and consider efficiency a natural and compatible aspect of democratic administrative governance.

Yiannis Gabriel argues that the twentieth century has been characterized by a decline in the influence and prestige of administration and a concomitant rise of management. Management has expanded largely on the back of the consumer, its political and ideological champion. By contrast, the champion of administration, the citizen, has become an increasingly distant figure, whose outlook, concern, and practices are continuously displaced by consumerism. While consumerism displays a remarkable ability to colonize most dimensions of human existence, the willingness and abilities to critique it have been undermined by the rise of postmodern theorizing. Critique, stripped of its humanistic heritage, is easily accommodated and defused by a set of consumer discourses which thrive on difference and celebrate controversy. He raises some doubts on the continuing ability of consumerism to accommodate the political, environmental, and technological challenges that lie ahead.

The article by Martin Parker is a re-thinking of the conditions of possibility for asking questions about "future challenges in organization theory." He suggests, through a variety of textual devices, that memory is central to this question. What counts as the "future," as a legitimate "challenge," and as "organization theory," are matters which are constituted through amnesia. His themes will therefore be remembering, forgetting, and the production of ignorance, not as a way of criticizing the present for the crime of having forgotten its past, but as constituent elements in the very making of disciplinary knowledge itself.

Peter Bogason reviews the recent publications from American and North European Public Administration, more or less postmodern in character, and presents two main themes which are not mutually exclusive: social constructivism and foundationalism, and deconstruction, narrative and language. Three themes for future research are identified: values (particularly the public interest), citizen participation, and public employees as intermediaries. These themes are considered most important in the new century. He argues that the more postmodern values prevail, the more people will demand to become involved in decisions that may affect them. Consequently, research must concentrate on societal values and the way they affect various interests within public administration, and in the links to the society it was designed to serve.

1

Moving On (Legitimacy Is Over): Millennial Consciousness and Its Potential

―――――――――――――――― O.C. McSwite

> This is an observation which allows us to grasp what it means to be a precursor. What it isn't, which would be completely impossible, is the anticipation of the categories which emerge later and which haven't yet been created—human beings are always immersed in the same cultural network as their contemporaries, and the ideas they have can only be theirs as well. Being a precursor means seeing what it is one's contemporaries are constituting in the way of ideas, of consciousness, of action, of techniques, of political forms, seeing them as they will be seen a century later.
>
> —Jacques Lacan

INTRODUCTION

Typically, exercises such as the one that occupies this book are little more than speculative larks carried out to satisfy the mundane hope that things are going to change in some interesting way simply because an extraordinary marker in time has been reached. More often than not, however, we exaggerate the significance of the marker, evoke more anticipation than is warranted, and, in much the same way (and to the same end) as weather reporters, dramatize our projections. I believe, though, that the advent of this millennium is an exception to this pattern. The structural changes that have taken place in the world are of such magnitude and kind that it seems no exaggeration to identify the Year 2000 as denoting the possibility for a quantum level, paradigmatic shift in human culture. The immediate manifestations of these changes are perhaps best marked by the rapid increase in the velocity with which capitalism is assuming a place of hegemony as a global organizing principle, and the concomitant technical innovations spewing out from the explosion of electronic information technology.

We are already experiencing cultural discontinuities so palpable that their effects on the normative order regulating social life can be seen even without the typically necessary historical distance. These discontinuities are occurring almost invisibly at the level of day-to-day life in seemingly innocuous innovations like cell phone technology (which is more than simply an extension of the telephone in the same sense that e-mail is more than an extension of "snail mail"), and at the symbolic level in phenomena like the ubiquity of the internet and the virtualization of almost everything. In light of these types of alterations, which affect the basic structures of human life and relationship, it would seem important to take the charge of this symposium with utmost gravity. We must be about the task of guessing what is around the very next corner; it is certain that something is there, and it could surprise us painfully. Even more important, though, is the task of identifying the potential of the future and being ready to shape it through our theorizing.

THE THEME: EMERGENCE OF A RADICALLY NEW MINDSET FOR THINKING ABOUT PUBLIC ADMINISTRATION

The theme of this essay is that public administration theory in the new century will need to be fundamentally reoriented. The focal issue that has occupied it literally throughout its history—the issue of (to put it in its colloquial form) bureaucracy in a democracy—is going to go flat and become a lifeless abstraction: of concern only to those of past generations. This theoretical concern will die in the same manner that Thomas Kuhn described paradigms as shifting when generations change: those believing in the old paradigm simply die off, and the proclivity toward seeing the world in a new way will authorize a new paradigm (Kuhn 1962). This is an inexorable change, driven by the mind-altering forces set loose when oncoming generations grow up under fundamentally altering conditions as is happening at present. Inevitably, a new focal problem and a new framework for understanding it will move onto the scene. This is what is going to happen in the field of public administration. The bureaucracy versus democracy problem is rapidly becoming a dead letter. The challenge public administration theorists face is finding a conceptual framework that can realize fully the possibilities constellated by the demise of the legitimacy issue and the paradigm that supported it.

Following the binary logic of my own "information age" (and reminiscent of Noah's preservation of species in the face of an onrushing flood), the remainder of this argument will be brought on in pairs. I begin with the conceptual shifts that I see in the immediate offing.

The First Conceptual Shift: History Really Is Over, at Least for the Present, and So, Consequently, Is the Friedrich-Finer Debate

The legitimacy issue has been argued within the field of Public Administration in a variety of forms (McSwite 1997). Originally, within the frame set by the famous Friedrich-Finer debate, it was seen as a question of administrative discretion—how much, what kind, and how to use it (Friedrich 1940; Finer 1940). With the advent of the empiricist mood, it became a matter of how administrators were to be allowed to involve themselves in the definition of the goals of the organizations they managed. One side (led by Herbert Simon) held that goals were to be taken literally and whole from the political element of government, and the other side held that administrators played an intrinsic role in setting the direction of society by how they enacted governance through administrative institutions (Redford 1958; Simon 1952; Waldo 1952). With the advent of the sixties, the issue took the form of a debate about citizen participation and equity (Marini 1971). Next it was defined as an issue of administrative responsibility cast as adherence to ethical guidelines (Burke 1986; Cooper 1983; Denhardt 1988; Frederickson, 1980). The Blacksburg group, with its "Manifesto," reincarnated the issue in its generic form, as one of defining the role of the "agential leader" in the context of democratic institutions (Wamsley et al. 1990). The current nominal heading of the issue is the question of how to achieve "civil society" and create government institutions that involve citizens beyond the venue of mere "participation" (Box 1995; Fox & Miller 1995; Frug 1993; Jun 1999; King & Stivers 1998; Morgan & Vizzini 1999; Racine 1995; Shinn 1999; Ventriss 1995; Zanetti & Carr 1999).

This "progression" of dialogue is actually organized around one repeating polarity; its dimensions defined by the pole of "elite rule by reasoned expertise" on one end, and the pole of "popular rule by open discourse" on the other. This is, of course, simply a nuance of the archetypal issue of authoritarianism versus democracy. It should afford little surprise that this noble issue has been the frame within which public administration has reflected about its role, mission, and identity through the course of its history. I want to argue that, nonetheless, in the century beginning the new millennium, this issue will reveal itself as finished, as lacking the rhetorical power to call forth further discourse. It is the death of this issue, in turn, that offers the great opportunity and distinctive challenge that administration theorists now face.

Research into the dynamics of leadership offers an interestingly congruent (and possibly instructive) example of the transition I am describing. After its initial phase of investigating whether effective leaders possess specific identifiable physical or psychological traits, this research became captured by the paradigm of authority (Hersey & Blanchard 1982). Leaders were seen as varying from democratic types (Roosevelt and Churchill) to authoritarian types (Hitler and Mussolini). There was a great deal of fascination with marking out, through social psychological research and theory, the stigmata of the authoritarian personality.

This period was no doubt influenced heavily by the fact that one of its originating proponents, Theodore Adorno, was a refugee from Nazi Germany.

The resultant boom in small group research studying the question of what style of authority constitutes effective leadership moved the field past the uni-dimensional, authoritarian-versus-democratic frame of thinking. Group dynamics research into leadership revealed, and then documented many times over, that human groups function with two different types of leadership activity. One came to be known as "task" leadership, or behavior that emphasized the completion of the work project around which the group was organized, and the other was designated "maintenance" leadership, or behavior that emphasized the psycho-social support and human relationship aspects of the group's functioning.

This discovery laid the foundation for two famous management training schemes, the Blake-Mouton Grid approach and the Hersey-Blanchard Situational Leadership model (Blake & Mouton 1964; Hersey & Blanchard 1982). Blake and Mouton were the major early innovators in bringing the new idea of dual-dimension leadership to the world of management. They were soon theoretically superceded by Hersey and Blanchard. Blake and Mouton were taken by many to have proposed a "one best way" approach to leadership, the famous "nine-nine" manager who could somehow maximize emphasis on both task and maintenance aspects at the same time. Hersey and Blanchard contended that optimal effectiveness was to be achieved by having leaders learn a repertoire of styles ranging from direction to delegation. Their idea was that each style was optimal for specific situations that were defined by the "task maturity" of the leader's followers.

This simple enough reconceptualization of leadership as involving more than one dimension opened up thinking about it and led to fresh new lines of thought and practical innovation in both training methodology and management practice. New possibilities were created, possibilities that finessed the blocking issues of past ways of thinking and led to improved effectiveness. Taking a sociology of knowledge perspective, it seems plausible to assume that changes such as these occur when socio-cultural conditions shift. In this case, the shift entailed gaining psychological distance from the troubled intellectual ethos that surrounded World War II. This war was the dominating event of the time and was, of course, fought explicitly as a battle of the good democratic forces against the evil fascist forces. This opposition made the unidimensional model the most plausible frame for thinking about any relationship involving power and authority.

Similarly, it seems that the socio-cultural conditions that have kept the legitimacy issue alive as the central focus for thinking about the identity of public administration are rapidly in the process of disappearing completely. I have argued at length elsewhere that the latent function of the legitimacy issue was to legitimate a certain form of elite rule by "Men of Reason" (McSwite 1997). The advent of the global economy, spreading the inexorable logic of market efficiency and its pervasive influence, is delegitimating this idea of authority relationships. That is, since, above all, the market abhors authority and advocates in its place the idea of decentralized choice, it allows no room for the Man of Reason. He is, in economic terms, a middle-man who does not add value to the process of pro-ducing wealth and therefore must eventually be eliminated.

This change has already produced the beginnings of a major generation gap in the field. Younger scholars and students are showing less and less interest in the question of what role the administrator should play in the process of governance. "Let's stop wasting time talking about this (the legitimacy issue) and get on with it!" is their mantra. The socio-cultural vectors that have produced the identity they carry, emanating, as they do so strongly, from the market, have evaporated the legitimacy issue from the world in which they live. To them it is not a problem because the "solution" (which is to say, the type of action) that seems natural to them does not fit the "problem" of legitimacy.

The Second Conceptual Shift: The Age of the Individual Is Over, and So, Consequently, Is the Principal-Agent Model of Administrative Responsibility

The generic structure of the legitimacy issue is a special version of the principal-agent relationship—viz., what are the conditions under which agents can appropri-ately act in the name of their principals (Wamsley in Wamsley et al., 1990). This is the structure of all the manifestations of the issue listed earlier. Again, we can see an analogous situation in a related field of research, where a conceptual break-through (in this case inspired by serendipitously discovered empirical data) cast an issue in an entirely new light and made it appear more tractable than before.

This arena of research is family systems theory. The difficulties of families troubled by the problematic behavior of a single member (perhaps most often an acting-out adolescent) were traditionally defined in terms of the pathology of the problematic individual. Under the auspices of the National Institutes of Mental Health, it became possible to bring entire families into consulting rooms for treat-ment. As a result, it was soon discovered that the family's pathological condition, rather than being produced by the individual, was actually the consequence of the relational field of the entire family (Kerr 1988). The problem person was recon-ceptualized as the "presenting patient," which is to say, the patient who was expressing the pathology of the family. The family, as a whole, became the cen-tral client. The motto of the Murray Bowen school of family systems theory (the history of which I have been recounting here) became "There is no such thing as an individual" (ibid.)

The idea of personal identity as a product of social interaction has, of course, been around for a good while, taking an especially prominent place in the theo-ries of pragmatist writers like Mary Follett and George Herbert Mead (Follett 1918; 1924; Mead 1934; 1938). Like pragmatism in general, though, this way of looking at the individual did not become influential in traditional social theory. It was perhaps too "collectivist" to fit the prevailing social ethos in America at the time of its emergence. Deriving from the empirical experience given by the clinical setting, family systems theory initially appeared to be quite a radical departure from traditional approaches. Bowen's theory, along with the many similar versions of systems theory in the field of family therapy, was, however, able to hold special power because it was clinically efficacious. Social context produced it in the sense that the developing reality of interpersonal relationships and the importance of mental hygiene led to the creation of institutions, like the Institutes of Mental Health, where clinical work was paramount. As Bowen sought to train people in his theory, though, he began to see that even trained professionals experienced great difficulty in understanding the idea of the person as the product of a field of interpersonal relationships. Even though his ideas were shaped by the surrounding social context, they were too far ahead of it to make their own reception easy.

The implication of a theory like Bowen's for the principal-agent model of administrative responsibility seems obvious: it radically undercuts its entire foundation. There can be no separate principal and agent if each exists as a product of interaction with the other. Responsibility begins to appear as a matter arising from the quality and texture of the relationship between the two. Were this kind of thinking to gain dominance, the field of public administration would find it necessary either to rethink, or else abandon, the entire question of administrative responsibility.

I suggest that the present theoretical climate of public administration has already shifted significantly in the direction of a systems theory idea of the human person. This change is, no doubt, partially a result of postmodernist/poststructuralist thinking. The notion of a socially constructed identity is one of the more conservative ideas dealt with in the discourses of postmodernism; it is fundamental, more than taken for granted (Rosenau 1992; Sarup 1989). The main venue in our field for this new thinking about subjectivity is the literature dealing with civil society and civil discourse. In this context, the idea of subjectivity is expressed as that of the "socially situated self"; it appears in a range of theorizing from Michael Walzer on the left to Michael Sandel on the right (Sandel 1996; Walzer 1992; 1997; 1999).

It seems safe to assume that the classical liberal image of the individual will continue to fade into the background of contemporary social thought—at least in the academic arena. This is ironic, given that the market ethos, which of course assumes the principle of individualism, is becoming global and dominating world culture. On the other hand, it is well to remember that the presently prevailing theory of the individual is a political one, a theory of citizenship. The citizen is defined by a cluster of rights and duties, and serves as the marker for delineating the legitimate sphere of action of the state: the liberal state is not to transgress the rights of the citizen. It is this theory of the individual that is being eclipsed by the new "individualism" of market theory. In the arena of the market, there is no boundary between the private and the public, which is becoming more and more evident as marketing methodologies enable marketeers to invade the private space of individuals to more and more intimate levels (Mulgan 1997). The market understands people merely as products of their demographics, produced by vectors external to their identity. It should be no surprise, then, that people may be coming to understand themselves in the same way, as produced by the socio-economic, demographic, and personal vectors that bear on them. In such a context, the "socially situated self" seems quite a compatible and plausible way to look at personal identity.

THE BROADER BACKDROP OF CONCEPTUAL CHANGE: THE WANING OF MODERNISM AND ITS PATHOLOGY

The conceptual changes I have sketched are only two of the many that are presently occurring; they are the ones that to me most obviously and directly bear on public administration theory. These, and the other changes of mind happening now, mark a broader pattern that seems undeniable: the coming end of the modernist era. This is not to announce the advent of a "new" age of postmodernism. We are already in a postmodern social condition, and there actually is nothing new about it. Postmodernism is (to repeat a commonplace remark) simply a slight extension of modernism, one that reflects modernism's core nature back to it. The prevailing discontent with the Anihilism and anarchy" perceived as implicit in postmodern literature actually reflects an unconscious fear of the implications of modernism itself.

The easiest way to see the truth in this is to look at the consternation and appalled critique with which the advent of the modernist mentality, especially its scientific aspect, was greeted. If anything, those outcries were even more strident and hysterical than the current caviling against postmodernism. The substance of it, though, was the same. Modernism was seen as bringing the end of truth, moral certainty, and the pursuit of the higher goals of the human spirit—not to mention probable social anarchy. Science, the centerpiece of the modernist mentality, was regarded as a new kind of wild and rootless religion, the priests of which paid no homage to anything but a constantly mutating body of fact. This new religious symbol, empirical fact, was accurately seen as powerfully corrosive of stabilizing belief, peace of mind, and ordered social relations. (To see the meaning of this, recall the trial of Copernicus.) This reaction has been carried forward, of course, through the modernist era. In the social sciences, one of the most persuasive contemporary articulations of this conservative critique of modernism has come from anthropologists and interpretivist sociologists like Peter Berger and his collaborators (Berger et al. 1974).

An interesting aspect of the continuing critique of modernism, the aspect that possesses the most relevance for understanding the future of public administration theory, is the psychoanalytic assessment of the modern mind. From the point of view of psychoanalysis, modernism becomes a pathway (indeed, one running down a slippery slope) to schizophrenic psychosis. Louis Sass's remarkable study, *Madness and Modernism*, suggests this theme not only on carefully laid conceptual grounds (the main theme of the book), but also in terms of empirical evidence comparing patterns of mental hygiene in contemporary traditional and modern societies (Sass 1992).

The power and relevance of such analyses for public administration theory are considerable. Psychoanalytic insight reveals modernist consciousness, which is to say, rationalism, to be grounded in conflicted, fault-ridden territory. The result is a fragile, unstable kind of mind, one that can survive only by forgetting, or when reminded, by denying outright its fundamental contradictions and their implications. Since public administration has so far been preeminently a modernist enterprise, it finds itself grounded in this same dangerous terrain.

The paradox is that postmodernism functions actually as a support to modernism. In the way that even painful therapeutic insight leads to greater self acceptance and stability, modernism came on the scene as a defense of the pre-modernist form of mind and social order. Ever since human consciousness shifted from the oral, Goddess-oriented, bicameral form to the modern literate, male god, left-brained form that it currently possesses, a symbolic Master has been present (Jaynes 1976; Logan 1986; Ong 1982; Shlain 1998). In traditional society, the Master was embodied in royalty; in modern society, he is manifest in the system of wealth and privilege that is the modernist equivalent of the system of royal lineage—capitalism.

The actual objective of all theory and forms of social organization arising under our literate consciousness is to make this Master happy. Such service is the most essential homage, the one that sustains this form of consciousness. The painful shift from traditionalism to modernism was merely a necessary adjustment to ensure the continuing hegemony of the Master. Postmodernism is a similar, painful attempt at shoring up this consciousness, one that in the end will turn out to be its death rattle, just as modernism was to the traditional world.

I bring up the point that modernism was actually conservative so as to ground the idea I want to explore next—that modernism is a defensive ideology of authority. As traditional authority, grounded on claims of transcendence, failed, modernism replaced it with a theory of authority drawing its legitimacy from the claim that it holds power over the non-transcendent, actual world, which is to say, reality. At bottom, this is a claim to be able to represent accurately, and as a consequence, to manipulate, the world seen as objects.

Such a project requires the familiar epistemology, methodological schema, and moral theory of rationalism: the realist hypothesis is not a metaphysical claim but is an actuality; words refer to things; there is at least an aspect of the human person that can freely calculate and decide; the mind as experienced (i.e., consciousness) is all there is to mind; moral sentiment can only function through the guidance of values. Each and every aspect of this rationalist framework, and their many corollaries as well, has been beset by powerful, devastating assaults. The critiques, though, no matter how convincing, are bootless and, in a sense, off the point. Rationalism is necessarily entailed by the current model of consciousness. Critique, therefore, which is after all a conscious enterprise, can never bring it down. Indeed, what the current proponents of modernism do not seem to realize is that postmodern critics are their allies. Their best strategy is to accept such critique and refound modernist artifacts such as "institutions" on the new bases that inhere in postmodernism. Deconstruction, after all, is an "ethic" that seeks "justice" (Derrida 1991).

All this is becoming moot—which will be amply clear, I predict, as the new millennium unfolds. The postmodern social forms that will develop as the capitalist market ethos pervades the world will enact the essential psychological pathology of modernist consciousness, i.e., schizophrenia. The first thing that happens when schizophrenia develops is a variety of manifestations of a process in which words become detached from, or unable to designate, things (Sass 1992). The world begins to appear as a flashing panorama of sliding, mutating surfaces (something like what one sees in contemporary advertising and music videos). This same process, which is, at its essence, the breakdown of the power consciously to represent, progresses until full-blown psychosis is experienced, wherein the boundary between "reality" and what exists outside it fails to hold.

This process is only pathological when viewed from the current perspective of modernist consciousness and when it is happening specifically rather than generally. When it begins to become normative to the entire social order, something other than a fall into insanity occurs—a new mode of consciousness begins to develop. Inklings of this can be heard in the comments of the young when beset with the carping of their elders about their tastes and life preferences. I had the experience of being brought up short on this count once while presenting a guest lecture to an open audience at a large university. I was contending that postmodernist life was superficial and vacuous, a melange of empty sliding surfaces in which young people were being induced to regard identity as an ability to "vogue" or pose. Suddenly a young woman in the back of the hall, shot up her arm and asked: "What's wrong with that? You are talking about my life. It's fine with me if it's superficial, evacuated, and gratification oriented."

Which comment brings us to the point of this discussion of the exacerbating pathology of modernist consciousness and its relevance as a backdrop to a discussion of the prospects for theory in public administration. Postmodernism marks the beginning of the end of modernism and the consciousness that goes with it. Since, however, modernism was a defensive ideology of authority for the mode of consciousness that underpins it, modernism is properly seen, on the one hand, as pathological and on the other, as providing, through this very pathology, the grounding of a new pattern of mind. This new pattern of mind offers the potential for conceiving of social patterns and social life without authority, rational judgment, and moral decision. I argue that this is a world not of problem, but of potential.

THE PROSPECTS FOR PUBLIC ADMINISTRATION THEORY

What then are the possibilities for theorizing public administration as it becomes increasingly unconstrained by modernist consciousness, the rationalist paradigm, and the assumptions setting its understandings of democratic governance and administrative responsibility? Any wise scholar would surely issue a number of provisos and caveats at the start of any attempt to answer this question. I shall settle for one obvious and overarching disclaimer: there is no definitive answer possible. Kuhn's view about paradigm change—that it involves a gestalt switch, a leap of faith, and a movement into a new, reconstructed reality—holds thrice times over with the magnitude of change I am suggesting. That is, I am arguing that public administration theorists of the future (even as immediate a future as the next twenty to fifty years) may well be working from not just a new paradigm, but from a new mode of *consciousness*. Given this, it is silly to pretend to describe what such a possibility might afford. If oxygen cannot be described from within the phlogiston paradigm, and the medieval artist cannot give an account of Picasso, I (passing through the far end of middle age and having lived more than half of the twentieth century) certainly cannot claim access to the mind of the future. Even if I were magically able to fully discuss dimensions and implications of a new consciousness, they would appear as absurd or crazy to the contemporary way of looking at things. What I can offer, then, are only dim, perhaps seemingly weird and non-sensical, glimmerings of the possibilities of our conceptual future. As is my apparent custom, I have organized them into two broad dimensions.

The First Dimension of the New Consciousness: From Knowledge to Truth

The baseline of the new consciousness will be a shift in human project from *knowledge* to *truth*. It will become increasingly clear that knowledge, currently defined as entailing the putative goal of correspondence with external reality, is a frustrating, indeed inherently problematic, style of mind. Very much like the sorcerer's apprentice who attained enough knowledge to make the broom start working but then could not keep it from becoming destructive, current consciousness wishes not to acknowledge to itself its own limitations and intrinsic contradictions; instead it barges ahead with applications of new partial knowledge.

Witness the future that is already upon us. Futurists claim that simple, reliable, straight-line projections using the rate of change predict eternal life within fifty years and computers with the power of the human brain long before that. The full decoding of the human genome and the subsequent ability to genetically engineer human beings (physically and psychologically) is, as the twentieth century ends, almost complete. Even the most cursory reflection should alert us to the immense difficulties entailed in asserting any form of conscious control over these processes (Shattuck 1996). (And I write "difficulties" advisedly, in light of the fact that developments of this sort push the mind all the way to its fundamental dilemma in the paradox of self-referentiality.) The current attitude regarding these issues seems to be on the order of "We'll cross that bridge when we get to it," an answer that ignores the likelihood that there is *not going to be a bridge there* when we get to it. Current producers of knowledge, those who should be building such bridges, seem more concerned with enhancing their own positions in the knowledge game than in drawing attention to the chasm at either end of the playing field. Even assuming an optimistic view of the future, in which we do not go down the path leading to a horrific *Blade Runner* condition of manufactured people and a ruined Earth, we can still plausibly assume that our traditional knowledge process will lead to fundamental disillusionment and thus replacement with a kind of mind that seeks another way of knowing.

This other way of knowing I call by the name "truth" because it carries an oxymoronic connotation appropriate to the meaning I intend. It is also the term used in the source material I want to employ in explaining it: Lacanian psychoanalytic theory. I wish to use Lacan here not in substance but in form. In other words, it is not the particular "truth" he offers in his psychoanalysis that is relevant, but the *theory of truth* that underpins it (Lacan 1977; 1981; 1990; 1991a; 1991b).

While Lacan is most often counted a "postmodernist," this is a serious mischaracterization. Indeed, postmodernism is anathema to his followers in the field of critical cultural studies and literature. Lacan would feel out of place in both the modernist and the postmodernist camps. His theory is a strange melange of what he called the "old" or "true" science, philosophy (especially Hegel), structuralism, logic, topography, linguistics, and semiotics, and of course Freud—among other things. He characterized the current mode of science, at least as spoken within what he called the discourse of the university, as based on an ideal of knowledge that is quite literally paranoid. That is, it induces an incessant, suspicious search for what is behind and underneath the surface appearances of reality. The ideal knowledge generated by conventional contemporary science pretends to certainty, at least to the level of reliability in application; yet by the tenets of its own methodology, it can never completely assure that this has been attained. Worse still, it cannot acknowledge that its process is a socially and politically interested one. The social and political conflicts inherent in knowledge production are, as a consequence, driven out of sight, leading to distortions in the knowledge production process, endless quibbling and argument, and a constantly shifting public definition of what currently is to be considered knowledge at all. In psychoanalytic terms, all this goes back to the problem that knowledge production is organized around ego processes, and in the Lacanian view, the ego is a neurotic problem.

Lacan's own intellectual endeavors were aimed at the goal of truth. While it is doubtlessly inadequate, "truth" seems as suitable a vehicle as any for describing the logos of the consciousness of the next century. One way to see Lacan's idea of truth is through the "ethic" that is attached to the study of Lacan. Lacan himself, and certainly his followers, insist that his work should be studied as closely as possible through original texts. In a sense this is not possible, since he wrote very little, and his teachings (the bulk of his extensive work) were delivered orally in his famous seminars spanning over thirty years. His son-in-law and heir apparent, Jacques Alain-Miller, has suggested that Lacan's meaning can only be grasped through listening to him in the seminar context. In order to overcome this problem, Alain-Miller has had to invent a way of editing Lacan's seminar lectures and discussions so as to make them convey in writing more of what they meant when heard.

Studying Lacan, or any theorist for that matter, through secondary sources tends to create a sense that the theory contains a wholeness or completeness— that, in a word, *knowledge* is being offered. Even when an exegete takes a critical stance and points out gaps in, and conceptual issues with, a body of work, this is necessarily done from an external perspective, leaving intact the possibility that the work could answer these on its own terms and retain its integrity. The reader, in turn, who expects the exegete accurately to report a body of work, tends to impute to the original work, on the strength of this expectation, the status of knowledge. The very existence of exegesis implicitly gives integrity to a body of work, an integrity that can never really be there.

A different effect is achieved when reading a theorist's work in the original. As is blatantly evident with Lacan, who viewed himself reflexively, any theoretical discourse in the original is as incomplete, partial, and self-contradictory as is the human mind. It succeeds in attaining integrity only through the creation of a rhetorical illusion. Lacan's incompleteness and inconsistencies are clear in his original work. Indeed, at points, he vigorously attacked himself and even shifted the centerpoint of his theory dramatically. Nonetheless, he claimed to be getting at the truth and demanded that his interlocutors attend to his every word. What could he have meant by this? Which is to say, what is the difference between knowledge and truth?

One way of making this point is to invoke the methodology of caricature. Lacan, heavily influenced by his friend Levi-Strauss, is often and plausibly considered a structuralist. As such, he was very much a caricaturist. He made positive claims (which are inevitably in one sense exaggerations) about a certain fundamental level of human reality; at the same time he never presumed the position of the meta-narrator who could see and account for his own entire construction. He never pretended, like the caricaturist, to be offering a truly complete and accurate picture. One gains a sense of trans-historical certainty from studying his work; at the same time, it becomes clear that there are only the most shifting and relative bases from which to describe this certainty. Thus, Lacan becomes a kind of post-postmodernist and a peculiarly appropriate metaphor for the emerging consciousness I am interested in caricaturing myself.

Knowledge, as I am using the term here, is like a putatively accurate line drawing; truth, as I am using the term here, is equivalent to caricature. Let us immediately recall, lest we too quickly accord credit to that which is deemed "accurate," that neither the line drawing nor the caricature achieves a complete representation of the subject. The difference between them lies in what they claim and what they do or do not conceal about what they claim. The line drawing (knowledge) claims to represent the reality of the subject: by seeing this picture, the viewer is led to believe that he or she will be able to know what is being depicted. The drawing gives no hint of what is left out; it has no interest in doing this, as such would contradict its claim. (Even though, it would say, it never claimed to be a complete representation.) Paradoxically, the drawing does not reveal to the viewer what is actually there, the thing in itself. In this sense, there is nothing positive about it; in fact, it tells the viewer nothing definitive. Confirmation of the picture can come only upon seeing the "real thing." Then, of course, each viewer making the comparison to the thing will likely have a differing opinion as to how well the picture captures the subject. This is precisely because all the picture offers is the possibility of comparison; there is nothing actually in it. This is how the ideal of knowledge functions, viz., to create a tendency toward dissent, toward discussion. The latent function of this pernicious effect, taken to the level of social theory, is to make it necessary to impose social order, as it cannot be achieved through a commonality of mind.

The caricature, on the other hand confronts us with positive content—*at the structural level*. When it succeeds, it gives the viewer the sense that something is now known about the subject, even though it is clearly incomplete. That is, this kind of picture makes no pretense to accurate representation. Instead it only suggests what is not there, what it is not showing by overemphasizing an aspect that is certainly there in the caricature. The caricature does not claim to present the reality of the subject such that the viewer may expect to "know" what is depicted. The expectation created by the caricature is one of intended distortion; the viewer expects only a partial image. The feeling upon seeing the real version of the subject of a caricature is, therefore, a sense of confirmation ("I knew that would be there") along with a sense of discovery ("I wondered what was left out"). The result is a sense of engagement with the process of knowing. Truth, as I am using the term here, means *incomplete certainty*. It provides a basis, a beginning place, for further, *cooperative* exploration or learning about the object in question. This mode of knowing implies a collaboratively created social order.

The Second Dimension of the New Consciousness: From Ego to Self

The first dimension of the change in consciousness, discussed above, is epistemological. This second dimension is ontological. It reflects the same post-post-structuralist point of view that undergrounds the epistemological dimension, and consequently, it, too, takes on the same appearance of strangeness. I want to employ Lacanian theory again as a venue for exploring this second dimension.

I noted that there seems to be an increasing acceptance of the view that human identity is socially produced. Lacan certainly appreciated this perspective—as in his oft-quoted pronouncement "I am not a poet. I am a poem being written." (Lacan quotation) He saw the field of language as a complex, but determinate, set of vectors acting directly on people. When one is born into this field and then given a specific place within it by being named, language begins, beneath awareness, to determine the course of a life in the way (to invoke a metaphor Lacan used) that the Roman slave's fate was sealed when the message inscribed on the top of his shaved head ordered the recipient of the message to kill him after reading it. This process of social determination takes place through the venue of what Lacan called the Symbolic Order.

The Symbolic Order is a polysemous term (as all the key Lacanian terms are) that was meant to designate, at the most general level, the register of language itself, the Law in both the official and unofficial senses, and, in the broadest sense, culture. The project of classical Freudian psychoanalysis, especially as practiced in the United States, is to bring the human subject more effectively under the purview of the Symbolic—to gain complete submission to it. Psychoanalysis takes its project from the virtually inevitable malfunctioning of the oedipal process. The oedipal event is the point at which the child should give up on its project of staying joined to, or possessing, its mother by accepting the authoritative place of the father as a barrier to access to the mother. Typically, though, the child relinquishes its desires grudgingly, and the resulting resentment is expressed as one form or another of neurosis. The heart of the psychoanalytic project is better adjusting the child to the authority of the Symbolic Order and thus resolving neurosis. This is the basic framework of ego psychology: to produce an effectively functioning ego in an individual, one that can come to terms rationally with reality and conform to social norms. This idea of the ego underpins the dominant rational individualist ideology of modernist consciousness.

Lacan accepted this paradigm of psychoanalysis until into the 1950s, when he concluded that a psychoanalysis functioning in this way, viz., to bring about social adjustment, was, in his terms, perverse. This turn in his thinking led eventually to the development of perhaps his most powerful idea, that each human being possesses what he called "desire." Human desire, as he conceptualized it, can never be brought fully under the hegemony of the Symbolic, and as a consequence, it can never be reconciled to the Symbolic. It is a kind of leftover from the pre-symbolic, fully embodied existence of the person in the organic world. The human condition, seen in this way, is one in which the subject's desire must be acknowledged and borne willingly. The project of this reframed psychoanalysis is to put the analysand in touch with his or her desire, and create the psychological conditions in which she or he can own and bear it.

This is another point at which the ethic of Lacanian study, mentioned earlier, is relevant. Lacan intentionally obfuscated his teachings; he simply rejected the rhetorical convention of clarity. He expected his students to apprehend him in a way other than ordinary "understanding." For him to be clear and to create clear understanding in the conventional sense was to impose the Symbolic Order on the student, to make it seem more complete, more sensible, than it actually is or has the possibility of being. Clarity is a pernicious trick when viewed in this light. As a result, the study of Lacan became a kind of Lacanian psychoanalytic experience itself. In struggling with the impossible riddles of Lacan's statements, the student is moved into a marginalized position at the edge of the Symbolic Order. At this point a kind of epiphany can occur, one that opens the venue for experiencing the full reality of one's desire.

While this may seem strange, it is actually quite close to what Kuhn described as the process of moving from one paradigm to another through a leap of faith and a changed vision that reveals a new reality—a reality with, for example, oxygen rather than phlogiston. Those who feel that it is possible to "be" in or to "use" more than one paradigm, i.e., to possess some transparadig-matic perspective, are wrong in precisely this manner. While it is quite possible to understand a paradigm in a cognitive sense, such understanding is not equiv-alent to actually apprehending it. For this, the epiphany that opens the way into it must be experienced.

I introduce desire here because it is key to bridging, as Lacan did, the social constructionist and structuralist perspectives on the self. Lacan shows us quite clearly how the self comes to be socially situated, and at the same time he shows us just as clearly how it is partially situated outside this process. This part that is outside is a result of a structural dynamic, one that precedes the dynamic of social construction and indeed, begins it.

This marks a transition from an ontology of the ego to an ontology that accepts reality of the ego but adds to it the idea of a transcendant personal aspect: desire. This is an ontology of the self, one that shows the person as more than what can be defined into it by culture and law. It is an ontolgy that opens the possibility for an image of people as both socially produced and connected, and at the same time as occupying uniquely personal positions. It also shows human beings as, by nature, both orderly and liberated from order. Something similar to this image of people will emerge as the consciousness of the next century unfolds.

IMPLICATIONS FOR PUBLIC ADMINISTRATION THEORY

Administrative Responsibility as the Creation of Solidarity

The traditional way of conceiving of the issue of administrative responsibility has already become anachronistic. Two examples suggest how. In her insightful study of the Orange County, California bankruptcy issue, Susan MacDonald has shown that our traditional conceptions of responsibility simply do not fit the emerging realities faced by public administrators (MacDonald 1999). The agent in this case, the county treasurer (a man named Citron), was given a mandate by the electorate and the County Board of Supervisors essentially to invest the county's funds so as to yield an extraordinarily high rate of return. He was also charged not to cut back existing social programs and not to raise county taxes. In attempting to do this, he ran the county into bankruptcy. As MacDonald points out, though, the fundamental issue was that high return on investment was the only context set for Citron. There was no framework set for defining inappropri-ate "riskyness" and there likewise was no corollary statement of the "importance" of the money involved. Lacking this referential context, there was no way he could judge what being responsible meant to them. Risk was not part of the dis-cussion surrounding Citron. It is not even clear that he contemplated risk and hence even understood the degree of risk in the county's portfolio of investments. That he alone was blamed for the disaster seems absurd. It is like blaming a per-sonal stockbroker for investment decisions when the investor had demanded that gains be maximized, but had not taken the time to discuss how much the funds involved were valued and how risk averse he was. A more suitable assessment of Citron's responsibility would be that he should have led the Board and the community through a mutual discourse that would have produced a coherent framework for making his investment decisions.

A second example is the recent case of *Cohen v. Brown University*, a class action suit over the alleged inequity of Brown's allocation of funds to women's athletics under Title IX (Caudill 1997). Brown's defense was that it had documented, through an opinion survey of women students, that they did not want more funds allocated to their athletic programs. On the basis of the women's self-reported preferences, Brown refused to re-allocate funds from the men's programs. In the subsequent class action suit, the court, rather than taking the survey as evidence of Brown's good faith, deemed it to be evidence of their failure to act appropriately. It reasoned that the survey responses were evidence of just how far the traditional failure to support women's athletics had oppressed the women students such that they were unable to conceive of themselves as athletes. Responsible action on the part of Brown's administrators would have been for them to create programs and facilities for women and to carry out a process of dialogue that would have encouraged the women students to [re-]create themselves and the role of athletics in their lives as a result of their participation in them.

Both of the examples illustrate that the idea of holding agents responsible to charges by principals is becoming impossibly complicated in the postmodern world of elaborated value and technical issues. Such an idea is based on the rational ego model of the human person. This model makes it appear that what principals can provide to agents is a statement of their interests in certain outcomes. Such a statement is supposed to set the boundaries for the agent's actions. This, of course, has never been true even in the most traditional world; it is rapidly becoming impossible even to keep up the pretense.

With the consciousness of the future, however, in which people experience themselves as having a positive, desiring identity at the same time that they are aware of how they are produced by their social relations, a new, collective and cooperative sense of responsibility has begun to appear. Ego consciousness blocks this possibility because it comes naturally to egos to think in terms of scarcity, zero sum games, and specific payoffs. Egos experience themselves as self identified, and therefore self interested, and they tend to be narcissistically tied to their group identifications. Such identifications are their only sense of solidarity. The Self, the alternative, personally-desiring, socially-connected sense of identity, seeks solidarity through a process of positive world construction that it realizes can never be appropriately closed off or brought to conclusion. The product of the Self is an open solidarity.

Engaging and carrying on such a process will be basis for a new theory of responsibility. In such a theory, the outlines of which have already been drawn by Michael Harmon, action and solidarity will be closely linked (Harmon 1995). There will be no agents and principals, and no question about the legitimacy of what is done.

"Governance" and Efficiency Reconciled

The retort of traditional public administration theory to the demand that agencies become efficient is: "Public administration cannot be primarily concerned with efficiency! We are part of the process of democratic governance, and as such we must deal with all the constraints that this necessarily messy, inefficient process generates." The current global market ethos has already given this rejoinder a hollow ring. Everyone likes efficiency. It is something close to, in this world, a universal value. The problem it poses is not its desirability, but the frame that governs how we think about achieving it.

With the "end of history" alluded to earlier, that is, the end of the opposition of capitalist democracy and central planning authoritarianism, we can see the issue of efficiency in a new and broader light. Just as was the case with the history I recounted of leadership, it will become possible to understand that efficiency (the equivalent of "task" in the group situation) and governance (the analogue to the "group maintenance" function) can be considered as two *complementary* processes. It is not necessary that the one should intrude on the attainment of the other.

The problem of efficiency in traditional public administration theory actually derived from the Man of Reason elite mode of governance that the impossible Friedrich-Finer question implicitly legitimated. Efficiency seemed problematic because it appeared as an outcome that the Man of Reason had to make *happen* in spite of the issues of public governance that beset the agency as it sought to carry out its mission. Much in the same way that university deans ensure the recalcitrance of faculty by pressuring them to be responsive to students and social changes, so men of reason make efficiency seem problematic by defining themselves as solely responsible for it.

Theorists of the future will perhaps take a lesson from micro-economics on this count, and theorize efficiency, as the market does, as a problem of structural/cultural organization (more effective linking of various production components and of consumers to providers) rather than one of hierarchical management and control. The challenge will lie in rethinking the entire current idea of government action as "programs" and reconceptualizing agencies in such a way as to dissolve the traditional boundaries and allow fluid interaction and direct engagement of all those involved in the production and consumption of services. For example, rather than attempting to attain efficiency/effectiveness as the current GPRA initiative does, by having agencies create performance measures that can serve as consumer information, a theory of the future will recognize that agency services are not like commodities. Information does not accumulate around these services in the way that it does around commodities, making performance measures difficult to develop, useless when they are developed, and, at any rate, quickly obsolete. The answer, rather, lies more in the direction of organizing agency service production and delivery in such a way that it is directly in contact with, and receives immediate performance feedback from, those it serves. Such a

reconceptualization renders moot the purported opposition between public governance and efficiency.

CONCLUSION

The idea that the Symbolic Order of the present era of modernism is failing runs
as an implicit theme through the entire foregoing essay. The premise of this theme
is that the generations coming to maturity now, the public administration theorists
of the future, are going to carry a different kind of consciousness as a matter of
default. The discourse of modernism, which is, in Lacan's view, the neurotic
(specifically, obsessional) Discourse of the University, is failing to the point at
which it will not be able to reproduce itself through socializating oncoming generations. These generations are going to be exposed to a kind of brute force psychoanalytic experience purely because they are coming of age in this moment.
There is the real possibility that they will be put in touch with their desire by virtue
of the fact that the Symbolic is losing its coherence.

There is great potential in such a moment but also great hazard. There is no
guarantee that the speculative scenario I have sketched will be the one that public administration theory or human consciousness will follow. At bottom, what we
face, as we move into the next century, is to see the wisdom in such pronouncements as Richard Rorty's, when he asserted that imagination, rather than reason,
is the central human faculty and, as such, is the primary hope that we will be able
to shape our future in a positive manner (Rorty 1989). The age of reason is soon
to be over. We, in public administration, have been a far larger part of it than has
ever been acknowledged in our philosophies of governance. The final and grand-
est hope that the field of public administration can have is that its theorists of the
future will realize this and will understand that if we are to replace the age of reason with the age of imagination, it is significantly up to them to do it. The theory
agenda of the new century is not one of writing grand, panoramic social and political narratives, but of thinking and feeling through the *ultimately important*
smaller, more practical questions involved in working out how we are to live
together day-to-day. This has always been the central responsibility of public
administration theory and will be as long as the field endures.

REFERENCES

Berger, P., Berger, B., & Kellner, H. 1974. *The Homeless Mind*. New York: Vintage.
Blake, R.R., & Mouton, J. S. 1964. *The Managerial Grid: Key Orientations for Achieving
        Production Through People*. Houston, TX: Gulf.
Box, R.C. 1995. Critical Theory and the Paradox of Discourse. *American Review of Public
        Administration*, 25(1): 1-19.
Burke, J.P. 1986. *Bureaucratic Responsibility*. Baltimore: Johns Hopkins University Press.
Caudill, D.S. 1997. *Lacan and the Subject of Law: Toward a Psychoanalytic Critical Legal
        Theory*. New Jersey: Humanities Press.

Cooper, T. 1983. *The Responsible Administrator*. Port Washington, NY: Kennikat.

Denhardt, K.G. 1988. *The Ethics of Public Service: Resolving Moral Dilemmas in Public Organizations*. Westport, CT. : Greenwood.

Derrida, J. 1991. *A Derrida Reader: Between the Blinds*, edited by Peggy Kamuf. New York: Columbia University Press.

Finer, H. 1940. Administrative responsibility in democratic government. *Public Policy*, edited by C. Friedrich. Cambridge, MA: Harvard University Press. 247-275.

Follett, M.P. 1924. *Creative Experience*. New York: Longmans, Green.

———. 1918. *The New State*. New York: Longmans, Green.

Fox, C.J., & Miller, H.T. 1995. *Postmodern Public Administration*. Thousand Oaks, CA: Sage Press.

Frederickson, H. G. 1980. *New Public Administration*. Tuscaloosa: University of Alabama Press.

Friedrich, C. 1940. Public policy and the nature of administrative responsibility. *Public Policy*, edited by C. Friedrich. Cambridge, MA: Harvard University Press. 221-245.

Frug, J. 1993. *Decentering Decentralization*. University of Chicago Law Review, 60, 253-338.

Harmon, M.M. 1995. *Responsibility as Paradox: A Critique of Rational Discourse on Government*. Thousand Oaks, CA: Sage Press.

Hersey, P., & Blanchard, K. 1982. *Management of Organizational Behavior*. 4th ed. Englewood Cliffs, NJ: Prentice-Hall.

Jaynes, J. 1976. *The Origin of Consciousness in the Breakdown of the Bicameral Mind*. Boston, MA: Houghton Mifflin.

Jun, J.S. 1999, The need for autonomy and virtues: Civic-minded administrators in a civil society. *Administrative Theory and Praxis, 21*(2):218-226.

Kerr, M.E. Sept., 1988. Chronic anxiety and defining a self. *Atlantic Monthly*, 35-58.

King, C.S. ,& Stivers, C. 1998. *Government Is Us: Public Administration in an Anti-Government Era*. Thousand Oaks, CA: Sage Press.

Kuhn, T. 1962. *The Structure of Scientific Revolutions*. Chicago: University of Chicago Press.

Lacan, J. 1977. *Ecrits: A Selection*, translated by Alan Sheridan. New York: W. W. Norton & Company.

———. 1981. *The Four Fundamental Concepts of Psycho-Analysis*, edited by Jacques-Alain Miller, translated by Alan Sheridan. New York: W. W. Norton & Company.

———. 1990. *Television*, edited by Joan Copjec, translated by Denis Hollier, Rosalind Krauss, & Annette Michelson. New York: W.W. Norton, & Company.

———. 1991a. *The Seminar of Jacques Lacan, Book I: Freud's Papers on Technique 1953-1954*, edited by Jacques-Alain Miller, translated by John Forrester. New York: W. W. Norton & Company.

———. 1991b. *The Seminar of Jacques Lacan, Book II: The Ego in Freud's Theory and in the Technique of Psychoanalysis 1954-1955*, edited by Jacques-Alain Miller, translated by Sylvana Tomaselli. New York: W. W. Norton & Company.

Logan, R.K. 1986. *The Alphabet Effect: The Impact of the Phonetic Alphabet on the Development of Western Civilization*. New York: William Morrow and Co.

MacDonald, S. March, 1999. *Civil Society in a Global Economy and the Problematic of Risk*. (Paper delivered at the National Conference of the Public Administration Theory Network. Colorado Springs, CO).

Marini, R., ed. 1971. *Toward a New Public Administration*. London: Chandler, Scranton.

McSwite, O.C. 1997. *Legitimacy in Public Administration: A Discourse Analysis*. Thousand Oaks, CA: Sage Press.

Mead, G.H. 1934. *Mind, Self and Society*, edited by Charles Morris. Chicago: University of Chicago Press.

————. 1938. *The Philosophy of the Act*, edited by Charles Morris. Chicago: University of Chicago Press.

Morgan, D., & Vizzini, D. 1999. Transforming customers into citizens: Some preliminary lessons from the field. *Administrative Theory and Praxis. 21* (1):51-61.

Mulgan, G. 1997. *Connexity: How to Live in a Connected World*. Boston, MA: Harvard Business School Press.

Ong. W.J. 1982. *Orality and Literacy: The Technologizing of the Word*. London: Routledge.

Racine, D.P. 1995. The welfare state: citizens and immersed civil servants. *Administration and Society. 26*:434-463.

Redford, E.S. 1958. *Ideal and Practice in Public Administration*. Tuscaloosa: University of Alabama Press.

Rorty, R. 1989. *Contingency, Irony and Solidarity*. Cambridge: Cambridge University Press.

Rosenau, P.M. 1992. *Post-Modernism and the Social Sciences*. Princeton, NJ: Princeton University Press.

Sandel, M.J. 1996. *Democracy's Discontent: American in Search of a Public Philosophy*. Cambridge, MA: Harvard University Press.

Sarup, M. 1989. *An Introductory Guide to Post-Structuralism and Postmodernism*. Athens, GA: University of Georgia Press.

Sass, L.A. 1992. *Madness and Modernism: Insanity in the Light of Modern Art, Literature and Thought*. Cambridge, MA: Harvard University Press.

Shattuck, R. 1996. *Forbidden Knowledge: From Prometheus to Pornography*. New York: St. Martin's Press.

Shinn, C.W. 1999. Civic capacity: Theory, research and practice. *Administrative Theory and Praxis. 21*(1):103-119.

Shlain, L. 1998. *The Alphabet Versus the Goddess: The Conflict Between Word and Image*. New York: Viking.

Simon, H.A. 1952. Development of theory of democratic administration: Replies and comments. *American Political Science Review. 46*:494-496.

Ventriss, C. 1995. Emerging perspectives on citizen participation. *Public Administration Review. 45*:433-440.

Waldo, D. 1952. Development of theory of democratic administration. *American Political Science Review. 46*:81-103.

Walzer, M. Winter,1999. Rescuing civil society. *Dissent*. 62-67.

————. 1992. The civil society argument. *Dimensions of Radical Democracy: Pluralism, Citizenship, Community*, edited by Chantal Mouffe. London: Verso. 89-107.

————. 1997. The idea of civil society. *Kettering Review*. 8.

Wamsley, G.L., Goodsell, C.T., Rohr, J.A., Kronenberg, P., White, O.F., Jr., Wolf, J.F., & Stivers, C. 1990. *Refounding Public Administration*. Newbury Park, CA: Sage.

Zanetti, L.A., and A. Carr. 1999. Exaggerating the dialectic: Postmoderism's "new individualism" and the detrimental effects on citizenship. *Administrative Theory and Praxis. 21* (2):205-217.

2

The Hegemony of the Consumer: Administration and Management at the End of the Century[1]

Yiannis Gabriel

Imagine a similar symposium taking place not at the close of the twentieth century, but at its opening. Imagine the delight of being able to invite scholars of a hundred years ago to speculate on the developments and changes that our century would bring about to administration, its theory, but more importantly its practice, while we passed judgement on them with the immense benefit and arrogant superiority of hindsight. We could invite our favorite authors, as well as some of our less favored ones, to see the former hit felicitously at some prophetic insights while the latter came undone with some wide-of-the-mark prognostications. How would, say, Weber, Durkheim, Freud, Bergson, Dewey, Veblen, Simmel, and Lenin envision administration in the century ahead? Undoubtedly such a symposium would reveal some very nineteenth century concerns, anxieties, and hopes, from which we feel very distant both intellectually and emotionally. It would also, however, reveal some concerns about justice, freedom, and the meaning of a good life, which are always live and pressing. More sobering, perhaps, is trying to imagine ourselves as participants in such a symposium. It quickly becomes clear that *even with the benefit of hindsight,* trying to establish the fundamental changes which our century has brought about to the field of administration and to the discourses with which it is enmeshed is a formidable task.

And yet—how invaluable it would be to have the papers from such a symposium of a hundred years ago, since they would give us a snapshot of those concerns which dominated the thinking of scholars then. We could learn much from the blind spots in their thinking, from their disagreements and from the tacitly shared assumptions which time has since broken down. It is in such spirit that I approach this symposium—as part of a process which will allow us in later years to identify some of the blind spots of our current thinking, some of our current pre-occupations which prove parochial and whimsical, and some of our current concerns which prove not merely appropriate, but which generate useful insights for the practice of administration in the future.

This symposium is far more challenging than an equivalent one a hundred years ago—for one thing, our *fin-de-siècle* is one of greater uncertainty and discontinuity than the previous one. In the wake of the collapse of the Soviet Union and its centrally planned economy, many of the givens of a political world order have been shattered. Unchallenged capitalism and free trade may appear to offer unlimited opportunities to some, but the future, with its technological, environmental, economic, and political developments holds immense uncertainties evident to all. These uncertainties undermine our faith that the future will in some meaningful way be a continuation of the present. As Hobsbawm (1994) has strongly argued, we are at a moment in history when the future has become less knowable than ever before while the past has become less valid as an indication of what lies ahead. We live with a profound sense of the end of an era and little idea of the future. We have lost faith in history as a march towards progress, prosperity, and enlightenment. Universal ideals and values have become suspect. Even our faith in science, the one unquestioned source of authority in our time, has become tinged with apprehension, mistrust, and foreboding.

And yet, in a paradoxical way, that same future has never seemed so one-dimensional as it appears at the present time. Unfettered capitalist markets, globalization, the disappearance of political alternatives, and the universal hegemony of the consumer have led not only to melodramatic pronouncements on the end of history, but also to a floundering of critical imagination, of an ability to envision a future at all other than as more of the same—more goods, more trade, more pollution, more natural catastrophes, more wars, and more inequality between the haves and the have nots. The critical consciousness of our social sciences has become blunted. Our theories, as social scientists, have mostly given up on the Marxist ideal of changing the world and even on the more modest one of understanding and critiquing it. Instead they increasingly seek to "deconstruct" it through playful, witty, or ironic engagement, getting endlessly trapped into linguistic vortices, coming and going with the regularity of fashion. "All that is solid melts into air" proclaimed Marx as he surveyed the rule of the bourgeoisie, exactly one hundred and fifty years ago. Yet, under this rule, concepts were (or so we seem to believe now) immune from the change. Modernity might have seen cities rise out of nothingness; distances shrunk through the powers of technology; family, political, and organizational forms revolutionized. But modernity respected concepts, it respected theories, and above all, it respected truth. Post-modernity has no such qualms. It extends the liquefaction to concepts, theories, and ideas, turning them into fleeting mirages, parodies, and *jeux d'esprit*.

WHITHER ADMINISTRATION IN THE TWENTY-FIRST CENTURY?

In addressing this question we must be very careful since the very concepts and ideas that we use to answer it are liable to melt in our hands, transmute into unexpected forms, and acquire unintended meanings. The meaning of the very word "administration" is one that undoubtedly has become seriously dislocated in the last hundred years. Yet, at the risk of sweeping over-simplification, I would suggest that throughout our century the prestige and authority of administration has declined. This is a century that not only saw the end of colonial administration, but also one that punctured for good any benevolent interpretations of it. To us, the idea that defeated and oppressed people in distant parts of the globe would willingly submit to being administered by their colonial masters seems preposterous. At the same time, our century has highlighted the unprecedented ability of administration to serve oppressive, inhumane, and even genocidal ends. Administration has inevitably acquired the meaning of a cold, compassionless, and often amoral order, frequently out of touch with the needs of the citizens it ostensibly serves (Jun 1999). To most laypersons, the very word administration has come to connote images of red-tape, pettiness, waste, and obsession, with regularity and control at the expense of all that is vibrant, charged, and enriching in human affairs.

The decline of administration throughout this century is brought into sharper relief by the concomitant rise of management. While many of our predecessors of a hundred years ago were sharply aware of the dangers and potential inhumanity of administration, virtually none of them could have envisaged the triumph of management during this period. The growth of management in the twentieth century is inextricably linked with the rise of the business corporation, consumer capitalism, free trade, global markets, and business education. It is not only that managers currently constitute one of the largest occupational groups in industrialized countries, that they control vast resources, that they are rarely accountable to anyone other than their peers, or that the most famous among them acquire heroic status. Rather, as Drucker has argued: "In less than 150 years, management has transformed the social and economic fabric of the world's developed countries. It has created a global economy and set new rules for countries that would participate in that economy as equals. And it has itself been transformed" (1988:65). Management has colonized every area of personal, group, and social activity as well as the ways we think about them. Thus, the intimate minutiae of personal life are experienced through the notion of management (management of emotion, stress management, managing the mid-life crisis, etc.); equally, however, management has encroached upon the vast panoramas of social life (crowd management, management of the economy, management of the environment, and even management of the planet).

Not for nothing then did MacIntyre (1981) view the manager as one of the three chief character archetypes of the twentieth century, the others being the therapist and the aesthete.

The manager represents in his *character* the obliteration of the distinction between manipulative and nonmanipulative social relations; the therapist represents the same obliteration in the sphere of personal life. The manager treats ends as given, as outside his scope; his concern is with effectiveness in transforming raw materials into final products, unskilled labor into skilled labor, investment into profits. The therapist also treats ends as given, outside his scope; his concern is also with technique, with effectiveness in transforming neurotic symptoms into directed energy, maladjusted individuals into well-adjusted ones. (MacIntyre 1981:30)

The interest in MacIntyre's arguments lies in the fact that while extolling the non-moral authority which has accrued to management, he punctures the two fictitious foundations of that authority—the claim to specialist knowledge and the claim to efficiency. While widely taken for granted, both of these assumptions are fictions, appropriate for an age which has given up rational systems of morality in favour of what he terms "emotivism"—"the doctrine that all evaluative judgments and more specifically all moral arguments are *nothing but* expressions of preference, expressions of attitude or feeling, insofar as they are moral or evaluative in character" (ibid.:11-12). Thus, the manager emerges as a cultural archetype in an age where moral discourse has become a discourse of tastes, preferences, and dispositions, rather than a discourse of justice, virtue, and truth. The conclusion which MacIntyre fails to reach is that management (as does therapy in its distinct way) draws its moral authority in our age from its ability to address the needs of the consumer, i.e. the solitary individual who seeks happiness and pleasure in making choices and offering no account or explanations for them. In his latest work, Ritzer (1999) has provided a convincing argument on how management addresses the consumer—offering the possibility of re-enchanting a disenchanted world through mass festivals in the new cathedrals of consumption, such as theme parks, cruise ships, and above all, shopping malls. What contemporary management does is to furnish, in a highly rationalized manner, an endless stream of consumable fantasies inviting consumers to pick and choose.

The cult of the consumer has now become a major feature of the ideological and political order of the business enterprise, legitimating, justifying, and supporting a wide range of management practices that would be regarded as intolerable had it not been for the belief that the customer is sovereign (Du Gay and Salaman 1992; Gabriel 1999; Long 1999; Sturdy 1998). Consumption has become an ever more important sphere of human existence, one in which meanings and identities are forged and communicated, in which fantasies and desires are acted out, in which group allegiances and antagonisms are fashioned. As Bauman (1988; 1992; 1998) has forcibly argued, in post-modernity, a consumer ethic dislodges the work ethic of past times, acting as the organizing principle for individual perceptions of self and other, restoring pleasure as the key objective of action, and casting the freedom of the capitalist marketplace as the absolute guarantee of individual freedom, fulfillment, and autonomy.

Where does this leave administration? In one way, it leaves administration entirely out of step with the spirit of our time. For if management has embraced the consumer as its brazen ideological and political champion, one who bolsters its authority and widens the remit of its practices, the champion of administration has fallen on very hard times. We are referring, of course, to the citizen, a figure of our political past, whose name may be regularly invoked, yet whose immediacy is scarcely present. Wexler has argued, "in this society, citizenship is an archaic term. It is not part of the language of everyday life. Its value for understanding this life is not evident either" (1990:166). While we have little difficulty in thinking of ourselves as consumers, we find thinking of ourselves as citizens far more problematic. Accustomed as we are to the consumer's privileges of ready gratification, tastes which need not be accounted for, fantasies which may be realized, and images which may be emulated, we find the civic ideal, along with the obligations and duties it entails, its demands on our time, autonomy, and freedom, less appealing.

This, then, seems to me to be the core difference between management and administration and their differing present fortunes. Management has redefined itself as a set of practices and discourses ultimately aimed at satisfying the requirements of a consumer who makes individual free choices and uses his/her money to realize his/her individual desires. In the interest of the consumer, no care is spared and no privation is too great—an "enterprise culture," dynamic, self-confident, attractive, and, of course, thoroughly spurious, has become part of our cultural landscapes. Administration, on the other hand, remains tarnished by its association with grey bureaucracy, resistance to change, ugliness, and the Nanny State, which makes decisions on behalf of the citizens rather than in response to them. Even among academics who adopt a nobler and more sophisticated image of administration, it remains defined by its commitment to serving a community of citizens who take an active interest in public affairs and whose needs cannot be addressed individually, but only collectively. Yet, this very community of citizens has been undermined throughout the twentieth century by a wide variety of forces, not least the professionalization of administration itself (Cooper 1991; Stivers 1990), the tribalization of political and cultural life (Bauman 1992; 1995; Maffesoli 1988), and the encroachment of market relations on political life (Gabriel and Lang 1995; Long 1999; Morgan and Vizzini 1999; Zanetti and Carr 1999). The very essence of modernity has increasingly conspired to disembed individuals from communities fixed in time and space (Giddens 1990; 1991), undermining the conditions for political discourse among citizens (Mulgan 1990).

CITIZENS AND CONSUMERS

The two ideas, consumer and citizen, have very different pedigrees. The citizen, the foundation of Athenian democracy, re-invented and expanded by the American and French revolutions, implies an equality among citizens, even if it denies it to others—slaves, immigrants or refugees. It is essentially a political concept, defining individuals standing within a state and a community, according them rights and responsibilities. The citizen is an impersonation of what Philip Rieff called "political man," the cultural ideal based on the notion that good life, justice, and happiness can be attained through political action rather than religious faith; the latter had been the recipe for salvation of political man's predecessor, the "religious man" (Rieff 1959; 1966). Common to both religious and political ideals was the presupposition that each individual is an organic part of a whole, unable to achieve full individuality and happiness except as a member of that whole. Where the ideal of the citizen dramatically deviated from that of the religious believer was in the inalienable rights of citizens to hold their own opinions and views. One can be a citizen while disagreeing with the government; in critique lies the citizen's thoroughly modern form of freedom.

The consumer, on the other hand, originates in a very different ideal, referred to by Rieff as economic man, who seeks the good life in market transactions. Here individuals act as atoms, unencumbered by social responsibilities and duties, free of the obligation to account for their preferences and choices. Like citizens, consumers are free to criticize; but unlike citizens, they are never required to endure sacrifices for a superior goal, nor do their actions represent anybody other than themselves. They need not defer to any collective majority. Consumers need not be members of a community at all, nor do they have to act on its behalf. As long as they are in a position to pay, they can make choices unburdened by guilt or social obligations. Both Marx and Simmel remarked on how the cash nexus dissolves social bonds, the former to criticize it as the root of alienation under capitalism, the latter to praise it as the liberation from the fetters of the gift economy (Marx 1844/1972; 1867/1967; Simmel 1978).

The idea of the citizen can be easily idealized, becoming the focus of nostalgia for a time when individuals were meant to be active members of political communities. However, if citizenship implies commitment and bonding, it also carries, since its earliest origins, disturbing resonances of exclusion and discrimination. Non-citizens, stateless persons, immigrants, refugees, exiles, people without official papers and fixed addresses, vagrants, these are people who may be legitimately harassed, exploited, and discriminated against in most societies, especially those which place a high premium on citizenship. Consumers, on the other hand, generally face no such discrimination. Through money they may acquire a wide variety of things, including, in many cases, "citizenship."

In spite of the decline of the citizen and the parallel rise of the consumer, recent years have seen something of a renaissance in citizen scholarship, as evidenced by the communitarian and the social capital movements. Both of these approaches have castigated the dissolution of values brought about by unchecked consumerism as well as the attendant dependence of "failed consumers" on the state (See contributions in Etzioni [1998] and Putnam [1995]). Some have sought to bring about a rapprochement of the ideas of citizen and consumer. Many on the left have sought to enlarge the consumer into a responsible consumer, a socially-aware consumer, a consumer who thinks ahead and tempers his or her desires by social awareness, a consumer whose actions must be morally defensible, and a consumer who must occasionally be prepared to sacrifice personal pleasure to communal well-being. In other words, the left has stretched the idea of consumer in the direction of citizen. Thus, Public Citizen and other organizations started by Nader have been prolific in campaigning and promoting the idea of the consumer as citizen. So concerned was Nader's team about the decline of meaningful U.S. citizenship by the early 1990s that it produced a civics package for use in schools. (Isaac 1992) This profiled a number of key citizens' movements representing the rights of women, minorities, consumers, unions, and environment. More importantly, the civics package took students through the options a citizen has for participating in civil society: whistle-blowing, pamphleteering, getting organised, arranging meetings, conducting research, legal action, direct action, becoming a shareholder activist, and so on. The book was a statement, as Nader wrote in the Foreword, of "practicing civics, becoming a skilled citizen, using one's skills to overcome apathy, ignorance, greed or abuses of power in society at all levels...". The message was that the only route to rebuilding citizenship from a consumer starting point was involvement with others.

The right, on the other hand, has sought to bring citizens and consumers together in a different way, by using the concept of "votes" and ballots. According to this argument, consumers vote in the market place in exactly the same way as citizens voted in the Athenian agora of old. The marketplace becomes a surrogate for political discourse, or, in their view, incorporates political discourse rendering it redundant. The citizen is being redefined as a purchaser whose "ballots... help create and maintain the trading areas, shopping centres, products, stores, and the like" (Dickinson and Hollander 1991:12). Buying becomes tantamount to voting, market surveys the nearest we have to a collective will (Ewen 1992:23). In this way, the more wealth or purchasing power the consumer has, the more "votes" she or he gets. So, when the idea of the citizen crops up in discussions of consumption, it assumes different meanings. Nowhere is this more clear than in discussions of television. Market enthusiasts want unregulated television where individuals choose to watch what they wish. If they do not like a program, they vote by switching to a different channel or by switching off. Public service advocates, on the other hand, believe that if individuals act merely as consumers, they end up with a profusion of virtually indistinct channels appealing to the lowest common denominator. Their choice is narrowed to minutiae (Brown 1991). If, on the other hand, they act as citizens, they seek to control and regulate what is shown on their screens, voting for a particular range of options and stopping others. Ultimately, the citizens do not take markets as given but will seek to regulate them, control them, and tame them. They seek to do so either through direct action and active participation, or indirectly, through the state. And this is where the state comes into discussions of citizens and contemporary consumption.

But state is far from a neutral observer of the discourses which have sought to bring consumers and citizens closer to each other. Under the rubric of empowering the citizen through "Citizens' Charters," privatisation of common assets, and the introduction of internal markets in public administration, the New Right sought throughout the 80s and 90s to commodify citizenship and establish the atomized consumer as the sovereign disciplinary agent in public administration. Tax offices, passport offices, prisons, and other government agencies increasingly treat their constituencies as customers, as they seek to fend off further privatization. Hospitals, universities, and schools are already undergoing a metamorphosis from sober and utilitarian deliverers of services to citizens into over-hyped providers of consumer fantasies; as Ritzer has argued:

> [University] administrators are coming to recognize that their educational cam-
> puses need to grow more like the other means of consumption to thrive. The
> high school has been described as resembling a shopping mall. The university,
> too, can be seen as a means of educational consumption. These days most cam-
> puses are dated, stodgy and ineffective compared to shopping malls, cruise
> ships, casinos and fast food restaurants. To compete, universities are trying to
> satisfy their students by offering, for example, "theme housing"—dorms
> devoted to students with shared special interests. As universities learn more and
> more from the new means of consumption, it will be increasingly possible to
> refer to them as "McUniversities." (Ritzer 1999:24)

The consequence of such trends is that many administrators turn increasingly into managers, dealing in the currency of fantasy, emotion, and enchantment. Not all, of course. The current consumer boom is not without its victims. As Bauman has argued, a new class of poor has emerged, one defined not by its absolute stan- dards of hunger and deprivation but by its disenfranchisement from consumer choice. Instead, as welfare recipients they must accept the state's choices on their behalf. "The radical unfreedom of welfare recipients is but an extreme demon- stration of the more general regulatory principle which underlies the vitality of the consumer-led system" (Bauman 1988:69). Far from treating these failed con- sumers as citizens with rights, pride, and dignity, the task of administration has increasingly become that of containing their anger so that they do not spoil the party for the many. The welfare recipients, then, are radically disenfranchised by their inability to consume as they choose and by having choices made on their behalf. A vast disciplinary machinery is set up, with its 'targeting of welfare ben- efits', its constant means testing, its distinctions between the deserving and the undeserving recipients, the bogus and the truthful claimants, a machinery with disciplinary mechanisms of surveillance, repression, and containment. This then becomes the residual domain of administration.

In contrast to attempts to resurrect the citizen as the character who will supply the big idea for the next century, we are impressed by the readiness with which the consumer becomes absorbed by consumerism, either as a disenfranchised and therefore powerless citizen, or as a particular type of citizen, whose wishes can be fulfilled in essentially the same way as those of other consumers. As one reads the emerging literature on social capital and communitarianism, one has the sense of revisiting some of the arguments of nineteenth century utopian socialists, if anything, with much blunted radicalism—wish-fulfilling arguments proceeding from a normative critique of the present. Marx's critique of those noble, but ultimately ineffectual attempts, was that the power of ideas alone is not enough to bring about social change. While ideas are vital in any change process, they must be underpinned by a political will as well as favorable economic and social conditions. In spite of numerous local initiatives, one looks in vain for a political will among citizens to take on the hydra of consumerism, let alone a will on the part of the state to take on the large-scale capitalist organizations which prosper on its back. If anything, it is the consumer (rather than the citizen) who, in a number of areas such as food additives, pesticide residues, genetically modified crops, and environmentally damaging practices, is taking on the producers, consciously or unconsciously boycotting their products and from time to time sending tremors down the financial markets. And by the same token, it could very well be capital that provides consumers with the experience of citizenship, living in small self-contained communities. If consumers get really tired of massive out-of-town cathedrals of consumption, if they desire to re-experience the feel of the small, the local and the rustic, it can all be simulated for their benefit, as the massively successful pseudo-village at Berkeley's Fourth Street with its bijou consumption "chapels" amply demonstrates. The city of Philadelphia provides a good example of how citizenship can be transformed by nostalgia into an eminently consumable commodity. Citizen theme parks may not be that far away in the future.

THE FUTURE OF CRITIQUE

While many have critiqued the culture of consumerism on psychological, political, environmental, economic, and even aesthetic grounds, few claim to have identified any political, economic, or cultural forces which threaten its underlying logic. The citizen, far from emerging as a genuine challenge to the consumer, has, to date, all too easily become part of the consumerist landscape, its spectacles, fantasies, and simulations. As we cross the millennium, there appears to be no end to consumerism and no convincing alternative in site. Thus Ritzer:

> The future will bring with it unimagined palaces of consumption filled to capacity with a cornucopia of goods and services. And they will be incredibly effective selling machines that will bring with them an even further escalation of the consumerism that already is such a dominant reality in the contemporary world.... The increase in consumption shows no signs of ebbing, let alone disappearing. People will need to get what they want somewhere. The landscape formed by the cathedrals of consumption is constantly changing, but though it may encompass a different set of settings, it will be filled with cathedrals. (Ritzer 1999:214-5)

According to this vision, the future will become a more concentrated version of the present—ever more individualistic, ever more materialistic, ever more looking for meaning and purpose in material possessions and exotic experiences to be obtained at a price. In such a future, the citizen, except as object of commodified nostalgia, would no doubt fade out altogether. Marginalized by management, its enterprise culture and its mission to re-enchant the world, administration would be restricted to an ever narrower, ever more repressive, ever more unpopular domain.

While faced with this truly one-dimensional scenario, a wide range of social scientists and cultural critics have moved away from the humanist critique of society. This was the critique pioneered by writers like Marx, Nietzsche, Freud, and the Critical School, which sought to unmask, analyze, and condemn exploitation and alienation, whether as intrinsic to the capitalist system of production, its political order, or its ideological legitimation supplied by the culture of consumerism (Rouanet 1998). It is a critique which has resurfaced through communitarianism but failed to provide the great idea which will challenge the paradigm of consumption. Most critical theorists have beyond doubt lost faith in the humanist ideal, with its mono-cultural, universalist, and rationalist heritage, one which they see as all too easily corrupted into different forms of totalitarianism and domination. Instead, a new range of approaches has emerged, inspired by postmodernist and post-structuralist perspectives which, on the one hand, seek to unmask power and domination in the most intimate interstices of language, while at the same time being determined to celebrate difference, diversity, emotion, and style.

So, what happens to critique in these postmodern times? In a trenchant and finely crafted "critique," Grey (1999) has argued that many and diverse attempts to critique postmodern organizational practices rooted in consumerism lapse into sentimental nostalgia for some presumed golden age of organizations which were characterized by justice, order, integrity, and a family-like ethos of caring. Grey has no difficulty is establishing that even the *modernist* critique of modernity (along not only Marxist and Critical theory lines, but also straight sociological ones inspired by Weber, Durkheim, Tönnies, and others) entails nostalgic elements for the presumed authenticity and integrity of the pre-modern. He then proceeds to undermine such critiques by arguing along lines that this writer had proposed (Gabriel 1993), that nostalgia is more a reflection of current discontents than the actualities of yesteryear. In the wake of the demise of humanism, he finds critiques of enterprise culture, consumerism, and McDonaldization on moral, political, and rational grounds, unconvincing and untenable. It makes no sense to argue that these contemporary trends dehumanize or alienate the human subject, that they disenfranchise the citizenry, or that they exploit worker and consumer alike, since the measure of all such assertions, namely what it means to be human, has melted away.

Having rejected a critique inspired by humanism, Grey proposes an aesthetic critique of postmodernity. Using Kant's idea of a disinterested aesthetic judgement, which is at once subjective and yet capable of being treated as objective, Grey puts forward an audacious critique of postmodern organizational practices, not as immoral, oppressive, or deceitful, but rather as ugly, indeed grotesque. He offers an amusing list of absurd abuses of language perpetrated by management gurus and their acolytes which he invites the disinterested reader to share. Indeed, one could extend Grey's argument by observing the revolting qualities of various features of contemporary culture, from body piercing to fashion in clothes, from popular music to postmodern architecture, and from corporate logos to what passes as haute-cuisine (curry of New Zealand mussels with avocado and oyster mushrooms, served *en-cocote* with a *gratin* of cabbage). Such critique, which can be both amusing and intimidating (see Bourdieu 1984), doubtless raises the critic above the foolishness of contemporary culture, yet, in a paradoxical way, post-modernity with its exaltation of the irreverent, the shocking, and the grotesque, renders it ineffective. Why critique the ugly, when we can celebrate it as an indis-pensable part of a postmodern carnival? Why disparage the ugliness of contem-porary management practices when they keep the workers quiet and the consumers happy? Indeed, how much uglier the dark corridors and cell-like offices of modernist administration may be when compared with the spacious atriums and open-plans of postmodern management.

A different attempt to resurrect critique in postmodern times is offered by Antonacopoulou (1999). Her argument develops from those aspects of critique which postmodernity *has* generated—the critique of discursive practices which marginalize or silence women and minority groups, and the critique of a language which incorporates power and muffles opposition (See, e.g., Alvesson and Willmott 1992; 1996; Carr 1997; Parker 1995; Thompson 1993; Willmott 1993). She argues that far from obliterating criticism, postmodernity allows new forms of critique to emerge, critique which is not overawed or powerless in the face of established conventions and practices, but surgically cuts through them when tra-ditional Marxist/humanist critiques have become increasingly blunt. The critiques of rhetoric, tradition, authority, and objectivity become more far-reaching when undertaken not from a fixed position, but as an affirmation of the ability to think differently, to see differently, and to act differently. Thus, in postmodernity, cri-tique becomes praxis and lived experience rather than a cerebral motivated process. In this way, Antonacopoulou seeks to vindicate critique not as the mech-anism for discovering a promised land of happiness and justice (something that is untenable in post-humanist times), but as a way of life, which leaves nothing unquestioned, not even the endlessly shifting grounds of its own motivation. In Antonacopoulou's argument, critique is not concomitant with some general rev-olutionizing project of society, but a restless quality of spirit which never stands still; it constantly seeks to create the space for new possibilities, not just alterna-tives. This is a strong argument which can be used to bolster even the communi-tarian and social capital critiques. It does, however, engender certain risks. It is perfectly possible to imagine a society of highly critical and judgemental individ-uals where nothing ever changes as a result of everyone criticizing everything, a society of possibilities dreamt but forever unrealized. Critique, too, can become a commodity, traded like other commodities, bought, sold, used, and discarded. You are critical of traditional administration/literature/architecture/music etc.? We can supply you with alternative administration/literature/architecture/music etc. Thus, in postmodern times we have a profusion of "alternative" offerings aimed at critics, just as we have numerous aimed at rebels. Like rebellion, commodified critique disintegrates into dandyism, a highly individualistic affirmation of one's difference and little else.

In fact, we could go further and argue that postmodernity both normalizes and emasculates critique. Nothing is sacred, nothing is above criticism. What is a cultural event nowadays if not an event which gets the critics excited and converts everyone into a critic? The more revered the object of criticism, the more iconoclastic the criticism, the easier it becomes an object of discussion, controversy and consumption. Critique proliferates to the point where meaning and value constantly disintegrate, swallowed into those semiotic black holes noted by Baudrillard (1983a, 1983b). Critique thus ceases to be *socially dangerous* (although it may be personally dangerous) and, like citizenship, becomes an easily accommodated part of the all-devouring processes of consumption.

While the hegemony of consumerism as a set of cultural, organizational, and political practices seems scarcely challenged by attempts at critique or at raising a convincing ideological alternative, it would be surpassingly naïve to disregard its precariousness in the face of material forces that will threaten it in the century ahead. Environmental degradation, widening social and economic inequalities, ever-increasing work insecurity, continuing erosion of community, massive political upheaval, and self-revolutionizing technology—these factors are likely to test the hegemony of consumerism in ways that have not been tested thus far. Will people continue to flip through their TV channels and click their way through internet sites engrossed in their consumer fantasies and dreams, or will they seek to make their voices heard and their actions count in ways different from that of entering their credit card details? Will the economy continue to deliver the goods? Will free trade continue to dominate? Will the capitalist state continue to sing to the tune of big business? Will the anger of the disenfranchised continue to be contained and silenced? In addition to such potential external checks on consumerism, internal checks could be even more important. Will the overspent and overstretched consumers continue to overspend and overstretch themselves, or will a new downshifting ethic take hold of them? Will their idyll with spectacle and fantasy lose its appeal? Will the capriciousness of their tastes and preferences continue to be accommodated within the system?

It is not possible to anticipate answers to such questions, although it would be very interesting to revisit them in thirty or forty years' time and judge their appropriateness. It seems to me indisputable that a consumer driven free-market world economy has answered successfully the questions that radicals and critics were asking thirty or forty years ago. Its capacity to resist both implosion and explosion, its abilities to metamorphose in the light of changing circumstances, to incorporate new cultural currents and trends, to instigate and take advantage of fantastic technological and scientific developments, to numb and absorb the discontents and malaise which it generated, would have surprised even its warmest apologists of the fifties and sixties. It remains to be seen whether it will continue to do so in the years ahead or whether it encounters a massive and unpredicted discontinuity.

NOTE

1. I would like to thank my friends Elena Antonacopoulou, Jane Gabriel, and Tim Lang for their many useful suggestions and comments.

REFERENCES

Alvesson, M. & H. Willmott, eds. 1992a. *Critical Management Studies*. London: Sage.

————. 1992b. On the idea of emancipation in management and organization studies. *Academy of Management Review*. 17(3):432-464.

————. 1996. *Making Sense of Management*. London: Sage.

Antonacopoulou, E. P. 1999. The power of critique: Revisiting critical theory at the end of the century. 1st International Critical Management Studies Conference, Manchester.

Baudrillard, J. 1983a. *In the Shadow of the Silent Majorities*. New York: Semiotext(e).

————. 1983b. *Simulations*. New York: Semiotext(e).

Bauman, Z. 1988. *Freedom*. Minneapolis, MN. University of Minnesota Press.

————. 1992. *Intimations of Postmodernity*. London: Routledge.

Bauman, Z. 1995. *Life in Fragments: Essays in Postmodern Morality*. Oxford, UK: Blackwell.

————. 1998. *Work, Consumerism and the New Poor*. Buckingham: Open University Press.

Bourdieu, P. 1984. *Distinction: A Social Critique of the Judgement of Taste*. London: Routledge.

Brown, D. H. 1991. Citizens or consumer: US reactions to the European Community's directive on television. *Critical Studies in Mass Communication*. 8:1-12.

Carr, A. 1997. Organization theory and postmodern thinking: The uncertain place of human agency. *Policy Organization and Society*. (13):82-104.

Cooper, T. 1991. *An Ethic of Citizenship for Public Administration*. Englewood Cliffs, NJ: Prentice Hall.

Dickinson, R. & S. C. Hollander 1991. Consumer votes. *Journal of Business Research*. 22:335-342.

Drucker, P. F. 1988. Management and the world's work. *Harvard Business Review*. (September-October), 66:65-76.

Du Gay, P. & G. Salaman 1992. The cult(ure) of the customer. *Journal of Management Studies* 29(5):615-633.

Etzioni, A., ed. 1998. *The Essential Communitarian Reader*. Lanham, MD: Rowman & Littlefield.

Ewen, S. 1992. From consumer to citizen. *Intermedia*. 20(3):22-23.

Gabriel, Y. 1993. Organizational nostalgia: Reflections on the Golden Age. *Emotion in Organizations*, edited by S. Fineman. London: Sage. 118-141.

Gabriel, Y. 1999. Beyond happy families: A critical re-evaluation of the control-resistance-identity triangle. *Human Relations*. 52(2):179-203.

Gabriel, Y. & T. Lang 1995. *The Unmanageable Consumer: Contemporary Consumption and its Fragmentation*. London: Sage.

Giddens, A. 1990. *The Consequences of Modernity*. Stanford, CA: Stanford University Press.

———. 1991. *Modernity and Self-Identity: Self and Society in the Late Modern Age*. Stanford, CA: Stanford University Press.

Grey, C. 1999. The future of critique in organization and management theory: From nostalgia to aesthetics. Paper presented at the 1st International Critical Management Studies Conference, Manchester.

Hobsbawm, E. 1994. *Age of Extremes: The Short Twentieth Century 1914-1991*. London: Michael Joseph.

Isaac, K. 1992. *Civics for Democracy: A Journey for Teachers and Students*. The Center for Study of Responsive Law and Essential Information. Washington, DC: Essential Books.

Jun, J. S. 1999. The need for autonomy and virtues: Civic-minded administrators in a civil society. *Administrative Theory & Praxis*. 21(2):218-226.

Long, S. 1999. The tyranny of the customer and the cost of consumerism: An analysis using systems and psychoanalytic approaches to groups and society. *Human Relations*. 52(6):723-743.

MacIntyre, A. 1981. *After Virtue*. London, Duckworth.

Maffesoli, M. 1988. Jeux de masques. *Design Issues*. 4(1-2).

Marx, K. 1844/1972. Economic and philosophic manuscripts of 1844. *The Marx-Engels Reader*, edited by R. C. Tucker. New York: Norton.

———. 1867/1967. *Capital*. New York: International Publishers.

Morgan, D. and D. Vizzini 1999. Transforming customers into citizens: Some preliminary lessons from the field. *Administrative Theory & Praxis*. 21(1):51-61.

Mulgan, J. 1990. *Politics in an Anti-Political Age*. Oxford: Polity Press.

Parker, M. 1995. Critique in the name of what? Postmodernism and critical approaches to organization. *Organization Studies*. 16(4):553-564.

Putnam, R. D. 1995. Tuning in, tuning out: The strange disappearance of social capital in America. *PS: Political Science and Politics*. 28(4):664-683.

Rieff, P. 1959. *Freud: The Mind of a Moralist*. New York: Doubleday.

———. 1966. *The Triumph of the Therapeutic*. New York: Harper & Row.

Ritzer, G. 1999. *Enchanting a Disenchanted World: Revolutionizing the Means of Consumption*. Thousand Oaks, CA: Pine Forge Press.

Rouanet, S. P. 1998. Modernity and its discontents. Http://www.ipa.org.uk/rouanet.htm

Simmel, G. 1978. *The Philosophy of Money*. London: Routledge & Kegan Paul.

Stivers, C. 1990. The public agency as polis: Active citizenship in the administrative state. *Administration and Society*. 22(1):86-105.

Sturdy, A. 1998. Customer care in a consumer society: Smiling and sometimes meaning it? *Organization,* 5(1):27-53.

Thompson, P. 1993. Postmodernism: Fatal distraction. *Postmodernism and Organizations*, edited by J. Hassard and M. Parker. London: Sage. 183-203.

Wexler, P. 1990. Citizenship in the semiotic society. *Theories of Modernity and Postmodernity*, edited by B. S. Turner. London: Sage. 164-175.

Willmott, H. 1993. Strength is ignorance; Slavery is freedom: Managing culture in modern organizations. *Journal of Management Studies*. 30:515-552.

Zanetti, L. and A. Carr. 1999. Exaggerating the dialectic: Postmodernism's "new individualism" and the detrimental effects on citizenship. *Administrative Theory and Praxis*. 21(2).

3

"Future Challenges in Organization Theory?" Amnesia and the Production of Ignorance

Martin Parker

FUTURE CHALLENGES IN ORGANIZATION THEORY?

In Jorge Luis Borges' short story, "Pierre Menard: Author of the *Quixote*," we find an intriguing intellectual puzzle. Among Pierre Menard's work, as well as many other things, we find "the ninth and thirty-eighth chapters of the first part of *Don Quixote* and a fragment of chapter twenty-two" (1981: 65). In the 1930s, Borges tells us, Menard has re-constructed, "word for word and line for line," parts of a book written by Miguel de Cervantes at the beginning of the seventeenth century. But this is no mere plagiarism, for Menard's *Quixote* is "almost infinitely richer" than Cervantes'. Indeed, how could it not have been, since three hundred years have passed in the interval between the two texts?

The point, or perhaps one of the many possible points, of this re-telling is to insist that texts can only gain their meaning from contexts—the weaving together of adjacent texts. Reading Menard is to read a different *Don Quixote* than the one that was written earlier. As Borges tells us:

> The latter, for example, wrote (part one, chapter nine):
> ...truth, whose mother is history, rival of time, depository of deeds, witness
> of the past, exemplar and advisor to the present, and the future's counselor.
> Written in the seventeenth century, written by the "lay genius" Cervantes, this
> enumeration is a mere rhetorical praise of history. Menard, on the other, writes:
> ...truth, whose mother is history, rival of time, depository of deeds, witness
> of the past, exemplar and advisor to the present, and the future's counselor.

History, the *mother* of truth: the idea is astounding. Menard, a contemporary of William James, does not define history as an enquiry into reality but as its origin. Historical truth, for him, is not what has happened: it is what we judge to have happened. (1981: 69)

And if I write that truth, whose mother is history, rival of time, depository of deeds, witness of the past, exemplar and advisor to the present, and the future's counselor? A wordy, confused, and perhaps rather sexist claim, for a contemporary of Michel Foucault.[1] The therapeutic implications of counseling are suggestive, but witnessing and advising must surely be meant ironically.

Borges' work is full of these puzzles—of books within books, paradoxes of time, and problems of consciousness. In another story in the collection, "Funes the Memorius," we meet someone who remembers everything. "In fact, Funes remembered not only every tree of every leaf of every wood, but also every one of the times he had perceived or imagined it" (1981: 93). What if we never forgot anything? What kind of library might be needed to hold a single life, let alone the output of an academic discipline? Now it seems to me that these are the sorts of questions which should inform any serious investigation into the past and present of any intellectual "project"—a word which conceals and dignifies at the same time. "Organization theory," like "administrative theory," is one such project, and in order to think about its new century it will undoubtedly be helpful to consider its past century. So, in this essay, I will explore some of the assumptions that commonly go unrecognized within common accounts of intellectual progress. My themes will therefore be remembering, forgetting, and the production of ignorance, not as a way of criticizing the present for the crime of having forgotten its past, but as constituent elements in the very making of disciplinary knowledge itself.

ORGANIZATION THEORY?

So perhaps, in order to write a text which addresses the ponderous question of "future challenges in organization theory?" I can repeat some fragments of a blind Argentinean librarian written fifty years before my time and leave it at that. That might make my point well enough, but the context of this essay demands rather more, so let me begin again.

The words we use to refer to intellectual projects are themselves rather instructive, even if they are not often reflected upon as topics in themselves. In the various "sciences" of organization, there is very little consensus on terminology. As Clegg and Hardy noted in the preface to their recent handbook (1996: xxiii), "organizational science," "organizational theory," and "organizational studies" all seem to mean slightly different things. I, as a (self-styled "critical") writer on organizations working within a Management Department in England, like to use the phrase "organization theory" to describe what it is that I do. I like "organization theory" because it seems to suggest a degree of conceptual sensitivity and because it preserves the tension between organization as an entity and organization as a process. In other words, it helps me to situate myself (for myself, and hence for others) as a sociologist and philosopher, and not a mere management scientist. An intellectual, and not a technician of managerial administration. Whether this self-other (and theory-practice) relation is warranted in any way is not the topic of this essay—though it may be exemplified through it.

"Organization Theory" aside, there are many other words that purport to describe this intellectual domain too. For me, they all have slightly different connotations—mostly ones that I would not wish to attach my writing to. "Organizational behavior" is the most commonly used. As exemplified in textbooks it seems to mean a catalogue of facts required to pass a business qualification in "people" and "organization"—or some such title. It is managerialist, but softly so, and scientific, but aware of the possible criticisms of hypothetico-deductive enquiry. A model liberal in fact, who sets himself (and it is still usually a "him") up as the good cop against the various bad cops of technical management. Not critical enough to get thrown off the MBA syllabus, but enough to be a little risqué sometimes. "Organizational analysis" and "organization studies" are alternative terms which cover the same kind of area. They are, perhaps, rather more academically respectable and have less of an emphasis on the people and groups parts of psychology. "Organization science" is another academically respectable term, primarily used in North America, but one that embraces performative and testable knowledges, this time with more of an emphasis on the psy-sciences and less on sociology. "Organizational psychology," "organizational anthropology," "organizational communication" (again in the U.S. primarily), and "organizational sociology" also appear to occupy parts of the terrain, but gain their legitimacy by referring back to another (perhaps more established) discipline from which they claim an authoritative ancestry. In the UK, "industrial sociology" is a slightly antiquated term to refer to something similar which also has some connections to "industrial relations," though in both cases with an emphasis on trade unions and industrial conflict. Like all lists, this is not an exhaustive one, but it makes my point well enough.

Now I am not claiming that all these terms refer to the same thing. Indeed, I am not even trying to claim that there is such a thing to be definitively named. This proliferation of names, their associated histories and boundaries, and the moral hierarchies which attach to them seem to suggest that some of the terms in my question are flawed. "Future challenges in...," in what? Perhaps the only answer is the time-honoured "it all depends what you mean by..." (The staple of social scientists for some considerable time now.) Which is really just another way of pointing to the relation between text and context. But I can also repeat myself, and hence demonstrate the contingency of my list. Since I claimed to be "a (self-styled 'critical') writer on organizations working within a Management Department in England," the divisions and distinctions I have made might not make much sense to someone who works somewhere else, in a different context, or a different time. Indeed, the very meaning of "a (self-styled 'critical') writer on organizations working within a Management Department in England" may have a rather less determinate reading than I was assuming it had when I first wrote it, just as it does in this text, because it meant something rather different a few paragraphs previously.

And now I can imagine one of my imaginary readers sighing, flicking forwards in the book, wondering what the point of this meandering might be. This seems to be another piece of pointless reflexivity, the beginnings of a meander that eventually becomes so convoluted that it connects back to where it started, a fold in the text that contains nothing of use. I will have to, for the third time, begin again.

FOUNDATIONS: FROM IGNORANCE TO KNOWLEDGE

There is a common story told amongst my people. It is a story of how, as Perrow put it rather neatly in 1973—"the forces of light and the forces of darkness" continue to battle with each other. This phrase I first saw cited in Roy Jacques splendid book on the history of U.S. management thought (1996: 137), but he may well have first seen it reprinted in Gareth Morgan's teaching resourcebook published seven years previously (1989: 41). Indeed Morgan himself was quite likely to have read the account, as it was paraphrased in John Wilkins' account of certain connections or affinities between Cartesian thought and organizational analysis (1981: 63) which was circulating at Lancaster around that time. The "original" text was, so the citations tell us, published in 1973 and was ironically entitled *The Short and Glorious History of Organization Theory*, but appears to borrow heavily (in a conceptual sense) from Alvin Gouldner's essay on organizational analysis first published in 1959. Gouldner cites (amongst others) Saint-Simon, Weber, and Comte, but in a footnote he writes:

> I have used Comte as a historical marker with the object of emphasizing his intellectual influence rather than his intellectual originality. *It is evident that thinkers prior to Comte held some of the ideas here associated with him.* (1959: 402, note 4, my italics)

So where did this story come from? Perhaps we can never be sure. Perhaps it would be more productive to re-tell the story, and see where that takes us in our quest for future challenges. Perrow's account begins something like this:

> From the beginning, the forces of light and the forces of darkness have polarized the field of organizational analysis, and the struggle has been protracted and inconclusive. The forces of darkness have been represented by the mechanical school of organizational theory—those who treat the organization as a machine. This school characterizes organizations in terms of such things as: centralized authority, clear lines of authority, specialization and expertise, marked division of labor, rules and regulations, and clear separation of staff and line.

> The forces of light, which by mid-20th century came to be characterised as the
> human relations school, emphasizes people rather than machines, accommo-
> dations rather than machine-like precision, and draws its inspiration from bio-
> logical systems rather than engineering systems. It has emphasized such things
> as: delegation of authority, employee autonomy, trust and openness, concerns
> with the "whole person," and interpersonal dynamics. (1973: 8, for a shorter
> version, see Jacques 1999: 209)

There are (at least) two possible economies at work in this story—one modernizing (or "foundational"), one rather more playful (or "relational"). The former is a glorious story of one hundred years of war on ignorance, a century of
intellectual and moral progress. Before bureaucracy and scientific management,
organizations were in the dark ages—rife with inefficiency, despotism, and
patronage. Turn of the century writers like Taylor and Weber (amongst others) are
suggested to have recognised or brought into being a new way of thinking about
organizations, which conceptualised them as logically structured machines.
Bureaucracies operated without hatred or passion, according to the legislative
rule book, and every member (but particularly those at the bottom) was subject to
the disciplines of work study and time and motion. Attendance was ensured by the
pay-packet, obedience with the threat of dismissal and efficiency by the man in
the white coat with the stopwatch and clipboard. Organizational science then built
up from these original foundations. Mayo invented human relations, Maslow a
hierarchy of needs, McGregor a Theory Y, culture replaced structure, and so on.
Organizational development and personnel management replaced hiring, firing,
and time sheets. Now, the proponents of this story suggest, organizational and
societal evolution has meant that the external coercions of bureaucracy and work
study are being (or should be) replaced by a new kind of flexible, virtual, post-
bureaucratic, commitment-based organization. In order that organizations
become more effective, these writers suggest that we must grow to love them, to
operate (as the introduction to this volume implies) *with* hatred and passion.

Whilst such labels are often misleading, this is an archetypal "foundational"
(or, if you prefer, "modernist") story. As Brech put it some time ago:

> Accumulated knowledge garnered by patient painstaking labours in the back-
> rooms is now borne in triumph to some board room ... for one thing above all
> else is receiving universal acclaim, that the harnessing of science and technical
> knowledge is a task for "management." (1963: 3)

The story posits an object of knowledge, a "one best" technology of knowing
and a recursive application of that technology to achieve progress. A discipline—
like organization theory or administrative theory—can then be built from the
foundations up. This is a highly enabling collection of concepts because it provides the conditions of possibility for specialists in research and consultancy, for
certain kinds of institutions to house these specialists, for books, journals, and
edited collections. In short, for criteria of success and failure. If such criteria were

not in place then contributors to a discipline would not know whether they had added a legitimate piece of intellectual masonry to the edifice. And, of course, once these material and social bits and pieces have been put in place and stabilised, we can then refer to a disciplinary history (a past) and a disciplinary project (the future). So it seems that the question of "*rethinking* organization theory" is not only a question which must assume "organization theory" (see above), but is also a mechanism which constitutes the "challenges" of the new century. That is to say, the routine discovery of "gaps in the literature," and the plea that "more research is needed." We may have resolved certain problems, but there are always more to be found. This is the paradox of the journey. Progress never stops, and the library always has empty shelves waiting to be filled.[2]

RELATIONS: THE PRODUCTION OF IGNORANCE

But, as I suggested, "Perrow's" story—for it is surely his now—can be read in rather a different way too. I hesitate to call this "postmodern," that is too easy, too glib. I will instead settle on the term "relational." His essay can, like any text, be re-read ironically, and its displacement to this essay, here, makes a modernising reading even more difficult. Perrow frames the trivial paper battle between warring intellectual factions as if it were a bloody military campaign, yet acknowledges that "the struggle has been protracted and inconclusive" (1973: 8). The implication is that the battle may never be finally won, not because there are always empty shelves, but because each side needs the other in order to ensure that the battle continues. The point here is that combatants would not be able to recognise that they were the forces of light without the forces of darkness being there also, and this point holds good whichever side the labels are attached to. (Which is usually a simple matter of where the author stands on whatever the matter at hand might be.) The logic goes like this—for illumination to be needed, some form of obscurity must be produced at the same time. Note that these terms are not simply descriptions, but that they contain a moral imperative too. They suggest the need for a certain kind of humble movement, away from the shadows of ignorance and towards the light of understanding.

Now, this is a "relational" understanding of knowledge because it doesn't assume that there is a single fixed place called ignorance a series of moves away from this place which can be called knowledge. It is relational because it doesn't assume that the disciplinary foundations for the production of knowing are always stable. This is to reverse the usual way of approaching such matters. Usually, adherents to a particular discipline will refer to knowledge production as if it were a matter of producing more and more lightbulbs that can finally illuminate a particular domain. However, following a more relational form of argument, it might equally be suggested that the production of ignorance is a process which occurs in parallel. This is not to give either "knowing" or "ignorance" a priority here, but simply to suggest that disciplines would not be able to achieve what they term "progress" unless they defined certain things as problems waiting to be solved.

They may not have been problems previously, and they may not sound like problems if they are translated into other areas of human activity, but their generation is essential if a discipline is to thrive and grow.

There are other matters at play here too, of course. The legitimation of problems is not simply a question for a community of neo-scholastics. To suggest that would be to assume two rather contentious descriptions of intellectual activity today. The first has already been alluded to, that there is often (perhaps always) no clear way to define where one intellectual "field" stops and another begins. In the 1860s Thomas Carlyle remarked of one of his contemporaries that he:

> does not enter on the field to till it: He only encompasses it with fences, invites cultivators, and drives away intruders; often ... he is reduced to long arguments with the passers-by, to prove that it is a field, that this so highly prized domain of his is, in truth, soil and substance, not clouds and shadow. (cited in Beer 1992: 1-2)

What counts as "organization theory" is clearly a contested field, and there are many shadowed areas which might be claimed by different disciplines. As a result, one discipline's rules for the production of ignorance partly depends on what these rules might be in other contextual fields. This essay is a case in point. My problem might be counted as a legitimate one within the philosophy or sociology of knowledge—one of the fields that I as "a (self-styled 'critical') writer on organizations working within a Management Department in England" would want to attach myself to. Whether it is legitimate within "organization behaviour," or "administrative theory," is a rather more questionable matter, but I doubt it. Yet, as domains shift and change, so do the rules for the production of ignorance, so there may be (as Menard's story would suggest) a re-reading and writing of this text in the future that will be very different to its context now.

The second issue is related to the first, but is concerned with the boundaries between intellectual disciplines and other forms of contextual practice. The kinds of problems that are given within a particular field are also necessarily related to some sense of the broader intellectual climate. This, I suppose, is what gets termed "politics," "economics," "history," "geography," and so on—though the divisions that produce these terms are themselves contextual, relational. The problem of "management," for example, is not a timeless one. It would not be self-evident to a seventeenth century Spanish author what this term meant, or what should be done with it. And, at the same time, old problems turn to dust from lack of attention. There is, to my knowledge, little contemporary interest in solving the problem of the substance of angels. Indeed, at the present time, there seem to be a wide variety of interest groups and institutions which are primarily concerned with defining ignorances. In the United Kingdom, academics are beset by research funding councils, publishers, professional bodies, audit exercises, and career structures which define and refine the valid and relevant problems of the day. Pressing social, psychological, and organizational problems are identified and research is solicited.

In this way, "stress," "knowledge management," "business ethics," or whatever are constructed as matters which require increasingly urgent attention. This is not to make a judgement on whether these matters are of "real" concern, they clearly are, but only to point to the ways in which their status as "gap" is produced.

But, for many of the reasons I have suggested so far, I cannot ignore the context of this text so willfully for so long. Chapters in academic books like this one require more than I have written. It is not enough to argue a point, however elegant I might believe such an argument to be, I must connect my argument to other texts more explicitly. For this chapter to count, for it to be countable, it should be firmly inserted into an existing problem. However, my problem is that there often seems to be no particular problem about asking questions about "future challenges in organization theory?" So, in order to construct some ignorance, I will begin (yet again), but this time in concert with some others.

SOME WORKED EXAMPLES

In a book entitled *The Practical Commercial Self-Educator*, published in 1947, we find the following paragraphs:

> A business, if it is a sound one, is something essentially dynamic, vital, *alive*. It possesses a mysterious collection of attributes to which we refer in an individual as personality; and it grows and develops, adapting itself to its environment and watching alertly for circumstances which it can turn to its own advantage. Here then is a more encouraging conception for the worker employed on some relatively humble job in a business. He is no mere cog in a soulless machine; rather he is one of many living cells in a purposeful, pulsating organism to the lifestream of which it is within his power to contribute his own individual share of vital energy. (Robinson 1947: 5, italics in original)

Pierre Menard in mind, would these words be out of place in the work of a contemporary management guru, or even a student "text" book? If we inserted some references to "teamwork," "trust," or "culture," would we notice that Charles Robinson wrote this over half a century ago? It seems to me that the problems, and hence ignorances, set in motion at least fifty years prior to Robinson are still informing the majority of academic work on organizations in our present age.

In Roy Jacques' recent book, this kind of archaeology is worked through in great detail. In charting the development of "management" (as a word, occupational title and academic discipline) in the United States, he grounds his argument in the gradual transition from Federalism to industrialism. For Jacques, Federalism is a way of describing the self-image of the early U.S. republican subject—a "conceptual language of frontier, community, small-town life, and individual self-sufficiency" (1996: xiii). As he argues, this was a discourse about character—the omnicompetence of the average citizen; a preference for action over words; and the harmony of self-interest and the wider social good. These ideas were rooted in a theology of Protestant perfectionism—that any man could achieve knowledge of God. He suggests that this ethos encouraged the development of a form of corporatism which made no easy distinction between sacred and profane, church and state, life and business. The notion of the "voluntary association of free, self determining citizens" (1996: 22) was one which reflected a middle class mentality, as well as a white male one, yet it continues to haunt the American dream to this day.

In historical terms, though the ghost of Federalism lives on, we can chart the demise of its "reality" from the U.S. Civil War onwards. Structurally, the organization of scale begins to dominate the business scene, and owner-operators become less common. The local discipline of small craft shops run by foremen and overlookers gives way to centralized administration—to the "files" as Weber put it (1948: 197). The new *employé*—originally a worker in a French *bureau*—is paid "wages" for his or her time, and the "job" comes to mean organizational work, rather than a parcel of work to be paid for on completion. At roughly the same time, the intellectual landscape changes too. The "labor question" arises in consequence of a fear of mass rule; the governance of large organizations becomes the "works management question;" and the "trust question" reflects the fear of oligopolistic control of markets by the emerging large corporations. So are problems defined, and ignorances emerge.

And here we can see the key change. The "ideal typical" Federalist worker controlled a particular work process from start to finish, was paid for outcomes, worked to gain enough capital to start an independent business, did not accept subordination to wage labor, and was potentially competent in all the roles of a citizen. The *employé* permanently "serves" a "boss" (from the Dutch *baas*—master) and is subordinated to become a resource for production. This new type of worker is deemed to be essentially childlike and ignorant, and therefore in need of instruction and classification by specialists. Taylor's famous "mentally sluggish" Schmidt may have been building a house in his spare time (Jacques 1996: 72), but within his work role he was necessarily subjected to the disciplines of his superiors. Yet the existence of this new organizational subject required other kinds of *employé*—the manager and the professional. *Il maneggio*, the handler (initially applied to horses, then man) replaces the foreman to solve the "works management question," and the scientific knowledge required to service both is supplied by the new organizational professional with "divine calling, vocation, being displaced by the notion of specialised expertise" (1996: 89). By the end of the nineteenth century these three industrial subjects—the employee, manager, and professional—are pitted against each other, each requiring the other for existence. In that sense they are all trapped within a relational web, defining the kinds of problems that must be addressed.

Importantly for this essay, the point that Jacques makes is that this history shapes U.S. understandings of what counts as "management" and "organization." He demonstrates this beautifully with a series of quotes from turn of the century texts which clearly prefigure the business revolution announced by authors like Drucker, Peters, Hammer and Champy, and so on. Take this one, for example, "It is an important part of [*the manager's*] duties to find out what [*the worker's*] ideas and opinions are ... and thus to make capital out of their originality and their suggestions" (1996: 3). This is not a quotation from Peter Senge, but an aphorism of Edison's cited in Shaw's *Handling Men,* published in 1917. Jacques provides the reader with many such archaeological surprises that turn claims to novelty into rememberings of what has already gone before. Similar arguments can be found in Pollert's dismissal of post-Fordism and flexibility as "old wine in new bottles" (1988); Grint's paper on Business Process Re-engineering, in which he claims that all of its key features can be dated to earlier literature (1994); Snider (1998) and Newman and Guy's (1998) claims about the contemporary relevance of Mary Parker Follett; and a later paper by Jacques which dates HRM back to the early years of the century (1999: 203). So, on the basis of these explorations, it would seem that accounts of "progress" in writing and thinking about management and organizations should be treated with caution. This might suggest, at least, the need to historicize our understanding of knowledge, particularly in an area which parades its breathless amnesia as an unique selling point.

If these ideas begin to demonstrate the importance of history in subtly shaping disciplinary "problems," some research I have been doing recently explores just how productive such forgetting can be. I'll borrow some of my own words here (but the full account can be found in Parker 2000).[3] I address the question of how contemporary management knowledge has been "invented" by investigating the addition of one relatively recent concept to its canon—"organizational culture." When U.S. management gurus began to write about organizational or corporate culture in the late 1970s and early 1980s, it was as if the idea had sprung from nowhere. The story told was one of the dominance of structural models of organization in management education, of functionalism in academic theory, and of accountancy in practice. An ignorance had been created and organizational culture was then proposed as an alternative way of thinking about managing. But much of this work was premised on the assumption that there was something new happening here, that something had been found that was not there before. By the mid 1980s, management academics were beginning to use the concept routinely, and yet the gradual erasure of a wide body of much earlier writings during that decade was quite remarkable. Increasingly, it seemed to me, the standard citations within works on culture became post 1980s writings from other management academics. Two exemplars will suffice. Andrew Brown's text *Organizational Culture* (1995) contains about 190 items in the bibliography, of which only 33 were published before 1980. If we discount general citations, we are left with 13 citations from 190 which might link post 1980s writing to earlier ideas. Similarly, Joanne Martin and Peter Frost's *review* of the culture debates (1996) contains about 180 citations. This time 30 were published before 1980. If we again discount general citations we are left with 14 citations relevant to culture. It seems evident that much earlier work is being written out of the canon, and since the two texts I selected above will themselves be used to reproduce the discipline, this is a revisionist project that is likely to continue. So, what is being forgotten?

As I suggested previously, from at least Weber onwards, a central problem for writings on organization was the tension between the formal and the informal, between structure and culture, or as Gouldner put it, between "rational" and "natural-system" models of organization (1959/1965). The "culture" of the 1980s was not really a new concept, but one that had been central in various guises ("climate," "atmosphere," "personality," "institutionalisation," "informal organization," and so on) in the study of organizations for at least eighty years previously. Indeed, we can find all of the constituent elements of organizational culturalism prior to its supposed "discovery"—liberalising and flattening bureaucracy, quasi-anthropological terminology, an attempt to insert accounts of meaning, the manager as character shaper, the humanization of work organizations, and so on. So the themes raised by the organizational culturalists in the early 1980s were far from new. That these strands found expression in the culturalism of the 1980s was simply the latest move in a relationship in which cultural accounts of organization have been framed as an "other" to structural ones. Light and darkness, yet again.

My point here is not only to make some dull scholastic point—that other writers had already been concerned with these matters—but to suggest that there is something interesting going on when so much writing gets effectively forgotten. It might be that this amnesia is related to the construction and legitimation of organization theory as a particular form of academic labor. It allows, in a sense, for wheels to be reinvented in order that further work can take place. So, historicizing the story of organizational culture can point to the ways in which the generation of the "new" idea itself was constructed through a form of forgetting, and also can allow us explore the implications of such amnesia for the social construction of what counts as knowledge (Douglas 1987). Such acts of referencing, the citation of authority, serve to construct and reproduce the proper canon of a discipline, and it seems that the case of culture illustrates their historical contingency. It is precisely by neglecting certain elements of the library that organization theory can come into being, as a contemporary management discipline which is *not* organizational sociology, or industrial relations and so on. Compare, for example, the disciplinary allegiances of Burrell and Morgan (1979) or Clegg and Dunkerley (1980) with Clegg, Hardy, and Nord's handbook (1996). Whilst the former were discipline-shaping works that drew heavily on sociology, the latter is not obviously indebted to any "other" discipline but itself. However invisibly, boundaries are being re-drawn, and they are boundaries which rely on forgetting.

Mary Douglas has observed that "the construction of past time... has very little to do with the past at all and everything to do with the present" (1987: 69). Where disciplines are concerned, stories about the past allow for legitimacy to be demonstrated through deciding what sorts of knowing count as proper—a tactic which both constructs and reinforces the discipline of discipline. Practicing "organization theory" involves all sorts of taken for granted assumptions about what kind of work matters, about the history of concepts and the provenance of ideas. In this sense it is an enabling strategy, one that allows for disciplinary reproduction to take place. We do not need to be aware of these matters, or to be "consciously" attempting to bracket off other ideas, in order for this process to take place. Indeed, perhaps it will work better if we do take our boundaries, our citations, and our teleologies for granted and not attempt to question them too much. Normal science can then proceed with speed, unhindered by the weight of memory.

Yet it is also possible to demonstrate these matters by doing more than looking in some forgotten corners of the library. The production of history is happening now, should we care to attend to it. The recent publication of a nineteen volume *History of Management Thought* constructed a version of the management canon which will undoubtedly be read by some as a definitive collection of knowledges. Volumes on "innovation," "governance," "entrepreneurship," and so on, refine a set of core disciplinary problems and set a variety of concepts and texts in a seemingly permanent relationship. But, in one of them, the footnotes cleverly suggest something else is going on too. In Marta Calás and Linda Smircich's *Postmodern Management Theory*—an interesting addition to the canon in itself—they explicitly speculate on the texts they have included (as "seminal") and those they have left out:

> The articles cited here appear in the reference section of this Introduction. As you already know, they are not among the selected articles, but they could have been; which, on saying this they, in fact, *are*. (1997: xxvii, footnote 3, italics in original)

What Calás and Smircich are attending to, through various textual devices, is the production of discipline. This is the warrant that attaches to a routine citation, a claim of ownership over particular ideas. Inclusion in the "history of management thought" is premised on the exclusion of other citations, but it guarantees a certain kind of intellectual immortality (until it is, in turn, forgotten). As Westwood exemplifies in his recent experimental text, the production of writing is a form of organization, and organization a form of writing (1999). Any form of organization elevates some matters, and leaves others "outside" as present absences. My "worked examples" in this section of the chapter do precisely this. Through this palimpsest of texts (my "own" and Others), I have now generated a legitimate domain of ignorance. A problem that can be recognised as a problem.

It seems that the inside—that is to say, the history—of "management," or of "postmodern management," or of "organization theory," is something that is made, not given. It is made through the ramified micro-politics of citations, of whose ideas count and whose are left to moulder unread—until they are resurrected by someone else under a new name, with, or without, citation. Claims to novelty can often, perhaps always, be undone by attending to some of the darker parts of the library. It seems that there is nothing completely new under the sun, and that includes the shadows. The "new" is always made by dividing it from what has gone before, just as re-membering requires a prior dis-membering.

According to this way of thinking there is no "origin" to be finally remembered here, no foundation from which this endless relational play of texts and contexts can be clearly seen. And, if there is no origin, then perhaps the question of destination (of "future challenges," of "the new century") is a question that cannot be answered either. There will be several directions, and they will in turn produce several more, but what those might be I cannot say.

BEGINNING AGAIN

I want to leave this chapter as open as I can, and to end with no moral sting in my tale. I do not claim to have discovered some kind of crime or conspiracy and I have no particular investment here in celebrating relationality over foundationalism. Both clearly do some rather interesting work, both are productive in their own way. After all, the kind of relational question I wanted to ask here was only made possible because of the foundational ignorances it claims to dissolve. The forces of light need the forces of darkness.

What interested me about this millennial rethinking was its presumption, and I wanted to turn the question back on itself, and to turn it away from where it might seem likely to go. So rather than thinking about discoveries, about uncovering knowledges that have not yet been seen, I have focused on forgetting and its role in the production of ignorance. (And here I must depart company from some that I have cited in my worked examples, and even from the introduction to this volume.[4]) Indeed, the role of forgetfulness in producing knowledge was understood by those cited as arch-rationalists—the Ancient Greeks. One explanation for the powers of reason was that it "could unblock secret caverns in the mind where *alethia*—things unforgotten—were buried at the creation of the soul" (Fernádez-Armesto 1997:100). The waters of Lethe, the river of forgetfulness, dissolve our memories and make the techniques of reason necessary. But for Plato, Lethe might even be the invention of writing itself. In the *Phaedrus*, he recounts a story about the invention of "number and calculation and geometry and astronomy, and checkers and dice, but especially letters." Theuth, the inventor, claims that letters will "make the Egyptians wiser and give them better memories, for it is a specific both for memory and intelligence." Thamuz, his partner in this conversation, replies:

> you, the father of letters, out of paternal affection are claiming for them just the opposite of what they do. This discovery will create forgetfulness in the learners' souls, because they will not use their memories, they will trust to the external written characters, and not remember of themselves. (...) You give your disciples not truth, but the appearance of wisdom (in Park 1996: 179-180)

Another reversal then. The very materials which we believe provide the conditions of possibility for intellectual progress—letters—also turn out to be constitutive of a distaste for slow contemplation. They scurry across the page too quickly. Or, as Lyotard puts it, "to go fast is to forget fast" (1993: 3). For Lyotard, to address the amnesia which attaches to the speed of modernity requires a re-appropriation of Freud's conception of memory. Psychoanalysis was centrally concerned with a surfacing of childhood memories that had been lost, suppressed, and so on. But, since these memories formed a kind of block on healthy develop-ment, this was not simply a "remembering" (in the sense of mere recall) but a "working through" (*durcharbeitung*), a coming to terms with, a not-forgetting, an analysis. It is this kind of engagement that Lyotard solicits, twists and re-names "anamnesis":

> anamnesis: the search for that which remains unthought although it has already been thought. (in Readings 1991: 137)

Rather than capturing a memory, and fixing its loss as a crime against Reason, this is what Readings calls "a refusal to forget the past either by con-signing it to oblivion or by making it present (believing that we can fully remember)" (1991: 138).

> Remembering, one still *wants* too much. One wants to get hold of the past, grasp what has gone away, master, exhibit the initial crime, the lost crime of the origin. (Lyotard 1993: 29)

My aim in this essay is similar. I do not intend to start the clock again from zero, nor to name the hidden facts of history in the name of some other conspir-acy. (Though I am aware that, by this point, I may be viewed as a scholarly revi-sionist, as someone engaged in the further production of ignorance.) Instead, I wanted to "work through," in a formal way, how a question could be built, legit-imated, and asked—but not answered.

So, "rethinking organization theory for the challenge of a new century?' It is certain that this text, and the others that I have invented, plagiarized, or cited along the way, will be rewritten by others in this "new" century—whether those future authors know it or not. And, as I am finishing with this chapter, only one thing is left that still disturbs me, and that is the inevitable truth that this text has already been written by someone else.[5] That it was not me that wrote it. As Borges would insist, we are all characters in other people's stories, and this author has no particular privilege over anyone else in this respect. In the story "The Library of Babel," he suggests:

> The certitude that everything has been written either negates us or turns us into phantoms. (1981: 85)

Perhaps our hubris is to imagine that we, or our knowledges, were ever any-thing but otherwise.

NOTES

1. These words of "Borges" are again rewritten in Michael Mulkay's essay on replication in scientific texts (1991: 90). Yet the context is different, and since that text is now attached to this one, it has changed again.

2. Or perhaps, there is always empty space on your internet server waiting to be filled. The material basis of information storage seems to make little difference in this regard.

3. I have borrowed my own words in several other places in this article too. I assume this is some form of plagiarism.

4. See, for example, Parker (1999) for an argument that anticipates many of the points I make here. Or even Foucault (1984), in whose name I deny the authority of this text.

5. See, for example, Parker (1999) for an argument that anticipates many of the points I make here. Or even Foucault (1984), in whose name I deny the authority of this text.

REFERENCES

Beer, G. 1992. *Forging the Missing Link: Interdisciplinary Stories.* (Inaugural Lecture.) Cambridge: Cambridge University Press.

Borges, J. L. 1981. *Labyrinths.* Harmondsworth: King Penguin.

Brech, E. 1963. Management in principle. *The Principles and Practice of Management,* edited by E. Brech, R. Aldrich, H. Betham, A. Field and R Lagdan. London: Longmans.

Brown, A 1995 *Organizational Culture.* London: Pitman.

Burrell, G, & Morgan, G. 1979. *Sociological Paradigms and Organizational Analysis.* London: Heinemann.

Calás, M. and L. Smircich. 1997. Introduction. *Postmodern Management Theory,* edited by M. Calás and L. Smircich. Aldershot: Dartmouth/Ashgate.

Clegg, S. and D. Dunkerley. 1980. *Organization, Class and Control.* London: Routledge & Kegan Paul.

Clegg, S., C. Hardy, and W. Nord, eds. 1996. *Handbook of Organization Studies.* London: Sage

Douglas, M. 1987. *How Institutions Think.* London: Routledge & Kegan Paul.

Fernádez-Armesto, F. 1997. *Truth: A History.* London: Black Swan.

Foucault, M. 1984. What is an author? *The Foucault Reader,* edited by P. Rabinow. London: Penguin.

Gouldner, A. 1959/1965. Organizational analysis. *Sociology Today: Volume II,* edited by R.K. Merton, L. Broom, and L. S. Cotterell. New York: Harper & Row.

Grint, K. 1994. Reengineering history: Social resonances and business process reengineering. *Organization.* 1(1):179-201.

Jacques, R. 1996. *Manufacturing the Employee.* London: Sage.

———— 1999. Developing a tactical approach to deal with "Strategic" HRM. *Organization.* 6(2):199-222.

Lyotard, J-F. 1991. *The Inhuman: Reflections on Time.* Oxford: Polity.

Martin, J. and P. Frost. 1996. The organizational culture war games: A struggle for intellectual dominance. *Handbook of Organization Studies,* edited by S. Clegg, C. Hardy, and W. Nord. London: Sage.

Morgan, G., ed. 1989. *Creative Organization Theory.* Newbury Park: Sage.

Mulkay, M. 1991. Don Quixote's double: A self-exemplifying text. *Knowledge and Reflexivity: New Frontiers in the Sociology of Knowledge,* edited by S. Woolgar. London: Sage. 81-100

Newman, M. and M. Guy. 1998. Taylor's triangle, Follett's web. *Administrative Theory and Praxis.* 20(3):287-297.

Park, C. 1996. The mother of the muses: In praise of memory. *The Anatomy of Memory,* edited by J McConkey. New York: Oxford University Press.

Parker, M. 1999. Pierre Menard's "organization theory": A fragment. *Administrative Theory and Praxis.* 21(4):502-507.

Parker, M. 2000. The sociology of organizations and the organization of sociology: Some reflections on the making of a division of Labor. *Sociological Review, 48*(1), (in press).

Perrow, C. 1973. The short and glorious history of organizational theory. *Organizational Dynamics.* 1(1):8-20.

Pollert, A. 1988. The "flexible firm": Fixation or fact? *Work, Employment and Society.* 2(3):281-316.

Readings, B. 1991. *Introducing Lyotard: Art and Politics.* London: Routledge.

Robinson, C. 1947. Modern business organization. *The Practical Commercial Self-Educator,* edited by M. Crooks and H. Crawford. London: Odhams Press Ltd.

Snider, K. 1998. Living pragmatism: The case of Mary Parker Follett. *Administrative Theory and Praxis.* 20(3):274-286.

Westwood, R. 1999. A "sampled" account of organization: Being a de-authored reflexive parody of organization/writing. *Studies in Cultures, Organizations and Societies.* 5(1):195-233.

Wilkins, J. 1981. *Philosophy and Organizational Thought.* London: Academic Books.

4

Postmodern Public Administration Research: American and Northwest European Perspectives[1]

Peter Bogason

SETTING THE STAGE FOR POSTMODERN PA-RESEARCH

Something is changing in the public sectors in the Western countries. The scope and magnitude of the changes may be discussed, but signs of change are easy to spot—themes like internationalization, decentralization, and network management are examples. While there may be a significant degree of agreement that this is something to watch, there is less agreement regarding how to treat the changes analytically. The problem for the analyst is first, whether there is any change in the object of research. Most agree that something is happening but they do not agree on how to conceptualize this. The second problem concerns research itself: is there any reason why research should change, given the changes in the research objects? Stated differently: If society is changing such that some postmodern conditions are found, must research then also change into something postmodern?

This is where we find quite sharp divisions among researchers. Below, we sketch some of those in crude alternatives—modern and postmodern. However, other researchers are somewhere in between the extremes, trying to compromise polarized research principles into something more workable.

Many *modern* theorists continue their work based on the traditional social science concepts and methods, using surveys, in-depth structured interviews, document analysis, and statistical analysis of existing (public) data. They structure their analysis by formal statistical categories, i.e. by level of government, by formal organizational divisions, by sectoral or program divisions, by formal categories of personnel, and by formal categories of recipients or clients. Recognizing that these categories are in one way constructed abstractions, they nonetheless subscribe to a "realist" (Sayer 1992) view of research and treat them as something that is "out there," independent of the analyst, and use the research results for (attempted) objective advice on how to make the public sector work better.

Other *postmodern* theorists denounce that line of research. They deny any interesting links between the formal categories and research questions. They do not accept the realist positions regarding what one may find whether or not it is perceived by the analyst; they follow an "anti-foundationalist" (Rosenau 1992: 81) view that links research results much closer to the approach of analyst and the interaction between the analyst and the objects of research. Formal categories are seen as instruments of power in that they force the analyst to do research on the basis of instruments that were not created for the research questions. Instead, research questions are channeled into what may be answerable from a formal point of view. In that particular sense, formal categories may be of obvious interest to the researcher. Otherwise, researchers must create categories on their own initiative.

Postmodernism is ambiguous as a concept, and it has created much controversy. Some of the problems are illustrated below; postmodernism is difficult to place in intellectual schools, and reactions to it are often overly negative, making its substantial message blurred, at best. Though discussion of these matters has not been limited to one field of social research, the discussion below is restricted to issues within the discipline of Public Administration. There are significant and connected discussions within several academic fields, particularly policy analysis and evaluation theory. We shall not deal with those discussions in any comprehensive way, but we may touch upon themes from them here and there to illustrate comparable features.

I have subsumed American and (Northwest) European postmodern writing on public administration under two headings: (1) social constructivism versus foundationalism, and (2) deconstruction, language, and narrative analysis. These are comparable themes across the Atlantic. There is more postmodern analysis, which we shall not discuss, but briefly mention. The American debate is treated in a larger summary in Bogason (1999). Publications after the Fall of 1999 are not included, and due to space restrictions, the literature cited is highly selective.

SOCIAL CONSTRUCTIVISM AND FOUNDATIONALISM

The basic theme in the discussions on social constructivism versus foundationalism concerns the stances on objective knowledge: is it possible to go along the classic Durkheimian (1965) line and measure social facts, preferably in a quantitative fashion and as something being there unrelated to the observer, or may we only understand the world around us as an ongoing discussion of our subjective perceptions of social conditions, as Berger and Luckmann (1966) contend?

In the Scandinavian countries, a first overarching article linking postmodernism and political science was Henrik Bang's discussion of the new institutionalism (Bang 1989). His concern at that time was targeting political theory more than public administration, and the article discussed principles, not actual social science research since there was practically none that could be termed postmodern in Denmark at that time. Bang saw the new institutionalism in March and Olsen's then new (1989) book as a step towards a liberation from the social science of Modernity. In particular, he saw indications towards a comprehension that one cannot perform social scientific analysis only as encompassing generalizations which in the last instance could be traced back to a basic essence, determining anything in society, regardless of time and space (Bang 1989: 249). Henrik Bang points to some essential features leading to a postmodern analysis. First, the time of the great generalizations is over, and there is no room for Big T-Truths—instead we have double hermeneutics. Secondly, we have to give up both objectivism and pure relativism, and instead understand the duality of structure as both result of, and medium for, meaningful agency of the collectivity. Third, we have to turn down a generalized understanding of power, whether based on the Marxian understanding of the state as the medium of the *bourgeoisie*, or based on the faith of Liberalism that an all-encompassing normative consensus can be gained, and that over time, no one will become permanently oppressed. Instead, we must understand the dialectics of power, meaning that no one must live in complete dependency, every one has some potential for opposing power (Bang 1989: 252-254).

Two British observers of public administration have expressed social constructivism as follows (Bevir & Rhodes 1998: 4-5): There is no external reality that social science can represent; the world outside is constructed as a mental makeup by the observer; all knowledge is intelligible and debatable only within their context, paradigm, or interpretive community; reality is a linguistic convention; and one must deconstruct, favoring negative critical capacity and demystifying a text. Bevir and Rhodes agree that knowledge is not certain, facts may be invented; and objectivity is provisional and a product of local reasoning and reconfirmation. They see narratives as being useful for providing the map, questions, and language with which we construct the framework of analysis. They presented the following bid for a socially constructed analysis: A field of study such as Public Administration may be understood as a co-operative intellectual *practice*, with a *tradition* of historically producing norms, rules, conventions, and standards of excellence subject to the critical debate, and a *narrative* structure and context which gives meaning to the activity of organizational analysis. Objectivity is then reached by encounters, and subsequently, comparisons between narratives, in field work (is it meaningful to people out there), in reconstruction processes of narratives (logic, consistence), and in processes of redefining and translating concepts based on judgments of the community. Rules for intellectual honesty apply: taking criticism seriously, using established standards of evidence and reason, and preferring positive theories that open new avenues of exploration. Objectivity, then, is a product of local reasoning. Decentering, dilemmas, and discontinuities are at the heart of anti-foundationalist social science: by giving room for individual action (within institutional constraints); by stressing the need for focusing on ways PA conceives of and responds to unsolvable features; and by underscoring that absolute generalizations may always be understood otherwise (Bevir & Rhodes 1998: 6-9).

In the U.S., an early indicator of calls for changing our understanding of organizations in a postmodern vein was Gareth Morgan's book, *Images of Organization* (Morgan 1986). Morgan suggested that we think in terms of imagination rather than organization to strengthen the creative side of our thinking, to break free from the past.

Morgan's concept of imaginization became the catchword for the American anthology *Images and Identities of Public Administration* (Kass & Catron 1990). The images used were several; thus, the following metaphors were used in articles dealing with the roles of public administrators in the political system if they wanted to get more legitimacy: the "phronemos" (practical reasoner) (Morgan 1990), a member of the "democratic elite" (Fox & Cochran 1990), the "steward" (Kass 1990) and the "responsible actor" (Harmon 1990). Other contributors discussed the challenges to Public Administration as a field: it should be reborn from the ashes, the "Phoenix project" (White & McSwain 1990), it should adopt an "unfinished democracy revolution," and it should be understood in terms of icons like the "pyramid" (old PA) and the "circle" (new PA) (Hummel 1990). The authors, then, were deliberately downgrading the traditional aspiration for conceptual precision. Instead, they wanted the reader to relate to the subject of discussion, contemplate, and let the imagination wander on the basis of the impulses from the metaphors used in the text.

The postmodern discussion was only emergent in the USA until Fox and Miller published their book on *Postmodern Public Administration* in 1995. They called for the refutation of several schools of thought on American Public Administration and expresses a need for discourse theory to be applied to the field. They based their analysis on interactive networks. Furthermore, they introduced a model for authentic discourse that led to their understanding of the active citizen as a worthy agent in public affairs.

The basic premise of the book (Fox & Miller 1995) is a dissatisfaction with the outcomes of the basic nineteenth century model of democracy, the "loop model." This is, in essence, the input-output-feedback understanding of democratic decision-making, with its connotations of dividing lines between politics and administration and the idea of the neutral public employee who lets the politicians deal with citizens and then faithfully executes the political decisions. Citizens' informed choices are exerted through voting: dissatisfaction with incumbents of political office will mean replacement by a competing candidate by next election. This understanding of the political process is out of step with reality, Fox & Miller maintain, and attempts by both the "Blacksburg manifesto" (Wamsley et al. 1990) group and the communitarians (Cooper 1987) deserve praise, but do not change the premises radically enough for democracy. Fox and Miller's alternative is authentic and sincere discourse. Habermas is used to define an ideal policy discourse, based on essentially equal participants in a dialogue that is authentic (i.e. based on reasonableness) to be justified by the thus active subject, who is supposed to give a substantive contribution to the discourse. The immediate consequences of the approach were that policy networks would become the focus of the analysis (the discourses would be related to various policy issues), and that democratic theory would be satisfied in terms of free participation for anyone with no one person having a special say, therefore, there would be no particular elite that could dominate the discourse.

However, the real challenge Fox and Miller find in the trends towards postmodern conditions in society is that words, signs, and symbols are increasingly unlikely to mean anything solid or lasting. We see media-induced consumerism, we watch the thwarting of political dialogue into one-way "political figure" utterances and increasing closure of politics into self-referential, introverted groups—a "neo-tribal" fragmentation of society. The self-conscious enlightened individual is transformed into a decentered self, identified perhaps mainly by external symbols like the Nike running shoes and your favorite brand of soda pop. Such conditions are not promising for democracy. The possible solution Fox and Miller see is based on the original Habermas, calling for inter-association democracy in the form which seems to be developing in "extrabureaucratic policy networks and other formations" (Fox & Miller 1995: 75). Participation in authentic discourse would require "warrants for discourse," meaning that one has to involve oneself with sincerity (creating trust), and intentionality in the situation (creating orientation towards solving a problem at hand). Furthermore, one must be attentive (creating engagement, but also the ability to listen), and give a substantive contribution (creating a sense that the process is going forward) (Fox & Miller 1995: 120-127). These are normative demands, expressing the authors' hope that there is, even under postmodern conditions, a possibility of sustaining a democratic system of governance, requiring increased levels of direct citizen participation in public affairs.

An observer might draw the conclusion that while Fox and Miller recognize and criticize the postmodern trends, their solution to the problems is hardly rooted in postmodern theory, it is more like the demands set up by the original modernists in the functioning of civil society. But those reformers probably had a solid understanding of the duties the enlightened elite needed to care for the rest of the society. Under postmodern and fragmented conditions, quite a few of the weakest, in economic and social terms, may fall through the gap and, hence, not get the attention they need. One may wonder whether this is an acceptable situation from Fox and Miller's perspective.

An article by Geuras and Garofolo (1996) is instructive regarding the debate between modernists and postmodernists on objective and constructed knowledge. The authors criticized the "subjectivist" theorists in public administration for not being able to state the ethical basis for the values they insist practitioners must apply to be able to make their decisions, bundling authors like Jay White, Michael Harmon, Richard Box, and Fox and Miller with Marcuse, Habermas, Denhardt,

Lyotard, and Jameson in a group whose members all would subscribe to a subjective perspective for public administration theory. Fox and Miller are seen as presenting modernism as having, comparatively, some advantages, yet "with all its flaws, we must wonder why postmodernism is more appealing" (which is what the authors derive from Fox & Miller's discussion), and "we need to wonder why, even in postmodern circumstances, it is not possible...to adhere to a set of fundamental moral principles that, we believe, transcend neotribalism, subcultures, and hyperreality" (Geuras & Garofolo 1996: 9).

As an alternative, the authors recommended reliance on Kant, whose "first principle is the self-evident law of non-contradiction to which all rational beings must adhere."

The rejoinders (Kouzmin & Leivesley 1997; Harmon 1997), which we shall not detail here, were quite merciless.

As a sequel to their first book on the *Blacksburg Manifesto* (Wamsley et al. 1990), the Blacksburg group wrote a new anthology. In the introductory chapter (Wamsley & Wolf 1996: 27-32), the editors leaned towards post-structuralism as a suitable approach in an era of postmodernism: analyzing text would become important in uncovering social relationships and then in deconstructing the context. They thus followed the trends towards denying privilege to any particular concept, and by questioning possibilities of representation, they recommended a sort of enforcement of dialogue on the participants, who were then creating a number of small-t truths—i.e., localized and contingent as opposed to generalized "grand narrative" Big-T truths.

But some went much further. In this anthology, McSwite (1996) integrates Continental skepticism from Derrida with American affirmative values. McSwite sees the development towards postmodernism as a possibility rather than a constraint. In McSwite's view, and following Derrida, postmodernism means a rejection of the possibility of unambiguous representation or identity. Places change, cities lose their meaning as locus of civilization, and people become disembedded. The personal identity becomes part of an open-ended, unspecified metaphor of personal development, which is relative, and thus explorable, for each individual (what does gender mean for an androgynous person?). In other words, the Big-T Truths (generalized visions) are gone, and small-t truth(s) (localized realizations) must be looked for at this time, showing relevant purpose. This means that American pragmatism in the tradition of Mary Parker Follett may reenter public administration. Thus, practical discourses are initiated, and this means new forms of involvement and relationship, "a process-based communitarian approach to governance," based on the ideas of the confederation and philosophy of pragmatism (McSwite 1996: 222).

DECONSTRUCTION, NARRATIVE AND LANGUAGE

Foucault has had a strong influence on European postmodern writing. A popular theme is finding boundaries in varied ways and establishing a difference. One may, for instance, analyze power as the constitution of borders (Andersen et al. 1995: 90): Power constitutes strategic possibilities of variance, thus it puts actors in a relationship. Boundaries are relations that constitute (organizational) fields, the analytical question is how games and processes elevate differences and relations to borders that constitute fields. This happens through discourse, putting the relations into speech terms. The focus of the analysis, then, is on networks of negotiation between actors and fields. The essence of power becomes control of communication in networks. Borders of organizations create limitations and impediments; they create a we/them distinction; they define roles, and they create a sense of what gives meaning (and what does not). The borders, however, are dynamic, and may even explicitly be a theme of contestation. Consequently, a field may become a territory to be conquered. Their stance is anti-foundationalist (Andersen et al. 1995: 100). Laclau (1993) is another frequently used theorist, who, with Saussure, held the view that language is an element in relationships. Analysis is not aimed at facts, but at their conditional possibilities. Language is a structure, and the meaning of a word is not its physical referent, but rather in our heads; language is form, not substance. As a consequence, relational and meaningful totalities are to be analyzed as discourses, they combine linguistic and extra-linguistic elements into a totality. They are dynamic regarding their identity, depending on the contexts they are linked to through language or social actions (Hansen 1996: 100). Consequently, there is no objectivity or Big-T Truth understanding of a discourse.

Yet another theorist inspiring postmodern analysis is Derrida. Thus, while planning is discussed as a modernistic concept, it is implemented under conditions of postmodernism (Pedersen 1996). Building on Derrida's understanding of signifiers in ambiguous structures always in play, vibrating, and under change, Pedersen analyzes how the planner cannot participate in a search for Big-T Truth, but must be a participant in a game of interpretation on how knowledge is constituted—oriented towards ambiguity and the unsettled. He also follows Lyotard in his understanding of the importance of difference as an ethical challenge for politics, and the death of metanarratives and the universal history. He refers to Foucault's concept of the creation of knowledge as a way of constituting power, and Laclau's concept of dislocation is introduced for its disruption of a social order with its consequential collapse. The consequence for the planner concerns the ability to see and change his role in the regime of knowledge and production of truth. Postmodern planning requires interpretation, contextuality of significance, ambiguity, plurality, empowerment, power, and the reciprocity of truth. Knowledge is produced for action, not for objectivity or reason, and it addresses the marginalized in society. The role of the planner is to problematize, and to create processes, searches, and mechanisms (Pedersen 1996: 67-68). The actor is understood as partly constituted by institutions and partly liberated from structural determination because of antagonisms. The actor has the possibility of acting differently through varying processes of identification. Planning, then, with Laclau becomes a hegemonic project, rearticulating various strategies, their actors, and the antagonisms they are concerned about, brought into a common project for the re-creation of a new, stable social order.

Putnam and collaborators' (1993) article on changes in democratic roles gives the basis for contrasting a postmodern analysis with a modernistic analysis. The (modern) theme is Putnam's view of social capital and the associated significance of unity, homogeneity, and consensus as the constituting elements of civil society. Bang and Sørensen (1999) have identified a—possibly common, but neglected by most analysts—role of the Everyday Maker, who is engaged in politics, not for the sake of keeping the state effective and responsive, but in order to make a concrete difference in daily affairs in the locality. This means having a political role in civil society, because the Everyday Maker sees his or her role as a political one (the examples are drawn from Denmark, a comprehensive welfare state with many political institutions present in local services). The claim of the authors is that Putnam "removes the focus (of analyzing civil society) from its political aspects: the handling of differences, diversity and dispute" (Bang & Sørensen 1999: 326).

Disinterest in central government politics is not the same as non-communality, uncivicness, or egotistic individualism. The Everyday Maker accepts democratic values and procedures in the handling of local governance. Putnam neglects the presence of political capital in the social realm. This is to some extent because of his (modernistic) approach which separates community and elite power, or the separation of politics and the social realm, separations that are found in most modern social science at the cost of recognizing how they may be intertwined.

Discourse is a concept uniting many analysts, but there are many versions, so the commonality may be somewhat superficial. One field open to discourse analysis is the creation of national policies and the roles of administrative agencies in such processes. Based on Luhmann's understanding of systems and Foucault's understandings of discourse, Andersen (1995) has analyzed how a national policy on administrative organization was created. His conception of discourse required an ideal to be ordered in three ways: it must have a descriptive order which regulates what may be object for the discourse; it must have a narrative order which regulates the roles of empowered subjects in the processes; and it must have an argumentative order that determines the range of acceptable ways to communicate among the subjects active in the discourse (Andersen 1995: 20-21). This understanding of discourse, however, is set up for that particular purpose; discourse analysis must be adapted to the particular purpose of each research project, and in that sense, it cannot be generalized. Difference has priority over the general. Discourse analysis should be understood as a range of possibilities from which one can pick and choose, depending on the aim of the analysis. Andersen sees it as follows: since Laclau permits himself to bring in elements of Foucault's discourse analysis together with elements of Lacan's psychoanalysis in spite of Foucault's aversion against Lacan, why not contemplate bringing in system analysis in a combination with an analysis of hegemony

(Andersen 1999: 179). This is not to say that anything goes; it must be done on the basis of a conscious and reasoned choice by the analyst.

Above we saw how Bevir and Rhodes (1998) would use narrative analysis, resulting in objectivity understood as something coming out of local reasoning, a standpoint which Rhodes first presented in his 1997 book. In that book, a narrative analysis would include several elements: institutional analysis, the ethnography and culture of networks, the behavior of core executives, conditions for governing structures to work, and contextual conditions such as the role of globalization and representative democracy (Rhodes 1997: 189-198). A narrative, then, is one of many possible stories about important phenomena like organization, and may vary in contents according to variations in the six elements, and variation comes about, depending on who does the narrative. It has nothing to do with the discourse analysis mentioned above.

A strong interest in narrative analysis has crystallized among some European postmodern scholars, particularly those working on the borders between public administration, evaluation, and policy analysis. A particular focus is on the interaction between citizens and public employees in policy-shaping, a focus where new forms of organization may be followed closely. Thus, Kensen (1999) studied how a reform of social renewal was implemented in different ways in different places, making local initiative a crucial parameter for the direction of change. This is where the role of administration—management—changes from creating sameness to helping diversity come forward. The analysis is based on the narratives as told by various actors in the localities; Kensen uses stories as carriers for paradigms of action in these cases of how local actors might understand and use the possibilities of decentralized social renewal for betterment of their neighborhoods. The differences between an approach based on difference and a more integrative approach to evaluation are detailed in an article by Kensen and Bogason (1999), in a non-adversarial confrontation between a modernistic and a postmodern approach.

The literature directly linked to public administration is more comprehensive in the U.S. A major American work based on the linguistic turn in the social sciences is Farmer's *Language of Public Administration* (Farmer 1995). We shall only draw upon those features that are most relevant to identify Farmer's own approach to the analysis of public administration. The basic approach is a reflexive interpretation concerned with why we see (understand) what we are seeing (understanding), and with the possibilities for seeing (understanding) something different by changing the lens. (ibid.: 13). The link to deconstruction—by changing the lens—should be obvious. And like Derrida, everything is seen as text, but of course it is beyond a registration of mere words. The direct elements of analysis are our languages as instruments for our understanding of public administration phenomena, and the analysis is reflexive in that it is focused on the lens(es) used for our interpretation rather than the objects we are interpreting. It follows that those objects cannot be but social constructions constituted through uses of language. The interpreter ascribes various prereqisites for the interpretation, perspectives that determine what can and what cannot be part of the analysis. A perspective may be derived from Frederick Taylor; then the observer would see activities through a lens of administrative efficiency. An observer from the school of "New Public Administration," on the other hand, would look for relevance, equity, and fairness of representation (Farmer 1995: 17).

Farmer's object for discussion is public administration theory. He explores how we understand what is going on in public administration as interpreted through administrative theory. He aims at developing understandings below the surface level by using a hermeneutic circle, i.e. a forward-and-back series of iterations of interpretations, starting with a general hypothesis which directs attention to parrticular features of public administration theory. Some features fit the hypothesis, others do not, creating a need for another interpretation, etc. The hypothesis Farmer uses as a starting point is that modernist public administration theory shows contraries, paradoxes, in each set of its major underlying lines of development. Hence, it is limited in its capacity to understand and explain what it set out to explain.

This, in turn, is a strong critique of the self-understanding of modernist scientific theory, based as it is on the Enlightenment and its demand for science to govern the development of the world—a unilateral understanding, and an appreciation of the one and only right solution being available. This approach is subject to the condition that a proper analysis has been carried out based on the pros and cons of alternative lines of action. The first half of the book is devoted to a critical analysis of features of modernity as they apply to theories of public administration. Regarding postmodernity, Farmer does not accept any one-sided definition of its nature, but relies on skepticism, "properly understood" (Farmer 1995: chap. 9). It concerns a comprehensive series of negations of hitherto accepted understandings of the (modern) world, denying: the centered subject, the foundationalist and epistemological project, the nature and role of reason, macrotheory, grand narratives, macropolitics, and the distinction between reality and appearance. Farmer's type of skepticism has consequences for the way research may be carried out: instead of getting "research results," we get extended discourse open to continuing processes of deconstruction. Compared with modernity, the status of researchers, and particularly theorists, is severely degraded (at least as perceived by a modern theorist); there is no longer a privileged position for any form of science.

For Farmer, postmodern analysis is the understanding of four analytical elements which may only be hinted at in this article. Imaginization was one of the first concepts (as we learned from Morgan (1986), referred to above), and it is for postmodern analysis what rationalization is for modern analysis. Through imaginization one thinks of a wide rage of possibilities (where modernity would tend to reduce possibilities to the "do-able"). Imaginization is placed between perception and intellect, and is used to transform impressions into thought. Thereby, particulars become important instead of modernist generalizing trends, which subsume any activity under a rule. Deconstruction, the second element, is a pervasive way of approaching an understanding of phenomena. It is not restricted to being an analytical method or a critique. It is a way of appreciating texts under particular circumstances with an aim to dismantle received views of what that text stands for. In the third element, deterritorialization, modern understandings of representation are negated; postmodernity means the end of the logocentric metaphysics of presence. This is where the social constructivist understanding of research activities becomes important—the realization that not much may be understood by itself, but instead as part of a human interaction about understandings of the phenomenon. Finally, alterity refers to a moral stance that counterweighs the standard bureaucratic-efficiency understanding of public administration, an anti-administration stance in Farmer's terms, reducing authority and helping service-orientation. There is no one, single way of understanding: diversity must be furthered.

Farmer has made a clever deconstruction of public administration as we know it, and thus he invites us to rethink the whole discipline; a challenge most public administration theorists probably would shy away from because they are forced to speak about it in concrete terms in their daily lecturing and coaching of students.

Farmer has subsequently edited a book on "anti-administration," published in 1998. In its introductory chapter, he characterized postmodern analysis as a liberating endeavor, aspiring towards full accomplishment of what citizenship should entail, enabling a radical "listening to the other." The overall idea of anti-administration is to negate administrative-bureaucratic, rational power (Farmer 1998a: 2-5). At the core is skepticism in its philosophical sense, holding that the capacity of human minds is limited, in contrast to the philosophers of the Enlightenment who saw rationality as our savior. Farmer uses deconstruction to question what lies under seemingly well-established categories of, e.g., the bureaucratic phenomenon. Gillroy (1997: 164-167) had a similar point of view, seeing an advantage of postmodern theory in that language does not have a timeless meaning, but reflects specific contexts. Postmodern analysis, then, can be used to make administrators reexamine their fundamental assumptions based on fixed paradigms and concepts—categories. The major concept of modernist administration is efficiency. Under postmodern conditions, alternative values like fairness, equality, utility, and autonomy may be furthered, but then they must meet the formal requirements of the modern strategy to get recognition—in the policy design phase.

The line of analysis of Tennert (1998) is that sentences are only true by their relation to other sentences; language cannot be isolated from the individuals who speak them. Following Rorty, science for Tennert simply is a forum for unforced agreement, where communities test other beliefs against their own. This is ethnocentrism in the sense that we are bound to our language and our own web of beliefs; our judgment of the beliefs of others are rational or reasonable depending on our attempt to weave their beliefs into our own. So questions of "big science" drop out. The notion of praxis in public administration—i.e. theory guiding practice—drops out. Constructing general narratives of accomplishments after the fact may be thought of as recontextualization rather than as theorizing. Public administration as Science is constructed as a series of language games, none of which has beforehand greater value than others. It can be defined and re-defined many times. The popular themes like accountability and democracy, then, become meaningless outside of a particular context and problem: one should avoid grand theorizing.

This stance is typical of a pragmatist way of arguing. McSwite's book (1997) on the general theme of how administrators may have a legitimate role in democratic affairs is important in that respect. They see, as a major problem under post-modern conditions, the decentering of the subject, which has been lost or alienated into limbo, in contrast to modernist discussions that seem to focus on a human nature that can be categorized, e.g. as an economic maximizing agent, or as an altruistic person in the community. Discourse oriented relationships, i.e., a mutual surrender to one another, is offered as an alternative understanding to the egoistic (rational choice) model. It is argued that the problem of legitimacy will evaporate once such a reframing of discourse and institutions is accomplished (McSwite 1997: 15). Corresponding to this image is that of a "facilitative" Public Administration, striving towards involving citizens in efforts towards collaboration. This movement, however, remains tied to traditional understandings of legitimacy and therefore may not succeed; instead, McSwite sees a need for using the "idea of reason" to deal with the problem of coming to terms with the "implacable, immutable sense of otherness" that is evoked in our human social relations. The advice is to let go of the "pointless" discussion about legitimacy because it has institutionalized and maintained a particular understanding and structure of government. Instead, one needs to go back to the true foundation of American Public Administration: Pragmatism. Fact/value, foundationalist/relativist, and phenomenology/positivism dichotomies are all bypassed by the continuing testing of hypotheses by the pragmatist, who denies the prerequisites of rational action by picturing social relationships as collaborative, grounded in a joint project and a joint action. In short, the idea is to assume a posture of permanent doubt, place experimentation in a collaborative context, and make the results the operational definition of truth (McSwite 1997: 135).

THEMES FOR PUBLIC ADMINISTRATION NOW—
AND AFTER THE YEAR 2000

Public administration, as a field, is linked to practice, but that is not to say that the focus must be on the practitioners in a narrow sense, as in how to organize for a particular purpose, or personnel administration. A broader perspective links the actors of the public sector to wider horizons. The European discussion is not developed enough to let us use it for setting new agendas. In the American discussions, several societal perspectives have come out with particular strength. These themes are: (1) the values of public administration; (2) public participation in decision-making; and (3) the role of the administrator as an intermediary between local political decisions and the community. All three themes are interrelated, but we shall discuss them under separate headings, and in that discussion relate them to the emerging European postmodern analysis of public administration.

Values in Public Administration

Postmodern values emphasize human autonomy and diversity instead of the hierarchy and conformity that are central to modernity. Inglehart (1997: chap. 1) summarizes the following trends of interest particularly to politics and administration. The bureaucratic (modern) state has met its limits because it strips away spontaneity, personal likes and dislikes, and individual self-expression and creativity. It has effectively coordinated many actions, but new values pay less attention to economic effectiveness and more to the quality of life: happiness is no longer equal to economic security. Social problematics have changed from the material distribution of goods (property, income, jobs) to distribution of bads which cannot easily be summarized as material (risk of nuclear technology, genetic research, environmental degradation). Since there is a sense of insecurity linked to these trends, there is now, in politics, less faith in hierarchy and more in individualism and participation, thus creating problems for the old political regimes.

A major general concept that has united the field of Public Administration has been the public interest or the common good—understood as the general value that administrators must adhere to. Several theorists have discussed how the common good fares under postmodern conditions. McSwite (1996) has discussed the concept on the basis of an understanding of postmodernism as beginning with a rejection of the possibility of representation or identity; thus, cities lose their meaning as locus of civilization and people become disembedded. Under modernism, the concept of the public interest makes administrators adhere to a number of constitutive rules or values that the term reinforces. But ethical codes do not operate unambiguously, "one person's ethical act is another's evil deed." Therefore, the need for arbitration arises, but when acceptance of the arbitration processes wanes, as may be the case under postmodern conditions, problems arise in this respect; the administrator oriented towards modern conditions cannot deliver the promised "heavenly city" (McSwite 1996: 204-206).

Gillroy (1997: 164) sees an advantage of postmodern theory in that language does not have a timeless meaning, but reflects specific contexts. The framework of postmodernism, then, can be used to make administrators reexamine their fundamental assumptions based on fixed paradigms and concepts—categories. But still, the major concept of modern administration is efficiency. Under postmodern conditions, alternative values like fairness, equality, utility, and autonomy, may be furthered, but then they must meet the formal requirements of the modern strategy to get recognition. This may be particularly important in the policy design phase and requires an understanding of how to create a "Comprehensive Policy Argument" to further alternative ideas—a demanding task.

McSwite (1998) has summed up many of the differences between schools of thought by discussing the relationship between the "New Normativism" (neoinstitutionalism and interpretivist organization theory, increasingly accepting social constructivism) and the "Discourse Movement" (process-oriented and postmodernists, focusing on the necessity of discourse because of the limitations of human consciousness). Common enemies are found among the "New Theorists," who are the real modernists, sticking to methodological individualism and empiricism. New normativists, like the Blacksburg Manifesto group, want values to be embodied in stable institutions where they can be expressed in the concrete practices of the institutions (since they cannot, anyway, be defined). This is where there is some degree of authoritarianism in the New Normativist point of view: they advocate for a solid foundation for the exercise of authority. Among discourse theorists—mainly postmodernists—authority is not at all an issue, but the consequences are. Or rather, the consequences are constantly questioned in processes that aim to create synergy—something that would not otherwise be there—where the essence of the process is doubt. A final difference is that New Normativists still take abstractions like values and generalized facts seriously, where discourse theorists want to keep our orientation concrete and empirical (McSwite 1998: 379-380).

In sum, then, there is an interesting gap between some postmodernists and most modernists. The question is whether postmodernist values will lead to a vacuum in terms of "usable" ethical rules of conduct for the administrator. An alternative may be a general acceptance of some principles, e.g. universal human rights, to be adapted locally with some discretion.

Public Participation and Community

As we have seen repeatedly above, there is much interest in community and the involvement of citizens in public affairs among many of those that approach postmodern thinking.

If we start out with values, Green (1996) argues that postmodernism is an iconoclastic philosophy, leaving dim prospects for current institutions because people become increasingly impulsive and ungovernable, and because public institutions are on the verge of disintegration. But on the other hand, some see this as a promising era, giving new hopes for family and community, churches, markets, etc., which were eroded by national policies. Developments in institutions towards communitarianism and, theoretically, towards new institutionalism and its insistence on processual views, structuration, reflexivity, and knowledgeable agents, transcend rationality in the modern calculative or instrumental sense. This, in turn, changes the role of statecraft away from determining accomplishments and instead focusing on conditions for life that will shape public life beneficially for a generation or more. The role of public administration is, then, to be active in the processes that bring those together who can create statecraft, being "knowledgeable agents" operating at all levels of an inter-institutional mire.

To form comparisons with the European scene: Frissen has a discussion of the "techno culture" of the information society, which is seen as a culture of images (Frissen 1998: 42), organized like the internet—that is, not an organization in the traditional (modernist) sense. This means that policy processes become parallel and interdependent, not linear and sequential, and that they occur along with a horizontal functional integration among small and fragmented organizations. There is a need to develop theories about such fragmentation and anarchy, and to rephrase theories of power into relational concepts (Frissen 1998: 46).

Spicer (1997) has some clear, normative suggestions for public organizing under postmodern conditions, arguing, much in line with Frissen, that the state, as a purposeful agent, is problematic in a postmodern understanding. He, then, sees the civil association as more appropriate. The problems coming from the postmodern conditions are that one would deny the possibility of such a shared political metanarrative that ties the ends sought by the state to a betterment of human conditions. Instead, we have a number of incommensurable language games (Lyotard), an atomization of society, resulting in multiplicity and diversity, which is a challenge for the state in the above understanding. In contrast, a civil association is a platform where people see themselves free to pursue own interests, but within rules of conduct that limit their individual spheres of action. It is a kind of procedural regime, permitting individuals to follow one's own ideas, and participate in a discourse about the commensurability of those ideas with the ideas of other people within the association. The role of public administration, then, is to limit the monopolization of political discourse by particular subcultures that try to reduce the range of language discourses in order to promote their own ends. Accordingly, public employees, then, should serve to solve disagreements among different interests and visions of the public good.

One does not have to be a postmodernist to support citizens' involvement. Moving towards another sort of solution, Box (1996) has discussed new forms of local governance, suited for the challenges of the twenty-first century, and incorporated some of Fox and Miller's (1995) ideas about the warrants for discourse. Postmodern thoughts refute rational collective action—the world is becoming too fragmented and contentious, such that large-scale institutional enterprises will fail. Long-standing agreements over values and goals are threatened, change is rapid, stability and trust is under siege. There is increasing interest in local communities regarding the relationships local citizens have with each other that are based on shared local experience. The present era is one of citizen governance, based partly on a communitarian understanding of citizenship. There is a transition taking place—from centralized, expert-based systems to decentralized, citizen-centered systems. In order to avoid the problems of the "loop democracy" that Fox and Miller (1995) have criticized, Box suggests an expanded use of citizen boards to direct local services and to put the traditional municipal in a mainly coordinating role.

From the European scene, one also sees, in some countries, discussions of local elites and their strengthened roles because of trends towards organizational fragmentation with stronger user influence on local services (Sørensen 1997). Whether one wants to call them "new elites" or something else is a matter of conceptual definition and, perhaps, dispute, but the idea behind the Everyday Maker (Bang & Sørensen 1999) is that clearly there is nothing of the traditional elite in such people taking on *ad hoc* responsibilities in the locality.

The problems of citizens and community in an "anti-government" era are discussed by King and Stivers (1998), and it is a distinct American theme. Although many Europeans are having second thoughts about the size of the welfare state, the interventionist role of the state is generally accepted (Andersen 1991). The anti-government sentiment of the American people is based on the anti-bureaucrat movement in the media and among politicians running for president. This sentiment communicates the notion that administrators overuse their powers; the perception that government policies are either ineffective or fail; and the sense of being powerless vis-a-vis government. The authors show that lawmakers in representative government use generalized knowledge about citizens based on statistics and comparable instruments. Citizens, on the other hand, think in personal terms, or "lived knowledge": U.S. government is not a democracy of lived knowledge; law aimed at citizens excludes us as individuals; administration works with cases, not individuals, thus, representation creates alienation. Using Arendt, the authors claim that democratic knowledge must be constructed from represented to experienced knowledge by opening up the public space, thereby easing processes that let human thoughts and ideas be tested by the examination of other citizens. Here, it is important to be able to put oneself into another's place, to understand from another viewpoint. Citizens create their sense of the common through active conversations with neighbors. That is when "government becomes us" (King & Stivers 1998: 46-48).

Public Administrators as Intermediaries

Several of the authors above, hinted at an intensification of the relations between public employees and citizens in the process of strengthening community. Already, when *Images and Identities* was published in 1990, the theme of "stewardship" was important. Catron and Hammond (1990) discussed, in their epilogue, possible images of the public administrator which came from the discussions in the anthology: (1) namely the functionary, who is the traditional subordinate administrator; (2) the opportunist/pragmatist who is the utility-maximizing employee; (3) the interest broker/market manager as the disinterested arbiter; (4) the professional/expert technician as the competent analyst; (5) the agent/trustee acting on behalf of the public; (6) the communitarian facilitator asking their colleagues to work in the "proximate" environment of the face-to-face group; and (7) the transformational social critic monitoring political processes on behalf of the citizens, against oppressing trends. Many of those images were conventional in the sense of being social roles, but the two last ones transcend our usual understanding of public administration employees. They invite practical discourse in the "projects of human life," where public administrators deepen their own appreciation of their roles and enhance the image of public service (Catron & Hammond 1990: 250).

Dennard (1996) has seen the role of the public administrator under modernism as based on a personal devotion, the Adubious and often unrewarding task of regulating society for its own good." The challenges of postmodernism should not be passively watched. The modernistic solution to problems has been to fight what is wrong in a system rather than analyze the potential for something different. Now is the challenge to look for adaptive processes to create a democratic environment. So citizens do not struggle for access within bureaucracy, they are integrated into it in a change of relationship. The trick is to see beyond opposites, the "we" in the organization and the "they" out there. Therefore, empowering people, or making representative bureaucracy, belongs to modernistic opposites. One should instead speak of the reengagement of government with its people, and participation of public administrators in their environments, as conscious actors in a democratic system. Prescriptions for democratic government would include several forms: personal involvement of administrators; address people in order to address the whole; listen actively to what people say; accept that people are different and not accessible through models; understand people's emotions about their situation; and assume responsibility for involving oneself into the difficult problematics.

Conclusions regarding the role of the admininstrator reached by McSwite, as we saw above, was that one has to assume a perspective of ongoing doubt; place experimentation in a collaborative context; and see the outcome as the working definition of truth (McSwite 1997: 135). "Collaborative pragmatism" was at the heart of the Confederation, in populism and progressivism in the beginning of the twentieth century, and is now present in postmodernism. Our perception of the world is socially conditioned, and we need to state our sense of purpose in order to be able to "measure" our world—we do not perceive in limbo. Such purpose is created in relationships with other people in the community. The relationship is reached by pragmatic collaboration between administrators and citizens, based on an understanding of "process theory."

In their book on citizen governance, King and Stivers (1998: 71-75) discussed possibilities and problems in citizen-administrator collaboration as an "us." The scientific, rationalized, professional knowledge is an obstacle in bureaucracy. On the other hand, there are problems with citizens' accountability, in their carrying out certain roles, and how much power they should get. Established societal interests may work against participation, as may organizational features. The book presents a great number of cases of how citizens and administrators may cooperate actively.

As to habits of mind, it is important to give up the hierarchical (dominance) way of thinking and understand the importance of having power with citizens, in horizontal relations, sharing authority, and thus, less emphasis on professional norms. In sum, the images of the active administration are: a transformative, facilitative, public-service practitioner; a task-oriented but inclusive and balanced convener; and a listening bureaucrat. Challenging positions! In comparison with European ideas, the Americans seem to have a less stringent or limiting role for the public employee.

CONCLUDING REMARKS

We can conclude that the theme of postmodernism in public administration is only emerging in Europe, whereas in the U.S., judging from the number of books in print, it is becoming an important topic of discussion. In journals, it is only a dominant theme in the journal of the PAT-Net, *Administrative Theory and Praxis*. It seems that a common theme for discussion across the Atlantic will be discourse analysis and deconstruction. This goes for the meta-theoretical side. In substance terms, forms of democracy seem to be of common interest, and the Habermasian ways of thinking are a challenge for participants in the discussions about how to conceptualize democratic theory under postmodern conditions.

We have restricted the discussion to literature within public administration. Since the theme of postmodernism is also present in neighboring and relevant academic camps of policy analysis and evaluation (Guba & Lincoln 1994), this might be a straightjacket. But limitations are inevitable for articles.

The themes discussed in section Four above will stay in the center of academic discussions for years. Most of those who are attracted to postmodernism are so, based on the affirmative perspective, and are involved in questions of democracy, marginalization, minority policy, feminism, human rights, and comparable movements of liberating citizens. Likewise, there is a wide interest in themes of ethics, legitimacy (of administrators), public administration as stewardship, justice, and the public interest—all highly value-laden according to most perceptions, but not necessarily in a narrowly focused way.

All postmodernists, and many of the critical theorists, are strong supporters of social constructivism, and most of them are anti-foundationalists: this goes for the U.S. as well as for Europe. An American feature of public administration discipline is that in one way or another, most of the postmodernists subscribe to pragmatism.However, you need not be a postmodernist to be a pragmatist. At the meta-theoretical level, pragmatism is the alternative to the utilitarian (rational choice) approach, demanding experimentation and learning through experience, based on democratic understanding with its multiple realities and conflict. This gives the analysis a certain flavor of liberalism, since the idea is to let changes be played out in order to let people learn by doing, and have principles accommodated at the local level to local wishes. The explicitly philosophic, pragmatic view is absent from the European debate, but much of the literature discusses experimentation and underlines the necessity for more democratic influence from the citizens, so the themes are much the same across the Atlantic.

A strong dividing line may be found in the stance towards narrative analysis, and closely-related deconstruction. The further this type of analysis is carried, the stronger the severance from traditional social science. As Wittgenstein becomes the centerpiece in theoretical terms, most of the participants in the debate declare their unease and lack of interest and understanding. As social scientists, they are more interested in approaching action research in a dialogue with their research objects. Full-fledged American postmodernists analyze their texts at some distance—this is where they tend to be classic academics, with almost an ivory tower distance from their research object. Discourse analysis, in various forms, is becoming an important vehicle for these analyses in Europe as well as in the U.S., and further development of discourse theory and methodology is a safe bet as a theme for many years to come.

Out of the debates have come strong demands for analyses that explicitly face the problems of values in our research; this again is closely linked to the anti-foundationalist trend. Furthermore, a large group of the theorists discussed above take a strong position in supporting an increased citizen participation in public affairs, and strengthening minority voices in that respect. Feminism stands out loud and clear as a central philosophic theme for several discussants. Finally, the theme of the role of the public employee in public affairs is of great importance to most of the theorists in the debates.

NOTE

1. Comments from Allan Dreyer Hansen and Eva Sørensen are gratefully acknowledged.

REFERENCES

Andersen, J. G. 1991. Responsible welfare support in Denmark. *Welfare Administration in Denmark,* edited by T. Knudsen. (Copenhagen: Ministry of Finance. 151-179.

Andersen, N. Å. 1995. *Selvskabt forvaltning. Forvaltningspolitikkens og centralforvaltnin-gens udvikling i Danmark 1900-1994.* København: Nyt fra Samfundsvidenskaberne.

————. 1999. *Diskursive analyseatrategier. Foucault, Koselleckm Laclau, Luhmann.* København: Nyt fra Samfundsvidenskaberne.

————. A. Born, and K. Majgaard. 1995. Grænser og magt. *Grus.* 45:88-102.

Bang, H. 1989. Nyinstitutionalismen og kritikken af det moderne. *Institutionalismen i samfundsvidenskaberne,* edited by C. Knudsen. (København: Samfundslitteratur. 237-266.

Bang, H. P. and E. Sørensen. 1999. The everyday maker: A new challenge to democratic governance. *Administrative Theory & Praxis.* 21(3):325-341.

Beck, U., A. Giddens, and S. Lash. 1994. *Reflexive Modernization: Politics, Tradition and Aesthetics in the Modern Social Order.* Cambridge: Polity Press.

Berger, P. and T. Luckmann. 1966. *The Social Construction of Reality: A Treatise in the Sociology of Knowledge.* New York: Doubleday Anchor.

Bevir, M. and R. A. W. Rhodes. 1998. Public administration without foundations: The case of Britain. *Administrative Theory & Praxis.* 20(1):3-13.

Bogason, P. 1999. *Public Administration and the Unspeakable: Postmodernism as an Academic Trail of the 1990s.* Roskilde: Department of Social Science. Available from http://www.ssc.ruc.dk/ Research/workingpapersmain.htm; INTERNET.

Box, R. C. 1996. The institutional legacy of community governance. *Administrative Theory & Praxis.* 18(2):84-100.

Catron, B. L., and B. R. Hammond. 1990. Epilogue: Reflections on practical wisdom—enacting images and developing identity. *Images and Identities in Public Administration,* edited by H. D. Kass and B. L. Catron. (London: SAGE Publications. 241-251.

Cooper, T. L. 1987. Hierarchy, virtue and the practice of public administration: A perspective for normative ethics. *Public Administration Review.* July/August. 320-328.

Dennard, L. F. 1996. The maturation of public administration: The search for a democratic identity. *Refounding Democratic Public Administration: Modern Paradoxes, Postmodern Challenges,* edited by G. L. Wamsley and J. F. Wolf. (London: SAGE. 293-326.

Dennard, L. 1997. A symmetry break: The ethics of a bifurcation in the sciences. *Administrative Theory & Praxis.* 19(3):380-394.

Durkheim, E. 1965. *The Division of Labor in Society.* New York: Free Press.

Farmer, D. J. 1995. *The Language of Public Administration: Bureaucracy, Modernity, and Postmodernity.* Tuscaloosa: The University of Alabama Press.

———. 1998a. Introduction: Listening to other voices. *Papers on the Art of Anti-Administration,* edited by D. J. Farmer. Burke, VA: Chantelaine Press. 1-10.

———. 1998b. Public administration discourse as play with a purpose. *Papers on the Art of Anti-Administration,* edited by D. J. Farmer. Burke, VA: Chatelaine Press. 37-56.

Fox, C. D. and C. E. Cochran. 1990. Discretionary public administration: Toward a platonic guardian class? *Images and Identities in Public Administration,* edited by H. D. Kass, Catron. London: SAGE. 87-112.

Fox, C. J., and H. T. Miller. 1995. *Postmodern Public Administration. Towards Discourse.* London: Sage Publications.

Frissen, P. H. A. 1998. Public administration in cyberspace. *Public Administration in an Information Age. A handbook,* edited by W. v. d. D. I. Th. M. Snellen. Amsterdam: IOS Press. 33-46.

Geuras, D. and C. Garofolo. 1996. The normative paradox in contemporary public administration theory. *Administrative Theory & Praxis.* 18(2):2-13.

Gillroy, J. M. 1997. Postmodernism, efficiency and comprehensive policy argument in public administration. *American Behavioral Scientist,* 41(1):163-190.

Green, R. T. 1996. Statecraft and institutions in the age of iconoclasm. *Administrative Theory & Praxis,* 18(2):74-83.

Guba, E. G. and Y. S. Lincoln. 1994. Competing paradigms in qualitative research. *Handbook of Qualitative Research,* edited by E. G. Guba and Y. S. Lincoln. London: Sage. 105-117.

Hansen, A. D. 1996. Strukturalisme, poststrukturalisme og subjektets plads. *Grus.* 49: 88-106.

Harmon, M. 1990. The responsible actor as "tortured soul": The case of Horatio Hornblower. *Images and Identities in Public Administration,* edited by H. D. Kass and B. L. Catron. London: SAGE. 151-180.

Harmon, M. M. 1997. On the futility of universalism. *Administrative Theory & Praxis.* 19(2):3-18.

Hummel, R. P. 1990. Circle managers and pyramidal managers: Icons for the post-modern public administrator. In.), *Images and Identities in Public Administration,* edited by H. D. Kass and B. L. Catron. London: SAGE Publications. 202-218.

Inglehart, R. 1997. *Modernization and Postmoderization: Cultural, Economic and Political Change in 43 Societies.* Princeton, NJ: Princeton University Press.

Kass, H. D. 1990. Stewardship as a fundamental element in images of public administration. *Images and Identities in Public Administration,* edited by H. D. Kass, Catron. London: SAGE. 113-131.

Kass, H. D. and B. L. Catron, (eds.). 1990. *Images and Identities in Public Administration.* London: SAGE.

Kensen, S. 1999. *Sturen op variatie. Sociale vernieuwing en de deense variant als bronnen van inspiratie.* The Hague: VNG Uitgeverij.

Kensen, S. and P. Bogason. 1999. Two approaches of narrative policy evaluation compared. Evaluating a Danish neighborhood council twice. *Telling Tales: On Evaluation and Narrative,* edited by T. Abma. Greenwich, CT: JAI Press. 79-108.

King, C. S. and C. Stivers. 1998. *Government is Us. Public Administration in Anti-Government Era.* London: Sage.

Kouzmin, A. and R. Leivesley. 1997. Ethics in U.S. public administration: Self-arrested or castrated agency?—A rejoinder. *Administrative Theory & Praxis.* 19((1)):92-98.

Laclau, E. 1993. Discourse. *Blackwell Companion to Contemporary Political Philosophy,* edited by R. E. Goodin and P. Petitt. Oxford: Blackwell.

March, J. G. and J. P. Olsen. 1989. *Rediscovering Institutions. The Organizational Basis of Politics.* New York: Free Press.

McSwite, O. C. 1996. Postmodernism, public administration, and the public interest. *Refounding Democratic Public Administration. Modern Paradoxes, Postmodern Challenges* edited by G. L. Wamsley and J. F. Wolf. London: SAGE. 198-224.

———. 1997. *Legitimacy in public administration. A discourse analysis.* London: Sage.

———. 1998. The new normativism and the discourse movement: A meditation. *Administrative Theory & Praxis.* 20(3):377-381.

Morgan, G. 1986. *Images of Organization.* London: SAGE.

Morgan, D. F. 1990. Administrative phronesis: Discretion and the problem of administrative legitimacy in our constitutional system. *Images and Identities in Public Administration* edited by H. D. Kass & B. L. Catron. (London: SAGE Publications. 67-86.

Pedersen, K. 1996. Postmoderne planlægning—mellem kritik og styring. *Grus.* 49:59-74.

Putnam, R., R. Leonardi, and R. Y. Nanetti. 1993. *Making Democracy Work: Civic Traditions in Modern Italy.* Princeton, N J: Princeton University Press.

Rhodes, R. A. W. 1997. *Understanding Governance: Policy Networks, Governance, Reflexivity and Accountability.* Buckingham: Open University Press.

Rosenau, P. M. 1992. *Post-Modernism and the Social Sciences: Insights, Inroads and Intrusions.* Princeton, NJ: Princeton University Press.

Sayer, A. 1992. *Method in Social Science: A Realist Approach.* London: Routledge.

Spicer, M. W. 1997. Public administration, the state, and the postmodern condition. A constitutionalist perspective. *American Behavioral Scientist.* 41(1):90-102.

Sørensen, E. 1997. Democracy and empowerment. *Public Administration.* 75(3):553-568.

Tennert, J. R. 1998. Who cares about big questions? The search for the holy grail in public administration. *Administrative Theory & Praxis.* 20(2):231-243.

Wamsley, G. L., and J. F. Wolf. 1996. Introduction: Can a high-modern project find happiness in a postmodern era? *Refounding Democratic Public Administration: Modern Paradoxes, Postmodern Challenges,* edited by G. L. Wamsley & J. F. Wolf. London: SAGE. 1-37.

Wamsley, G. L., Bacher, R. N., Goodsell, C. T., Kronenberg, P. S., Rohr, J. A., Stivers, C. M., White, O. F., and J. F. Wolf. 1990. *Refounding Public Administration.* Newbury Park, CA: Sage.

White, J. D. 1990. Images of administrative reason and rationality: The recovery of practical discourse. *Images and Identities in Public Administration,* edited by H. D. Kass & B. D. Catron. London: SAGE. 132-150.

White, O. F. J., and C. J. McSwain. 1990. The Phoenix project: Raising a new image of public administration of the past. *Images and Identities in Public Administration,* edited by H. D. Kass and B. L. Catron. London: SAGE Publications. 23-59.

PART TWO

Challenges in Public Service, Values, and Ethics

INTRODUCTION

Louis Gawthrop discusses that if reality is in the relating, then the relationship that exists at any given point in time, between the visions-values-virtues of democracy and the actual implementation of public policy, represents a critical determinate in defining the moral essence of civic republicanism and the common good in our systems of governance. The manner and extent to which the virtual hopes and promises of democracy can become existent realities are determined, in no small measure, by the magnitude of the ethical-moral consciousness that prevails among those who have committed themselves to serve the commonweal. The moral interface that binds the visions of democratic values to the practical dynamics of public service represents a point of convergence where the nature of this relationship determines the quality of life evidenced at all levels—national, state, and local—of our society. Gawthrop further argues that the burden of maintaining the integrity of our civic republican system of governance falls heavily on the career public servants. To them, substantial responsibility is delegated to insure that the laws are faithfully executed. But even more significantly, they become, by default, our guardians of the moral interface, implicitly charged with maintaining the eschatological visions of our Founding Fathers.

As we enter the new millennium, one of the most salient issues facing the field is the substantive meaning of the public. Ventriss argues that as much as we use the word "public" in our lexicon, it is often regarded as a mere abstraction, or is associated with the meaning of government or the state. For the most part, the field has stripped the centrality of the public from its substantive meaning in public affairs resulting in, what John Dewey referred to as, the eclipse of the public. Ventriss explores some of the issues related to the substantive meaning of the public and the challenges it poses to administrative theory and the future role of both public administration and public policy in societal matters.

Hendrik Wagenaar argues that the need for administrative ethics arises from the by now generally accepted insight that the work of administrators inevitably is part of politics. Most authors on administrative ethics propose a normative solution of how to guide and account for this administrative discretion. He argues that the problem with these solutions is twofold: they suffer from an undercharacterization of discretionary space, and they generally proceed from a deontological, rule-based approach to ethics. With regard to the first objection: this paper proceeds from the assumption that irresolvable value conflict, a condition that in moral philosophy is called value pluralism, is intrinsic to contemporary political and administrative life in liberal societies. In fact, it is argued in this chapter that value pluralism should be the starting point of administrative ethics. With regard to the second objection he makes: careful, ethnographic observation of administrative work shows that administrators do not so much arrive at moral judgments by reasoning from large principles, as a deontological approach suggests, but by acting upon the case at hand and by giving meaning to their actions by telling stories about it afterwards. He calls this, in contrast to the rule-based approach to administrative ethics, a practice-based approach. Building on a concrete example of administrative value conflict, the chapter then analyzes the case respectively from a rule-based and a practice-based perspective. The chapter closes with an outline of a practice-oriented approach to value pluralism in administrative ethics.

The essay by Dvora Yanow and Hugh Willmott considers the role of passion and humility in the theory and practice of public administration in response to one of its central conundrums: how to act in administrative capacities with "passionate" commitment and conviction, while at the same time entertaining the possibility that, in its formulation and/or application, this commitment might be misplaced, misguided, or wrong. Although assuming humility is difficult for experts and managers, humility is an indispensable quality of a civic-minded administrator.

5

Public Service as the Parable of Democracy

— Louis C. Gawthrop

INTRODUCTION

At that particular moment in time when the last year of one century fades into the first year of the new century, I suspect there has always been a strong tendency among social commentators of the era to describe the event in such terms as "watershed," "sea change," "dramatic," etc. when, in fact, the transitional impact was more mirage than real. I recall one delightful passage from Walter Rauschenbusch's (1914), *Christianity and the Social Crisis*, in which the gray-bearded Father Time of the Nineteenth Century enters the "vaulted chambers of the Past, where the Spirits of the dead centuries sit on granite stones together." The solemn figure of the nineteenth century announces to all those who are gathered, "I am the Spirit of the Wonderful Century. I gave man the mastery over nature....I freed the thoughts of men....I broke the chains of bigotry and despotism....I have touched the summit of history." Hearing all of this, it is the voice of the First Century that asks whether the mastery of nature has really made humanity free from want, whether increased human wisdom is anything more than cunning, whether people have learned to control their passions, or have learned how to dispense justice? Alas, the Spirit of the Nineteenth Century concedes that the long-promised redemption did not come in his time. "But it will come," all of the Spirits of the centuries past assure each other—"it will come" (Hutchison 1976: 168-69; *see also*, Rauschenbusch 1914: xii, 211-13).

Unfortunately, this kind of serious reflection marking the end of the twentieth century was (or will be, depending on that sect of calendar keepers with whom one affiliates), obscured by the glitz and glamour, as well as the gloom and doom associated with the passage of the second millennium and the start of the third. To coin a phrase, it's not everyday that a new millennium comes along.

For now, however, no more dire predictions, no more giddy celebrations; the year 2000, the twenty-first century, the beginning of the third millennium *anno*

Domini are no longer virtual realities. They are real-time events that provide us, as a profession and as professionals, with a convenient baseline position from which we can project our benchmarks for the future. That is to say, the year 2000 provides us with an excellent milestone to assess what we need to do—as a profession and as professionals—in order to achieve a dramatic rebirth of public service activity in a manner so striking that the twenty-first century will be marked as one of the great moments in the development of democratic visions, values, and virtues. One way to approach this proposition might be to take a step back in time in an effort to discern the extent to which the future generated by our professional past yielded a public service true to the spirit of democracy. In other words, what was the future of our past?

THE FUTURE OF THE PAST

From a European perspective, the historical framework of the nineteenth century began in the midst of the Napoleonic era and ended with the demise of Queen Victoria (January 1901). In America, it marked the dramatic and breathtakingly-rapid growth of a nation from infancy to childhood to brash and robust adolescence. According to one British historian, the two main features of the Victorian era, which he sets from 1837 to 1901, were the growth of democracy and the expansion of the empire (Gooch 1933). In less dignified terms, this meant that the major Western European powers were not adverse to infusing their democratic ideas and ideals among the backward nations of the world, at gunpoint if necessary. The British author Rebecca West tells us, in her delightful chronological memoir entitled simply, *1900*, that, by the end of the nineteenth century, there was:

> a vague feeling everywhere that all men had a right to be free; at the same time, white men felt that they had the right to walk into any country belonging to people of a different civilization and tamper with their customs and their thoughts by controlling their government and education. (1982: 48)

With the end of the nineteenth century, the U.S. flag was raised in a number of locales outside the continental limits of the country, and wherever the flag is raised, can public administrators be far behind? Turn-of-the-century Americans were bullish on democracy and effusive in their pretense of Victorian morality, and by 1901 the presidency indeed became the "bully pulpit" for a man who had no hesitancy in, and offered no apology for, cultivating the field of democracy with the nurturing seed of moral zeal. As noted by one scholar:

> For whatever reasons, moralism became more central in Anglo-American culture, at least its educated middle-class ranges in the decades after 1850 than at any previous period. It was hardly coincidental that the second half of the century saw the greatest flowering of ethical studies in the annals of Anglo-American philosophy, from John Stuart Mill's *Utilitarianism* in 1853 to G. E. Moore's *Principai Ethica* in 1902. There is no evidence that Victorians on either

side of the Atlantic actually behaved better than their ancestors or descendants. That is not the point. An intensely self-conscious moralism—we call it, generically, "Victorian"—loomed larger in their world view. (Turner 1985: 222)

Without question, the situation in the United States, following the Civil War, created an ethical-moral tension of the first magnitude insofar as the newly-defined status of blacks in American society was concerned. This issue, however, was pushed aside primarily because of the steady, systemic degeneration of our democratic political systems at all levels that loomed menacingly in the two decades following the end of the Civil War. How were the thirteenth and fourteenth amendments to be implemented when, by all accounts, federal, state, and local governments were so eaten away with political corruption that the notion of racial equality was viewed solely in the nihilistic terms of corrupt power politics that varied from region to region and state to state.

Leonard White began the concluding chapter of the final volume of his American administrative history with a homey allegory:

A perceptive Rip Van Winkle who fell into slumber on the banks of the Potomac at the close of the Civil War and awoke at the close of the Spanish-American War would have remarked both [sic] the tenacity of tradition and the inevitability of change. (1958: 386)

But old Rip's sleepy-eyed generalizations would have missed quite a bit. He would have missed the full force and effect of the reform movement that, as described by White, attacked the steadily degenerative corruption on three fronts—civil service reform, election reform, and municipal government reform. And despite the Victorian moral template that was cemented firmly in our social system at the time, no great evangelistic moral crusade was launched to eliminate the corruption that had become endemic in these three areas. Rather, the primary efforts of the reformers were aimed at fashioning systems of governance that were impervious to the corrosive effects of political spoils. The net result was the development of detailed techniques, procedures, and methods that were intrinsically and explicitly impartial, apolitical, and objectively impersonal. Political neutrality was the key to corruption-free government as seen by the nineteenth century reformers and, within that context, administrative neutrality was measured as the key component.

The manner in which administrative neutrality could be effected was by detaching and insulating—categorically and absolutely, in mind as well as in deed—all administrative processes, functions, and procedures from the political currents that swirled around public servants. It was simply assumed that the administrative elements that serviced the public sector were mechanistic systems that could be controlled in a completely deterministic—i.e., scientific—manner. Scientific management was the engine that would eradicate the cesspools of political corruption suffocating the nation. Moreover, it promised to restore democracy to the nation through the implementation of scrupulously devised sets of procedures, methods, and techniques that were intended to enforce the uniform standardization of public sector administrative systems, and the absolutely uniform application of law and policy.

When Teddy Roosevelt assumed the presidency in 1901, the dynamic symbol of social and political reform in America became squarely based in the White House. As for public administration, one commentator noted:

> After 1900, the doors of power opened to those who saw a national administrative apparatus as the centerpiece of the new government order. The central question in institutional development was correspondingly altered. It was no longer a question of whether or not America was going to build a state that could support administrative power, but of who was going to control administrative power in the new state that was to be built....Packaged in the rhetoric of "good government", the rise of the new professional public servant in America merged hopes for a responsible new democracy with the hopes for a responsive new political economy. The bureaucratic remedy represented at once a narrowing of political alternatives and an obfuscation of the distinctions among them. By transforming ideological conflicts into matters of expertise and efficiency, bureaucrats promised to reconcile the polity with the economy and to stem the tide of social disintegration. (Skowronek 1982: 165-66)

What was envisioned by the reformers was not a miraculous cleansing of the inevitable political power struggles that shaped the initiation and formulation of public policy programs, but rather the construction of an administration system that would filter any impurities contained in the policy mandates and then deliver the mandates in the most efficient, responsible, and detached manner possible. Writing in Germany at the time, Max Weber's observations on public sector bureaucracies overlapped neatly with the views of the reformers in America, and particularly with Woodrow Wilson's seminal statement on administration. "Bureaucratization offers above all," wrote Weber:

> the optimum possibility for carrying through the principle of specializing administrative functions according to purely objective considerations....The "objective" discharge of business primarily means a discharge of business according to calculable rules and "without regard for persons"....When fully developed, bureaucracy also stands, in a specific sense, under the principle of *sine ira ac studio* [without passion or enthusiasm]. Its specific nature...develops more perfectly the more the bureaucracy is "dehumanized," the more completely it succeeds in eliminating from official business love, hatred, and all purely personal, irrational, and emotional elements which escape calculation. This is the specific nature of bureaucracy and it is appraised as its special virtue. (quoted in Gerth & Mills 1946: 226)

The convergence of these two perspectives—the view that the intricacies of public sector management could be controlled by the rigors of the scientific method, and the view that a totally dehumanized cadre of public servants was basic to the attainment of operating efficiency—served to create a value-free administrative system. The principal characteristic of this system was the total absence of any sense of the spiritual essence of democracy so basic to those founders who joined together one hundred years earlier to create a new republic. The value visions of democracy that served us so well in the first half of the nineteenth century were, of course, severely tested by the Civil War. Moreover, in the post-war decades of the 1860s, 70s, and 80s, when political corruption reached epidemic proportions, any ethical-moral sense of a covenantal commitment to the pursuit of a common good could only be viewed in the most skeptical, if not outright hypocritical light. For some—indeed, probably for many—the dynamic and insurgent, if not revolutionary, force of reform was seen as a new hope for the humanistic values and virtues reflected in the promise of an American life, as Herbert Croly so aptly titled his 1912 book. But such a hope was not to be. The value-free administrative systems that emerged in the opening years of the twentieth century were governed by the objective tenets of scientific management and were as dehumanized as they could be.

The tone and the temper of this period of scientific enlightenment gripped the emerging social sciences in America with a firm, unrelenting grasp. For the scientific management apostles who were energized by the good government reform movement, the early decades of the twentieth century were an extraordinary period of social experimentation and application of a new "mind set," so to speak. The new centurions celebrated the dawning, not of the age of Aquarius exactly, but certainly the age of economy and efficiency. Moreover, the enthusiasm for this new positivism continued for an extended period of time despite the critical concern aimed at its amoral precepts.

Viewed from the perspective of the good government reform dynamic and its scientific management component, both of which were in high gear by 1912, the whole thrust of the economy and efficiency movement was designed to transform (emancipate, if you will) the public sector—government at all levels and in all branches—from its illusions of the past. The mentality that bred the concept, "To the victor belong the spoils," did not create a system that simply needed to be amended or corrected in certain respects. It needed to be eradicated completely. Moreover, given the industrial giant that America had become, even at that time, there was certainly no returning to the simple governmental systems of the pre-Civil War era. From a perspective of political governance, and especially from a perspective of public administration, the advent of the twentieth century marked a radical departure from the past, and the beginning of a new mentality that animated our administrative systems for...well, just how long can we say? Perhaps the best way to approach this question is to determine the extent to which the past defines the present.

THE PAST DEFINES THE PRESENT

Ironically, to a certain extent some of the colorful figures of speech employed by Leonard White to describe the period of administrative history covered by his last volume, *The Republican Era,* seem just as applicable when applied to our current situation. For example, it would certainly strike me as a completely reasonable proposition to state: A perceptive Rip Van Winkle who fell into slumber on the banks of the Potomac at the end of Teddy Roosevelt's presidency and awoke at the close of Bill Clinton's second term in office would have remarked at both the tenacity of tradition and the inevitability of change. Although the differences between the two eras are obvious and inevitable, the similarities are really quite striking in many respects.

For instance, despite the dynamic impulses of reform that spread throughout the nation during the Theodore Roosevelt years, a debilitating mood of social, moral , and environmental degeneration continued to prevail. In 1907, a key figure in the Progressive movement, Walter Rauschenbusch noted:

> the pall of coal smoke hanging over our industrial cities is injurious to the eyes; it predisposes [individuals] to diseases of the respiratory organs; it depresses the joy of living; it multiples the labor of housewives in cleaning and washing. (1914: 371)

And although Rauschenbusch's comments were aimed literally at the horrendous problem of urban air pollution, his comments can also be interpreted figuratively as a commentary on the squalid ethical-moral conditions that were then shaping the nation's emerging industrialized society.

The opening years of the twentieth century clearly bore the imprint of Rauschenbusch and his Social Gospel movement—a movement that principally was aimed to stir the ethical-moral conscience of the nation into confronting the social and economic evils that were the inevitable by-products of a totally unregulated industrial society. Drawing heavily from the secular socialist thought of the nineteenth century, the Social Gospelers saw the inner being of every individual invariably malformed by the unregulated social and economic institutions that dominated their lives. The good of an industrialized society, however, could be realized by all citizens given a beneficent, responsive, and active administrative state, operating under the watchful eye of a positive, dynamic national government, and inspired by a strong ethical-moral consciousness. The Social Gospel movement proclaimed that this goal could be attained only by collective, not individualistic, endeavors. Thus, the true distinctiveness of the Social Gospel movement was that, first and foremost, it was a *social* movement designed to raise the ethical-moral temper and tone of a society committed to the theological notion that social salvation was logically prior, temporally and substantively, to individual salvation. (Hutchison 1976: 165, fn. 36)

Walter Rauschenbusch and his Social Gospelers, along with the Progressive movement in general, left their imprints on society and gradually faded from the scene by the middle teen years of the twentieth century. But something of a legacy, or perhaps a nagging universal and perennial question remained and is present still as we begin the twenty-first century: namely, what is the proper place of values in a world of facts? In contrast to the value-free, mechanistic systems advanced by the acolytes of the scientific management movement, the main vision of the Social Gospel followers focused on a holistic ethical-moral social system that bound all individuals together in community. In this value framework, one commentator noted, "Society is not a sand heap of atomistic individuals but a dense texture of organic relations, in which no single self exists except as a self-in-relation" (Beach & Niebuhr 1973: 448).

Extending this same argument well after the Social Gospel left the scene, Mary Parker Follett informed us that the objective facts generated by the methods of scientific management do not represent reality—reality is only to be found in the relating of one individual to another and in the endless evolving of these relatings (1924: 54-55). Where, then, is reality? In the objective situation or in "the people"? In neither, she answers, but in that relating that frees and integrates and creates. Creates what? Always fresh possibilities for the human soul, she responds in her book, appropriately titled, *Creative Experience* (Ibid.: 130). The same value-based perspective is revealed in her earlier book, *The New State,* in which she argues that the State, the Nation, the Republic—the Union—is forever in the process of evolving, creating anew, unifying; it is constantly in the process of becoming the center of moral authority for the commonweal. But as Follett points out in a manner that is not unfamiliar to many of us today:

> The federal state can be the moral state only through its being built anew from hour to hour by the activity of all its members....This means a new ethics and a new politics. Citizenship is not a right nor a privilege nor a duty, but an activity to be exercised every moment of the time. Democracy does not exist unless every [person] is doing [his or her] part fully every minute, unless every one is taking [his or her] share in building the state-to-be. This is the trumpet call to [citizens] today. A creative citizenship must be made the force of American political life, a trained responsible citizenship always in control, creating always its own life....the doctrine of true democracy is that every [individual] is and must be a creative citizen. (1918: 335)

This sentiment of Follett's is thoroughly consistent with the themes advanced by Raushenbusch and his Social Gospelers, and is also strikingly similar to the emphasis currently being placed on concepts such as communitarianism and the common good. Let Mary Parker Follett speak for them all:

> [individuals] advance toward completeness not by further aggregations to [themselves], but by further and further relatings of [themselves to others]....The spirit craves totality;...the process of getting it is not by adding more and more to ourselves, but by offering more and more of ourselves. Not appropriation but contribution is the law of growth....The deeper truth, perhaps the deepest, is that *the will to will the common will* is the core, the germinating center of that large, still larger, ever larger life which we are coming to call the true democracy. (Ibid.: 65, 49)

From the beginning of time, and most certainly from the beginning of the twentieth century to its concluding months, public sector administrative operations, functions, and processes associated with the intricacies of social intercourse, however defined, have been described as systems possessing either mechanical or organic attributes. While Rauschenbusch and Mary Parker Follett described their perceived realities in terms of organic systems, the scientific management forces of Wilson, Weber, Taylor, Fayol, et. al. defined their administrative visions solely in terms of mechanistic systems. As noted by one disciple of the new and modern passion for mechanized efficiency:

> Our political machinery...[indeed] our whole political machinery in all its parts must be adapted to all the changing purposes of government....it is of small advantage that each separate government wheel turns with noiseless ease, if the system *as a whole* is ill-geared. If in a government there is a lack of coordination among the parts, if certain parts are weak which should be strong, and certain parts are strong which might be weak, ...if there is fluctuation where there should be stability, and a stiff unchangeability where there should be elasticity and change—if there are these or any of these, then no true efficiency can be maintained. (Weyl, quoted in Skowronek 1982: 177)

This mechanical vision informed our thinking throughout most of the twentieth century and yet, as we begin a new millenarian chapter in time, there are many observers who conclude that we are on the verge of a cataclysmic moral meltdown. In 1918, Follett observed, "There is no use denying that we are at a crisis in our history....The world is at present a moral bankrupt" (4, 333). And very probably this is one instance in which our awakening Rip van Winkle could say that nothing has changed. To be sure, strong objections could be raised to such an assertion. It is much too glib and superficial, one might conclude. Moreover, it could be argued that people like Follett, and those who embrace her gestalt-styled management approach, can hardly be cited as authorities on public sector systems of management and administration. Rather, we would be much better advised to follow the lead of someone like Luther Gulick who was one of the major figures who helped pull public administration from the quagmire of politics, and who created a mechanistic, value-free context in which public administrators committed themselves solely and totally to the dictates of efficiency. What would Gulick say to us as a profession and as professionals at the start of this new millenium? We have no way of knowing, but we do know what he told us twenty-four years ago on April 1, 1976 in an address delivered at Indiana University's fledgling School of Public and Environmental Affairs.

> [While] we in public administration have been quick to point out that the lack of "good management" is at the bottom of most...[of our] disappointments and failures....we must admit that there is now a deeper failure, a fundamental *political and moral failure*....This challenge is significant; ...it is first of all ethical and political. And it is aimed at the core of our democratic faith....It is obvious that we face an epochal challenge in human history....We must change our fundamental paradigms...or we will not survive. (Gulick 1977: 707)

And then there follows a line of thought that is quite extraordinary and remarkable, given the mechanistic position with which Gulick came to be associated, especially as reflected in his *Papers on the Science of Administration.* "There is good reason for dropping the idea that government is a *machine,*" he stated.

> We never should have abandoned the notion that any team of people working together for a purpose is an "organism", not a machine....If we think of government as an organism, a living organism, we have a totally different and more accurate and constructive understanding of the nature of a government organization....The staff are no longer cogs, they are suborgans....They do not merely transmit the energy imparted to them from above, they each make an added contribution to the total effort, influenced by what they see, feel, and are doing. (Gulick 1977: 709)

To the extent that public service, and even democracy for that matter, are currently perceived in purely procedural and mechanistic terms, then it seems reasonable to conclude that many of the commentaries of the past do, in fact, accurately define our present plight—that is to say, we are presently faced with a political and moral failure of the first magnitude. If it is true, however, that the future is the only place that you can change the present, then we must seriously pursue the assumption that the future begins in the present.

THE FUTURE BEGINS IN THE PRESENT

Slightly more than thirty years ago, F. E. Emery wrote an intellectually rigorous and conceptually imaginative article entitled, "The Next Thirty Years: Concepts, Methods, and Anticipations" (1967: 199-237). Emery's basic proposition was that the future exists in the present in the form of latent, embryonic, developing systems. As Emery explained:

> If social life is properly characterized in terms of overlapping temporal *gestalten*, then many of those processes that will be critical in the future are already in existence in the present....Granted that there are genuine emergent processes...,then we must accept...that we have to live for some time with the future before we know it. (ibid.: 209)

Such latent processes are potentially dynamic systems of change, and in their embryonic stages of development they are referred to by Emery as "the leading parts." In other words, given the multiplicity of component parts characterizing every emergent system, there will be one part, Emery argues, "whose goal achievements at t_0 tend to determine the goal achievements of all the parts at t+" (ibid.: 208). This he defines as "the leading part."

Having taken a quick glimpse at how the nineteenth century blended into the twentieth century, and having scanned the twentieth century to determine the linkages and contrasts that are evident between the beginning and ending of the century, can we apply Emery's teleological notion of a future purposefulness existing in the present to our current set of circumstances? Perhaps the most prudent approach is simply to acknowledge that if the future is the only place where we can change the present, as well as the only place where we can negate the negatives of the past, then the task before us, as a profession and as professionals, is to focus on "the leading parts" that dominate our current thinking and to determine how to configure those parts in order to attain the type of purposeful future that embodies the values and virtues of our democratic being.

Certainly one dominate theme that effects our immediate future is the specification of a new definition of publicness. Posing under many different labels (e.g., contracting, out-sourcing, etc.) privatization is currently an integral element in the reinventing government literature. Moreover, it is a clearly defined vision in the futures of many different private sector industries. Conjunctively, the dramatic growth in numbers as well as influence of the non-profit sector, when combined with the increasing role of private sector corporations, constitute an obvious "leading part" of a future scenario that clearly requires a new definition of publicness. If the motivating forces of the private and nonprofit sectors continue to progress without conforming their public sector activities to the categorical imperative of democratic ethical-moral values, then the following comments by Luther Gulick seem just as applicable today as when they were originally presented twenty-four years ago:

> The American people...have not been able to decide where they as a people want to go, and have not selected leaders of ability and character to guide them in dealing with the growing problems of the present and the future. If this aimless political incompetence and dishonesty continue over the next decade, it may be said that the American dream has failed. (Gulick 1977: 707)

Of course, the skeptics can correctly note that we have gone well beyond the doomsday decade projected by Gulick—just as we managed to dodge the apocalyptic thunderbolt of God's wrath at the Y2K mark. Nevertheless, the twentieth century clearly ended on a note that harked the demise of the classic dichotomy not only between the public and private sectors, but also between public and private behavior and public and private values.

Clearly what is needed is a new conception of publicness that, as Mary Parker Follett might define it, incorporates the different "leading parts" within the rubric of democracy as "an infinitely including spirit. We have an instinct for democracy because we have an instinct for wholeness; we get wholeness only through reciprocal relations, through infinitely expanding reciprocal relations" (1918: 157). In the final analysis, democracy is really about creating wholes. Indeed, for those who view the promise of democracy as being integrally dependent on a wholesome and holistic public service, one principal issue that cannot be ignored is the manner in which the core of democracy—i.e., its essential sense of publicness—provides the energetic dynamic that creates and maintains an enduring sense of wholeness.

In this regard, democracy itself needs to be viewed as the fundamental "leading part" that establishes our handrails to the future. That is to say, democracy provides something of value, something that has genuine worth, something dear, perhaps even precious that one is ready to suffer or sacrifice for, which gives one a reason to live and, if need be, a reason to die. Democracy provides life with an essential dimension of meaning. It identifies a person, and it provides one with a character and a set of motives. Democracy defines the quality of one's life, its breadth and depth. In other words, democracy not only tells me that a life of service is essential and worthwhile, but that its worthiness is basic to my very being, and I am, in turn, affected by its worth. To this end, we are reminded of a turn-of-the-century observation that fits quite neatly as an end-of-the-century commentary. As Herbert Croly noted in 1912:

> There comes a time in the history of every nation when its independence of spirit vanishes, unless it emancipates itself in some measure from its traditional illusions; and that time is fast approaching the American people. They must either seize the chance for a better future, or else become a nation which is satisfied in spirit merely to repeat indefinitely the monotonous measures of its own past. (Croly 1912: 279)

Certainly one disturbing pattern of the last half of the twentieth century that needs to be reversed if we can realistically entertain any serious hope for a better future, is the steadily progressing public mood of not caring. As one theologian has noted:

> Man's most debilitating proclivity is not his pride. It is not his attempt to be more than man. Rather it is his sloth, his unwillingness to be everything man was intended to be....Sloth describes our flaccid unwillingness to delight in the banquet of earth or to share the full measure of life's pain and responsibility. In means to abdicate in part or in whole the fullness of one's own humanity. Sloth is admittedly an ugly word....Perhaps, therefore, we would do better to resurrect the word *acedia.* (Cox 1967: xi, xv)

Stemming from the Latin, *acedia* translates into "not caring," and in the context of democracy, the cardinal sin is not to care. And yet, in our insistence to repeat indefinitely the monotonous measures of the past, public administrators all too frequently are unwilling to deviate from the deeply embedded Stoic tendency that views caring as a most dangerous thing. The risk that is incurred when public servants commit themselves to enhancing the qualitative well-being of another citizen and neighbor, is that, like the biblical mustard seed, the tiniest bit of personal ethical-moral commitment can grow into a complex existential reticulation. In his epigraph in *The Human Factor,* Graham Greene (1978a) quotes from Joseph Conrad: "I only know that he who forms a tie is lost. The germ of corruption has entered into his soul." The germ of corruption referred to is the force of one's conscience, the sense of moral obligation. Such a sense of moral consciousness has an effect that clearly runs counter to the rational order of complex public sector organizations. The point is, that every public servant who labors in the service of democracy is bound to the transcendent good that the concept of democracy entails—that is to say, a common good that elevates the sanctity of every human being to the highest level of compassion and service. And it is in this respect that one can say positively that caring is the most dangerous thing.

We learned long ago from Robert Presthus that both public and private sector administrators can allow themselves to be drawn into the existential wastelands of an organizational's self-centered interests and join the ranks of the upward mobiles. Alternatively, they can view their parent organizations with complete indifference and use them as vehicles to fulfill their own personal agendum without developing any concern whatsoever for either the policies or programs of their respective organizations. Finally, there is a third direction that one can attempt to follow—an ambivalent course that veers between a reluctance to commit to the self-serving ends and means of the organization on the one hand, and on the other, an equally sincere ethical-moral commitment to a transcendent good, however defined.

As far as the public sector is concerned, the individuals who constitute this latter subset of managers—the ambivalents—learn "to stay, to love, to accept responsibility, to lie" (Greene 1978b: 187). Moreover, by all accounts, much more pain than pleasure is incurred by those who attempt to maintain a sense of ethical-moral commitment to the values and virtues of democracy. Those who attempt to integrate the language and habits of the heart with those of the mind must walk across "the razor's edge." As described by the ancient Hindu philosopher, Katha, "The sharp edge of the razor is difficult to pass over; thus the wise say the path to salvation is hard." In the world of the ambivalents, the razor's edge is the narrow boundary between loyalty and disloyalty, between fidelity and infidelity. And in the end, the saving grace of most foot-scarred public sector managers and administrators is that at various critical junctures in their professional lives—in those instances when each was confronted with the heart of the matter—they often responded as truly authentic human beings. Aside from these personal epiphanies, however, the overall contour of public administration remains essentially unaltered. For those ambivalents of the future who will continue to labor in the vineyards of public sector management, wherever they are located, the message seems clear:

> Neither [should you] hope for reward for good deeds nor fear punishment for evil deeds; moralists cannot shake the wicked from the surface of the earth and God will not. The laws of the natural order and those of the moral order are not of one piece. If you decide to do good, do it because it is good. (Tsevat 1980: 33)

CONCLUSION

And so, we end as we began. Let us surmise that the ghost of the twentieth century joined all of the other Spirits of the centuries past with such understandable boastings as: "I gave them mastery over the most infinitesimal biological and genetic organisms contained in the human body; I left them with an unimaginable sophistication of the workings of the outer space; and the age-old barriers of time and space, that from earliest centuries have isolated the many cultures and civilizations of the world, have been diminished beyond comprehension." What kind of reaction might be expected? Particularly in connection with the latter point, we all can share the excitement of identifying a "leading part " to our future in the sentiment expressed by one observer: "The sooner we learn that this earth is a very small planet and getting smaller every year, and that our welfare is bound up with all the other passengers, the better it is for us." Who can disagree with such an observation? Indeed, it is just as valid today as when it was originally published in the *Rochester Democrat and Chronicle* on February 13, 1899. And before we get too smug about the twentieth century legacy we leave to the annals of history, keep in mind that the author of the preceding words, Walter Rauschenbusch, also wrote at the end of World War I, "Modern pessimism drains the finer minds of their confidence in the world and the value of life itself. At present, we gasp for air in a crushing and monstrous world" (quoted in Hudson 1984: 35, 197). How do we find ourselves responding to this point today? As one staff writer for the Baltimore *Sun* phrased his opening paragraph of an article on the twentieth century, "Call the twentieth century advanced if you like, but it also has been bloody. The bloodiest. Ever. A century of organized death." And his article was focused on deaths (military and civilian) resulting solely from warfare (big and little) among and within nations during the course of the twentieth century. As reported in *The Sun*, "In the last ninety years...three times more people have been killed in wars than in all the previous 500." (Imhoff 1999: 2A). In a totally separate context, the same point is echoed by Nobel Peace Prize winner Oscar Arias. "We began the twentieth century, the bloodiest in history, with a war in the Balkans and we are ending it with a war in the Balkans," the former president of Costa Rica noted. "We cannot survive the twenty-first century with the values of the twentieth century" (*The Sun*, March 30, 1999: 3B). Perhaps Michael Walzer can summarize it best as he addresses the argument that the value dimensions of democratic societies suffer from the absence of rigorously defined ethical-moral theories.

> Liberty, justice, democracy, domination, oppression, exploitation, cruelty, violence, terror, mass murder, totalitarian rule—this is the language of politics in the twentieth century, a time of large hopes, high risks, desperate efforts, fearful culminations. Who can doubt that this language is better employed by a person of moral sensitivity without a theory than by an amorally obtuse person with the grandest possible theory. (1988: 88)

We still have not made humanity free from want; we are still not certain that the increase in human knowledge translates into wisdom; and we clearly have not learned how to bring a sense of love and compassion to our fellow citizens—our neighbors—in attempting to implement the impulses of democracy. But, then, one is again reminded of Robert Michels—the German sociologist who authored the iron law of oligarchy. It was Michels who, in talking about democracy, relates a fable of a peasant on his death bed who tells his sons that a treasure is buried somewhere in their dry, dusty, impoverished fields. As Michels then describes it:

> After the old man's death the sons dig everywhere in order to discover the treasure. They do not find it. But their indefatigable labor improves the soil and secures for them a comparative well-being. The treasure in the fable may well symbolize democracy. Democracy is a treasure which no one will ever discover by deliberate search. But in continuing our search, in laboring indefatigably to discover the undiscoverable, we shall perform a work which will have fertile results in the democratic sense. (1962: 368)

To a very real extent, public service is a parable of democracy, which, itself, is a parable of human civilization. Public service is like the sons working in the field, trying to locate the treasure lode of democracy. This parabolic nature of democracy was also described quite accurately by Socrates in his response to Glaucon's assertion that such an ideal city governed by an absolutely virtuous sense of the common good does not exist anywhere on this earth. Socrates explains, "...whether such a [city] exists or ever will exist in fact, is no matter; for he will live under the manner of that [city] having nothing to do with any other." And, then, Socrates adds, "in heaven there is laid up a pattern of it, methinks, which he who desires may behold, and beholding, may set his own house in order" (quoted in Jowett 1941: 360).

Public service *is* a parable of democracy. It contains and reflects all the mysteries, contradictions, challenges, and surprises that we associate with parables. And in attempting to comprehend the substantive essence of "ad-ministering" to the commonweal, one is drawn ever-closer to the perennial parabolic mysteries of democracy. The two are integrally related. In fact, the only hope there is in drawing closer to the visions, virtues, and values of democracy is through the engagement of public service.

Service in the name of democracy activates ethical-moral impulses that are deeply embedded in the psyche of our national character. From Athens to Philadelphia—and at numerous points in between—an abiding faith in the common good was the primary impetus for civic action imbued with the spirit and the faith of democracy. For well over the past two hundred years, that faith in democracy and that spirit of the common good have served us well in creating always new possibilities, as Mary Parker Follett would say—in achieving a life lived in the service of democracy. But, probably, we have learned all we can from the major figures whose wisdom and kindness, whose unselfishness and insightfulness have guided us to where we are today. And in this regard, it is important to continue to remind ourselves that although the ethical-moral impulses of democracy are capable of ascribing character to the human side of public administration, administration in action can infuse or defuse the dynamic spirit of democracy. The measure of those who labor in the service of democracy is a measure of the vitality of democracy itself. To serve in the name of democracy is both the alpha and omega point of our journey over time. The Founding Fathers envisioned an eschatological future of hope and promise. Certainly the democratic eschaton they (and the men of Athens before them) envisioned continues to elude us as we assess the challenge of the twenty-first century—"but it will come," the spirits of our Framers murmur in unison, "it will come." And who are we to doubt their visions and wisdom, their insights and outlooks, however elusive they may be? To end their elusiveness, however, is to confront their challenge.

REFERENCES

Beach, Walter and H. Richard Niebuhr. 1973. *Christian Ethics*, 2nd ed. New York: John Wiley.

Cox, Harvey. 1967. *On Not Leaving it to the Snake*. New York: The Macmillan Co.

Croly, Herbert D. 1912/1963. *The Promise of American Life*. New York: Dutton.

Emery, F.E. 1967. The next thirty years: Concepts, methods, and anticipations. *Human Relations*. 20(3):199-237.

Follett, Mary Parker. 1918. *The New State*. New York: Longmans, Green.

Follett, Mary Parker. 1924. *Creative Experience*. New York: Longmans, Green.

Gerth, H. H. and C. Wright Mills, eds. 1946. *From Max Weber: Essays in Sociology*. New York: Oxford University Press.

Gooch, G. P. 1933. Introductory: The Victorian Age, 1937-1901. *The Social and Political Ideas of Some Representative Thinkers of the Victorian Age*, edited by F. J. C. Hearnshaw. New York: Barnes & Noble.

Greene, Graham. 1978a. *The Human Factor.* New York: Simon & Schuster.

———. 1978b. *The Heart of the Matter*. New York: Penguin Books.

Gulick, Luther. 1977. Democracy and administration face the future. *Public Administration Review,* 37(6) (Nov.–Dec.):4, 333.

Hudson, Winthrop S., ed. 1984. *Walter Rauschenbusch: Selected Writings*. New York: Paulist Press.

Hutchison, William R. 1976. *The Modernist Impulse in American Protestantism*. Cambridge, MA: Harvard University Press.

Imhoff, Ernest. 1999. Looking back on a cruel century. *The Sun*. Baltimore, 10 January, 2A.

Jowett, B., trans. 1941. Plato's *The Republic*. New York: The Modern Library.

Michels, Robert. 1962. *Political Parties*. New York: Collier Books.

Rauschenbusch, Walter. 1914. *Christianity and the Social Crisis*. New York: The Macmillan Co.

Skowronek, Stephen. 1982. *Building a New American State: The Expansion of National Administrative Capacities, 1877-1920*. Cambridge UK: Cambridge University Press.

The Sun. Baltimore. 1999. 30 March, 3B.

Tsevat, Matitiahu. 1980. *The Meaning of the Book of Job and Other Biblical Studies*. New York: Ktav Publishing.

Turner, James. 1985. *Without God, Without Creed: The Origins of Unbelief in America*. Baltimore, MD: Johns Hopkins University Press.

Walzer, Michael. 1988. *The Company of Critics*. New York: Basic Books.

West, Rebecca. 1982. *1900*. New York: The Viking Press.

White, Leonard D. 1958. *The Republican Era*. New York: The Macmillan Co.

6

A Democratic Public and Administrative Thought: A Public Perspective

Curtis Ventriss

INTRODUCTION

In his insightful final chapter to the *Preface to Public Administration*, Richard Stillman (1991) discusses the various theoretical perspectives concerning the role of the state and their implications for public affairs. In that chapter, he also posed the following salient issue about what he so aptly referred to as the "pro-stater," which can also be equally applied to many of the theoretical approaches presently in vogue in administrative theory:

> Much can be learned in the various specialties and technicalities contained in this literature for advancing the multitude of particulars of modern administration. Yet, there in lies the rub, for specialized analytics do not necessarily add up to meaningful and purposeful administrative action. Keeping the trains running on time may be a worthy enterprise, but it can also miss the larger issue: Are the trains going in the right directions? Should they even be moving in the first place? Without worrying about the worth of the central purpose or fundamental goals, Big Questions and Big Issues can be overlooked or missed entirely. (1991: 226)

One of those big questions we tend to ignore in administrative theory is the nature of the public. It is interesting to me that as ubiquitous and commonplace as the word "public," or publicness, is in our administrative and policy lexicon, we still regard this term as a rather muddled and murky abstraction. This is due, in part, because the notion of the public is difficult to quantify with any empirical precision; hence, most theorists tend to avoid defining this term altogether. Why bother, one can argue, in attempting to define such a vague and amorphous

concept that defies scientific clarity? Yet, the notion exists. When we have tried
to grapple with the term, it is viewed as somehow being inexorably linked with
the role of purpose of the government (or the state). Given the expansive role of
the state in the twentieth century, this quotidian view is somewhat understandable. However, it is a notion, I contend, that warrants some serious rethinking
among theorists and practitioners alike. In fact, from an etymological perspective, the public goes well beyond what is associated with the government or the
state. Terry Cooper, for example, correctly put it this way:

> Thus the etymology of the term public indicated a breadth and depth of mean-
> ing that transcends government. Its most fundamental denotations are the
> shared, communal, universally accessible dimensions of collective life...the
> realm of interdependence. The normative connotations of the word, as found in
> *res publica*, have to do with the common good or well being. The state is clearly
> included in the meaning of public, but in a secondary, apparently derivative sta-
> tus. (1991: 177)

If Cooper's assertion is correct, then, this raises some rather intriguing questions for the field: what is the substantive meaning of contemporary "public"
administration or public service, for example, when publicness is often conceptualized, more or less, in exclusively market or governmental terms? And, equally
as important, as a result of this proclivity in public affairs, can there be such a
notion as "public" citizenship in regards to the issue of public accountability, public trust, and civic involvement? There are, no doubt, many other questions that
can be posed, but my point is that given the centrality of "publicness" to both public administration and public policy, it is an issue that will not—and should not—
go away. I will argue that what we are seeing—to use John Dewey's term—is an
eclipse of the public occurring in both fields (notwithstanding the efforts of
Frederickson (1997) and some others) which has stripped it of its substantive
meaning in public affairs. I know that this view stands in sharp contrast to the
Panglossian tone often expressed in the literature today. My basic argument
echoes a point articulated by the exegetical pen of C. Wright Mills:

> The images of the public of classic democracy which are still used as working
> justifications of power in American society...are not adequate even as an approx-
> imate model of how the American system of power works. The issues that now
> shape [the individual's] fate are neither raised nor decided by the public at large.
> The idea of the community of publics in not a description of fact but an assertion
> of an ideal, an assertion of legitimization masquerading as a fact. (1957: 300)

The sober implications of C. Wright Mills' perceptive contention must, I think,
be appropriately sorted out in order to readdress, and perhaps even reconceptual-
ize, both public administration's and public policy's relationship to the historical,
philosophical, and political concerns of the role we should—and ought—to play
in a democratic polity. When all is said and done, this stands as one of the most
critical challenges that lies before us as we enter the twenty-first century.

CONCEPTUALIZING THE MEANING OF THE PUBLIC: A THEORETICAL AND PRACTICAL CUL-DE-SAC?

Critical social thought in the United States, then, suffers from the absence of a counterproject, an alternative view of historical possibility.

—Norman Birnbaum

In one of his more disconcerting observations, Max Weber argued a point that has been, interestingly enough, overlooked by many administrative theorists that warrants a reminder: that democracy itself, in many respects, is the most elaborate form of domination in that it obscures its potential authoritarian inclinations by wrapping itself neatly around the need for bureaucratic rationality and popular rhetoric (1958: 182). This rather troubling point, of course, raises a related and equally poignant issue; namely, whether a democratic public can truly exist at all, when, as Habermas has so eloquently contended, the public sphere under modern conditions has been largely undermined, manipulated, and misused by a pervasive adherence to instrumental goals and procedures (1979). This notion begs the larger question concerning the meaning of the public, particularly in regards to its substantive meaning. Let us briefly examine some of those meanings as exemplified in the literature.

Writing in a style strangely devoid of his typical polemic tone, Herbert Marcuse once argued that "the masses are not identical to the [public] on which sovereign of a free society [is] to be established" (1970: 60). To Marcuse, a genuine publicness denotes the saliency of "autonomy" whereby the public can act free of societal heteronomy (as he called it) or social groupism based upon an ubiquitous technological rationality running rampant in modern society. From a different theoretical angle, Robert Ezra Park stated it even more succinctly back in 1904: "When the public ceases to be critical, it dissolves or is transformed into a crowd" (1904: 20). Park's observation, in part, was in recognition that a crowd (or mass), unlike a public, lacks any fundamental moral responsibility to one another or the community. John Dewey' s influential definition of the public is also worth pondering: [the public] is "all those who are affected by the indirect consequences of transactions to such an extent that it is deemed necessary to have those consequences systemically cared for" (1927: 243-344). What has occurred, according to Dewey, is that the "public" has become unable to understand these consequences and the ability to control them. Dewey's salient argument merits quoting him at length:

> Indirect, extensive, enduring and serious consequences of conjoint and interacting behavior call a public into existence having a common interest in controlling these consequences. But the machine age has so enormously expanded, multiplied, intensified and complicated the scope of the indirect consequences, has formed such immense and consolidated unions in action, on an impersonal rather than a community basis, that the resultant public cannot identify and distinguish

itself. And this discovery is obviously an antecedent condition of any effective
organization on its part. (1927: 314)

Borrowing heavily from Dewey, William Sullivan (1986) has recently argued
along similar lines that any viable and substantive view of the public must be separated from the instrumental outlook of modern liberalism and reinstituted within
the context of a republican tradition that emphasizes mutual interdependency,
civic virtue, and character development.

As interesting as these views seem to be, public administration and public policy scholars have approached this issue of publicness, by and large, through the
lens of a public-private distinction. For example, the insightful works of Rainey,
et al (1976), Emmert and Crow (1988), Bozeman (1984; 1987), and Nutt and
Backoff (1993) have reported on the organizational overlap and blurring between
the two sectors, as well as the emerging role of quasi-public organizations at all
levels of government. As laudatory as these empirical approaches have been in
assessing one aspect of publicness, they tend to ignore how publicness itself is
being slowly transformed into the pedantic values of efficiency and expediency,
thus displacing the substantive content of publicness from any of its constitutive
concerns dealing with social justice, equity, and human dignity. In this regard, it
is crucial to examine Jürgen Habermas's work, *The Transformation of the Public
Sphere* (1989), in which he traces the historical developments of the public sphere
and how publicness has been undermined by what he so aptly referred to as the
"refeudalization of society." This refeudalization of society, as he explained,
refers to the blurring of the public and private realms, and how this has inevitability contributed to the emergence of an acquisitive, consumptive society composed
of relatively passive individualized consumers. This stands in stark contrast to the
eighteenth century, according to Habermas, that gave birth to the ideals of free
communications:

> Since the eighteenth century, the features of a form of life in which the rational
> potential of action oriented to mutual understanding is set free have been
> reflected in the self-understanding of the humanistically imbued European mid-
> dle classes—in their political theories and educational ideals, in their art and lit-
> erature. (1987: 328)

What we are seeing presently, he claims, is a bourgeois public sphere that rose
within the emergence of a market society that reified critical discussion in terms
of only accentuating those factors that contribute to maximizing one's particular
economic (or political) interests. What is new, Habermas infers, is a public being
reduced to merely their economic roles as primary agents of entertainment; that
is, as a passive audience for advertisers to manipulate public demand and public
needs. Put bluntly, the bourgeois public sphere has become a reified spectacle for
a citizenry that no longer yearns to critically discuss the relevant role of democracy in society, but a public too easily manipulated, among other things, by tech-

nocratic public relation experts. What Habermas correctly warns us about, concerning any discussion of the public, is the critical need of focusing and recognizing those societal forces which can undermine the capacities of achieving a democratic citizenship.

While space does not permit an extensive review of Habermas' complex argument here, it is critical to remember that Habermas believed that a way of counteracting this transformation of publicness is in the emergence of social movements that can address the porous boundaries between public and private as well as the divisions between civil society and the state.

The issue, I believe, that arises from these various, albeit selective, theoretical perspectives—regardless of their conceptual differences—is that both public administration and public policy are beset with inherent *public* paradoxes that continue to wreak havoc on both fields. Let me just mention two such *public* paradoxes. First, while we still use the word public before administration and policy, which, one would assume, conveys some kind of guiding set of priorities that makes these disciplines different from others, we are presently in an era (and this is not just confined to the United States) where we are seeing the eroding publicness of the delivery of public services. There is, in short, still an ambivalence amongst most citizenry and scholars about the meaning of publicness as it relates to the role of government, even as we continue to define public administration and public policy primarily in governmental or quasi-governmental terms (Dyckman 1978). To some, this paradox is also expressed in the dilemma, as Daniel Bell has argued, "[that] the state has become too small for the big problems of life (e.g. tidal waves of capital and currency markets) and too big for the small problems (e.g. the problems of neighborhood and community)" (1990: 54). In the next breath, Bell concluded with this piquant assertion:

> The demand for a return to civil society is the demand to a manageable scale of social life, particularly where the national economy has become embedded in an international frame and the national polity has lost some degree of its independence. It emphasizes voluntary associations…arguing that decisions should be made locally and should not be controlled by the state and its bureaucracies. (1990: 55-56)

Bell's argument, although provocative in its ramifications, misses a more basic point that I find particularly troubling as we wrestle with the meaning of public: that an economic or market perspective has increasingly become the conceptual yardstick in determining what is to be regarded as public or private—a perspective lacking in normative considerations (Box 1999: 30). Moreover, public administration theorists have been, for the most part, ineffective in rebutting this intellectual propensity that has impacted the practice of public administration (and public policy). The public paradox here is simply this: while, generally speaking, we have tried to become more sensitive to public concerns regarding the publicness of our obligation to the citizenry; on the other hand, there has been a relative indifference or disdain by most administrative theorists as to the substantive meaning of the public, whose task it is to reflect on political and administrative realities in some systematic, coherent manner. This paradox takes on, however, a slightly different and more serious twist when we consider that the lack of attention may, to some degree, be related to our comfortable, rather than awkward relationship with modern power. The point leads to the second public paradox we face.

As public administration and public policy have become more professionalized—with all that this implies—they are as intellectually bound to the framework of the bureaucracy and its successful managerial and policy operations. The paradox is, that given this cognitive relationship, we tend to define our publicness congruent to a procedural rationality that reinforces how things are "done" rather than what they "imply." In this regard, publicness becomes merely an extension of bureaucratic life. To be sure, this trend is somewhat inevitable given the complex nature of modern life and the subsequent growth of government. I think the public paradox in this state of affairs—and why we often find ourselves going in intellectual circles—is that we have become so effective, relatively speaking, at adapting our managerial practices and policy strategies to changing economic and political realities (Stillman 1991), that we have forgotten, as John Dyckman has tried to remind us, "that intervention in complex interdependent systems of action cannot be predicated [solely] on the concept of efficiency" (1978: 282). Assuming the validity of Dyckman's point, we have come to believe that our publicness was (and is) part and parcel of a pragmatism in achieving workable managerial procedures to achieve governmental ends. This belief, while certainly laudable, nevertheless, raises the question whether our sense of publicness may in fact be a disguised tautology that merely reflects a certain assumptive belief system unique to a particular social system (Ramos 1981). Following this line of logic, is it really surprising that most contemporary administrative theorists have failed to distinguish between the substantive and formal meaning of publicness and what that might mean for the field? This lacuna, for example, has left public administration particularly vulnerable to the charge that, while the field gives much lip service to its public role and obligations, "publicness" is, in reality, primarily viewed by how well it abides by externally derived organizational prescriptions. My point is that this public paradox manifests itself, among other things, in the public administration's (and public policy's) legitimacy being built essentially on a duality; namely, that there needs to be democratic controls to ensure "public" accountability of public organizations, while, at the same time, publicness by definition implies that we try to maintain some kind of independent intellectual role that can critically explore the substantive role of citizens in a democratic polity. But can public administration and public policy realistically do the latter without undermining their own impartial and professional role as primarily an instrument of the state? Assuming the validity of these paradoxes, the notion of publicness posits at least two challenges for public administration:

- What are the basic constitutive aspects of a substantive concept of the public and what would be the societal implications for both of the fields?; and,
- How can such a substantive meaning find its way into the rough-and-ready world of administration and public affairs, and present a viable alternative to the prevailing motifs dominating much of our attention?

A SUBSTANTIVE VIEW OF THE PUBLIC AND ITS RELEVANCY TO PUBLIC AFFAIRS

I am concerned with the fact that the displacement of human reality never goes so far that no forms of solidarity exist any longer. Plato saw this very well: there is no city so corrupted that it does not realize something of the true city; that is what...is the basis for the possibility of practical philosophy.

— Hans-Georg Gadamer

Hannah Arendt (1958) has argued that what is especially troubling in our age is the loss and disappearance of the public realm in modernity. For Arendt, the implications of this loss was both stark and clear: the concept of the public in our modern age has lost its power to bring citizens together to act. Consequently, she added, we no longer have plurality but rather the mere fragmentation of passive, isolated individuals. Specifically, Arendt's message to administrative thought in general, and public administration in particular, is rather disconcerting. Administration, she claimed, is inherently prepolitical in nature. However, administration has become too often mistaken for the very stuff of politics, thus, inevitably denaturing (her term) the public realm. There is little ambiguity in her thoughts when she argues that "when the government has degenerated into mere administration the public realm has vanished" (1962: 237). Arendt's real fear is that the public will also become increasingly massified (her term) which she voices in this disturbing manner:

men have become entirely private, that is, they have been deprived of seeing and hearing others, of being seen and being heard by them. They are all imprisoned in the subjectivity of their own singular experience, which does not cease to be singular if the same experience is multiplied innumerable times. The end of the common world has come when it is seen only under one aspect and is permitted to present itself in only one perspective. (1958: 58)

One can, of course, argue that this is another example of an overdrawn conclusion devoid of any empirical support. Yet, what she hints at here—in her own awkward manner—is something worth pondering in public administration and public policy: that inadvertently, and, with probably the best of intentions, we have narrowed rather than broadened the moral syntax of public affairs by the mystification of a managerial kind of politics—a politics comfortably confined within the interstices of governmental institutions. The broadening of the moral syntax of public affairs is, I contend, at the heart of trying to ascertain a substantive view of the public. So how would we come to define a substantive meaning of the public? I have argued, in 1987 for example, this particular approach:

> *The primary reason for not having a theory of public administration is that we have been unable to formulate any meaningful theoretical linkages to the meaning of the public...* At the heart of any theory of the public, then, is the conception of political education [which means that] the capacity, the maturity, and the learning process of the public must be inexorably linked with the activities of public administration to facilitate a political educative process between the public and the administrators. The theory we have been so desperately looking for may be only a process: an asymptotic—to use Alfred Whitehead's (1929) term—exercise in deliberative public learning, a public learning that jointly links public administration and the public in furthering their capacity, maturity, and knowledge. (Ventriss 1987: 35)

While other scholars have also tried to define the public, most notably by Frederickson (1997), Hague (1996), and Matthews (1985), they have—as I did in 1987—neglected to seriously confront the socialization process in modern society that can excoriate any resemblance of a public to a mere oracular and demiurgic populace devoid of any independent critical thought. And here is the rub: the public—following in the theoretical footsteps of Park's formulation—"must always be critical because unlike a crowd it can never submit to the influence of a collective drive [that] it obeys without criticism." (1904: 15). In other words, a democratic public implies employing a critical learning process "that involves the process of improving public action through knowledge that critically examines the domain assumptions and the normative implications of public policies in an interconnected political environment" (Ventriss & Luke 1988: 338). This conception of a democratic public, I believe, would directly challenge the following administrative assumptions that have become such an integral part of contemporary administrative thought:

- An excessive preoccupation with organizational adjustment, the monitoring of individual and organizational performance and the necessary adjustments of behavior in order to achieve established organizational goals and objectives.
- A goal of implementing new managerial techniques and policy processes that contribute to the more efficient or effective achievement of intended organizational goals.
- An emphasis on organizational means to larger organizational ends that is typically assumed as a given.
- A focus on managerial processes for guiding or motivating individual behavior for organizational purposes of organizational efficiency, effectiveness, or adaptation.
- A predominant focus on the immediate moment; on immediate organizational needs, predicaments or errors of immediate practical interest (Ventriss & Luke 1988: 347-348).

A democratic public would utilize what I call a "maieutic analysis," that is, an analysis that would attempt to disclose those societal or political factors which tend to only divert or camouflage the citizen's knowledge of the true source of society or political problems. Writing in 1978, Vaclav Havel echoed a similar view on exactly this point: "[It is always dangerous] to promote the principle of outward adaptation, whereby the citizen is offered benefits befitting an obedient member of a consumer herd in exchange for political quiescence." (1986: 12) To Havel and Park, "publicness" is not some felicitous metaphor for passive citizenship, but rather a critical learning process by which citizens ascertain, or try to ascertain, those societal and political factors that only obscure what Alberto Ramos referred to as cognitive politics (1981: 76). It is, perhaps, symptomatic of the field today, with its mawkish sentimentality to citizenship and ethics, that we still have no real debate concerning the meaning (or role) of a democratic public or democratic citizenship; a citizenship confronting—to borrow Arendt's rather stern wording—"the instrumentalization of the whole world and earth" (1958: 157).

But what pragmatic importance is there for such a field like public administration or public policy to take serious any approach to substantive publicness particularly in the rough-and-ready world of administration and policy? After all, it can be argued that such a question only reflects the theoretical dead ends that we need to avoid in order to win acceptance by our critics (Dubnick, 1999). This response, however, only begs the question whether in our attempt to be more "accepted" we believe that we must mimic, "the cognitive patterns inherent in a market-centered society" (Ramos 1981: 79).

In this respect, it is worth thinking again about Havel's wonderfully plangent message:

> the basic political lesson… is the recognition that the only kind of politics that makes sense is a politics that grows out of the imperative, and the need to live as everyone ought to live and therefore—to put it in somewhat dramatically— to bear responsibility for the entire world. People lucky enough not to have to live under totalitarianism may never have learned this lesson with the same urgency as those who did. But so much the worse for them. (1999: 54)

Although Havel's language can be accused of being inflated, and almost condescending in its tone, he is asking his audience to reach for something gallant and noble, even if it means that we bear alone the responsibility of this task on our shoulders. This gallant endeavor in public administration and administrative theory will not alone come from intoxicating ourselves with more empirical data and methodological acuity. Nor will it come from new management perspectives, as important as their contributions may be to the field. Instead, this gallant endeavor rests in our desire to wrestle with the "publicness" of public administration and public policy. The clumsiness of this concept should not preclude our efforts in giving it the theoretical dignity that we often warrant the other managerial and policy interests that dominate our thinking. Arguing along similar lines, George

Frederickson (1997) has posited that we should develop a general theory of the public, which is consonant with the normative values of the public service. He contends that such an attempt will promote better knowledge and understanding of the field. As noble as these intentions happen to be, Frederickson misses a much broader and obvious point: *when we discuss the public we are not trying so much to advance the knowledge or understanding of the field as we are trying to understand our intellectual role in relationship to modern power, and concomitantly, the purpose and role of the citizenry in maintaining a public sphere in which ethical deliberation and responsible action can take place.*

With this recognition comes the following realities that a democratic public will confront, and the new changes that administrative thought must ultimately grope with:

- Public action with public, private, and nonprofit sectors is now occurring in expanding and crowded environments in which everything depends on everything else and power is dispersed and shared by a multiplicity of publics and public actors (Bryson & Einsweiler 1987; Ventriss & Luke 1988; Ventriss 1987; 1994).
- There is a significant increase in unforeseen, unintended or indirect policy consequences which increase vulnerability and openness to outside influences, with policymakers and administrators becoming increasingly dependent on other individuals, publics, and organizations outside of ones' view (Thompson 1973; Ventriss & Luke 1988).
- The normative consequences of policy choices and public action are often far-ranging, delayed, and have direct or hidden costs beyond the normal externalities; desirable and undesirable consequences are difficult to separate, and important and often critical second, third-order effects of policy choices can go unnoticed (Stone 1985; Ventriss & Luke 1988).

How we address these issues, as difficult as it may appear, is the beginning of any endeavor in our ongoing search for a substantive meaning of the public as the twenty-first century stands at our doorstep.

CONCLUSION

Vital to the contemporary bureaucratic...democratic state is its clerisy [that is]...intellectuals and scholars dedicated to the state precisely as their medieval forebears were to the church.

—Robert Nisbet

Looking back on the early beginnings of public administration, it is fair to conclude that the field—and for that matter, public policy—have had virtually no outstanding philosophers, perhaps with the exception of Dwight Waldo and perhaps a few others. Into this vacuum has come an amalgamation of well-intentioned economists and managerial experts who have had a lot to say about administrative and policy functions, most of it focused on the process of decision-making. These economists and managerial theorists have been attractive to both fields because their approaches are both pragmatic and have the trappings of a "bona fide" science. As we enter the twenty-first century, the influence of these conceptual forces, I believe, will hardly wane. On the other hand, the vexatious normative questions facing us, however, will most likely continue as well. This makes for an interesting clash of ideas since one approach, to a large extent, steers away from any discussion about ends, while the other approach is fixated on such questions concerning the democratic responsibility of the field to the public.

The intellectual bridge between these two different perspectives may rest on the theoretical and practical focus we give to the "public." For, in the end, if the field believes it can always be neutral towards given ends, it runs the risk of becoming nothing more than a form of economics with a managerial and procedural emphasis. Yet, public administration and public policy is much more than this perception—or at least it should be. As we struggle with the substantive meaning of the public, it is worth pondering what Max Weber told us long ago: "a new [approach] emerges where new problems are pursued by new methods and truths are thereby discovered which open up significant new points of view (1949: 68). If we stumble—as we assuredly will—along the way in our attempt to open up significant new points of view in exploring the normative meaning of the public, we need only remember this sage advice from Rabbi Tarfon: "It was not granted you to complete the task and yet you may not give it up" (Cited in Gitlin 1989: 438).

REFERENCES

Arendt, H. 1958. *The Human Condition.* Chicago: University of Chicago Press.

Arendt, H. 1962. *On Revolution.* New York: Penguin Books.

Bell, D. 1990. The return of civil society. *Kettering Review.* Winter:47-56.

Box, R. 1999. Running government like a business. *American Review of Public Administration.* 29(1):19-43.

Bozeman, B. 1984. Dimensions of publicness: An approach to public organization theory. *New Directions in Public Administration,* edited by B. Bozeman and J. Straussman. Belmont, CA.: Brooks/Cole. 46-62.

Bozeman, B. 1987. *All Organizations are Public.* San Francisco, CA: Jossey-Bass.

Bryson, J. and P. Einsweiller, eds. 1987. *Shared Power.* Washington, DC: University Press of America.

Cooper, T.L. 1991. *An Ethic of Citizenship for Public Administration.* Englewood Cliffs, NJ: Prentice Hall.

Dewey, J. 1927. *The Public and its Problems.* New York: Holt.

Dubnick, M.J. 1999. Demons, spirits, and elephants: Reflections on the failure of public administration theory. Presented at the American Political Science Association, Atlanta, GA, September 2–5.

Dyckman, J. W. 1978. Three crises of American planning. *Planning Theory in the 1980s,* edited by R.W. Burchell & G. Sternlieb. New Brunswick, NJ: Rutgers University Press. 279-296.

Emmert, M.A. and M. M. Crow. 1988. Public, private and hybrid organizations: An empirical examination of the role of publicness. *Administration and Society.* 20(2):216-244.

Frederickson, G.H. 1997. *The Spirit of Public Administration*. San Francisco, CA: Jossey-Bass.

Gitlin, T. 1989. *The Sixties*. New York, NY: Bantam Books.

Habermas, J. 1979. Consciousness-raising or redemptive criticism: The contemporary of Walter Benjamin. *New German Critique*. 17(3):30-59.

———. 1987. *The Theory of Communicative Action: Vol. 2. Lifeworld and System: A Critique of Functionalist Reason*. Boston: Beacon Press.

———. 1989. *The Structural Transformation of the Public Sphere*. Cambridge, MA: MIT Press.

Hague, M.S. 1996. Public service under challenge in the age of privatization. *Governance*. 9(2):186-216.

Havel, V. 1986. Letter to Gustav Husak. *Living in Truth*, edited by V. Havel. London: Faber & Faber. 9-15.

———. 1999. Paying back the West. *The New York Review of Books, XLVI*(14). 1:54.

Marcuse, H. 1970. *Five Lectures*. London: Allen Lane.

Mathews, D. 1985. The public in practice and theory. *Public Administration Review*. 44(3):120-125.

Mills, C.W. 1957. *The Power Elite*. Oxford: Oxford University Press.

Nutt, P.C. and R.W. Backoff. 1993. Organizational publicness and its implications for strategic management. *Journal of Public Administration Theory and Practice*. 3(2):209-231.

Park, R.E. 1904. *The Crowd and the Public*. Chicago: University of Chicago Press.

Rainey, H.G., R.W. Backoff, and C. H. Levine. 1976. Comparing public and private organizations. *Public Administration Review*. 36(2):323-386.

Ramos, A.G. 1981. *The New Science of Organizations*. Toronto: University of Toronto Press.

Stillman, R. 1991. *Preface to Public Administration*. New York: St. Martin's Press.

Stone, C. 1985. Efficiency versus social learning: A reconsideration of the implementation process. *Policy Studies Review*. 4:484-496.

Sullivan, William M. 1986. *Reconstructing Public Philosophy*. Berkeley, CA: University of California Press.

Thompson, J. 1973. Society's frontiers for organizing activities. *Public Administration Review*. 33:27-335.

Ventriss, C. 1987. Two critical issues of American public administration. *Administration and Society*, 19(1):25-47.

Ventriss, C. 1994. The impact of trade and direct foreign investment in the subnational levels. *Comparative Public Administration*, edited by R. Baker. Westport, CT: Praeger.

Ventriss, C. and J. Luke. 1988. Organizational learning and public policy. *American Review of Public Administration*. 18(4):337-355.

Weber, M. 1949. Objectivity in social science. *The Methodology of the Social Sciences*, edited by E. A. Shils and H. A. Finch. Glencoe, IL: Free Press. 57-72.

———. 1958. *The Protestant Ethic and the Spirit of Capitalism*. New York: Scribner's Sons.

7

Value Pluralism in Public Administration: Two Perspectives on Administrative Morality[1]

Hendrik Wagenaar

INTRODUCTION: DISCRETION AND THE PROBLEM OF ADMINISTRATIVE ETHICS

In concrete situations rules, as experienced administrators know, only go so far. To make a decision about a real client with real needs, worries, anxieties, idiosyncrasies, a particular personal history, and the confusing welter of details making up the case at hand, the law does not quite tell which way to go. In such situations administrators rely on formal rules and procedures, organizational routines and conventions, personal beliefs, strong feelings, professional experience, advice from colleagues, and traditional ways of getting things done. The precarious balance between these constraints, resources, and personal tactics is what is meant, in the literature, by administrative discretion. Differently put, decisions of weighty and momentous significance to the average citizen who comes into contact with public agencies are made by officials who are not elected and therefore not responsible to the electorate (Denhardt 1989; Rohr 1989). In this sense, administrators, as much as elected officials, make "policy." The question this raises is this: if the ordinary means of electoral control are unavailable, and given the organizational fact of life that the large majority of decisions made by administrators are never reviewed, by what standards, guidelines, norms, or values are bureaucrats guided in the exertion of their discretionary space? How do administrators succeed in making decisions that, with relatively few exceptions, are considered to be just, fair, appropriate, and acceptable? This, in a nutshell, is the problem of administrative ethics.

Among scholars of administrative ethics, several attempts have been made to fill the void of discretionary space with a positive ethical theory. What these attempts have in common is that they are normative suggestions of how to guide and account for administrative authority. Rohr (1989) suggests, for example, that administrators take their cue from the values that are embedded in the American constitution. By informing themselves of the interpretations of the core values of the American polity as they are interpreted in Supreme Court decisions, administrators, according to Rohr, will stay in touch with the values of the American people. Denhardt argues that administrators should balance their political role with the constraints of the political belief system. In addition to adherence to constitutional values, these constraints include stewardship and impartiality in the exercise of democratic power (1989: 190). Frederickson (1974) suggests that administrators should not only be guided by the traditional bureaucratic ideals of efficiency, accountability, and due process, but that they should also actively promote social equity. And Kass (1990) argues that administrative authority should be based on stewardship, which he defines as being an effective and ethical agent in carrying out public programs.

The problem with this way of framing the issue of administrative ethics and the normative solutions it spawns, is twofold. First, it suffers—to continue our spatial metaphor of the preceding paragraph—from an undercharacterization of the topography of discretionary space. Discretionary space is usually seen as the absence of something: legal rules, rational procedures, binding norms. Yet everyday administrative life is far from empty. It is dense with the confusing detail of clients, colleagues, chefs, related agencies, budgets cuts, and media attention. In one of the rare examples to bring order to this confusion and to characterize the work environment of administrators, Harmon and Mayer see public agencies as "solutions to wicked problems" (Harmon and Mayer 1986). Public agencies are victims of their own suggested success in that they have solved most of the tame problems—building roads, spanning bridges, connecting sewers, designing a public pension system—that were out there to be solved. What is left are the problems for which no certifiable solution exists: protecting children, combating traffic congestion, preventing welfare dependency, providing affordable housing, implementing affirmative action programs, regulating immigration, securing equal access to health care, and the like. Wicked problems have contested problem definitions and, *ipso facto*, spawned no agreed upon solutions. Usually, the unintended consequences of programs dealing with wicked problems are so overwhelming that the solution quickly becomes part of the problem. Wicked problems are, as a result, stubborn and persistent. In combination with narrow margins for error, they represent to politician and administrator alike a *risque professional*: the risk of failure is infinitely higher than the chances for success.

The ethical consequences of this view of administrative life are large. Instead of carrying out well prescribed tasks, administrators are constantly solving problems. And solving problems, according to Harmon and Mayer, implies dealing with conflicting demands. As they observe:

> Increasingly (…) "to administer" means something much more complex (than to carry out a task. HW), including sorting through interests, accounting for consequences, and justifying actions. Government activity deals almost exclusively with the mediation between one part of society and another. Although this mediation is not a new activity, our recognition of its pervasiveness is relatively new, as is our recognition of the role of the public administrator in that mediation. (1986: 8. Emphasis in original.)

Discretionary space, inevitably, is rife with conflict, and in particular, value conflict. While it is probably impossible to estimate how often administrators are faced with choices which involve conflicting values,[2] there are at least three reasons why difficult discretionary value judgement is unavoidable in public administration: (1) public programs express important, but often conflicting, social values; (2) information constraints in the implementation of public programs force the administrator to rely on moral judgment of beneficiaries as a proxy to full information; and (3) beneficiaries pursue their own goals in the use of public programs which puts administrators in the uneasy position of having to choose between the rules of the program and the moral demand to assist the poor or the helpless.[3] Normative prescriptions that suggest that discretionary authority be guided by one or a few overriding values or principles beg the question of how to apply such values or principles in concrete situations of value conflict. Such prescriptions take for granted what should be explained: how administrators manage to deal with conflicting values in a generally appropriate, legitimate, and effective way.[4]

This taking for granted of the ethical work of public administrators leads to a second problem with the normative solutions of dealing with discretionary authority that are common in administrative ethics literature. What these have in common is their *a priori* framing of the solution as one of large ethical principles guiding everyday behavior. This deontological approach is vulnerable to several well-known criticisms: that it is hard to know the proper universal principle, that it easily results in moral rigidity, and that it has a hard time dealing with exceptions to the rules (Denhardt 1988 #1: 47-48). A more fundamental critique, however, is that a deontological approach is unable to explain how administrators apply the rules to the particulars of a situation at hand. Deontological, or rule-based approaches to ethics have difficulty accounting for the conditionality of values: the insight that, in their realization, values always depend upon their context. For example, deontological or rule-based approaches to ethics have difficulty accounting both for the conditionality of values (the fact that the realization of values in concrete situations always depends on their context) and their plurality (the condition that one ethical principle clashes with another equally desirous ethical principle). In those cases, the rules themselves do not provide guidelines of how to arrive at feasible compromises, and in the deontological universe, administrators are left in the lurch. In actual practice, experienced administrators usually know quite well how to deal with situations in which values clash, and are able to arrive at solutions that most people—clients, peers, and chefs—in most situations find acceptable. Yet, we know little, in a descriptive sense of the word, of how administrators manage to deal effectively with value conflict. I will argue in section 3 that, instead of a deontological, rule-based approach, they apply a practice-based approach.

This chapter has the following outline: in the next section I will briefly characterize the rule-based and the practice-based approaches to administrative ethics. In section 3, a concrete case of value conflict in public administration is presented. In section 4, I will discuss the case from a rule-based perspective. I will show that the more-or-less self-evident deontological approach to administrative ethics that is common in the literature has the effect of pushing values and the discussion of value conflict into the realm of the emotional, and, by implication, irrational. It also conceives of resolving value conflict as attaining a moral certainty. Moral certainty is arrived at by careful reasoning from universal principles that are supposed to shield the administrators from the intrusion of affect and emotion. In the final section, I will suggest a way of handling value conflict that centers around the concept of practice. I will argue that the work of administrators should be seen as a form of practice, and that part of that practice is dealing with value conflict. Practical conflict resolution has two characteristics: (1) it builds upon the concrete, situated character of the conflict at hand; and (2) it consists of an ongoing, careful perception and interpretation of the facts of the situation, including the feelings and personal identity of the administrator himself. That means, among other things, that the perception of emotions, far from detracting from the resolution of value conflict, is in fact an invaluable, albeit, tacit, ingredient of it. By returning to the case of section 3, I will demonstrate what is involved in practical ways of dealing with value conflict.

TWO MODELS OF ADMINISTRATIVE MORALITY

How do administrators deal with value conflict in everyday administrative practice? I will argue that in the discourse on administrative ethics, two distinct modes of thought can be distinguished. These modes of descriptive and normative ethical analysis describe the relation between everyday administrative life and morality in strikingly different terms.[5] The traditional mode of discussing value conflict in public administration, namely the ideal that administrative ethics should be guided by a comprehensive, all-embracing moral view, is reflective of what I call a *rule-based* orientation towards administrative ethics. In such a perspective, administrative ethics is seen as a set of distinct rules and principles that, together, form a coherent and more or less complete moral code. These principles, such as equality, efficiency, liberty, justice, and impartiality, are seen as large abstract ideals whose meaning is independent of the specifics of time and place. They form a separate domain of the "ethical," to be distinguished from the factual, legal, and mundane aspects of administrative situations. Taken together, they form a coherent moral code which, in practical circumstances, functions as a term of reference, as a guideline or arbiter in situations of moral doubt (van der Burg 1999: 71). The task of moral actors is to apply the relevant principles in a logical and consistent way in order to arrive at sound moral judgements. The rule-based approach is best exemplified in the work of John Rohr, George Frederickson, and, at times, Kathryn Denhardt.

In contrast to the rule-based orientation, in a *practice-based* orientation towards administrative ethics, ethics is not seen as something distinct from every-day administrative behavior. Morality is embedded in the thousands of social interactions that, together, make up the work of public administrators. It is not something that hovers over such activities as those of an impassive final arbiter. Morality is not something out there, called upon in situations of conflict or doubt, but instead is part and parcel of the lived experience of administrative practition-ers. In this sense, moral judgement can not be distinguished from everyday prob-lem solving. Whatever, with hindsight, we call moral judgement or ethical principle is literally created in the ongoing interactions of administrative workers going about their jobs. That does not mean that administrators who make value choices are at a loss. Their moral perceptions express not so much big values as a shared practical experience in public administration. Moral judgment is embed-ded in administrative practice. In a practice-based perspective, the axiological is continuous with the epistemological. The practice approach is less common in the public administration literature (Morgan's discussion of administrative phronesis is illustrative of this approach [1990], and elliptical references to it can be found in Kathryn Denhardt's work on "political judgement" [1989]).

The importance of the distinction between a rule-based and a practice-based approach to administrative ethics is the recognition that it literally colors every aspect of the way we conceive of ethical issues in public administration. For example, the rule-based approach clearly demarcates the "ethical" from the "fac-tual" as a separate domain. Certain ways of framing "ethical" issues, then, pre-sent themselves to the analyst as a more or less logical and inevitable consequence. So, for example, from a rule-based perspective, value conflict eas-ily comes to be seen in terms of irresolvable dilemmas between incompatible or incommensurable social ends. From a practice-based perspective, such conflicts, while by no means denying their conflictual character, come to be seen as practi-cal problems for which more or less feasible and acceptable resolutions can be found. Similarly, what constitutes solutions and standards for rightness and acceptability in moral judgement is determined by the choice of perspective. In a rule-based perspective, the emphasis is upon certainty in rightness. It is the task of the analyst to bestow upon his judgement the certainty and authority of the original ethical principle. From a practice-based perspective, what counts above all is to stabilize a difficult situation in such a way that it allows the administra-tor to find workable and acceptable solutions that do not close off the resolution of comparable future situations.

Also, both perspectives conceive of the way administrators deal—or, as descriptive and normative stances intermingle here, *have* to deal—with values in different ways. In a rule-based perspective, as I will argue, administrators reason from principle to ethical conclusion. The correctness of a moral judgment is established if it is a logical consequence of the relevant ethical principles and the facts of the case. Alternatively, in a practice-based perspective, moral judgment is seen as a form of discourse with strong narrative elements. Through discourse, administrators shape their interaction with everyday administrative reality, simultaneously reflecting and shaping the administrative order (Jaworski and Coupland 1999: 3). Finally, even the notion of value differs in both perspectives. Underlying the product perspective is an emotive understanding of values. Values are logically distinctive from facts (Weber 1949; Harman 1977). Epistemologically speaking, values carry no cognitive information; they are the expression of the emotional attitudes of the person expressing the value. Between facts and values exists an unbridgeable gap. In a practice-based perspective, on the other hand, facts and values are seen as continuous. In everyday administrative practice, both value-statements and factual statements serve as observations about the surrounding world. The way we arrive at moral judgement has more in common with perception than deliberation (Harman 1977), and both have their warrants in the theoretical preconceptions that make up the ontology of the everyday world. This includes events both external and internal to the actor. Although in extreme situations man can be swayed by emotion, in regular administrative practice, feeling and affect are not things to be suppressed in the name of neutrality or impartiality. Commitment doesn't preclude perspective; the perception of personal feeling and identity is an intrinsic part of effective moral judgement. The proper use of value statements, similar to the proper use of factual statements, requires that one is a competent member of a particular community.

In the remainder of this essay, I will discuss value conflict in public administrative practice from both the product perspective and the practice perspective. As I will show, both have important things to say about ethical issues in administrative life, and illuminate different aspects of the issue of administrative ethics, yet, the emphasis will be on the practice perspective. In fact, one of the purposes of the essay is to develop a practice perspective on administrative value conflict. But let's edge into the difficult subject of value conflict in public administration by first looking at a concrete example.

VALUE CONFLICT IN EVERYDAY ADMINISTRATIVE LIFE: AN EXAMPLE

The example is taken from an interview with a certifying physician in the Dutch disability administration. The physician's task is to assess patients' eligibility for disability benefits:

> Yeah, why do I find this difficult? The problem in this case is that what you find
> in terms of objective deficiencies, if there is any objectivity in this, does not

correspond with the seriousness and the degree to which my patient experiences her constraints, and she deals with those in a rather agitated way. What makes it even more difficult is that the woman makes a very realistic impression both on me and on her general practitioner. So you're stuck with a kind of internal conflict. You receive conflicting information. On the one hand you think, nice, friendly, realistic woman, not a trace of hysterical behavior, not a trace of looking for secondary gains from her illness, just someone with whom you can get along well, and then she experiences a tremendous inability and then you examine her again and again. So in this case too I requested additional information because I didn't find the answer myself, and that information tells you there's nothing there, neither physically or mentally. Yet this woman experiences incapacitating tiredness that leaves her unable to work for more than two or three hours a day, so I tried to reintegrate her into her own job but that failed. So her employer says, and her partner says , it has been proven that she wants to work but that she simply is unable to, and then you get the 64,000 dollar question: to what extent can you justify this for the insurance, because it has that damned rule that there must be an objective illness…. That is what makes this case very difficult.

What does this example of value conflict in public administration tell us? The problem that confronts the analyst is that the perspective from which he discusses the case, rule-based or practice-based, determines the very vocabulary in which he discusses the case. Or rather, his language reveals the assumptions of the perspective that he, knowingly or unknowingly, has embraced. There is no Archimedean point which avoids either perspective. So, in the remainder of this paper, I will discuss the case from both perspectives; first, the rule-based, then the practice-based. Each, as we will see, contributes to an understanding of value conflict in public administration.

A FIRST CUT: VALUE-CONFLICT IN THE RULE-BASED MODE

The physician in our example experiences an acute conflict between his impressions of his patient and a central rule in the disability program that states that only illnesses that are objectively determinable will be eligible for reimbursement of lost wages. The conflict is a value conflict because it involves a clash of important social ends. Program rules, as we have seen, point towards collective values. On the one hand there is the rule that is designed to contain the number of persons eligible for disability. As Stone has argued convincingly, each decision to award disability benefits has, in our society, strong moral overtones, as it goes against the deeply ingrained ethos that work defines man, and that anyone worth his mettle should earn his money through his own labor. Under certain circumstances (work-related accidents, prolonged illness) exemption from this moral obligation is possible, but these should be sporadic and surrounded by careful screening methods (Stone 1984). On the other hand there is the professional judgement of the physician that, to the best of his knowledge, the woman suffers from a genuine, and as the evidence suggests, chronic and debilitating illness. This fact brings the values of security and altruism on board. Not only does the client's illness give her the right to treatment, but also the right that she shouldn't suffer catastrophic loss of income because of her illness. Boiled down to its rule-based essentials, the conflict is one between two equally desirable value systems: obligation versus compassion.

To proceed in the rule-based mode, technically speaking, this makes the case an example of *value pluralism*.[6] Value pluralism describes the condition in which conceptions of desirable social states are plural *and* in which the realization of these conceptions mutually exclude each other. As the moral philosopher John Kekes puts it: "Pluralists are committed ... to the view that the conceptions of a good life and the values on whose realization good lives depend are plural and conditional. These conceptions and values, however, are often related in such a way, according to the pluralists, that the realization of one excludes the realization of the other." (1993: 21) "Conditional" in this phrase means that no value or moral code exists that is sufficiently authoritative to always override other values in case of conflict. Instead, pluralists assert that every value or combination of values may be defeated by some other value or combination of values that, in the specific context, is more important (ibid.: 20).

What makes value pluralism attractive is that it allows for an analysis of value conflict that is both level-headed and subtle. For example, although value conflict is ubiquitous, both in public administration and life in general, there is no need to assume *a priori* that each and every instance of conflict is intractable. Value pluralists would be skeptical of the inflationary use of the term "dilemma" in the literature on public administration and public policy. Most conflicts involving values amount to nothing more than a clash between two desirable ends, of which the relinquishing of one entails no great loss to the actor. For example, in deciding on how to spend a limited budget, I may be faced with a conflict between buying theatre tickets or taking my friend out to dinner. While it would be great to have the means to do both, the foregoing of one of these options does not amount to a grievous loss. Similarly, some value conflicts may be the result of careless planning, deficient organization, or the lack of information. For example, an administrator handling applications for rent subsidy might be faced with the conflict between rejecting an application because the client, despite his low income, has a balance in his savings account that slightly exceeds the maximum allowed, or making use of her discretion to grant the client the subsidy because without it he would face an acute housing problem. Yet, had the administrator known that the client leases the apartment to illegal immigrants for usurious rents, she would have rejected the application out of hand.

Finally, a conflict between two important ends may arise that, on closer inspection, turns out not to be a conflict at all, as the conflicting ends can be subsumed under a larger and more compelling value whose authority all reasonable people would recognize (Kekes 1993: 52). For example, a psychiatric worker may be faced with the dilemma between admitting a patient who is brought to the hospital with acute psychotic symptoms, or delaying the admission for two days because the hospital is filled to capacity. Yet, when the diagnostic interview reveals that the patient is severely suicidal and would quite likely end his life when sent home, this fact overrules the original dilemma and puts the admission officer under the legal obligation to hospitalize the patient immediately. I do not call these conflicts genuine value conflicts—complicated and distressing as they may be to the actors involved—because the alternatives which form the horns of the dilemma either are of no great moral weight and do not entail a great loss to the actor, or the conflict is structured in such a way that a viable solution exists, if not now, then certainly in comparable future situations, or, an overriding value can be formulated that takes precedence over the values involved in the initial conflict, and thereby suggests a necessary and binding solution to it.

Incompatibility and Incommensurability of Values

From a rule-based perspective, genuine value conflict presents itself to the individual as a situation with no obvious way out. The alternatives can be both so compelling, necessary, or binding that the foregoing of one of them is experienced as a genuine loss (Berlin 1997: 11), or, on the contrary, the alternatives that present themselves to the actor can both be so repulsive that the forced choice of one of them amounts to a sense of irreparable damage (Stocker 1990). What makes these conflicts intractable is the circumstance that the values involved are both incompatible and incommensurable. These are complex concepts, and for the purpose of understanding serious value conflict in public administration, we need to be clear about their meaning.

Incompatibility arises when "some values are so related as to make living according to one totally or proportionally exclude living according to the other" (Kekes 1993: 55). The incompatibility derives nor from any external source (lack of knowledge, deficient organization), but from qualities intrinsic to the values themselves or to human nature. We can't pretend to be a dedicated father, yet spend sixteen hours a day, seven days a week, at the office. Commitment to our children and blind ambition cannot be reconciled. These are incompatible values because either one implies the denial or negation of the other, and because of the biological fact that human organisms need, at the very minimum, five hours of sustained sleep. Incompatibility of values is very common in the everyday work of public administration. The following example is from an interview with a welfare worker who administers a program for the homeless. She talks about her physical repulsion for a particular client:

> Well those are the kind of things you may encounter…uh…often yeah very sad situations. Yeah at some point actually a young girl walks in. She looks terrible, someone whom, I hate to have to say this, whom you don't want to shake hands with. I find those situations difficult, because I think, you work for a service oriented organization and everyone to me is equal, no matter if he walks in as an unemployed college graduate or a homeless. We are all human beings and we

all deserve the same kind of respect. But sometimes it happens that someone enters the office that you think: Jeez, what a disaster. Dirty hands or covered with open wounds or sores, and then it goes through your mind (mumbles) but I don't really do it, but I do find it hard. Yeah, I am here to do my job, and you have to take care that you're not being influenced by your personal norms and values.

The administrator is at the epicenter of a number of conflicting forces. She feels it her obligation to treat all her clients equally and with respect, yet, some of her clients evoke in her an impulse for self-protection. The interview fragment is a good example of the moral and emotional struggle that such incompatibility of values brings forth in the lived experience of the administrator. She describes the situation as "sad," she is rueful about admitting that she can't live up to her personal and professional ideals, and characterizes the whole situation as "difficult." The example also illustrates that the conflict is rooted in the values themselves, and not in some deficiency of the administrator. No reasonable person has trouble identifying with the administrator's physical repulsion to some of her most ravaged clients, while at the same time we agree with her professional standards of personal respect and equality. Yet, the incompatibility of values in this situation, no matter how difficult it may be to the actors involved, does not in principle exclude a rational solution. It is very well possible that the administrator is able to strike a balance between the incompatible claims. (For example by temporarily overcoming her repulsion and shake hands anyway, or by refraining from shaking hands and to compensate for this by verbal demonstrations of personal respect.) Incompatibility of values generally leads to the kind of situations we call a conflict of obligations. And while conflicting obligations can, under certain constraints, lead to hopelessly difficult situations (Lukes 1991: 5), it is, in principle, possible to strike some balance, to find some reasonable compromise to meet both incompatible demands somewhere halfway.

Incommensurability, on the other hand, leads to irresolvable value conflicts. Incommensurability is a complex concept that can best be summarized with the statement that no common denominator or overriding value exists to which we can reduce the conflicting claims. Lukes states it most succinctly: "The key idea, then, is that there is no single currency or scale on which conflicting values can be measured, and that where a conflict occurs no rationally compelling appeal can be made to some value that will resolve it" (1991: 12).[7] A sure signal that some conflict is the result of the incommensurability of the values involved is the experience of a sense of loss. It is not only that the actual choice between the conflicting claims, even by compromising on one or both, entails an irredeemable sense of loss, but even inactivity would evoke the experience of loss as it is the situation itself that is tragic.[8] Being confronted for the first time with incommensurable values is what we have come to call the loss of innocence, and is seen as an inevitable, even required, element of maturation, both in private and professional life.

Value pluralism arises when values are both incompatible and incommensurable. According to rule-based pluralists, there is, strictly speaking, no way out when confronted with such value conflicts. No compromise, appeal to higher order values, or fixation on desired outcomes, or conversely, no denial of the conflict by reducing it to mere emotions or passions will make it go away. There simply is no common ground in these cases from which to arbitrate rationally between the conflicting values.[9] From the rule-based perspective, the case of the certifying physician is an example of genuine value pluralism. The physician is confronted with a stark choice between two courses of action that are both reasonable and, at the same time, completely exclude each other. Denying the dilemma, for example by a legalistic following of the letter of the rule, is not a viable option, for following the rule of law would not in any way compensate for the loss of justice towards the client. The client could perhaps be persuaded of the rightness of the rule of law, and grudgingly accept the loss of income, but it would nevertheless amount to a major sacrifice on her part. Or, the administrator can be persuaded on good grounds that his client, given her condition, has a right to be declared eligible for disability, yet, he still has to face the fact that he broke a rational and sensible program rule, the violating of which eventually would undermine the integrity of the whole program. The upshot is that the values in this case cannot compensate for each other. They simply exclude each other. Moreover, from a practical point of view, a denial of the dilemma by choosing one of its horns would probably result in an formal appeal by the client, or an overturning of the physician's decision by his superior. The dilemma would probably return in a different court.

What make cases like this so difficult and hopeless in the rule-based ethical universe are their underlying epistemological assumptions. Rule-based analysts assume a strict separation between facts and values. Moral principles, they argue, simply cannot be tested the way we test scientific principles. Values differ from facts in that they are no more than the expression of the actor's emotions, feelings, attitudes, or intentions. As Harman expresses it, "To value something is to be in an emotional state, not in a cognitive state" (1977: 28). For that reason, values inhabit a different logical realm than facts (Weber 1949). Value statements can never be deduced from factual statements. No matter how precise and complete our factual observations are, the factual observation that something is the case can never lead to the value position that therefore we ought to follow a particular course of action. The later statement requires that one believes a certain moral principle, or, in other words, that one has the proper feeling about the facts. A deep, unbridgeable chasm exists between statements of fact and statements of value.

But if values are only expressions of emotion, how can we ever hope to establish the rightness of an ethical judgement? The answer of traditional ethics is: by logical reasoning from universal ethical principles. The purpose of such ethical reasoning is to bestow the certitude and reliability of scientific reasoning on the shifty and ambiguous domain of moral judgement. How does it work? The ideal of systematic ethical reasoning is modeled after the Covering Law model of

deductive-nomological explanation (von Wright 1971: 11). The explanandum E
is a particular action in a concrete situation. The action is arrived at by reasoning
from a universal principle or general ethical law V (for value) and certain initial
events or states of affairs $E_1,...E_n$. So, for example, if an administrator obeys the
ethical-administrative principle that income support must be provided to employees who experience invalidating illness for which they are not the blame (V), and
the state of affairs (E_1) is that this particular employee has had a work-related
accident that has left him partly paralyzed, than the correct course of action (E) is
that he should declare this employee eligible for disability benefits. The yields of
systematic ethical reasoning are that the outcome can be predicted, that it is independent of the person doing the reasoning, that it is accessible to outsiders, and
that the syllogism imparts the truth of principle V to the behavioral injunction E.
It thus succeeds in making value discourse immune to the irrationalities of feeling and affect.[10] However, for systematic ethical reasoning to be able to function
as an "ethical algorithm" (Jonsen and Toulmin 1988: 7), it is essential that the
value V must be a universal. It must be a general law or principle that is independent of the particulars of time and place. When this condition is met, we have
attained the ethical ideal that certain situational contingencies $(E_1...E_n$ in our ethical syllogism), are determined by the general principle V, instead of the other,
subjectivist, way around in which the particulars of the situation influence the
moral principles involved, and thus, the outcome of our judgement.

Clearly this Kantian, deontological image of ethical judgement is philosophically outdated and hardly plausible,[11] but dealing with values through careful reasoning is still by and large the received view in public administration and the
policy sciences. Despite the erosion of the politic-administration dichotomy,
administrators are still widely expected to execute political decisions in a technically competent, value-neutral way, and the accusation that they engage in unwarranted politicking is never far away. The traditional policy sciences still perceive
themselves as providing reliable, scientific observation and analysis to inform
political decision making, and the accusation that one policy conclusion or
another is "subjective" instead of "scientific" is all too ubiquitous in the debate
between policy analysts. To see proper moral judgment as a form of deliberation
is part of the cultural institution of facts and values in public administration. Even
if people are willing to admit that we use formal ethical syllogisms only rarely,
and that ordinary people usually don't *conclude* that something is right or wrong
but *see* it, they would still insist that any moral judgement that is deserving of that
name requires the explication of some general ethical principle, or that the kind
of reasons that carry weight in a moral dispute are grounded in some explicit general principles (Gutmann and Dennis 1996: 52). In fact, what counts as a moral
argument in the public mind—and this conclusion applies just as much to the professional literature on administrative ethics[12]—is something that involves universal principles and some attempt at systematic reasoning.

Thus, to wrap up the analysis of the case of the certifying physician, from a
rule-based perspective of administrative ethics, there is no way for the physician

to resolve the conflict without entailing a loss. The two values exclude each other. Either he honors the woman's claim, in which case he will violate the program rule and its associated values, or he will deny her benefits, in which case he violates his professional values and the larger value of compassion. The conflict is irresolvable because no criterion, no common ground, exists that will reconcile the conflicting values. Even doing nothing, or walking away from the conflict, is not an option. First, the conflict is acute; the woman needs a decision about her eligibility as soon as possible or she will suffer a loss of income, and walking away will only transfer the conflict to one of his colleagues.[13] But more importantly, the conflict is unavoidable. The physician could not have prevented the conflict by a more effective organization of his work, a more exhaustive examination of the woman, or by a better reading of the program rules. The conflict is not in his actions. It does not originate in a lack of judgement on his part. The conflict is inherent in the program itself. The disability program strives for two equally desirable ends which, in our society, simply cannot be reconciled.

But couldn't we find some firm ground in this morass by appealing to a practical value such as reasonableness, an overriding value such as equality (Frederickson 1974), or a general guideline such as "stewardship" (Kass 1990)? Reasonableness, equality, and stewardship are important guiding principles, but they do not occupy a higher, let alone overriding, position in a cluster of values that includes equality, responsible management of public funds, and responsiveness to the client's needs. Quite likely, all of these values would play a role in a decision about this case, but the situation is structured such that they do not allow for a decisive ranking that is based on characteristics that are both intrinsic to the values and acceptable to all reasonable persons (Kekes 1993: 56). Also, in the rule-based universe, a compromise is ruled out because of the absolute, all-or-nothing character of the choice. And, finally, even a careful consideration of the consequences of his actions doesn't help the physician in arriving at a definite solution. Such a reasoned exploration of consequences could very well lead to a good and informed choice, but not to the resolution of the dilemma for the simple reason that the two conflicting options are an intrinsic feature of the situation that the administrator finds himself in. As Raz observes, "even where they [an understanding of consequences] guide one's choice they may fail to determine its outcome...(T)hey may well fail to yield a determined outcome, a definite right or wrong, wise or foolish decision" (Raz 1986: 335). The physician in our example is faced with an impossible situation; a choice for which no easy, satisfying, definitive solution exists. He finds himself in the position of Agamemnon at Aulis, who could either save his fleet or his daughter, but not both at the same time. He is faced, in short, with a tragic choice.

Yet, if we if we are willing to shift our perspective, there is, I believe, a way out. In public administration, as in everyday life, occasion drives principle, instead of the other way around. It is probably no coincidence that examples of moral debate in the literature of the ethics of public policy and public administration generally revolve around big and entrenched public controversies, such as affirmative action, the right to euthanasia, or medical rationing. Such controversies usually know no end, and are dealt with by prolonged and principled debate (Denhardt 1988; Gutmann and Dennis 1996). Moral judgment, thus, becomes identified with irresolvable ethical issues and the exchange of principled arguments. Rightness in moral judgment becomes more procedure than outcome, and the quality of a particular moral assessment can be recognized by the explicitness of its justification (Denhardt 1988: 172).

My argument here is not that this kind of moral reasoning is wrong or misguided. Clearly good, systematic reasoning from explicit general principles can help us to clarify complex moral issues in many situations. My argument is, rather, that this kind of explicit ethical justification is one-sided and incomplete. It identifies everyday moral judgment with the kind of intractable controversies around big ethical questions that fill the newspapers. It conceives of values as abstract, disembodied principles that can only function as *causa sui generis* in explicit ethical arguments. It creates an impenetrable boundary between values as ultimately groundless, subjective principles, and facts which are grounded in objective, observable reality. And finally, by framing moral judgment as explicit calculation, the hope of dealing in feasible, acceptable ways with genuine value conflict recedes, for if universal principle V_1 contradicts universal principle V_2, then behavioral injunctions E_1 and E_2, are derived from these two conflicting principles, will be both true and conflicting. In such cases, systematic reasoning will not be able to resolve the conflict. Yet, conflicting moralities are a fact of life, certainly, as we saw, of administrative life, and people usually do not shrink from them but accept them as something they will have to deal with in the course of a regular working day. Sometimes these conflicts will be painful, sometimes they are routine, but in the lived experience of ordinary people, they are not something out of the ordinary, and resolving them is part and parcel of what it means to be a functioning human being in a particular community, be it professional or otherwise. How administrators go about resolving everyday value conflict will be the subject of the next and final section.

A SECOND CUT: VALUE CONFLICT IN THE PRACTICE MODE

Value pluralists, as we saw at the start of the preceding section, believe values to be conditional. They think that the context in which values are realized determines their weight relative to one another. In that sense, there is common ground between a rule-based and a practice-based analysis of value conflict. Where the practice-based mode differs from the rule-based mode, however, is in the importance it attaches to the context of value conflict. In fact, it believes that although value and context can be distinguished, values cannot be seen apart from their context in the everyday experience of individual administrators, similar to the way that in the act of listening, the pitch and the typical sound color of a violoncello cannot be separated. Practice-based analysts argue that the conditionality of values is so important that it requires a radically different approach to the study of values and value conflict. In particular, they feel that the primacy of conditionality obliges analysts to get out of their university offices and analyze value conflict in the settings where everyday actors act out value conflicts in real-life situations. This ethnographic turn in the study of values, they then argue, changes the discourse on value conflict in almost all important respects. To prepare the way for a practice-based analysis of value conflict, let's return to the case of the certifying physician once more.

In a rule-based ethical universe, the case was framed as a conflict between two values that exclude each other. Yet, even a cursory reading of the interview reveals that the physician doesn't experience the value conflict *in abstracto*, but concretely. From the point of view of his lived experience, it is not a clash between two general principles, but a conflict that involves real people with real worries, pains, and interests. He needs no reminding of the fact that his decision will have a large impact on the life chances of his client and her family, and that he is responsible for these consequences. The problem derives from his professional charge to act upon the matter at hand; that is, to make eligibility decisions no matter how they present themselves to him. There is no walking away from the conflict. Moreover, this being a wicked problem, he has no right, as Harmon and Mayer say, to be wrong (1986: 11).

Related to the preceding point, is that there is nothing remarkable or noteworthy about the conflict. It was one of many difficult or less difficult cases that he dealt with in the course of a regular working day. They are part of the job. In fact, as the physician remarked in the interview, it was the constant recurrence of situations such as these that defined the job as challenging, demanding, and, at times, unrewarding. His usual way of handling difficult cases was either to find some course of action himself, or to informally consult one or more of his colleagues. He presented extremely difficult cases to a weekly meeting of certifying physicians in his unit. Yet, common as they may be, these situations are by no means routine. Standard solutions are not available, and there is often no satisfying solution at all. Yet, as one survey after another reveals, although mistakes are being made and clients are sometimes dissatisfied or angry with the way that they are treated, most people express satisfaction about their encounters with administrators (Goodsell 1985). Whatever administrators do to resolve real life value conflict is recognized by their immediate clients as reasonable and acceptable.

An Account of Everyday Moral Judgment

How, then, do administrators, and people in general, deal with value conflict in ordinary circumstances? How can we conceive of everyday moral judgment without the deliberative bias of traditional ethical reasoning?[14] In summary form, everyday moral judgment is immediate, intuitive, concrete, interactive, pragmatic, personal, and action-oriented. Moreover, this kind of everyday moral judgement is something that comes natural to people. It is something they do in the course of their everyday activities, usually without giving it much thought. Moral judgment is problem-oriented; it is an integral part of peoples' problem solving activities in which it functions simultaneously as a mode of perception and discernment, and as a way of giving meaning to facts, events, and behavior under circumstances of uncertainty. Also, moral judgement, contrary to received opinion, is not something that happens inside the mind of individual actors. Rather, it both emerges and is accounted for in people's continuous interactions with each other.

Everyday moral judgement aims as much at good results as at proper procedure. But what counts as result is not the definitive resolution of a conflict, but the temporary stabilization of a situation that is unhinged or threatens to become so. To test their judgements, people deliberate; but it is not the kind of systematic, principled reasoning typical of traditional moral philosophy. Rather, judgment emerges through discourse. As a result, moral judgment is not a one-shot affair, but evolves slowly, often tentatively and haltingly, in conversation with others. Everyday moral judgment is tacit, and sometimes, as we will see, dealing with value conflict can be painful or unsettling, but this does not mean that it is seen as, in principle, impossible. Some solutions are better, more feasible, or more acceptable than others, but the public assessment of the quality of the solution is part of what everyday moral judgment is all about. As I said before, to be able to engage successfully in everyday moral judgment is what being a competent member of a community is all about Moral judgment, as Dewey saw it, is aimed in sustaining an agent in a social environment (Welchman 1995: 3). Let me, before I apply these insights to the case of the certifying physician, clarify the main characteristics of everyday moral judgment in a more systematic manner.

Values are embedded in concrete situations.

One of the most pernicious consequences of the deontological, rule-based approach in ethical thought is to conceive of values as large, disembodied, abstract, "first-cause" principles, such as liberty, justice, or equality. Most of the values that count in everyday situations, however, are neither large nor abstract. They are embedded in, and cannot be seen apart from, the particulars of a situation. In everyday situations, most values are "thick" values. Examples can be found in the normative qualifications our administrators applied to their clients: "realistic," "uncanny," "modest," "restrained," and "courageous." Conceiving of values as situated in concrete reality allows us to go beyond the noncognitivism of the traditional fact-value dichotomy. Schematically speaking, valuative terms such as "modest" or "uncanny" contain a cognitive and volitional component. They are based on the perception of certain observable facts and the simultaneous appreciation of these observations; an appreciation that is equivalent to an injunction to act in a certain manner (respectively: "Treat this person with respect," and "Be on guard in your dealings with this person").

But, someone could object, by distinguishing between a cognitive and a volitional component in value terms, don't you bring in through the back door the old, time-worn, fact-value dichotomy that you have just laid to rest? The reply would be that the cognitive and volitional component, in value terms, can be distinguished analytically, but that they cannot be seen apart in the way value terms function in their natural context. There is simply no way to describe the cognitive component of value terms without referring to the evaluative interests in which these terms makes sense, and vice versa. As Iris Murdoch puts it: "It is especially characteristic of normative words, both desirable and undesirable, to belong to sets of patterns without an appreciation of which they cannot be understood" (Murdoch 1985: 33). Normative qualifications such as "modest" or "uncanny" are part of a recurrent, patterned situation in which the use of such terms is both called for and meaningful to the actors involved.

Value-terms are embedded in practices.

Another way to put this is to say that the use of value terms is part of a practice. Those can be specific practices that are tied to particular domains of life (such as farming, teaching, or in terms of this paper, assessing eligibility for disability or deciding upon the legal status of refugees), or general practices (such as following rules, having a conversation, greeting, or answering questions), which are dispersed over a large variety of specific practices (Schatzki 1996: 91). To say that value terms are situated in practices is to say that the culture, or collectivity, contains not only the conceptual schemes that we share with each other, but also the procedures for applying these conceptual schemes: the criteria for judging the results of our valuations, the criteria by which we decide that we prefer to change the criteria because we are pleased with the result and not with the standard of judgment, the experience that it is not clear beforehand if and how a moral term applies to a particular person or situation, the mutual understanding between the parties involved that our valuations are always provisional and subject to change when circumstances change, and so on.

We can now grasp the deeper implications of this observation for moral judgement in real-life situations. In concrete everyday situations, people are constantly faced with the task not only of figuring out what to do, but also how to account for whatever they did. Moral judgements are a representation of this ongoing process, presenting an account not only of the actions and the situations that occasioned those actions, but also of the warrants for those actions in that they convey the message: "For most people, this action will do for this particular situation with these particular constraints." There is considerable evidence that this everyday moral judgement is something that has become second nature; that it is a routine that even children master at a quite early age (Bruner 1986: 67). In other words, far from being the arbitrary application of moral epithets on unsuspecting people, in ordinary circumstances moral judgment is a carefully balanced and informed act of a competent member of a community of practice.[15]

Moral judgment is interactive.

In the traditional view, moral judgment is seen as a private activity that takes place in the mind of the individual. Surely, people engage in moral debate, but that is only to exchange positions already taken or to persuade others of the fallacy of their moral assessments. The position I take in this paper is that everyday moral judgment, being part of practices, is both interactive and public *in a constitutive sense*. By this, I mean to say that, generally, people construct their moral assessments by engaging in a discourse with other people. What does it mean to engage in discourse? The theory of oral discourse that underlies this question is too comprehensive to discuss here in any detail,[16] but in broad brush-strokes, the argument goes as follows: people make sense of situations by engaging in discourse. A discourse, according to the sociolinguist Gee, is any stretch of language, spoken or written, that is sufficiently coherent to make sense to a community of people who use that language (Gee 1990: 103). Sense-making in language involves a lot more than being able to use words in a grammatically correct manner. In fact, language is always embedded in a larger framework of social relationships and social institutions. By using language, speakers always communicate more than just the literal message. By the manner in which language is spoken, speakers express points of view, refer to shared contexts, communicate how they want to be seen by the other, and so on.[17] Differently put; by engaging in discourse, people drag into the conversation a huge shared context, which the parties involved implicitly assume but are hard put to fully articulate.[18] This shared context functions as a common reference point both for developing positions vis a vis new and difficult situations, and for assessing the rightfulness and acceptability of those positions. It is important to realize that the vagueness that is inherent in oral discourse is not some drawback or deficit of the oral style compared to the more precise language of formal deliberation. In fact, as we shall see, speakers in everyday situations, such as administrators, capitalize on this inherent vagueness in everyday discourse to deal with large, intractable issues.

Moral judgment involves emotion and identity.

To be able to engage in discourse in this way, a person obviously has to be a competent user of a language. But what does it mean to be a competent user of a language? As Gee makes clear, to use a language means to use in the right way, and that entails not saying the things in a grammatically proper manner, but in saying the right thing, at the right time, in the right place. In fact, the socially embedded nature of language use also requires that one acts in the appropriate way when saying whatever one has to say at some point. For example, if the certifying physician would tell his story of value conflict with a cheerful smile, no one would hesitate to call him insincere. Discourse expresses life forms. To engage in a discourse means to express what it entails to live a certain recognizable way of life. Although contemporary popular language suggests that we choose the life form that suits us best, in reality we slowly grow into a particular way of life. Gradually, over the years, the conventions, habits, speech patterns, expectations, aspirations, and values that, together, make up a particular life form will have become second nature to the person living that particular life. Discourse, thus, reveals not only a way of life, but also a particular identity. As Gee states it: "(L)anguage is always spoken (and written for that matter) out of a particular social identity (or social role), an identity that is a composite of words, actions and (implied) beliefs, values and attitudes" (1990: 140). The way a person engages in discourse, and the meaning he comes to attach to a particular situation through his use of discourse, has to fit the way he sees himself and the way he feels about the situation at hand. Differently put, for a situation to make sense, meaning, affect, and identity have to more or less correspond with each other, both for the speaker and his audience.

Everyday Moral Judgment in Administrative Practice

Does this account of everyday moral judgment help us to understand how administrators deal with genuine value conflict? Let us return to the certifying physician at the beginning of this paper. As I will make clear shortly, a somewhat extended account of the case is required:

> After the initial description of the situation, the physician continues by explaining how he interprets his professional role. He says that he always informs his clients that he is not a "helping doctor, like your psychologist or psychiatrist or your internist or your general practitioner. I am a physician who assesses you. I translate your medical circumstances to your insurance contract. That's what they need me for. But I work within the framework of your insurance, so something that isn't in the contract or that the contract doesn't allow, I can't offer you, so that that is totally clear." He even adds that he thinks that the professional demands that are made upon the certifying physician are inherently contradictory because "naturally you're trained as a physician to help people so people could label you as a benefit-raider and that can conflict with your own feelings about it. I am pretty good at taking a neutral stance towards this because I'm convinced that I'm not here to help them but to assess them. That is what I explain to them, and if I at the very least inform them of that, I think that I have fulfilled a moral obligation because I made my position clear." When asked how he experiences the conflict he described, he reacts as follows: "I find it unpleasant for her. On the other hand I occupy a position in which I don't see myself as a provider of benefits. I know colleagues who see themselves like that." This seems a clear general statement of how he perceives of his role. Yet, deeds speak louder than words, and the remainder of the interview is a long explanation of his unceasing efforts to obtain the medical information that might demonstrate a certifiable illness with his client. Alas to no avail.
>
> He then decides to strike a balance between the requirements of the law and his impressions of his client. He declares her fifty percent disabled, stressing that by doing this he is in fact breaking the rules. He also schedules a reassessment for over six months in the hope that in the mean time the medical picture will have become clearer. The client disagrees with his decision and

announces she will appeal at court. At first the physician states that in general he has an open mind about clients who appeal his decisions, but further on he reveals that he had strategic motives with this decision. Although he had obtained information from every relevant medical specialization, he had knowingly refrained from asking for a psychiatric report. His official reason is that no one, including himself, felt that the woman had psychological problems, but there turns out to be an ulterior motive. He knows that the client's lawyer will ask for a psychiatric assessment on the grounds that the certifying physician had been negligent in not asking for one. He also knows that, given her address, she will be sent to a psychiatrist in her catchment area who is very good at finding "hidden depressions," and that the judge will use the report as a justification for overturning his decision and give her full benefits. As he concludes: "I took that risk [to have his decision overturned] more or less deliberately, because I can't feel sorry for that in this case. Perhaps a little bit a feeling of yeah what I haven't been able to give you, you were able to get indirectly through an appeal, although I would contest the interpretation proposed in the appeals case on the grounds of: can you motivate that in a convincing way?

At the end of the interview the physician becomes reflective. He muses that the case would have been easier if the woman had been unpleasant: "although that is of course really subjective. You're not allowed to think like that, but it is human, and it would have been less hard. That's why I wanted to discuss this case in this interview, particularly because it affects your personal experience of your job, of how you have to do it, and what your role towards your patients has to be. And that lady is genuine, I'm still convinced of that. And that creates a situation of in a substantive way your assessment is really not right. If everyone is honest and genuine then something must come out of it that we can all live with, and yet I have too little...(End of interview).

The transcript of the interview stretches over twenty-four densely typed pages. It is made up of long detailed stretches of medical information, reflections about the profession, descriptions of the agency's organizational structure and functioning, vignettes of colleagues, hypothetical scenarios of the same case, references to similar cases, expressions of personal feelings, and so on. The course of action the physician chose is arrived at gradually, almost hesitatingly, through long asides about the nature of the profession, the role of his colleagues, his interpretation of his professional role, moral judgements of his client, and expressions of personal feeling—all of which somehow feed into his actions. Reading through it with the scientist's bias towards parsimony, it is tempting to skip most of the material as irrelevant and select the passages in which the physician discusses his moral dilemma. That would be a misrepresentation of what the transcript represents. All twenty-four pages of asides, reflections, and conjectures, form a comprehensive discursive account of what it means for this administrator to deal with this particular moral conflict.[19] In reconstructing an actor's choices, we tend to distinguish decision from context, signal from noise, but in everyday moral judgment, context is decision; the signal is in the noise. A more precise way to put this is to say that the discourse of this administrator is composed narratively (Gee

1990; Wagenaar and Hartendorp 1999). This is not merely to impose another analytic structure onto the administrator's discourse or imply that narrative structures are used to give a syntactical or thematic coherence to speech, but to convey that narrative is integral to the effort of actors to make sense of the situations they face.

Values conflict because they are rooted in coherent life forms. Different life forms make different demands on people, and, as in contemporary society, most people inhabit several life forms simultaneously; people end up struggling with situations that make conflicting demands upon them. As one life form is not *a priori* superior to another, the demands can be incompatible and/or incommensurable. This is not an unusual or exceptional situation, but a fact of life; harmony being the exception rather than the rule (Hampshire 1983: 152). Being confronted with value conflict is part of what it is to be human. Administrators are, in this sense, not different from anyone else. The question this raises for administrative ethics, however, is: what distinguishes good solutions from bad solutions in cases of value conflict? Or more generally: can we draw normative conclusions from this "thick," practice-based description of everyday moral judgement? How do we know that the physician's solution is a good one?

The answer is: it depends. It depends on how we weigh the values involved, what information we deem relevant to the case, how we weigh that information, how long we can or want to stay with the case. One administrator will chart a different course through the case and arrive at different, and not necessarily worse, conclusions than another. This is not a plea for moral relativism but the acknowledgement of moral pluralism in administrative life. Relativists believe that moral judgment is dependent upon a specific historic-cultural setting, that it does not travel beyond that setting, and that actors from different cultures are unable to understand each others positions. Pluralism more or less agrees with the first condition and disagrees with the second and third. Some values, pluralists argue, such as equality, liberty, or efficiency, as well as the core meaning of "thick" values, such as "uncanny," "modest," and "realistic," are "objective" in the sense that they can be understood in many cultures, although their concrete form may vary across these cultures. We have access to other ways of life, through discourse of the kind shown above, in which actors communicate not only the moral valuation, but also invoke large segments of the embedding situation which gives meaning to the valuation. People might even agree on a few broad standards of judgment. For example, that evenhanded judgements are better than one-sided ones, that a detailed justification of the case is better than a cursory one, or that a careful procedure is better than a careless one. Moral pluralists assert, in short, that there are different ways of life, that one is not *a priori* better than another, but that ordinary people are able to discuss with each other, in a meaningful way, the merits of one versus another. Practice-based pluralists, in other words, deny the hopeless incommensurability of the rule-based pluralists.

If these are inconclusive answers to the question about the merits of one moral judgement over another, they are meant to be. As the examples from administrative life make clear, value conflict in everyday administrative situations is "dealt with" rather than resolved. "Dealing with" may involve many different things: evenhanded exposition of the situation, making general declarative statements, introspection, soul searching, painstaking inquiry to obtain the relevant facts, even subterfuge and calculating behavior. Yet, in the end, as we saw in the physician's case, there is no closure. At best there is temporary stability; a transient moment of understanding in a moving field that enables the administrator to continue doing his job. A pause in a never ending stream of events. The world that administrators inhabit is uncertain and unpredictable. The best way to chart such a world is by "reassessing," "redefining," or by "modifying" their appraisals of people and situations (the language is from Murdoch). Differently put, administrators must be impartial and open-minded. Because often they are not quite certain what they are looking for, and during the search they have to modify their valuation of the situation and the norms they use in valuing simultaneously. This reassessing and redefining is not restricted to particular moments of hard choice, but occurs within a continuous stream of patterned action. In our pluralist and fragmented world, value conflict is a thing to stay. The challenge for public administration is to design organizational settings that allow for the kind of moral attention that is the prerequisite for good administrative decisions in situations of value pluralism.

NOTES

1. This article has benefited greatly from comments made by Wibren van den Burg, Marc Hertogh, Paul Hart, Robert Weiss, participants of the luncheon-seminar at the Schoordijk Institute, Tilburg University, and the participants of the panel "Practice and Discourse: Dealing with Conflicting Values in Public Administration" at the Third Public Sector Ethics Conference, Portland, Oregon, May 18-19, 2000.

2. We asked the certifying physicians who participated in our research what proportion of the eligibility decisions they had to make they considered "difficult," as opposed to "routine." The answers varied from roughly half to two-thirds. Interviews about difficult decisions, they said, always involved some form of value conflict.

3. In the philosophical literature, the unavoidability of value conflict has been argued for on different grounds. According to Berlin, value conflict is a conceptual truth: "The notion of the perfect whole, the ultimate solution in which good things coexist, seems to me not merely unattainable—that is a truism—but conceptually incoherent; I do not know what is meant by a harmony of this kind" (Berlin 1997: 11). Hampshire argues that the unavoidability of value conflict springs from the existence of different forms of organized social life: "I have been arguing that nature has so designed us that, taking humanity as a whole and the evidences of history, we tend to have conflicting and divergent moralities imbedded in divergent ways of life, each the product of specific historical memories and local conditions" (1983: 162). For a description, as lucid as it is entertaining, of the inevitability of value conflict—and even conflict between different interpretations of the same value—in political life, see (Stone 1997).

4. Some of the authors discussed recognize that the values that they suggest as guidelines may conflict. For example, Kass, in his discussion of stewardship, observes that "since these criteria [to be effective and ethical] are often in conflict with one another, being a good stew-

ard is extremely difficult in practice" (1990: 126). Yet, they do not explore the consequences for administrative behavior, or describe how administrators deal with these conflicts.

5. This insight has been suggested by Wibren van der Burg. In the discourse among legal theorists, the relation between law on the one hand and society and morality on the other, is a central issue. It is common to distinguish between a formal, or "product," and "process" model of law. In the first, law is considered to be the sum total of the formal statutes, rules, and judgements by courts. Whatever morality or views law expresses are sufficiently captured in the formal texts of statutes and rulings. In the process, or practice, model, on the other hand, it assumes that law cannot be isolated from social reality. In fact, "law" emerges, and is shaped, in the thousands of interactions between citizens and organizations that, taken together, make up society. In the process model there exists a strong continuity between social exchange and formal law. Law, in this sense, is seen as practice, that is not the exclusive domain of legal experts. (For an excellent discussion of these two models, see (van der Burg 1999)

6. I do not mean to identify the rule-based, neo-Kantian mode with value pluralism. In fact, pluralist ethicists can be located on a scale from rule-based to practice-based, with, for example, Berlin occupying a position nearer the rule-based pole and Hampshire nearer the practice-based pole. What makes the discussion difficult is that in most pluralist analyses, rule-based and practice-based elements intermingle. A good example is Kekes analysis. While he recognizes the conditionality of values, he often seems to treat them in a reified, emotive way as distinct, autonomous entities.

7. For a more extended and formal treatment of incommensurability, see (Kekes 1993: 56), and (Raz 1986: ch. 13). Raz defines incommensurability as a breakdown of transitivity: "Two valuable options are incommensurable if (1) neither is better than the other, and (2) there is (or could be) another option which is better than one but is not better than the other" (1986: 325). One of the main reasons for such a failure of transitivity is an "incomplete definition of the contribution of criteria to a value." That is, the criteria that make up the value of the options are so numerous, and in addition, are themselves evaluations, that we are unable to arrive at any stable and definitive ranking. This, in turn, makes it impossible to compare such a complex option with another, usually equally complex option, be they the relative merits of great writers or the rightness of two great values.

8. Loss as a concomitant of tragic choices has been described by several authors on value conflict; a particularly eloquent description comes from Kekes: "The sense of loss, therefore, is a frequent experience in our lives. It need not be due to having made a choice that we come to regret. For we can feel that we have lost something important even if we are convinced that we have made the right choice and that we would make it again if we had to. If the loss is accompanied by regret, the regret is about life's being such as to exclude the realization of all the values we prize" (1993: 54). See also (Hampshire 1983: 155; Stocker 1990; Berlin 1997: 11).

9. It should be noted that we assume here that the choices that confront administrators are significant. That is, the choices involved are comprehensive in that they affect large portions of a person's life (Raz 1986: 32). Generally speaking, the significance of value incommensurability is not a given, and should be demonstrated. Many incommensurable value choices, as Raz and Lukes rightly observe, are not significant at all, and quite a few are downright trivial, such as the question if Hemingway or Proust is the better writer. The question is unanswerable, and amounts to real incommensurability because their work is so different on many dimensions that we cannot think of a single characteristic on which to rank order them in any decisive way (Lukes 1991: 12).

10. The apex of this kind of thinking is to be found in the work of Hare, but is also associated with the work of Kant and Sartre. As Hare put it: moral philosophy was nothing but "the logical study of the language of morals" (as cited in Welchman 1995: 1. See also Hartman 1977: 115-116).

11. See Hartman (1977) for a critique of the Kant-Hare approach to ethical reasoning and a lucid description of a less strict "naturalistic theory of reasons."

12. For example, Denhardt (1988) states: "What has been argued throughout this book is that public administrators must consistently and conscientiously make decisions on the basis of *ethical deliberation* if the ethical tenor of the field is to be improved" (emphasis in original). Or, in a particularly sophisticated example of the genre, Gutmann and Thompson declare: "We address the challenge of moral disagreement here by developing a conception of democracy that secures a central place for moral discussion in political life."(1996: 1). Gutmann and Thompson argue that their model of deliberative democracy is philosophically "neutral" in that it is based on, what they claim is, everyday moral judgement. Everyday moral judgement, however, is also seen as a form of explicit reasoning: "We treat the method as an informal reconstruction of a form of moral reasoning familiar in everyday life, a pattern of argument that many people use when they try to justify to others, in moral terms, the positions they take and the decisions they make"(1996: 5). Probably, these authors have the naturalistic moral reasoning in mind that aims for a plausible instead of a logical relation between principles and particular judgements.

13. In fact, as the physician explained in the interview, this is how the woman became his client. He had taken the case from a colleague who had been unable to come to a decision.

14. The deliberative approach to moral judgement has been criticized widely in moral philosophy and occasionally in policy theory. One of the earliest, and still most cogent critiques, is that of Dewey (Welchman 1995). For recent critiques of the deliberative approach and its associated concept of value, see Murdoch (1970), Hampshire (1983), and Putnam (1981). Jonsen and Toulmin have formulated a casuistic approach to moral deliberation that goes a long way in addressing the problems of the traditional approach. In policy theory, the work of Martin Rein (Schön and Rein 1994; Laws and Rein 1999) is particularly important. The argument in this section has been influenced by all these sources.

15. That doesn't mean, of course, that unreasonable or willful moral judgement never occurs. But the very fact that we recognize certain qualifications as instances of unreasonable judgment requires that a practice of competent moral judgment should be in place.

16. For a detailed statement of a theory of discourse and society, see Gee (1990). For an earlier statement, see Gumperz (1982). For an application in public administration, see Wagenaar (1999 #37).

17. Speakers do this by employing the prosodic aspects of spoken language. The prosodic characteristics of a text, such as pitch rises and falls, rhythmic patterns, and hesitations, function semantically by signaling information that is not contained within the text's lexical aspects.

18. As Gee states, referring to the discourse among professional linguists by way of example: "Every act of speaking, writing, and behaving a linguist does as a linguist, is meaningful only against the background of the whole social institution of linguistics, and that institution is made up of concrete things like people, books, and buildings; abstract things like bodies of knowledge, values, norms and beliefs; mixtures of concrete and abstract things like universities, journals and publishers, as well as shared history and shared stories" (1990: 143) This statement applies with equal force to other professions such as welfare officer, certifying physician or legal clerk in the Immigration Office.

19. As Hampshire argues: "The argument in these last two chapters requires that sometimes, and with some moral concerns, the complex description of a whole way of life, does fill the place occupied in other moral contexts by general principles of utility or justice: that is, the justification stops when the interconnections of practices and sentiments within a complete way of life are described" (1983: 5).

REFERENCES

Berlin, I. 1997. The pursuit of the ideal. *The Proper Study of Mankind. An Anthology of Essays.* London: Chatto & Windus.

Bruner, J. 1986. *Actual Minds, Possible Worlds.* Cambridge, MA: Harvard University Press.

Denhardt, K. G. 1988. *The Ethics of Public Service. Resolving Moral Dilemmas in Public Organizations.* Westport, CT: Greenwood Press.

————. 1989. "The Management of Ideals: A Political Perspective on Ethics." *Public Administration Review.* 49 (March/April):187-193.

Frederickson, G. 1974. "Introductory comments." *Public Administration Review.* 34 (January-February).

Gee, J. 1990. *Social Linguistics and Literacies. Ideology in Discourses.* Basingstoke, Hampshire: The Falmer Press.

Goodsell, C. T. 1985. *The Case for Bureaucracy. A Public Administration Polemic.* Chatham, NJ: Chatham House Publishers, Inc.

Gumperz, J. J. 1982. *Discourse Strategies.* Cambridge: Cambridge University Press.

Gutmann, A. and T. Dennis. 1996. *Democracy and Disagreement.* Cambridge, MA: The Belknap Press of Harvard University Press.

Hampshire, S. 1983. *Morality and Conflict.* Cambridge, MA: Harvard University Press.

Harman, G. 1977. *The Nature of Morality.* New York: Oxford University Press.

Harmon, M. M. and R. T. Mayer. 1986. *Organization Theory for Public Administration.* Glenview, IL: Scott, Foresman and Company.

Jaworski, A. and N. Coupland. 1999. Introduction: Perspectives on discourse analysis. *The Discourse Reader.* A. Jaworski and N. Coupland. London: Routledge.

Jonsen, A. R. and S. Toulmin. 1988. *The Abuse of Casuistry. A History of Moral Reasoning.* Berkeley: University of California Press.

Kass, H. D. 1990. Stewardship as a fundamental element in images of public administration. *Images and Indentities in Public Administration.* H. D. Kass and B. L. Catron. Newbury Park: Sage.

Kekes, J. 1993. *The Morality of Pluralism.* Princeton, NJ: Princeton University Press.

Laws, D. and M. Rein. 1999. Reflection, reframing, and the institutions of policy discourse. *Theory, Policy and Society Symposium.* Leiden, the Netherlands.

Lukes, S. 1991. *Moral Conflict and Politics.* Oxford: Clarendon Press.

Morgan, D. F. 1990. Administrative phronesis: discretion and the problem of administrative legitimacy in our constitutional system. *Images and Identities in Public Administration.* H. D. Kass and B. L. Catron. Newbury Park: Sage.

Murdoch, I. 1985. *The Sovereignty of Good.* London: Routledge.

Raz, J. 1986. *The Morality of Freedom.* Oxford: Clarendon Press.

Rohr, J. 1989. *Ethics for Bureaucrats. An Essay on Law and Values.* New York: Marcel Dekker.

Schatzki, T. R. 1996. *Social Practices. A Wittgensteinian Approach to Human Activity and the Social.* Cambridge: Cambridge University Press.

Schön, D. A. and M. Rein. 1994. *Frame Reflection. Toward the Resolution of Intractable Policy Controversies.* Basic Books.

Stocker, M. 1990. *Plural and Conflicting Values.* Oxford: Carendon Press.

Stone, D. 1997. *Policy Paradox. The Art of Political Decision Making.* New York: W.W. Norton & Company.

Stone, D. A. 1984. *The Disabled State.* Philadelphia: Temple University Press.

van der Burg, W. 1999. "Two Models of Law and Morality." *Associations.* 3(1):61-82.

von Wright, G. H. 1971. *Explanation and Understanding.* Ithaca, New York: Cornell University Press.

Wagenaar, H. and R. Hartendorp. 1999. *Bureacratic Order and Personal Order: The Narrative Analysis of Administrative Practice.* Symposium Theory, Policy & Society. Leiden, the Netherlands.

Weber, M. 1949. *The Methodology of the Social Sciences.* New York: The Free Press.

Welchman, J. 1995. *Dewey's Ethical Thought.* Ithaca, New York: Cornell University Press.

8

Passionate Humility: Toward a Philosophy of Ethical Will

———— Dvora Yanow and Hugh Willmott

If you know that you are not sure, you have a chance to improve the situation.

—Richard P. Feynman

Some years back, the head of redevelopment for a large California city closed a nightclub downtown, over its owner's protests. One of the area's newspapers reported the story (Hazle 1992) and quoted the agency head as saying about the owner: "Kevin and I have a history. Mine is right. His is wrong."

A similar certitude was evident in Lager's study of Ben and Jerry's, the ice cream manufacturing company. About Ben's management style, the author wrote: "Ben was usually so single-mindedly convinced that he was right about something that he often didn't even acknowledge the legitimacy of alternative points of view." His "management style was at odds with how he wanted the company to treat its employees" (quoted in Henriques 1994).

These stories suggest a key desideratum and illustrate a central conundrum for administrative theory—including its manifestation in public administration education—as we move into the next century, and it is one that follows us out of the century that is closing. Conviction becomes dogmatic and oppressive unless it is tempered by humility. If we wish to avoid having the potential virtues of commitment degenerate into the vices of arrogance and domination, then we need to better understand how it is possible to act in administrative capacities with commitment and conviction while at the same time entertaining the possibility that, in its formulation and/or application, this "passionate" commitment might be misplaced, misguided, or wrong. And we need to learn better how to educate a cadre of administrators who can and will engage in the same questioning. This will involve encouraging and fostering an alertness to the humane dimensions of administrative practices, including an ethic of care (Noddings 1984; Tronto 1993) and compassion alongside technical expertise. It will require, that is, a commitment to "passionate humility" (Yanow 1997). By developing such a reflective awareness, administrators, as actors with local knowledge in addition to their professionally-developed expert knowledge, may be better placed to make informed, practical judgments even to the extent of refusing to implement policies or take administrative actions that they regard as inhumane, even when charged to do so. The exercise of such judgment may also increase their alertness to the possible limitations of their own local knowledge and impel them to seek to access others' local knowledge (whether in their organizations or in the communities potentially affected by policy acts) as needed. We are pointing here to the need to balance the will to act—with passionate commitment—against the humbling possibility that one might be wrong.

Such concerns, of course, are neither entirely novel nor restricted to the sphere of public administration. The requirement to balance the will to act, on the one hand, with an ethical and humane stance, on the other, is found in the domain of corporate management as well. This is evident from a recent news report that received considerable publicity as we were writing this. It seems that the Clinton administration, following on a proposal made in 1997 by Vice President Albert Gore, proposed legislation that enjoins the U.S. Federal government from contracting with any corporation that does not have a "satisfactory record of integrity and business ethics" (Mokhiber & Weissman 1999). What is more intriguing, for our purposes, is the response: the U.S. Chamber of Commerce, joined by a multitude of business trade associations, mounted a massive lobbying effort against the bill—suggesting, as the reporters note, that it is the source of great concern in the carpeted halls of capitalist enterprise. Apparently, there is some difficulty in reconciling a will to act in ways that are commercially viable, with demonstrating and preserving even a modicum of ethical integrity.

In this essay, we consider the role of passion and humility in the theory and practice of public administration. The postmodern mood of epistemological pluralism has simultaneously unsettled and opened up previously held certainties concerning acts, behaviors, and views. This has been accompanied by contemporary disillusionment with grandiose visions of change and progress. The challenges of practice and education can be located within this conceptual ferment. We see such a challenge emerging both within the context of local implementation of a legislative program and within organizational practices. We suggest that the development of ethical will, centered upon a practice of passionate humility, offers relevant guidance for the future development of the practice and teaching of public administration.

POSTMODERN PLURALISM VERSUS ADMINISTRATIVE CERTAINTY

It is characteristic of beliefs about this postmodern era that we see ourselves living in a pluralistic world where there are multiple, competing beliefs and associated value standpoints. No longer is it possible to take for granted the existence of homogeneous ethical values (whether or not they ever existed) or the humane and ethical intentions of those in positions of power and authority. Doubts about the existence of a single, universal set of beliefs and values are further fueled as national boundaries between ideas, not to say people, collapse or become more permeable. In the arena of national politics, for example—Clinton in the U.S., Blair in the UK, and others—a postmodern play of images offers competing representations of, and promises to, the middle ground as established divisions between "left" and "right" have been de-differentiated, with attendant confusion and uncertainty for those wedded to their respective (individualistic and collectivistic) beliefs and values.

This loss of established bearings and the associated ethical disorientation can produce a moral vacuum in which a fascism of the center can take hold. Fascisms of the right and left are well documented. Their seductive and destructive power has been demonstrated repeatedly during this century. Currently, both stand discredited, lending greater appeal to the seemingly moderate ideas of the center—the Third Way. The door is then opened to an authoritarianism, if not a fascism, of the center, in which ideas of moderation and progress, based upon commonly accepted, uncontested (and uncontentious) values, become the new, and seemingly the only, basis for government. In this context, centrist leaders (and their apologists) present legislative possibilities as certainties in a technocratic program that appeals directly to those disillusioned by right and left extremisms, but also bewildered and threatened by postmodern open-endedness.

This development, which is facilitated by the appointment of large numbers of special advisors, spin doctors, and public relations specialists, has disturbed seemingly settled positions and postures. Dilemmas circling around ethical action become particularly acute in such an environment, where there is simultaneous pressure upon politicians and others (e.g., business executives and public administrators) both to adopt an ethical stance and to make room for pluralistic meanings. Where and how does one find the locus of ethical action in such seemingly relativistic circumstances?

One of the implications for administrators/managers of these contemporary developments is the end of unfettered certainty about the rightness of their actions. The question—and it is one not only for practice, but for education as well—is, how does one proceed under such conditions? A possible answer, we want to suggest, is not with further layers of intermediaries (e.g., spin doctors or their equivalents) or with redoubled insistence on the rightness of one's position, but with what we will term "passionate humility." Such a response combines a conviction that one is right with a recognition that convictions are indeed inherently problematic and, therefore, could well be wrong; or, at least, that their truth is context-dependent. This brings to mind the words of the physicist and Nobel laureate Richard Feynman (in the context of an appreciation of democracy over Soviet Communism), who called for:

> a satisfactory philosophy of ignorance, and the progress made possible by such a philosophy, progress which is the fruit of freedom of thought. I feel a responsibility to proclaim the value of this freedom and to teach that doubt is not to be

feared, but that it is to be welcomed as the possibility of a new potential for human beings. (quoted in Ferris 1998)

Feynman celebrates the importance of ignorance and doubt, as contrasted with the more common placement of positive value upon knowledge and certainty. Such a position of doubt entails humility about what one believes, or assumes, to be incontrovertibly true. A further condition of doubt is the possibility of dialogue in which ideas that unsettle or contradict one's certainties are explored and appreciated, leading to "the possibility of a new potential for human beings." Instead of desiring certainty and fearing doubt, Feynman commends the reversal of such passions. Instead of striving to escape doubt, he encourages its passionate embrace on the grounds that it is the condition of democratically governed progress.

This understanding can be illuminated further by reference to a distinction made by Bauman (1987) between two kinds of communication. Communication may be preoccupied with prescribing for, or "legislating," others' beliefs and actions. This form is based upon the unshakable conviction that the prescription is correct, and it is often accompanied by the understanding that others, in general, will be the beneficiaries of its application. Such conviction, when untempered by humility, can produce fascisms of the left, right or center. Alternatively, communication may strive to interpret or understand the other, without prescribing action or belief. The impetus here is not to impose a predetermined set of requirements upon the other but, rather, to facilitate a process of dialogue and negotiation in which mutual learning is fostered.

Passionate humility is clearly more consistent with interpretation than with legislation. Any inclination or compulsion to impose prescribed beliefs or acts upon the other is checked and qualified by a humbling acknowledgment that the other is a subject, not an object, and is, therefore, endowed with the human capacity of independent agency, including thought, feeling, belief, value, and judgment. Indeed, the other is only fully recognized as an active, participating subject through a process of dialogue. Thinking and talking together—exchanging words—makes feeling together—compassion—possible. A condition of humility, perhaps, is a willingness to "let go" (symbolically, if not also materially) and to accept that one's life might be enriched, rather than impoverished, in the process. It is in the pairing of passion with humility that compassion is enabled.

In principle, at least, action inspired and guided by passionate humility contains within it the possibility of engendering greater mutual understanding and closer, more direct communication. Such understanding and communication is predicated upon ideas associated by Foucault (1986) with the care of the self. Care of the self acts in conjunction with efforts to increase one's awareness of the inclination to legislate others' behaviors. Taken together, self-care and reflexive awareness seek to interpret or understand these behaviors instead. Such an approach poses a challenge to the traditional vision of administrative practices deriving from management science and a mood of modernism. It is, instead, more open-ended and more resonant with a postmodern mood in which multiple realities and possibilities for action are acknowledged and celebrated.

CARE OF THE SELF AND OF THE OTHER

Whether in the context of implementing policies or in the context of organizational practices, how is an administrator to deal with desires and fears that are stimulated in pluralistic settings? Administrators may be reluctant to communicate about certain tendentious, taboo, or otherwise "delicate" matters because they anticipate, more or less consciously, that their ambitions (e.g. for their clients or themselves) will be frustrated or that their fears (e.g. of retribution) will be realized. They may experience a tendency either to act out, or project, these feelings onto others without paying attention to the latters' sensibilities, or to bottle up these feelings for fear that they will be questioned, rejected, ignored, etc. An alternative path would be to give voice to these feelings in a way that is passionate—that gets expressed—but that is also humble—that recognizes that there are competing desires, fears, agendas.

This view can be illustrated by reference to the classroom. Lack of passion in teaching risks conveying the understanding that the material must be dull or unimportant because the lecturer is clearly bored by it. A lack of humility, on the other hand, risks students feeling that they are being used as a captive audience for the confirmation of the instructor's (closed) agenda. In neither case are students engaged in a Buberian I-Thou manner. Instead, they are treated as depersonalized objects.

In a public agency, the administrator who is passionately committed to a particular view of the world (whether with respect to internal matters vis-à-vis colleagues and subordinates, or with respect to implementation vis-à-vis clients and other members of the public) risks not serving those others. Without humility, their respective views simply collide, as in the cases of the redevelopment director and the nightclub owner, and Ben and his employees. Only a dialogue permits mutual acknowledgment of the possibility of different understandings and interpretations, and the prospect of crafting programs that address local social realities.

Such an ethic of compassion builds on the idea of public administration as public *service* (as contrasted with its not uncommon application as top-down control). This idea of a service ethic does not imply that the administrator or worker becomes subordinate, like an object, to what the public demands as s/he humbly does the bidding of "the customer." But neither does it mean that the administrator becomes the master of the public, arrogantly imposing an impassioned will upon clients who are deemed incapable as active agents ("targets" of service "delivery," in earlier policy implementation language). Instead, it calls for a mode of acting that recognizes and values the presence and contribution of those with local knowledge of the situation in which public services are provided. Public administration then works with the grain of local circumstances and those who have intimate knowledge of local domains. For this to happen, however, technical expertise must be balanced with acknowledgment of the range and relevance of local expertise. Otherwise, a passionate effort to take administrative action and "do something" is likely to provoke resistance and resentment as decisions and programs are imposed upon agency staff or local community "targets."

This argument for passionate humility has affinities with the rejection of the fact-value dichotomy (see, e.g., Rein 1976) and the politics-administration split (e.g., Baier, March, & Saetren 1986; Fox 1990; Yanow 1987; 1990). For if facts (Kuhn's "conceptual boxes") are called into being by theories, and the observer affects that which is being observed, the certainty afforded by singular, "objective" knowledge no longer obtains—especially when implementors are no longer seen as "merely" carrying out administrative "orders" (but, rather, are seen themselves as interpreting legislative and other directives). In such conceptual circumstances, the authority of the non-local technical expert is not automatically privileged over those attuned to local circumstances.

The problem we are addressing is akin to one that Argyris and Schön (1974) discussed at some length, identifying the behavior as, among other things, self-sealing. They documented the inclination of executives and managers to be committed to their own ways of seeing, and their inability not only to see from another's point of view, but also to reflect on their own knowledge and its limits. In calling for the development of double-loop learning—learning to learn—and in later work on reflective practice, Schön, with his co-author and solo, sought a solution to the behavioral limitations of blinkered passion. In calling for such passion to be wedded to humility, we are treading a parallel path, but one which is, we feel, less mechanistic, more humanistic, and simpler in a way: we are calling on administrators to look beyond themselves and consider others and (as Schön did) to check their assumptions and test their attributions (e.g., of motives to others), but without requiring them to develop, recognize, or make explicit a theory about learning that commends this process.

When a valued standpoint or agenda is challenged, there is a tendency to defend it or to deny allegiance when mounting a defense is too onerous. Metaphorically speaking, heels are dug in or one takes to one's heels. In each case, there is a preoccupation with protecting routines and, ultimately, with (pre)serving identity in the face of challenges to their continuation. Less common is a response that sees in the challenge, and seizes on it as, an opportunity to appreciate and potentially learn from competing viewpoints. The task for administrative practice is to acknowledge feelings of "fight" and "flight" and to endeavor to take care of (and care for) them. This involves taking care of the self—by developing alternative "strategies," based upon a combination of passion and humility, that strengthen the ability not to be frozen or overwhelmed by such feelings. "Ethical will" is then exercised as, following Kohlberg, a morality based upon habituated adherence to received wisdom, with unexamined convention progressively questioned. In this process, morality becomes more attuned to the uncertainties and complexities of local circumstances (Willmott & Kronstad 1995).

By locating the exercise of passionate humility in the context of dialogue with others, be they co-workers, clients, or community members, we are broadening the individualistic or psychologistic focus of Argyris and Schön's analysis. Administrators, after all, are not solo practitioners: their work is carried out conjointly with others, in the office and outside of it. It is this working encounter with other modes of thought, other modes of being, other passionate convictions concerning appropriate ways to proceed, organizationally and/or programmatically, that requires a measure of humility to leaven those convictions. In this, we are taking a position analogous to Forester's (1999), which calls on practitioners to "deliberate" about their acts, not just to reflect on them. For while reflection is a solo act, deliberation is done in concert with those others involved in the administrative event. As he notes about planners and policy analysts, public administrators, too, rarely can act unilaterally. More typically, they "work in between...interdependent and often conflicting parties..., parties whose mutual distrust and strategic posturing regularly undermine their collaborative problem solving" (ibid.: 2). The passion is there; what makes the deliberative dialogue work is the consideration of others' passionate commitments—that is, the willingness to listen, actively, with the intent of grasping the other's meaning; that comes from humility.

PRACTICAL JUDGMENT AND LOCAL KNOWLEDGE

The exercise of passionate humility depends on an appreciation (in Vickers' [1965] sense) for local knowledge and calls it into play. Local knowledge is contextual knowledge—the knowledge that develops in interaction with the people and programs, operations or objects (physical artifacts) that are specific to a local context. It develops out of experience with the situation in question; and much of it is tacitly known—"a kind of nonverbal knowing that evolves from seeing and[/or] interacting with someone [or some setting or practice] over time" (Hafner 1999). Local people and local workers are far more knowledgeable about the situation than those without such experience. Local knowledge is, then, the mundane, yet nonetheless expert, understanding of, and practical reasoning about, local conditions derived from lived experience.

Local knowledge involves a practical, embodied understanding of the particulars of local situations. It is often unhelpfully juxtaposed against "expert" or "scholarly" knowledge—a term used usually in reference to technical and/or professional expertise that derives from academic training. The former is "scientifically constructed knowledge," based in the academy, while the latter derives from practical reasoning about context-specific events (Greenwood & Levin 1998). In this comparison, "everyday knowledge" is routinely assigned an imperfect and inferior status. However, as Greenwood and Levin note, local knowledge "systems are complex, differentiated, and dynamic" (ibid.: 109). These features enable them to be much more finely attuned to the specificities and lived experience of the locality. In their own way, local knowledge systems embody forms of expertise that suggest their relevance, as well as the importance of paying increased attention to, and placing a higher (than heretofore) value upon, them (Yanow 1999; 2000).

The exercise of passionate humility also links to the question of "closure" in respect to administrative decisions. It calls for keeping in mind a certain indeterminacy in face of the impossibility of knowing that all the actors and all their diverse concerns have been recognized and appreciated. Administrators are faced with pressures to act, often in the face of missing data, missing information, and missing or silenced stories. Passionate humility would suggest continuing to keep the dialogue open as much, and as long, as possible. As Patsy Healey notes (1999), we require decision-makers to reflect upon, and to be prepared to justify, the inclusion and exclusion of particular actors and particular stories in their decisions. In this process, it may well become apparent that the presence and contributions of some groups have been excluded, ignored, or otherwise marginalized in indefensible ways. Cultivating humility and openness about existing procedures and programs is one way of incorporating the insight that we never know what we might understand tomorrow that would change those values and practices in which we passionately believe today.

CONCLUDING REMARKS

An argument for passionate humility is especially needed in a world characterized by the possibilities of "administrative evil" (Adams & Balfour 1998), in which the increasing professionalization of administrative training and practice rests ever more on a logic of technical rationality and its associated shortcomings (Ingersoll & Adams 1992; Yanow 1996). Associated with this development is a marginalization and managerialization of ethics in the provision of public service.

It is ironic that the very rationalist values and related organizational mechanisms—bureaucracies and their officers—which aspired to develop a better and more orderly society, and which Weber saw as controlling human (specifically, monarchic, and ecclesiastical) whim, are now themselves becoming tools for containing tensions and contradictions in the operation of capitalist societies, rather than operating as media of progress. In this regard, the challenge is not to sweep away bureaucracy—which is critical for maintaining any complex society—but to minimize its needlessly irrational and destructive effects. One way of facilitating this, we have argued, is to foster an ethos of passionate humility in which commitment to finding ways of improving administrative acts, for example, is coupled with, and guided by, an awareness that all "solutions" are imperfect and that a viable and sustainable way forward is more likely accomplished through dialogue including a sensitivity to local client and employee contexts. As Richard Feynman noted at the end of the passage quoted earlier (in the sentence that forms the epigraph of this essay): "If you know that you are not sure, you have a chance to improve the situation" (quoted in Ferris 1998).

Accordingly, it is attendant upon us to reflect briefly upon the status of our argument for passionate humility as a guiding ethos of the theory and practice of public administration. In commending this ethos, are we not ourselves assuming the role of Bauman's legislators rather than interpreters? Certainly, we have taken a position that we have sought to articulate in a compelling way. We hope that our arguments have been persuasive, or at least provocative, otherwise there would be little point in making them. We do not, however, understand ourselves to be legislating in the sense of seeking to impose an ethos. Nor are we seeking to devalue or displace technical expertise by championing a sentimental or romantic idea of humility. A commitment to developing the traditional, technical expertise relevant for public administration remains undiminished, but it is tempered by a revitalized appreciation of its limits.

Our self-understanding is one of contributing to a debate about what ethos will underpin and guide the theory and practice of public administration as we move into a new millennium. We acknowledge that our argument could conceivably be converted into a program of indoctrination designed to create a cadre of public administrators circumscribed by the doctrine of passionate humility. But this would be a travesty of the ethos of passionate humility that, as we have seen, is concerned to value multiversity and doubt, not to override their importance in the pursuit of its own ethos. Our commendation of passionate humility is intended, at least, to be a contribution to an ongoing process of reflection and interpretation through which the practices that comprise public administration are identified, represented, and transformed.

To this end, it is important to acknowledge the limits of passionate humility as an ethos of conduct. A willingness to engage in dialogue by being open to other values and practices gives no guarantee of reciprocity or influence. Those who are wedded to some alternative ethos and its related set of practices may be unreceptive. If sufficiently threatened, they may indeed even mobilize material and/or ideological resources to marginalize or silence an ethos that does not confirm their own positions, sense of identity, and/or prejudices. Although an ethos of passionate humility may give the best chance to democratic forms of change, it must be recognized that the presence of anti-democratic forces and elements may impede or effectively subvert this potential. In the face of such opposition and setbacks, it is the presence of compassion—thinking, talking, and feeling together in the marriage of passion with humility—that can help forestall the degeneration of a commitment to public service into cynical conformity with its routine public administration.

REFERENCES

Adams, Guy B. and Danny L. Balfour. 1998. *Unmasking Administrative Evil*. Thousand Oaks, CA: Sage.

Argyris, Chris and Donald A. Schön. 1974. *Theory in Practice: Increasing Professional Effectiveness*. San Francisco, CA: Jossey-Bass.

Baier, Vicki Eaton, James G. March, and Harald Saetren. 1986. Implementation and ambiguity. *Scandinavian Journal of Management Studies*. 2(3-4) (May): 197-212.

Bauman, Zygmunt 1987. *Legislators and Interpreters: On Modernity, Postmodernity, and the Intellectuals*. Oxford: Polity Press.

Ferris, Timothy 1998. Mr. Feynman wasn't joking. Review of *The meaning of it all: Thoughts of a citizen scientist*. By Richard P. Feynman. Reading, MA: Helix books/Addison-Wesley. *New York Times Book Review* May 17. 50.

Forester, John 1999. *The Deliberative Practitioner*. Cambridge: MIT Press.

Foucault, Michel 1986. *The Care of the Self*. Harmondsworth: Penguin.

Fox, Charles J. 1990. Implementation research. *Implementation and the Policy Process*, edited by Dennis J. Palumbo and Donald J. Calista. chap. 13, Westport, CT: Greenwood.

Greenwood, D. J. and M. Levin. 1998. *Introduction to Action Research*. Thousand Oaks, CA: Sage.

Hafner, Katie 1999. In real life's shadow, virtual life can pale. *The New York Times*, 26 August. D10.

Hazle, Maline 1992. S.J. Nightclub closes its doors, blames city. *San Jose Mercury News*, 14 May. 1B.

Healey, Patsy 1999. Comments at the theory, policy, and society colloquium. Leiden University, NL. 25-26 June.

Henriques, Diana B. 1994. The emperors of ice cream. *New York Times Book Review*, 19 June. 12.

Ingersoll, Virginia Hill, and Guy Adams. 1992. *The Tacit Organization*. Greenwich, CT: JAI Press.

Mokhiber, Russell and Robert Weissman. 1999. Weekly column, in Focus on the corporation. Internet list-serve corp-focus@essential.org. Posted to the Critical Management Studies Workshop list c-m-workshop@mailbase.ac.uk August 24.

Noddings, Nel. 1984. *Caring*. Berkeley, CA: University of California.

Rein, Martin. 1976. *Social Science and Public Policy*. New York: Penguin.

Tronto, Joan C. 1993. *Moral Boundaries: A Political Argument for an Ethic of Care*. New York: Routledge.

Vickers, Sir Geoffrey. 1965. *The Art of Judgment*. London: Chapman & Hall.

Willmott, Hugh and Bjorn Kronstad. 1995. Business ethics: Restrictive or empowering? *Journal of Business Ethics*. 14:445-464.

Yanow, Dvora. 1987. Toward a policy culture approach to implementation. *Policy Studies Review*. 7(1):103-115.

———. 1990. Tackling the implementation problem: Epistemological issues in implementation research. *Implementation and the Policy Process*, edited by Dennis J. Palumbo and Donald J. Calista. Westport, CT: Greenwood. Chap. 14.

———. 1996. *How Does a Policy Mean? Interpreting Policy and Organizational Actions*. Washington, DC: Georgetown University Press.

———. 1997. Passionate humility in interpretive policy and administrative analysis. *Administrative Theory and Praxis*. 19(2) (September/October):171-177.

———. 1999. Collective organizational learning and local knowledge. Prepared for the panel "Collective, non-communitarian ways of knowing," Society for Organizational Learning Research Greenhouse on Managing knowledge, learning and change, Cambridge, MA. 8-9 October.

———. 2000. *Conducting Interpretive Policy Analysis*. Newbury Park, CA: Sage.

PART THREE

Challenges in Public Organizations

INTRODUCTION

Francesco Cerase explores the further implications of adopting market and managerial principles in conducting public action. The focus is on the risk of losing sight of public interest, blurring the distinctiveness of publicness, and turning citizens into customers. Furthermore, the article argues that behind the curtain, which announces the triumphant advance of marketization and managerialism, the scene is quite confused both on the side of theory and on that of action plans. With the demise of the public sector, the dismantling of the public administration and its regulative buffers, the new century may find itself with a much higher degree of social inequality and a much more defenseless citizen than the developments of the previous one had produced. As an answer: a move for the comeback and recovery of public administration is foreseeable, and here lies the challenge to administrative theory and practice. The challenge concerns reinventing government—this time by reinstating a notion of publicness—and it concerns public administrators' ethos and practice. But a third issue underlies the first two, and it concerns agency. Who is going to pick up the challenge?

Michael Diamond questions the future of organizational membership. New technologies such as e-commerce and wireless Internet access, globalization, and atomization, are external factors that will inevitably impact the future of organizations and the meaning of affiliation and employment. His essay is a step in beginning to address this quandary from the perspectives of chaos, complexity, and psychoanalytic theories.

Clarke and Clegg point out that new forces for change have acted as a catalyst in transforming much of public sector provision: the insistent interventions of impatient government politicians; new demands created by social change; transformed thinking about the nature of effective management; and heightened consumer awareness. These have combined with much tighter financial controls; close external scrutiny of spending and performance; and renewed commitments to quality in public service delivery, to encourage a climate of improved performance. The authors argue that the new wave of management thinking in the public sector has an explicit emphasis on the management of change with the object of a metamorphosis in organization culture. The aim is to improve the quality of service by moving the locus of managerial authority and budgetary responsibility from the policy center, closer to the point of delivery, getting closer to the public and attempting to shift the balance of power in favor of those who the organization is intended to serve. While the financial and political constraints imposed by central governments, which have lost sympathy with the values and practices of public enterprise, have limited the possibilities for innovation, often public organizations have responded to their newly insecure position with a creative engagement that has seen positive results. A boldness and innovation has been released where, before, there may have been conformity and tradition. Critical for the survival of democratic public enterprise will be the capacity to change and respond to new social demands as they arise.

Ralph Hummel introduces to public administration a long-standing dispute between Herbert Simon and the philosopher Hubert Dreyfus over the assumptions underlying artificial intelligence. His argument pursues the likelihood that computers will never encompass human intelligence as a whole, but that human intelligence is being reduced to the level of computers.

9

The Demise and Forseeable Comeback of Public Administration

———————————— *Francesco P. Cerase*

ON MARKETIZATION AND MANAGERIALISM:
IMPLICATIONS FOR THE PUBLIC ADMINISTRATION

At the turn of the century, *public* administration appears to be shaken in its very foundations. The emphasis on due process and rules appears to be old-fashioned and dysfunctional. In its place, all over the world, market ideology and managerialism are being upheld as the guiding ideas and principles to sustain public action and inspire the reform of the public sector (Olsen and Peters 1996; Kettl 1997).

Conceived as a shift towards a new paradigm often described as the "new public management" (Hood 1996: 268; Wright 1994:103-108), couched in the term "reinventing government" (Osborne and Gaebler 1992; Gore 1993), or expressed simply as running government like a business, the ubiquity of the process is further reflected in the spreading of "managarialese" as the new Latin (Czarniawska 1999:108). All over the world, privatization and entrepreneurism, together with "accountingization" (Hood 1995: 93), downsizing, cost-efficiency, competitiveness, have become dominant, central themes and catchwords in public administration discourse.

This is not to say that no attention has been paid to "variations" on the theme, such as different "initial endowment" and national experiences, the problems of forcing complex context-rich realities into abstract, or simple categories and summary productivity numbers (Hood 1995; 1996; Olsen and Peters 1996; Bekke, Perry, James, and Toonen 1996). Indeed, the specific features of the national contexts often emerge as the decisive variables in explaining the intensity of the process, the means and contents of which distinguish one national case from another (including the different capacity for learning the process on the part of public administrators). Yet, the emphasis has been less on differences and variations than on homogenization.

Two major concomitant developments make the process appear irreversible. On one hand, marketization and managerialism are often conceptualized and analyzed both as being part of the globalization process which is encompassing the world, and of the subsequent demise of the nation-states; on the other, they are considered a remedy to the ills of public bureaucracies and a valid answer both to shortcomings and failures of bureaucracy, and to its inadequacy as an organizational form in the new context.

Although it involves social, political, cultural, and economic dimensions and relationships, globalization appears very much dominated by the same market ideology (with the market as the primary steering mechanism) behind economic rationalism and neo-liberalism doctrine. More to the point, inasmuch as globalization implies both a new dynamics of accumulation (Tickell and Peck 1995) and a new regulatory system (transnational agreements and conventions, international standards and so forth). The dynamics of national economies is no longer considered autocentric, and it is assumed that nation-states' regulatory power will inexorably be superseded. Indeed, national borders are revealing an increasing vulnerability in the face of global networks and communication, and states are losing control over an increasing number of aspects related to the organization of social life. Whether conceptualized in terms of "hollowing-out" (Rhodes 1994) or "retreat" (Wright 1994) the nation-state is being increasingly called into question as an adequate institution for understanding and regulating social life.

Of course, the question is far from being settled. Because, from quite a different perspective, in spite of flexible production, flexible labor systems, and new enterprise systems, the so-called "global-local nexus" is not yet sustained by a new "institutional fix" (Tickell and Peck 1995), but more to the point, as Cooper and Yoder aptly put it, not everyone is ready to admit that the nation-states "will ... evaporate anytime soon" (Cooper and Yoder 1999: 198). Although the action of Western European states, in the context of the EU for example, has become more "indirect, more discreet and more bartered," still the central states "retain a nodal decision-making position" (Muller and Wright 1994: 8). Ample evidence shows that states are reshaping strategies and positions in the continuous attempt to safeguard national interests (Jacobsson and Morth 1998), and, in many ways, vulnerability, paradoxically, leads to a new emphasis on cultural and economic boundaries (Kouzmin 1998). Furthermore, Majone argues that privatization in certain fields, inasmuch as it is accompanied by the strengthening and expanding of the state's regulatory capacity in other fields (like competition, environmental or consumer protection), can be interpreted as redefinition of its function rather than a retreat (Majone 1994: 80).

As to implementing administrative reforms aimed at banishing bureaucracy (Osborne and Plastrik 1997) and adopting managerial approaches, the diffusion of the process seems to be even more widespread (Halligan 1996). Next to public administration and civil service systems where the "movement" was put in motion, like in Great Britain (Fry 1995), the process embraces systems that are notoriously affected by various problems of malfunctioning and inefficiencies—the Italian case appears to be one of these (Cassese 1993: 9-10; Cerase 1990: 14-20). In the latter case, the adoption of managerial principles may indeed be considered as the only possible way to face these problems. But the process is also under way in cases of "self-confident and powerful civil service systems" like France (Olsen and Peters 1996:19), or in Japan, where top state bureaucracy was a pillar on which national identity and stability was built and still rests (Muramatsu and Krauss 1996; Cerase 1999).

That the retreat of the state, or its "reconceptualization" as more softly put by Olsen (1998: 324), deeply affects public administration systems is quite understandable. It is the fact that these implications will be different according to the size and scope of the existing public sector, government policies, ideological commitment, and other factors (Wright 1994). Specific state apparatuses may have become obsolete, may need downsizing, merging, and restructuring. Whether this also implies doing away with public bureaucracies, however, is quite a different question. There is an expectation that the adoption of managerial rules and practice will do away with red tape and many types of maladministration, such as diseconomy, counter productivity, inertia, ineffectiveness, wastage, and delayed responses (Caiden 1991). However, that managerialism implies superseding bureaucracy as a way of organizing administrative activity is, to say the least, doubtful. In arguing with postmodern imagery, Thompson reviews some of the basic features of bureaucratic work organization—in particular centralization and hierarchy—and maintains that the burial of bureaucracy is once more premature (Thompson 1993: 190-194). His argument can be directed *a fortiori* to the managerial critique. Aucoin goes even further. He also reviews hierarchy, specialization, and standardization as the basic features of bureaucracy and sees in them the "organizational means to promote democratic control, direction and accountability" (Aucoin 1997: 295). If the latter—he argues—as well as effective public policy, productive public management, and responsive public service, are the ends that public management must serve, then "the bureaucratic model is essential to good public management and good public management is essential to good governance," and this is why bureaucracy will survive into and in the twenty-first century (ibid.: 291-292). But is there room for *public* management in the coming century, and if so, what space should it occupy? And what is to be understood by *good* public management?

In spite of counter-arguments, the prevailing view is that marketization and managerialism will lead to a demise of the public sector and public administration, at least in the way these have emerged in the course of the past century up to the most recent developments. As Hood recalls, new public management is in contrast with *progressive* public administration and is supposed to be pushing it into extinction (as models, of course). But as an organizational model, progressive public administration upheld, among other things, the principles of distinguishing clearly between the ethos of the public sector and that of the private one. It also maintained "buffers against political and management discretion by means of an elaborate structure of procedural rules..." (Hood 1995: 93-94). What is at stake, then, is much more than red tape; in question is a way of organizing and managing administrative activity in order to put into effect a new organizational design and management practice more consistent with market principles and ideology.

Nowadays disentanglement and disengagement are the words most often associated with government strategies related to public action at all levels. Dismantling the public sector, relinquishing public ownership, and direct management responsibility in all fields are proposed as the only viable ways of getting out of budget deficit and turning the provision of services to an efficient and effective practice. That some of these proposals are well based is indisputable. But before throwing away the baby with the bath water, it is worth paying at least cursory attention to their further implications.

LOSING SIGHT OF THE PUBLIC INTEREST

One basic task of government in the modern state, at least in its most advanced democratic form, is that of interpreting and safeguarding the general interest of the polity and society, and seeing that the pursuit of legitimate individual interests fits with it. Of course, the contents of this "fitness" cannot be defined *a priori* and once and for all. They depend, among other things, on the way interests coalesce, organize, and mobilize. Yet, there lies the crux of the regulatory capacity of a modern public administration as an institution and the specific challenge and difficulty of *public* management: in facilitating the satisfaction and fulfillment of individual needs and pursuits by reconciling them with the fostering of social betterment. Combining one with the other is not a simple task. It involves many tensions and cross-pressures, which are not easy to manage. It requires a great deal of interpretation and, unavoidably, it rests on the exercise of discretion. Nevertheless, only inasmuch as it succeeds in doing so, does public administration contribute to the strengthening of civic virtues and social development.

Facilitation consists, primarily, of reducing uncertainty and transaction costs in social relations. It is on that ground that institutions can provide, in North's terms, the regulative frame to sustain economic growth (North 1990). But with the welfare state or, more precisely, with the shape it took in the post WWII period, in the European context, as a *centralized welfare state-project* (Olsen 1998: 323, italics in the orig.), public intervention has embraced redistributive measures and spread to direct satisfaction of individual needs as a way of advancing the contents of fairness, equity, and well-being in social life one step further. Therefore, the pursuit of *public* interest has become even more complex. The tension arising from the individual's expectations, and his feeling he has a right to see public action facilitating the pursuit of his own legitimate interests as well as granting given-free services according to universalistic principles, has become even more difficult to manage. The task of legitimizing a given social order and ensuring social integration attributed to administrative action has become much more differentiated. The major tasks of administrative action have been, increasingly, to advance the substance of common good, such as buffering conflicts of interests between groups, movements, and single individuals; providing a channel for social mobility; giving voice to new subjects; and absorbing and neutralizing the destructive impact of social discrimination and marginalization.

These developments are well reflected in the increasing contrasts within the concept of citizenship. Legal elements of citizenship based on an "atomistic and rights-carrying self" have come to clash with ethical elements based on "an embedded social self" (Zanetti and Carr 1999:206). The "liberal" notion that the only purpose of society is that "of allowing maximum individual liberty," has come to clash with the social democratic notion of ethical citizenship which "incorporates commitment to the public good, popular control of government, some meaningful degree of substantive (material) equality, acceptance of civic virtue, and commitment to active participation by the citizenry in government" (ibid.: 207). But, up to a point, the contrasts have been managed: legal and ethical elements, rights, duties, and obligations have found a way to coexist, giving substance to an enlargement and enrichment of citizenship. Moreover—a point worth noticing in the context of this discussion—it is the ethical dimension of citizenship that "provides the normative foundations for the role of the public administrator" (Cooper and Yoder 1999: 196).

But once market ideology extends to public action, the notion of a public administration called to safeguard the public interest risks being obfuscated (Box 1999; Wright and Hart 1996). At the societal level, marketization emphasizes and fuels a process of fragmentation of interests. The awareness of societal ties, which hint at the existence of a common interest, tends to be lost and the commitment of the individual part to the polity as a whole obscured or neglected. Each individual part tends to perceive itself independently of the "other" and of the "whole." Alliances and connections are finalized to strengthen competitiveness. Relationships are conceptualized in terms of exchanges and negotiations. Even mutuality and reciprocity are "rediscovered" as a mere mechanism of exchange and allocation of resources. But what counts most—once again—is that all elements and aspects of human and social life tend to be reduced to commodities. The fiction of generalized commodification appears, once more, to be "the organizing principle of society," and the self-destructiveness of this notion (Polanyi 1944: chap. 6 in particular) appears to be forgotten.

Running government like a business is probably the most crude and compact translation in managerialese of the adoption of market principles in public management. With managerialism, fragmentation tends to extend itself to public action and administrative tasks. Once each one of these has become a "business" in itself—whatever that might be—building a cooperative spirit and ensuring coordination between the different administrative units and sectors may turn out to be hardly less difficult than it is in a bureaucratic arrangement. Moreover, keeping sight of systematic links between administrative actions in the different fields is no longer a major concern. Links are rather perceived as contingent, shifting ties according to convenience and circumstance. Make the administrative units as autonomous as possible and more manageable, reduce operational costs, eliminate waste, increase productivity, raise the performance standards—to mention only a few—these are the arguments behind the introduction of managerialism. This may indeed be what the public sector needs if it is to operate according to the principle of "value for money." But what measures the product of administrative activity may not correspond to what measures its results in terms of satisfaction of social needs or demands (Kettl 1997; Cerase 1998, chap. 3). This fact should not be overlooked, otherwise the risk is high that objectives conceptualized in terms of standing up to given productivity standards, cost-cutting, and so on, may turn into ends in themselves. The fact that the connection between output—in terms of product of administrative activity—and outcome—in terms of its social impact—is not easy to establish, is not a good reason to forget that it is on the basis of the latter that public action claims legitimacy. And legitimacy, Brunsson and Olsen remind us, is based on beliefs about what organizations and institutions are for (Brunsson and Olsen 1998:19).

In a paper of not too many years ago, Frederickson, referring to theory and practice in U.S. public administration from the 1940s up to the 1960s, stated, "In running government the administrator's job was to be efficient (getting the most service possible for available dollars) or economical (providing an agreed-upon level of services for the fewest possible dollars)." "It should be no surprise, therefore that issues of inequity and injustice were not central to public servants or to public administration theorists" (Frederickson 1990: 228). His argument was that, after that, a theory of social equity as a "third pillar" for public administration developed in order to reconcile economy and efficiency with fairness in public action. The same issues may very well be raised today with the adoption of managerial arrangements all over the world. Indeed, the difficulties of reconciling market values and managerial principles with social equity and fairness may be even more acute for two concomitant reasons: the fact that a distinctive notion of publicness may get lost, and that citizens may turn into customers.

BLURRING THE DISTINCTIVENESS OF PUBLICNESS

One of the two doctrine reversals on which new public management is based, states Hood, is that of "lessening and removing differences between the private and the public sectors" (Hood 1995: 94). In the reformed management setting, recalls Box, "the public-private distinction is "essentially obsolete," and management is generic across sectors" (Box 1999: 21). The implication is clear (and what has been discussed in the previous paragraph has already hinted at it): organizing public activities is not different from organizing private business. The distinction between the logic of managing public activities and that of pursuing private concerns is blurred in the name of the superior rules of the market. What are we to retain, then, of the specificity and distinctiveness of publicness?

"Publicness" is (was) usually associated with the formal legal structure, or ownership, of an organization as well as the influence of political authority. In short, the *public* nature of the resources being used represented the basic element of publicness. That "public administration is politically authorized, funded by the enforced collection of taxes and other revenue enhancement devices," is the starting statement adopted by Luton in his search for an answer to the question "what does it mean to say, 'public' administration" (Luton 1996: 143). The statement, however, comes after having pointed out the differences between *business* administration and *public* administration. "Business administration has as its ultimate purpose, maximizing profit, but in the allocation of public goods and services, public administration's ultimate purpose is promotion of the public interest" (ibid.: 141). Moreover, "public administrators have a public-interest attitude, a sense of responsibility to the public. They look beyond the interests of their agency, having a concern for the more general impacts of their professional activities" and "in order for a good or service to be 'public,' it needs to be available to people who have not participated in a market exchange" (ibid.:140 and 139). In other words, the notion of publicness assumes that a market orientation is extraneous to public action and that the latter aims at safeguarding and enhancing the public interest and is inspired by public spiritedness. But the previous discussion on the effects of the pervasiveness of market values and rules casts doubts that a public interest perspective may remain dominant in orienting public actions.

Paradoxically, managerialism in no way questions the fact that public administrations are assumed to act in order to safeguard the public interest. It is because of that that public administrations are legitimated to claiming and using *public* resources. Indeed, inasmuch as the emphasis on "value for money" calls for a management able to combine maximum efficiency with best results, it appears to be fully oriented to public interest. Yet, this remains the crux of the question. The *public* nature of the resources used to fund public administrations' budgets calls also for a guarantee—in terms of democratic procedure, control, and accountability—that the citizens have their say in what they are used for. And it is with this guarantee that market values and managerial principles may turn out to be even harder to reconcile than the bureaucratic arrangements they are suppose to supersede.

TURNING CITIZENS INTO CUSTOMERS

"Public administration," argued Frederickson, "understands and practices social equity" (Frederickson 1990: 235). This was possible because it was *public*, because administrators perceived themselves as *public* servants and people perceived directing their demands to a *public* administration. If citizenship is the concept which has mediated between the individual and the public spheres and unified them at the same time, public administration has provided the ground on and through which this mediation and combining have occurred. As Cooper and Yoder point out, the ethical tradition of citizenship, embedded in the community of interest, has gradually democratized public life and provided a normative basis for public administrative ethics (Cooper and Yoder 1999: 199). The specific trust and fiduciary element in the relationship between public administrations and citizens, insist Cooper and Yoder, is still based, among other things, on the assumption that they work for the public interest, i.e. on public spiritedness. "Public spiritedness is about respecting and enhancing the public good and the rights and obligations of the citizenry over one's personal interests and contributing to the process of citizens' development. Public spiritedness also places service to the citizenry over service to one's department, organization, or political superiors" (ibid.: 203). How much of this can be retained once running government like a business leads to a removal of the distinctions between public and private sectors and to an obfuscation of the notion of public interest? Or, once the commitment to public service is reduced "to technical-instrumental market functions not unlike the manufacture and marketing of a consumer product" (Box 1999: 19)?

In public administrations, superseding bureaucratic rule in favor of managerialism is usually presented as a way of paying more attention to individuals' demands and needs and ensuring higher satisfaction, and this may indeed be so. Yet, the inspiration to market values and the adoption of managerial principles may deeply affect the concept of citizenship and radically change the relationships between public administration and citizens. First of all, the reliance on market mechanisms tends to extend commodification to the public sphere and, with it, to citizenship (Zanetti and Carr 1999). Commodification tends to recast the concept of citizenship by unbalancing the coexistence of legal and ethical elements in favor of the former. Citizens become mainly identified as owners, consumers, and customers, and this has many faceted consequences. From the citizen's side, customerization makes people more aware, alert, and watchful of what they are getting for what they are paying. The importance of this should not be underestimated, especially in countries where the notion that public services should be appreciated also for what they cost to the tax-payer is quite weak. But at the same time, customerization of citizenry may weaken solidarity and social equity. Commitment to public good and obligations to the polity tend to become less cogent than expecting satisfaction to one's own rights. "Customers are people to be persuaded and sold an image, a product, or a service rather than people who deliberate and decide" (Box 1999: 36). The mediation and combining of individual and public spheres performed by the concept of citizenship appears to be less needed. A customer is a person who thinks in terms of convenience and self-interest in the face of what he/she is about to buy; his/her focus is on individual equity.

From the public administrator's side, customerization introduces an element of direct transparency in the relationship between the individual "citizen-customer" and the administration, facilitates the measurement and evaluation of the performance of the single administrative actor, and makes the latter more directly accountable. The professional skills required become more clearly connected to the contents of the specific demand addressed to the administration than to the regulations about how to deal with it. All this, also, should not be underestimated, particularly in countries where administrators often tend to conceive of themselves as being responsible only for legalistic interpretation of the "rule." Yet, not necessarily does all this spur civic-mindedness. Nowadays, argues Jun, one major difficulty in encouraging public administrators to become civic-minded "stems from an emphasis on strong professionalism and managerialism in public administration, which focuses more on the improvement of internal management, rule enforcement, program implementation, and employee performance. The pressure for internal efficiency and productivity often undermines administrator's sense of social responsibility to citizens and community" (Jun 1999: 218).

Finally, without undermining the importance of actions undertaken to safeguard consumers' rights or that of consumers' associations, what counts in the context of this discussion is that the emphasis on "pleasing the customer" may push into the background the fact that some may have less means than others to buy and "be pleased." It introduces a subtle distinction between those who can and those who cannot afford buying and "being pleased." Moreover, inasmuch as customerization encourages citizens to act in self-interest, it may bring with it a tendency to question whether everyone is contributing their fair share (Zanetti and Carr 1999: 209), and have a new, oblique divisive impact. More in general, the closer connection of state action to economic conditions has evident effects on social exclusion. Since the 1980s, welfare regimes have become less oriented towards generalized standards and norms. State regulations have become much more differentiated. As it is, they no longer appear to favor those who are economically underprivileged. On the contrary, both new state regulations and measures aimed at restricting eligibility for benefits—and in some cases the outright elimination of benefits—as well as state inactivity have made the distribution of welfare benefits even more subject to economically uneven conditions, and the state has lost ground to the market and the family as an essential factor of social reproduction (Falkner and Talos 1994: 71-72).

A CONFUSED SCENARIO

To doubt the one-directedness of the implications of marketization and managerialism, to address attention to their further implications for public administration, citizenship, and social inequality, is only one side of the story. The other is that behind the curtain, which announces the triumphant, self-celebrating, homogenizing advance of marketization and managerialism, the scene is quite confused both on the side of theory and on that of action plans. Contrasting "moves" and "voices" make up a very noisy and paradoxical scenario. Not that, in themselves, confusion and chaos are detrimental. However, a brief glance at some of the contrasting elements and paradoxes is enough to realize that it is hard to say how this scenario will evolve. Indeed, what is being said, or the courses of action being suggested on the scene, can be concocted in many stories and articulated in many plots (on this notion, cf. Czarniawska 1999: 64-66) that not only escape one single "direction," but risk colliding with one another. A few examples drawn from the previous discussion may be enough to make the point.

On the Effects of Globalization

At the beginning of this discussion, attention was addressed to globalization. Its implications go quite beyond the retreat and reshaping of the regulatory functions of nation-states. They extend, among other things, to the emergence of a globalizing culture and to the erosion of national citizenship that has evolved with the transformation of the nation-state. Reference to the global village, to the borderless society, has become a common way to summarize the new development project beyond the horizon of the single nation state. Yet, seldom in history has there been a similar outburst of fragmented pushes for recognition in independent "states" as the only way to assert ethnic national identities and safeguard nationalistic interests. Localized cultures and institutions continue to be emphasized as one major interpretative variable to make sense of events around the world. In spite of official declarations of international bodies and frequent evocation in media discourse, global citizenship remains a hollow-concept.

On the Distinction Between Policy Making and Implementation

Administrative and organizational thinking appears to be pervaded by the conviction that the two-stage models implying "a clear distinction between policy making and implementation, or politics and administration, have been found inadequate" (Brunsson and Olsen 1998: 17). But, at the same time, a lot of energy and effort are being spent on trying to draw a line between what are to be the responsibilities of the administrators and those of the elected officials in charge, under the assumption that they do not impinge on each another. Consequently, great emphasis is being put on corporatizing the public sector in autonomously run units, while the need for cooperative synergic actions within the administration is felt to be more acute than ever.

On the Authoritative Structure of Bureaucratic Arrangements

One recurring attack to bureaucratic arrangement concentrates on the stifling effect its authoritative structure has on creativity. Furthermore, the escape from the bureaucratic "iron cage" is envisaged as the only way to "humanize" administrative work. Yet, few things appear as paradoxical as the obnubilation with which the fierce rejection of bureaucratic authoritarianism is replaced by the acquiescent acceptance and submission to managerial rule and control. That the latter may impose flexibility, undermine work-niches, and upset self-pleasing routines and what not, is indisputable; that it can spur imagination and creativity remains an open question.

On the Implications of Standardization

As Brunsson reminds us, modern society is possible because human action is highly coordinated (1998: 203). To hierarchies and markets considered as the principal forms of social coordination and control, he adds standardization. With norms and directives, standards represent a third type of rules. Whereas the main characteristic of norms concerns their internalization, and that of directives their imperativeness, standards are different inasmuch as they are voluntary (Brunsson and Jacobsson 1998: 14-17). Besides a coordination function, the importance of standardization concerns a more effective use of information, simplification of procedures, and large-scale production advantages (ibid.: 23-24). Standards are spreading and gaining increasing attention in all fields—comment Brunsson and Jacobsson—and the growing influence of standard-setting organizations on the global scene is emphasized. A great deal of networking (and conflicts) of interest accompanies the issuing of standards. The more they are adhered to, the more influential standard-setters become. But the more difficult it also is for potential recipients to disregard them, the more standards assume the character of directives. But then to continue to refer to the control they exercise as stemming from a voluntary acceptance is a euphemism. "How did the state gradually get a handle on its subjects and their environment?" asks Scott (1998: 2). By creating standard grids whereby anything could be "centrally recorded and monitored." Indeed, in due time "these state simplifications, the basic givens of modern statecraft" acquired "the force of law" (ibid.:3).

On the Rejection of Instrumental Action

Criticism, if not rejection, of the notion of instrumental action, and with it of means-end rationality, is a recurrent theme in organizational and administrative literature. Concern with communicative behavior and discourses on ethics and values, an interest in sense-making—note Brunsson and Olsen (1998: 17)—have taken the place of instrumental action in explaining cooperation and civilized conflict resolution, and led to a renewed interest in the development of loyalties in human interaction. Against the domineering managerial discourse and commodification, however, a great deal of this may turn out to be little more than the wishful outcome of criticism. For one thing, an undercurrent of means-end rationality is still the prevailing tone in discourse on managerial predicament and control. Next, commodification is an all-embracing, generalized process.

Communication, itself reduced to fiction, is a commodity, and at the core of the concept of commodity is the notion of instrumentality.

On Learning and Purposeful Action

In management discourse, growing emphasis is placed on learning (organizational learning and learning organizations) (Gherardi 1995). Indeed, reform itself has been conceptualized as a "learning process" (Olson 1993) through the development of adaptive capacities, organized collective efforts directed at problem-solving, purposeful actions, the stress on better ways to manage and induce cooperation, and on planning and design. But there is also ample recognition that the learning process itself is hampered by ambiguity and uncertainty; that, whatever the actors' intentionality, they are afflicted by uncertainty and powerlessness; and that projects are subject to tentativeness, and flow of events to quasi-casualness. The discrepancy on this point is made clear by comparing the claim supporting experiential learning in reforming processes to the way in which learning from experience functions in practice. As Olsen and Peters point out, on one hand it is expected that "experience should improve the intelligence, effectiveness, and adaptability of governance and institutional design"; on the other hand, ample evidence shows that "causal and normative beliefs, behavioral patterns, and institutional designs do not easily change in the light of experience" (Olsen and Peters 1996: 2-3).

On Customer-Satisfaction Oriented Action

In the previous discussion, attention was given to the fact that managerial principles and rules in running public administrations are introduced in order to enhance the administrative capacity to meet citizen-customers' needs or to make administrative actions more responsive and accountable to citizen-customers' demands. The underlying assumption is that administrators deal with citizens who are able to translate their needs in customers' demands and be watchful that they receive adequate satisfaction. In fact, whatever the number of potentially eligible citizens may be, not all of them are equally able to turn needs into actual demands or, even more precisely, into properly formulated requests to the administration institutionally in charge. Nor are all of them equally able to check that administrative actors be accountable to their demands. Indeed, not only may people have different possibilities and capacities to express their needs and expect that they be met, but some may not be able to do so at all (Cerase 1998: 63). This disparity hides a subtle, but no less pernicious, form of exclusion. Moreover—and the previous discussion on the implications of customerization has hinted at this—public actions oriented to satisfy customers' needs may not at all be congruent with measures addressed to citizens in need (Haque 1999). Quite paradoxically, privatization and cuts in public spending are often associated with the purpose of enhancing customer satisfaction, but the fact that they may imply elimination or reduction of measures for citizens in need is overlooked.

THE CHALLENGE FOR THE NEW CENTURY

It might very well be that the contrasting "moves" and "voices" mentioned in the above paragraph are expressions, like many others, of the different languages that make up the vital "polyphonic and polysemic" world some authors refer to (Czarniawska 1999: chap. 7). As such, they may be able to coexist and enliven the scene for quite some time. But it may also turn out that the noise they make is an attempt to distract attention from the hard fact that purposeful *public* action is being dissolved in a market fiction, and that with it, citizens may have a much less active role than expected. Once they are turned into customers, they may have a lot to say about how their demands are to be met. But substantive questions related to who is going to decide which demands deserve priority, and which claims are legitimate and how this is going to be decided may escape their control. In spite of so much emphasis on accountability and responsiveness, the meaning of their deeper social implications may be lost.

With the demise of the public sector, the dismantling of the public administration and its regulative buffers, the new century may find itself with a much higher degree of social inequality and a much more defenseless citizen than the developments of the previous one had produced. As an answer, a move for the recovery and comeback of public administration is foreseeable. But the answer can hardly come as a mere swinging back of the pendulum, as an attempt to restore the past. Here lies the challenge to administrative theory and practice, and it is two-fold. On one hand it concerns a way to reinvent government, but this time by reinstating a notion of publicness. Indeed, government is *not a business*. Surely, as Box puts it, to bemoan the condition of the public sector we have known in no way represents a constructive suggestion to approach the issue. However, "to preserve and enhance the essence of public service within the market context" (Box 1999: 20-21) may be too soft an approach. As Ventriss aptly puts it, market society may "provide the form but not the substantive content of public life" (Ventriss 1998: 98). On the other hand, the challenge concerns public administrators' ethos and practice (at all levels). Quite certainly, in no way can they be thought of—assumed they ever have been—as functionaries *sine ira et studio*. But neither can they be thought of as "employees" devoid of a specific awareness of the public good and civic virtues and attentive only to the goals of their business.

But a third issue underlies the previous two, and it concerns agency. Who is going to pick up the challenge? The development of the modern state can be ascribed to the work, choices, and ambitions, however conflictive, of "historical subjects," "collective actors" who, although gradually and slowly, have learned to confront each other through a civilized, democratic procedure. Today, these subjects appear to be dissolved. The issue itself, with its "modernist" overtone, is superseded by postmodernist thinking. Subjects are "disposed" of. Their place is taken by individuals with a fragmented identity (Zanetti and Carr 1999: 209-10). Here lies, then, the final paradox. A lot of the noise that goes on the scene is due to the attacks of postmodernists. Symposium issues in the journal presumably meant to find a communicative ground in order to conduct a dialogue in a spirit of collegial discourse (Fox and Miller 1996) instead end up with each side restating its own position. Modernization continues to be called for as a panacea to all kinds of public management issues.

REFERENCES

Aucoin 1997. The design of public organizations for the 21st century: Why bureaucracy will survive in public management. *Canadian Public Administration.* 40(2):290-306.

Bekke, H. A. G. M. Perry, L. James, and T. A. J. Toonen, (eds.). 1996. *Civil Service Systems in Comparative Perspective.* Bloomington, IN: Indiana University Press.

Box, R. C. 1999. Running government like a business. Implications for Public Administration Theory and Practice. *American Review of Public Administration.* 29(1):19-43.

Brunsson, N. 1998. Standardisering. *Standardisering,* edited by Nils Brunsson and Bengt Jacobsson. Stockholm: Nerenius & Santérus. chap. 11.

Brunsson, N. and B. Jacobsson. 1998. Den viktiga standardiseringen. *Standardisering,* edited by N. Brunsson and B. Jacobsson. Stockholm: Nerenius & Santerus. chap.1.

Brunsson, N. and J. P. Olsen. 1998. Organization theory: Thirty years of dismantling, and then? *Organizing Organizations,* edited by N. Brunsson and J. P. Olsen. Norway: Fagbokforlaget. 13-43.

Caiden, G. E. 1991. What really is public maladministration? *Public Administration Review.* 51(6):486-493.

Cassese, S. 1993. Introduzione. *Rapporto Sulle Condizioni Delle Pubbliche Amministrazioni.* Rome: Presidenza del Consiglio dei Ministri, Dipartimento per la Funzione Pubblica.

Cerase, F. P. 1990. *Un'amministrazione Bloccata. Pubblica Amministrazione e Società Nell'Italia di Oggi.* Milan: F. Angeli.

———. 1998. Pubblica amministrazione. Un'analisi sociologica. Rome: Carocci.

———. 1999. Winds of change in the Japanese public administration: How strong are they? *Japan and the Mediterranean World,* edited by F.P. Cerase, F. Mazzei, and C. Molteni. Naples: Fridericiana.

Cooper, T. L. and D. E. Yoder. 1999. The meaning and significance of citizenship in a transnational world: Implications for public administration. *Administrative Theory and Praxis.* 21(2):195-204.

Czarniawska, B. 1999. *Writing Management. Organization Theory as a Literary Genre.* Oxford: Oxford University Press.

Falkner, G. and E. Talos. 1994. The role of the state within social policy. *West European Politics.* 17(3):52-76.

Fox, C. J. and H. T. Miller. 1996. Modern/postmodern public administration: A discourse about what is real. *Administrative Theory and Praxis.* 18(1):41-42.

Frederickson, G. H. 1990. Public administration and social equity. *Public Administration Review.* 50(2):228-237.

Fry, G. K. 1995. *Policy and Management in the British Civil Service.* Hemel Hempstead: Prentice.

Gherardi, S. 1995. Organizational learning. *International Encyclopedia of Business and Management,* edited by M. Warner. London: Routlege.

Gore, A. 1993. *Report of the National Performance Review: Creating a Government That Works Better and Costs Less.* Washington, DC: U.S. Government Printing Office.

Halligan, J. 1996. The diffusion of civil service reform. *Civil Service Systems in Comparative Perspective*, edited by H. A. G. M. Bekke, J. L. Perry, and T. A. J. Toonen. Bloomington, IN: Indiana University Press. 268-287.

Haque, M. S. 1999. Citizens' needs vs. market demands in public governance: An extended view. *Administrative Theory and Praxis.* 21(2):288-317.

Hood, C. 1995. The "new public management" in the 1980s: Variations on a theme. *Accounting, Organizations and Society.* 20(2/3):93-109.

———. 1996. Exploring variations in public management reform of the 1980s. (eds.), *Civil Service Systems in Comparative Perspective,* edited by H. A. G. M. Bekke, J. L. Perry, and T. A. J. Toonen. Bloomington, IN: Indiana University Press. 268-287.

Jacobsson, B. and U. Morth. 1998. Paradoxes of Europanization. Stockholm: Score working paper 1998:2.

Jun, Jong. S. 1999. The need for autonomy and virtues: Civic-minded administrators in a civil society. *Administrative Theory and Praxis.* 21(2):218-226.

Kettl, D. F. 1997. The global revolution in public management: Driving themes, missing links. *Journal of Policy Analysis and Management.* 16(3):446-462.

Kouzmin, A. 1998. Globalization and public administration: Enhancing, dismantling or protecting distinctive administrative capacity? An introduction. *Administrative Theory and Praxis.* 20(4):434-438.

Luton, L. S. 1996. What does it mean to say, "public" administration? *Administrative Theory and Praxis.* 18(1):138-146.

Majone, G. 1994. The rise of the regulatory state in Europe. *West European Politics.* 17(3): 77-101.

Muller, W. C. and V. Wright. 1994. Reshaping the state in Western Europe: The limits to retreat. *West European Politics.* 17(3):1-11.

Muramatsu, M. and E. S. Krauss. 1996. Japan: The paradox of success. *Lessons from Experience. Experiential Learning in Administrative Reforms in Eight Democracies*, edited by J. P. Olsen and G. Peters. Oslo: Scandinavian University Press. 214-242.

North, D. C. 1990. *Institutions, Institutional Change, and Economic Performance.* Cambridge: Cambridge University Press.

Olsen, J. P. 1998. Institutional design in democratic contexts. *Organizing Organizations*, edited by N. Brunsson and J. P. Olsen. Norway: Fagbokforlaget. 319-341.

Olsen, J. P. and B. G. Peters. 1996. Learning from experience? *Lessons from Experience. Experiential Learning in Administrative Reforms in Eight Democracies,* edited by J. P. Olsen and B. G. Peters. Oslo: Scandinavian University Press. 1-35.

Olson, O. 1993. Reform as a learning process. *The Reforming Organization*, edited by N. Brunsson and J. P. Olsen. London: Routledge. chap. 11.

Osborne, D. and T. Gaebler. 1992. *Reinventing Government: How the Entrepreneurial Spirit is Transforming the Public Sector from Schoolhouse to Statehouse, City Hall to Pentagon.* Reading, MA: Addison-Wesley.

Osborne, D. and D. Plastrik. 1997. *Banishing Bureaucracy. The Five Strategies for Reinventing Government.* Reading, MA: Addison-Wesley.

Polanyi, K. 1944. *The Great Transformation. The Political and Economic Origins of Our Time.* New York: Holt, Rinehart & Winston.

Rhodes, R. A. W. 1994. The hollowing out of the state: The changing nature of the public service in Britain. *Political Quarterly* (65), pp. 138-151.

Scott, J. C. 1998. *Seeing Like a State: How Certain Schemes to Improve Human Condition Have Failed*. New Haven, CT: Yale University Press.

Thompson 1993. Postmodernism: Fatal Distraction. *Postmodernism and Organizations*, edited by J. Hassard and M. Parker. London: Sage.

Tickell, A. and J. A Peck. 1995. Social regulation *after* Fordism: Regulatory theory, neoliberalism and the global-local nexus. *Economy and Society.* 24(3):357-386.

Ventriss, C. 1998. Swimming against the tide: Reflections on some recent theoretical approaches of public administration theory. *Administrative Theory and Praxis.* 20(1):91- 101.

Wright, V. 1994. Reshaping the state: The implications for public administration. *West European Politics.* 17(3):102-137.

Wright, N. D. and D. K. Hart. 1996. The "public interest": What we are not leaving our posterity. *Administrative Theory and Praxis.* 18(2):14-28.

Zanetti, L. A. and A. Carr. 1999. Exaggerating the dialectic: Postmodernism's "new individualism" and the detrimental effects of citizenship. *Administrative Theory and Praxis.* 21(2):205-217.

10

Adapting to Chaos and Complexity: Organizing the Potential Space

Michael A. Diamond

The future of organizational membership may be in question. New technologies such as e-commerce and wireless Internet access, globalization, and atomization, are external factors that will inevitably impact the future of organizations and the meaning of affiliation and employment. This paper is a tiny step in beginning to address this quandary from the perspectives of chaos, complexity, and psychoanalytic theories. If we accept the premises of chaos and complexity theories, then what are the psychological prerequisites for organizational membership? For example, to what extent are ego strength and an integrated core self necessary requirements of individuals to adapt and manage at the so-called "edge of chaos"? Beyond organization-environment adaptation, what may be required of leaders and followers for a good enough fit between individual and organization?

At the manifest level, I will submit that future leaders and organizational participants need to embrace a new action strategy of (what I will call) *organized disorder*; while at a subliminal level, the ability to do so will require *good enough* emotional development and maturity—a well-*integrated* core self. The ability to humanely and effectively lead and manage organized complexity and chaos will depend upon (1) self-system integrity and authenticity and (2) the capability of leaders to promote and facilitate *good enough organizational cultures* at work.

In the following discussion, I examine chaos and complexity theories of social systems and, simultaneously, proffer some observations of people in changing organizations. Then, in order to fully understand the human challenges of future systems as outlined by chaos and complexity theories, I provide an overview of emotional development from psychoanalytic object relations. It is my assumption that we require a theory of self that fits the adaptational systemic requirements of constantly changing environments, whether or not we describe these landscapes as complex or chaotic. Contemporary psychoanalytic object relations theory is best suited to the task because it is a truly open systems model of mind because the mind is dialectical and relational at its core (Greenberg & Mitchell 1983; Modell 1984; Ogden 1989). This object relational theory of self will, then, provide a deeper comprehension of the necessary and requisite character of relationship between individuals and organizations of the future.

From the perspective of chaos and complexity theories, organizations are non-linear adaptive feedback networks that operate "far from equilibrium." Yet, these systems are often led and managed as bureaucratic structures existing in stable states. If we are to better understand this contradictory phenomenon and the changing fit (misfit) between individual and organization, a re-conceptualization of organizational systems will require a deeper comprehension of the adaptive and maturational dynamics of self-systems. This article addresses that concern. I begin with some observations of changes in the workplace.

OBSERVATIONS ON THE CHANGING WORKPLACE

As we enter the twenty-first century, many companies and public agencies experiment with "bottom-up" processes for strategic planning, dialogue, and organizational change. In some instances, organizational members closer to their constituents and customers and, thereby, farther down the flatter hierarchic structures, are affecting planning and corporate/agency direction. Hence, some cultural, structural, and strategic changes are evident. For instance, organizational visions and policy implementation are becoming better integrated via cross-functional teams, bottom-up processes of participation, and double-loop learning. However, despite attempts at integrative problem solving and decision making, organizational hierarchies and their divisional silos persist with few exceptions. Visions and policies are continually set at higher levels than where the actual work with citizens, customers, and constituents takes place. Divisions and sub-systems are "loosely coupled" and are often well-defended domains within which information is withheld and responsibilities are well-guarded. Some instances of innovative and collaborative planning signify a genuine delegation of authority and power from the top and are frequently, and ironically, a consequence of draconian executive acts of downsizing, re-engineering, and right-sizing, otherwise, euphemisms for job eliminations.

Despite these instances of downsizing in the late 1980s and early 1990s, there is hope in many struggling companies, hospitals, and public agencies as we turn the corner of the new millennium. One can increasingly observe counter-cultural and horizontal and bottom-up organizational activities that reflect leaders' struggles to contend with chaotic processes of social, political, and economic change. Innovative work processes such as cross-functional teams and "team-based" strategic planning may be more commonplace. These horizontal and integrative strategies foster a greater system's reflexivity and double-loop learning, which promote greater adaptation and fitness to complex landscapes and unpredictable futures. Nevertheless, the organizational majority in public and private sectors face familiar and persistent problems with participants' (cognitive and emotional) attachments to over-routinized and over-rationalized social structures. Corporations, in particular, place increasing emphasis on psychological testing and rigorous interviewing of recruits, searching for the "best fit" with their peculiar organizational identity. In some instances, organizational culture assumes a "cult-like" quality promoting homogeneity and illusion of predictability in subordinate performance. Such "strategic" preoccupations and misdirected intentions will have to be overcome so that creativity, adeptness, and resilient boundary maintenance can occur.

Many team-based activities can look and feel as if members (often with the aid of consultants and leaders) are willingly promoting disorder rather than attempting to cope with chaotic external forces. Familiar boundaries between and among organizational members and their constituents (if only momentarily) begin to wither and breakdown as if the empty space at the center of the work group becomes a fantasized image of a whirling funnel or trap door through which traditional organizational culture (e.g. status quo)—artifacts, values, underlying assumptions, strategies and structure—unwittingly escapes. Under these human conditions of organizational change, chaos and complexity aptly describe participants' inner states as well as their external realities. Chaos and complexity are phenomena that exist both inside and outside of self and organization. However, at an intra-personal level of experience, these states are more often associated with primitive anxieties and emotional *disorder*. Not surprisingly, psychological regression and concomitant anxieties over loss of control and uncertainty are often linked to these personal experiences of chaos and complexity. It is partly for this reason that I introduce the concept of organized disorder, because it best signifies the psychological challenge and contradiction of living and working with chaos and complexity. In addition, it depicts the human experience of disorder in an organized context.

Organizational participants' best efforts to adapt to what they perceive and understand about the changing nature of their environment may lead them to willingly question, and sometimes replace, well-worn structures and strategies. In some instances, they may show a willingness to face their anxieties over loss of control, unpredictability, and unfamiliarity. In fact, organizational and personal change is more often a consequence of members' perceptions of crises and their collective sense of urgency, which they assume requires some sort of action.

Nevertheless, environmental landscapes are in constant flux. If organizations and economies are to survive and prosper, they require resilient adaptive feedback networks to do so. Generally, however, organizations have evolved into defensive systems. Hence, resilient, open systems capable of second-order learning and relational authenticity are rare. Management continues to *react* to these challenging transformations of task environment from unconscious and unwitting to collective panic and fear of organizational annihilation.

For many leaders, adaptation to, and planning for, change assumes a collective struggle of making sense out of the non-sense of complexity at many levels of human performance. For instance, complexity and chaos theorists character-ize organizations as adaptive feedback networks that are: (1) non-linear, such that there is no proportionality between cause and effect; (2) fractal, such that measurement is scale dependent and concepts are indeterminate; (3) recursive between scale levels, such that it is easy to get lost; (4) sensitive to initial con-ditions, such that the system is experienced as volatile; (5) replete with feed-back loops and potential bifurcation points; and (6) subject to emergence (Lissack 1999).

Non-traditional methods and strategies for gaining insight and more effectively adapting to change become necessary for members and action researchers. "Organizational diagnoses" (Levinson 1972) based upon narrative data and inter-pretation of "organizational texts" (Kets de Vries & Miller 1987), which incorpo-rate paying attention to thematic patterns and repetitive linguistic structures, proffer greater meaning and deeper understanding of organized complexities than studies grounded in solely factual and quantitative data of organizational performance. In part, leaders' actions designed to fit chaotic and complex environments result from a rejection of old assumptions underlying systems management (such as "stable equilibrium") and a willingness to embrace new assumptions (such as "bounded instability") (Stacey 1996). These new assumptions include a recognition that cre-ativity and innovation emerge out of disorder and chaos. Managing at the so-called "edge of chaos" implies learning in the "here-and-now," skills and competencies of reflective practice that are rarely observed (Argyris & Schön 1996).

Influenced to some degree by chaos and complexity theories, organization the-orists and analysts are beginning to more fully comprehend the non-linear, emer-gent, and unpredictable nature of systems. Mathematicians and natural scientists have recently made discoveries that make it more difficult to deny the complex behavior of organizations. These scientists observe that certain kinds of systems, *nonlinear feedback systems*, operate in a state "far from equilibrium"—at the edge of chaos. In this state, the system generates behavior that is unstable, but because it is unstable within limits, that behavior is called *bounded instability* (Stacey 1996:11).

This organizational state of affairs requires adaptive feedback networks that function as evolving and emerging systems. Despite management's clinging to the mind-set of "stable equilibrium," organizations with ambiguous boundaries, and fluid strategies and structures are becoming more typical when observed in the context of their task environments. When combined with the mind-set of "bounded instability" and practice of "organized disorder," these systems become open, resilient, and somewhat amorphous, crucial instruments of the delivery of services and goods.

Adaptive feedback networks are capable of "self-organizing" and "double-loop learning" (Argyris & Schön 1996). They are reflexive, open, and self-correcting, systems in contrast to more typically bureaucratic, closed, and defensive organizations (Diamond 1993). Hence, they are able to more readily fit the changing environmental landscapes. These adaptive feedback networks signify survival strategies among and between subsystems within systems—communities of evolving systems (Stacey 1996: 81). Such social systems evolve and survive in ways analogous to the natural adaptive strategies of antibiotics. In other words, as Stacey writes: "We use antibiotics as a survival strategy against viruses, but the response of the viruses is to mutate resistant strains; our antibiotic survival strategy only works until the virus changes its survival strategy" (ibid.:81).

Leaders of adaptive feedback networks will have to relinquish bureaucratic strategic mind-sets, which assume stable equilibrium as an appropriate and functional goal. And, in its place, leaders will assume bounded instability, or what I prefer to call organized disorder. While bounded instability signifies a new mind-set for management, organized disorder is a new practice rooted in the psychodynamic prerequisites for leaders of the new millennium. It is an action strategy grounded in resilient object relations that foster the facilitation of potential space for creativity and imagination at the boundaries between self and others, between and among better integrated and less hierarchic structural divisions, and between and among organizations and their environments. Embracing organized disorder implies that leaders and managers will move closer to the so-called edge of chaos and come to experience the organization as a "good enough holding environment" (Winnicott 1971) positioned in a perpetual "transitional space" (ibid.) between order and chaos.

Many companies, government agencies, and healthcare organizations, are presently attempting to adapt to chaos and complexity. As they engage in bottom-up processes of strategic planning and "fitness" (Stacey 1996), they will come to find that complex learning can be derived from tension and disorder. Members find they have to trust the unfamiliar process of "emergent organization" (ibid.). These are evolving and perpetually changing organizations with strategies and structures that transform to better fit their environmental landscapes. Their futures are unpredictable. Organizational participants will have to overcome their anxieties associated with unknowable outcomes. Members will come to acknowledge the wisdom of unconscious knowing and the power of what Daniel Goleman has called "emotional intelligence" (1998). Similar to the trail-laying behavior of ants, members have no apparent "boss" or central programmer once the rules are established, nevertheless, through bottom-up self-organizing, they produce emergent patterns of behavior out of chaos. These emergent outcomes are essential "properties of the process of adaptive nonlinear feedback" (Stacey 1996: 75).

However, humans are not ants. In fact, humans may often appear to be less strategic than ants. Unconscious motives often lead people into (what appear to be) maladaptive and counter-productive strategies. Possibly, it is because humans fear death and desire security and safety as well as competence and success. Or possibly, it is due to many underlying and latent emotional factors that groups and organizations fail. If so, we need to understand the human nature of the evolution and emergence of self so that we can better understand what it will take to lead and manage chaos and complexity into the future. In so doing, I explore the meaning of organized disorder in greater depth.

THE MEANING OF ORGANIZED DISORDER

As a framework for thinking about twenty-first century organizations, organized disorder describes a perpetual, paradoxical state of affairs confronting businesses, government agencies, and healthcare systems. However, it is intended to convey much more. While organized disorder represents the objective reality of "organized" postmodern life, it also signifies psychic reality and the quality of human experience and perception. Thus, it becomes a governing factor in organizing strategies and the means of adaptation to the task environment. If one embraces the disorder of organizational life, and at the same time acknowledges and searches for organized patterns and emerging structures, then one can construct action strategies at the organizational boundaries. These strategies will promote better open systems adaptation to chaos and complexity. Therefore, in addition to its grounding in transitions of economy and markets, it reflects a psychological (relational and inter-subjective) position for people and organizations as well. Ultimately, it is this psychological position that governs its action strategy.

Organized disorder works at the virtual space located at the boundary between organizations and their complex and chaotic task environments. It is strategy that promotes a psychological space that is transitional in nature and that proffers a "potential space" (Winnicott 1971) from which creativity and innovation can emerge. Organized disorder is characterized by dialectical and non-linear modes of interaction at multiple levels of analysis. These include dynamic relationships between an organization and its environment, between systems and their subsystems, across groups, roles, and interpersonal relationships—the *Janus-face* of administrative complexity and the psychodynamics of human relatedness. Organized disorder is, fundamentally, a function of boundary maintenance in the midst of chaos. As an action strategy, it differs from Stacey's (1996) concept of bounded instability, which is more narrowly a description of the state of affairs.

As an individual and organizational *theory of action*, organized disorder assumes integrated, strategic thinking that enables effective management of unstable and impermanent boundaries. And, despite the nature of what chaos and complexity theorists describe as evolving and emerging (organizational) structures of fitness to transmuting landscapes, organized disorder assumes goal-oriented and mission-driven practice. In other words, it is plausible to manage unpredictable task environments, markets, and hierarchies, if the basic assumptions and practices of managers and leaders are radically transformed through more consciously reflective practices. Such reflective actions ought to signify a validation of organizational participants' experiences of disorder.

For instance, the current emphasis on visioning and the future will in part need to be replaced by a more reflective and insightful focus on the present and the "here-and-now" of theory and practice. Theoretical and practical adaptation and adjustment to the dialectical nature of organized tension between stability and disorder will need to occur. The field of organization analysis and change will become more and more dominated by the human sciences and hermeneutic principles of truth and action. Ethical principles of honesty, openness, and candidness will become essential operating doctrines. Paying attention to psychic reality and the significance of organizational perceptions will become increasingly valued in the study of organizations.

At a micro level and within institutions, organized disorder will signify a loosening of controls from the top-down—a minimization rather than an elimination of hierarchies. It also will imply a minimizing of everyday psychological defenses at work that foster excessive demands for control of others and their tasks. Hence, structure will become less often an unwitting outcome of social defenses and more often a conscious strategy for adaptation to constantly changing environments. Ironically, organized disorder may be viewed as a form of play at work—a psychological space between reality and fantasy from which culture and imagination emerge. There are rules, however implicit, but the future is unpredictable—the outcome of the game is unknown. Participants concentrate in the present, the here-and-now of reflective practice and double-loop learning. However, prior to acquiring the administrative competencies of organized disorder, members experience chaos and complexity with anxiety that often promotes psychologically-regressive actions.

For instance, adults in traditional organizations are unaccustomed to relinquishing control over their roles, tasks, authority, and expertise, particularly in a manner that suggests members can learn from, and collaborate with each other, regardless of status and position. This ideal form of playful regression is in stark contrast to more typically destructive and counter-productive manifestations of regression at work, such as actions driven by unconscious fantasies and persecutory anxieties (Diamond 1998).

Organized disorder (as I use it here) does not refer to psychologically regressive actions per se. Rather, it signifies a relinquishing of organized fantasies of domination and control for a *playful flight into learning, transformation, and adaptation to chaos and complexity*. Organized disorder is a productive alternative to destructive, defensive, and regressive actions often taken in response to unmanageable anxieties. It is a strategy for managing at the boundary between order and chaos. In the next section, I will further develop a psychoanalytic understanding of organized disorder with a discussion of the object relational model of emotional development and well-being.

In his article, "Chaos, Complexity, and Psychoanalysis," Miller argues that "in complexity theory, the transitional chaotic phase is replaced with the idea that dynamic, living systems exist and maintain themselves at the edge of chaos, balancing themselves between predictable order and chaos. Rather than traversing chaos to adapt to an ever changing environment, the many different elements that make up a complex system interact with one another and with their environments in such intricate ways that a stable yet constantly evolving order emerges" (1999: 358). These systems avoid falling into perpetual chaos because they are open systems in reciprocal interaction with their environments. The system and the environment continuously feed off one another and "are said to exist at *far from equilibrium* conditions," whereas closed systems are subject to entropy (ibid.: 358).

   In the following section, I explore the psycho-dynamic foundations of adaptive feedback networks and open systems located in the emergence of self and self-object relations. I begin with a discussion of maturation as states of transition from the total dependency of infancy to relative autonomy of mature adulthood in the context of a "facilitative environment" (Winnicott 1971). This contemporary psychodynamic view of change parallels the chaos and complexity theorists' open systems view of adaptation to change as occurring in a space that is "far from equilibrium," one in which we manage the necessary tension between order and chaos—otherwise referred to here as organized disorder. Akin to Freud's notion of the Ego in his essay *The Ego And The Id*, contemporary psychoanalysis refers to the Self as maintaining an adaptive function between the internal and external world of object relations (1923).

PERSONAL ADAPTATION TO CHAOS AND COMPLEXITY: TOWARD REQUISITE SELF-SYSTEM INTEGRITY AND AUTHENTICITY

The evolution of psychoanalytic thinking is influenced by many factors including a century of clinical studies, infant observational research, and advancements in brain research and the neurosciences, in addition to cultural, societal, technological, and economic transformations in the post-industrial world. Post-Freudian and Kleinian psychoanalysis has shifted from the study of drives and the preeminence of sexual and aggressive instinctual motivations to the psycho-dynamics of relations and the elevation of object-seeking patterns of inter-subjectivity and desire (Fairbairn 1952; Winnicott 1971; Greenberg & Mitchell 1983; Kohut 1977; Modell 1984). In its most simplified paradigmatic shift, it is a transformation from an emphasis on Oedipal (triad of mother, father, child) to pre-Oedipal (mother and infant) development, and thus, a turn from a one-person to a two-person psychology (Modell 1984). In the following section, I present an overview of human (ego/self) development and adaptation according to contemporary psychoanalytic object relations theory. In so doing, I want to further elaborate for the reader the symmetry between chaos and complexity and psychoanalytic object relations theories as avenues of deeper understanding about the future of organizations and organizational membership. In other words, I try to address the question: What are the psychological requisites of social character for non-linear adaptive feedback networks or the ability to embrace (what I call) organized disorder?

A TRANSITIONAL JOURNEY FROM TOTAL DEPENDENCY TOWARDS RELATIVE INDEPENDENCY

Human development and maturation occur along a continuum from total dependency at birth and early infancy to relative autonomy in adulthood. Object relations theory, as pioneered by post-Kleinians such as Fairbairn and Winnicott, views humanity as primarily object-seeking (Fairbairn 1952; Winnicot 1971). Rather than driven primarily by sex and aggression, object relations theorists claim people are essentially motivated to form and establish meaningful and life-sustaining relationships. The concept of self, for instance, cannot be comprehended without the concept of object or other.

Maturational processes start from a dedifferentiated position. Self and other boundaries are absent in the cognitive mind of the infant. This undifferentiated position is then followed by the baby's earliest acknowledgment of the presence of the mother. The sense of self or subject emerges in relation to the primary care-giving other. Differentiation is experienced while total dependency of the infant on the mother is still present during what Bowlby and others call attachment (Bowlby 1969). As the child develops physically and cognitively in the second, third, and fourth trimester of life, it comes to recognize the presence and absence as well as the accepting and rejecting qualities, of the primary care-giver. This experience triggers feelings of love and hate, acceptance and rejection, separation and loss, often signified by panic and separation anxiety in the child.

This transitional experience of separation and loss is crucial to the emergence of a self as differentiated from others—the roots of subjectivity and identity (Bowlby 1973; 1980; Winnicott 1971). Winnicott views infancy as the earliest state of subjective omnipotence (often called primary narcissism) in contrast with objective reality. Healthy maturation, indicative of coming to view the other as subjective object, is contingent upon what Winnicott calls the "good enough holding environment" (Winnicott 1971). During this transitional experience, the facilitation of development requires adequate nurturing of the emerging and evolving "true self." It is the true self that contains the essence of authenticity and the ability to "be oneself." In contrast, the experience of "not good enough" care-giving or parenting can force the nascent self into hiding behind the veil of a compliant, "false self."

ORGANIZATIONAL CULTURE: THE CHALLENGE OF FACILITATING GOOD ENOUGH HOLDING ENVIRONMENTS

For Winnicott, when change is embraced and nurtured, it becomes a transitional experience that requires a facilitative or good enough holding environment, which signifies the psychological and potential space for discovering one-self through creativity, imagination, and play (Winnicott 1971). This requirement does not conclude with childhood, although it is critical to the development of a core and authentic sense of one-self. Managing and leading organizations into complexity and chaos demands a good enough holding environment in the organizational culture. Self and organizational identity are vulnerable to change. Change will promote loss and separation anxiety. It is crucial that processes of transformation foster a transitional experience that allows organizational participants to grieve and mourn as well as to reject and resist change that contradicts the values of true self.

The predicament of the false self may be observed among adults in organizational settings (Diamond 1993). It is commonplace within organizational cultures that promote role compliance, or aggrandizing and adoring followers to observe the false self phenomenon. Hence, change and adaptation cannot be coerced or even unilateral. Organizational participants need to share in the rationale for strategic, structural, and cultural change. Narcissistically held organizational members will find adaptation difficult in a culture that fosters inordinate power and influence at the top and inadequate empowerment and responsibility among workers.

The recognition among complexity theorists that organizations are emergent has led to various perspectives on how organizations change. For example, Butz has described dynamic systems as evolving through four states: (1) stable, (2) bifurcation, (3) chaos or complexity, and (4) a new and more complex adaptive order. As the instability of a system grows, it enters what appears to be a chaotic state. The system looks chaotic because, on the local level, you cannot predict the next state of the system. Yet, there is an underlying order to the states of a system that emerge that does not derive directly (linearly) from the previous state of the system. It is often somewhere between "bifurcation" and "chaos or complexity" that organizations enlist outside change agents thereby further opening their systems to the possibility of reflection and insight. These evolving states of organizational change share much in common with contemporary psychoanalytic views of individual transformation (Butz 1997).

For example, according to Ogden, we begin life in a pre-verbal, pre-symbolic, and sensual state of attachment he calls "autistic-contiguous" (Ogden 1989). It is a "stable" state of oneness and dedifferentiation in which hard and soft shapes, smells, sounds, and feelings dominate the pre-subjective state of infancy, and no distinction exists between where self ends and the other begins. The "paranoid-schizoid" mode of experience follows, and is characterized as one of, "bifurcation" and polarization. Psychological splitting coincides with the experience of differentiation and separation between self and other. However, self and other are viewed in black and white, experienced as either good or bad, rejecting or accepting, loving or hating. It is a time in which the emerging child begins to experience omnipotent subjectivity and a perspective of the world evolving around one-self. The depressive mode of experience follows in which the child comes to acknowledge the coming and going of mother and the good and bad characteristics of one and same parental object of desire. It is a time when the child begins to acknowledge the chaos and complexity of human relationships and one's loss of innocence and the ideal of perfection. In this phase of reparation, split-objects integrate and assume a truer multi-dimensional and inter-subjective character.

Embracing organized disorder requires the depressive position; however, that alone is insufficient. Acknowledgment of the state of constant change demands consciousness of the perpetuation and dialectical interplay of these three modes of experience throughout life. Hence, managing at the edge of chaos requires our psychological management of regression and the emotional forces of more prim-itive states of experience while finding comfort in the necessity of disorder for innovation and double-loop learning. These earlier infantile positions remain within our internal world of object relations and affect our ability, productively and unproductively, to adapt to external reality. With their acknowledgment of the unknown, latent, and "illegitimate" systems, complexity and chaos theories rein-force the value of paying attention to unconscious systemic forces as they impose their will on our best efforts at organizational change. A good enough holding environment for organizational change is a necessary step in facilitating partici-pants' willingness to embrace organized disorder and better cope with an unpre-dictable future.

In conclusion, one might ask: Have chaos and complexity theories added any new knowledge to our understanding of organizations as open systems? I submit that these theories raise issues that organization theorists and analysts have addressed for many decades. In fact, any claims that organizations have radically changed might be over-stated and over-generalized. It is my observation that organizational membership may be challenged by the impact of new technologies, globalization, and atomization. Markets and hierarchies change daily.

However, the actual cognitive, emotional, strategic, and structural barriers to transformation and adaptation have changed very little. Organizational partici-pants still engage in defensive routines and psychologically regressive behaviors that protect the status quo. Therefore, the challenge for organizational members of the future is not terribly different than it has been for some time. In fact, the issue of adaptation to complexity and chaos may assume that all changes on behalf of adaptation are "good" organizational strategies because they ensure viability and survival. This very assumption might be questioned on a case-by-case basis.

Nevertheless, organizational participants and their leaders will continue to work at developing their adaptive capabilities. Consequently, their sense of orga-nizational identity and its inherent meaning and integrity will become more sig-nificant rather than less so. Awareness of organizational identity is becoming increasingly under attack in a world of constant change in the form of policies, mergers and acquisitions, and "downsizing" and "rightsizing." Organizational distinctiveness, uniqueness, and ethic will become more important, strategically and socially.

In sum, organizational leaders will need to promote creativity and innovation among participants at a time when their unconscious proclivities may force exec-utives and management to become more obsessed with control and predictability. If it is true that leaders and followers produce and perpetuate organizational cul-tures, then the maturity and quality of object relations and the facilitation of a "good enough holding environment" within organizations is crucial. Organizing the "potential space" for learning and reflectivity in the moment will produce non-linear feedback systems that are humane, effective, and adaptive to chaos and complexity.

REFERENCES

Argyris, C. and D. Schön. 1996. *Organizational Learning II: Theory, Method, and Practice*. Reading, MA: Addison-Wesley Publishing Company.

Bowlby, J. 1969. *Attachment*. New York: Basic Books.

————. 1973. *Separation*. New York: Basic Books.

————. 1980. *Loss*. New York: Basic Books.

Butz, M.R. 1997. *Chaos and Complexity: Implications for Psychological Theory and Practice*. Washington, DC: Taylor & Francis.

Diamond, M.A. 1993. *The Unconscious Life of Organizations*. Westport, CT: Quorum Books.

————. 1998. The symbiotic lure: Organizations as defective containers. *Administrative Theory & Praxis*. 20(3):315-325.

Fairbairn, W.R.D. 1952. *Psychoanalytic Studies of Personality*. London: Tavistock.

Freud, S. 1923. *The Ego and The Id*. New York: Norton.

Greenberg, J. R. and S. A. Mitchell. 1983. *Object Relations in Psychoanalytic Theory*. Cambridge, MA: Harvard University.

Goleman, D. 1998. *Working with Emotional Intelligence*. New York: Bantam.

Kets de Vries, M.F.R., and D. Miller. 1987. Interpreting organizational texts. *Journal of Management Studies*. 24(3):233-248.

Kohut, H. 1977. *The Restoration of the Self*. New York: International Universities Press.

Levinson, H. 1972. *Organizational Diagnosis*. Cambridge, MA: Harvard University Press.

Lissack, M. R. 1999. "Complexity: The science, its vocabulary, and its relation to organizations." Unpublished manuscript.

Miller, M. L. 1999. Chaos, complexity, and psychoanalysis. *Psychoanalytic Psychology*. 16(3):355-379.

Modell, A. H. 1984. *Psychoanalysis in a New Context*. New York: International Universities Press.

Ogden, T. H. 1989. *The Primitive Edge of Experience*. New York: Jason Aronson.

Stacey, R. D. 1996. *Complexity and Creativity in Organizations*. San Francisco: Berrett-Koehler Publishers.

Winnicott, D. W. 1971. *Playing and Reality*. London: Tavistock.

11

Future Paradigms for Public Service

———— Thomas Clarke and Stewart Clegg

INTRODUCTION

New forces for change have acted as a catalyst in transforming much of public sector provision: the insistent interventions of impatient government politicians; new demands created by social change; transformed thinking about the nature of effective management; and heightened consumer awareness. These have combined with much tighter financial controls; close external scrutiny of spending and performance; and renewed commitments to quality in public service delivery, to encourage a climate of improved performance. In recent years, traditional public sector practices have been successfully challenged, and a change in orientation is taking place:

- from an emphasis on internal procedures to a concern for outcomes;
- from an emphasis on hierarchical decision-making to an approach stressing delegation and personal responsibility;
- from a focus on the quantity of service provided to one also concentrating on quality;
- from a culture that values stability and uniformity to one that cherishes innovation and diversity (Hambleton 1992: 10).

Before, there was in the British civil service what Metcalfe and Richards refer to as an impoverished conception of management: thinking of management as an executive function with a clear definition of objectives; management as an intra-organizational process concerned with internal routines and procedure; coordination and control achieved through well defined hierarchies; and that these broad principles would apply with minor adaptation to all organisations. "These elements in combination impose severe restrictions on the scope of management. They limit the role of public managers to programmed implementation of predetermined policies. They disregard the problem of adapting policies and organizations to environmental change. If this is all management means, giving more weight to it is likely to cause confusion and frustration rather than lead to long term improvements in performance.... Civil servants need a richer and more precise language for diagnosing complex management problems and developing workable solutions to them" (Metcalfe and Richards 1990: 17, 22). In the absence of a more creative and dynamic approach, the critics of the public sector are free to equate cutting expenditure with efficiency gains, assuming greater productivity is the only realizable management goal.

The new wave of management thinking in the public sector has an explicit emphasis on the management of change with the object of a metamorphosis in organization culture, improving the quality of service by moving the locus of managerial authority and budgetary responsibility from the policy centre closer to the point of delivery, and getting closer to the public and attempting to shift the balance of power in favour of those who the organization is intended to serve. This emphasis on listening to the customer, and delegating as much decision-making as possible to the operational level, has achieved positive results (Thomson, P. 1992; Hambleton 1992). The public sector is changing in many countries. In the UK, "In order to survive, local government has had to develop a stronger sense of strategic leadership, an increased emphasis on performance, quality, and better financial management and a greater concern for the consumers of local services" (Buckland and Joshua 1992: 21).

Accepting that the public sector is likely to remain a substantial presence in most countries for the foreseeable future, the importance of these efforts to transform the performance of the sector is considerable. It does seem a little premature to suggest the state is about to wither away; there remain vital functions for public enterprise in defence, industry, environment, transport, housing, social security, health, personal social services, education, employment and training, and law and order. In the UK, where the most sustained attempt has been made to erode the public sector, though the extensive privatisation programme has returned most of the former nationalised industries to the private sector, the remaining parts of the public sector—the civil service, NHS, and local government—have displayed a remarkable resilience despite imaginative government attempts with contracting-out, market testing, independent trusts, and the Next Step Agencies, to return them to the market system. During the entire period of Margaret Thatcher's governments from 1979 to 1990, though there was a substantial reduction in employment in the nationalised industries and public corporations, employment in central and local government was largely sustained. Moreover, though planned increases in public expenditure may have been restrained, public expenditure did continue to rise. This suggests the work of discovering ways of making the public sector more efficient and accountable is essential, and the argument is not simply about how to roll back the frontiers of the state.

FUTURE PARADIGMS FOR PUBLIC SERVICE

A series of questions have been posed by Sue Richards of the Public Management Foundation which are inescapable for anyone involved in the provision of public services: "Who defines the public good? Who decides who gets what, when, where and how? Who makes the crucial decisions that turn an infinite number of demands for service into a manageable number of legitimate needs to be met?" (Richards 1992: 7*).* Clearly a shift is emerging in how public service management is governed:

> The paradigm which has underpinned public service during the first part of the post-war period involved balancing two powerful forces, the political domain and the producer domain. Changes in the underlying political economy led to that paradigm being challenged, and the emergence of an efficiency paradigm, driven by principles of performance rather than balance. The efficiency paradigm is associated with private sector management methods and market-like mechanisms. Now the efficiency paradigm itself may be under challenge. New patterns of behaviour are developing, emphasising the significance of the consumer. This seems to be happening both as the unintended consequence of strategies to produce greater efficiency, and out of the rediscovery of the older public service values. What may be happening is the development of a third paradigm which seeks to synthesise the balancing and involvement values of the first paradigm and the performance orientation of the second. We refer to this as the consumer paradigm. (Richards 1992: 5)

Before, questions of the legitimacy and accountability of the public sector were simpler, with politicians who represented and were accountable to citizens, professionals who understood and served clients, and managers administering an uneasy truce between the two (Goss 1991: 25*).*

In the present reshaping of public service provision, as Sue Goss suggests, the systems of accountability and legitimacy have come loose. In the trend towards the creation of quasi-markets—the separating of purchasing and commissioning roles; enabling and providing; the creation of a plurality of providers; the bringing in of the private sector; the devolution of management decision-making; moving down to the front line; locality management; or the move to quasi-autonomous agencies—the origins of legitimacy become more obscure (Goss 1991: 26). Yet this is the direction in which much of the public sector seems to be headed. "The debate on the future of local government in the UK has centred on the idea of the enabling authority, with the role of the centre conceived as the strategic management of service delivery through partnerships and contracts with external private, voluntary and not-for-profit organisations" (Lawton and McKevitt 1993: 282). In a survey of European local authorities, Stoker has suggested that changes in the organisation of service have tended to converge around the enabling authority, and he defines the enabling role as "working with and through other organisations to achieve service delivery" (1991: 9).

Placing developments in the public sector within a broader political economy, Murray (1991) has suggested the manifest deficiencies of traditional forms of public service provision, with standardised services, delivered by routinised work in bureaucratic organisations, are the characteristics of a quasi-Fordist state in which the emphasis was upon quantity—universal mass provision, rather than quality. The post-Fordist emphasis is upon batch production, customised goods for segmented markets, and product and process quality; with decentralisation and autonomy within big firms, and new forms of network relationships between firms, facilitated by advances in information and communication technology. "If the postwar public sector was integral to, and modelled on, industrial Fordism," Geddes argues, "the current scenario for the public sector and public services is a post-Fordist one of quality production for a more diversified consumer market through more decentralized and plural structures" (Geddes 1991: 9).

As Metcalfe and Richards argue, the concept of efficiency has been wielded very uncritically in the public sector: "The connotation of efficiency as a politically neutral, no-nonsense way of improving performance is a useful weapon in political debate. Efficiency, portrayed as a purely technical, instrumental means to politically approved ends is often presented as an unqualified good ..." (Metcalfe and Richards 1990: 29). They illustrate the distinction between economy, efficiency, and effectiveness, and how they are providing a technical framework for national choice.

"Improvements in efficiency may be achieved by increasing outputs relative to inputs, reducing inputs relative to outputs, or, ideally, doing both at the same time. Within this framework, greater economy is achieved by making savings in actual resource inputs relative to planned resource inputs. Effectiveness is increased by achieving a better ratio between desired objectives and actual outputs" (ibid.: 30). Efficiency can easily be reduced to what is readily measurable, which can have a damaging impact upon overall organizational performance:

> Concentrating exclusively on measurable efficiency has three undesirable consequences. First, because costs are more easily measured than benefits, efficiency often reduces to economy. Savings in money and manpower become the sole measure of improvement; the quest for efficiency becomes a search for cuts. Second, because social costs are more difficult to measure than economic costs, externalities are often ignored. Individuals units concentrate on improving their own efficiency even though the overall effect is suboptimal. Third, economic benefits are more easily identified than social benefits and efforts to increase efficiency lead to a redefinition of performance criteria in ways that lend themselves to easier measurement. (Metcalfe and Richards 1990: 31; Mintzberg 1982)

In the UK, the Audit Commission, which has been charged with evaluating local authority management, has been accused of falling into precisely this trap in the development of a management diagnostic tool of the performance of service delivery responsibilities, ranking from "good" to "poor." "It is entirely quantitative. It equates performance exclusively to the efficient throughput of standard units—a mass production model. It does not also recognise the reality of differentiated markets of public services, the need for innovation, diverse and variable services, and the importance of outcome and effectiveness. It assumes that the "facts" on such measures exist merely to be objectively reflected and, indeed, that there is an uncontested perspective on good performance. The auditor assumes she has access to it, without access to information about particular services, or explicit criteria for assessing quality management or methods of ascertaining user's views" (Thomson,W. 1992: 39).

To clarify the issues, governments must distinguish several efficiency concepts: technical and economic efficiency; allocative and production efficiency; and static and dynamic efficiency (Metcalfe and Richards 1990: 31). Technical efficiency measures the physical use of resource inputs in relation to physical outputs. Economic efficiency measures the cost of using inputs in relation to the value of outputs. Allocative efficiency is the optimal distribution of resources, guided by prices, to ensure resources are distributed among producers to serve consumer wants in ways that reflect the cost of provision. Production efficiency, or X-efficiency, concerns productivity in the utilisation of resources, that is, producing at minimum cost. Economic theory focused on allocative efficiency, believing organisations had incentives to minimise costs. However, X-inefficiency occurs when organisations fail to minimise costs due to managerial inadequacies. This is most relevant to the public sector which depends more on the performance of organizations than markets. The difficulties of eliminating X-inefficiency in government were indicated by Peacock:

- outputs are often difficult to define, let alone measure;
- output indicators are flawed by their inability to pick up qualitative differences in performance;
- the incentives and opportunities for managers to seek ways of minimising costs are limited by agreements, and regulations that restrict management discretion;
- administrations cope with these uncertainties by withdrawing from the task of evaluation (Peacock 1983: 133).

Empirical evidence is abandoned in favour of elegant argument, "Bureaucratic politics becomes frequently 'the art of the plausible'" (ibid.). Finally, operational efficiency stresses cost-consciousness in performing existing functions, with a tight specification of objectives and performance standards, according to long term plans and detailed programmes of activity. Adaptive efficiency requires flexibility in the reformulation of objectives, and ready adjustments to environmental change. Adaptive efficiency is assisted by information flows which signal the need for change early (Metcalfe and Richards 1990: 32).

An orthodox view is that it is possible in most circumstances to clarify objectives, assess effectiveness and thereby improve efficiency, as in the management by objectives movement. However, the business environment does change rapidly and extensively due to competitive, economic, technological, and social forces that frequently render previously formulated business objectives obsolete. Organisational effectiveness becomes dependent upon the capacity to reformulate objectives, innovate, adapt, and manage change. Metcalfe and Richards (1990: 34) catalogue a growing management literature in which there is a strong emphasis upon the importance of organizational responsiveness to change:

- the self-designing organization (Hedberg et al. 1976; Weick 1976)
- the self-evaluating organization (Wildavsky 1972)
- the self-correcting organization (Landau 1973)

- the experimenting organization (Staw 1977)
- the learning organization (Argyris and Schön 1974; Hedberg 1981; Garratt 1990; Hayes et al. 1988; Senge 1990; Pedler et al. 1991)
- the role of strategic management of the relations between organizations and their environments in facilitating learning (Metcalfe 1981)

The "tidy" approach to management involves applying proven principles to create neatly structured organisational hierarchies with well-defined tasks and clearly allocated responsibilities. Orderly management is assumed to be superior to muddling through because it establishes firm control, streamlines processes, and defines purposes (Metcalfe and Richards 1990: 35). This neglects the problem of how to achieve effective performance in organisations with less firmly-defined, and more frequently changing, objectives. Leavitt suggests the management process concerns pathfinding, problem solving, and implementing. "Pathfinding ... is about mission, innovation, vision; problem solving is about analysis, thought, reason; implementing is about acting, changing, doing. Good management not only requires competences in each of these areas but also skills in managing the relationships among them" (Leavitt 1983: 4). Conceiving of this creative aspect, Metcalfe and Richards propose a general definition of management as "taking responsibility for the performance of a system." They continue,

> This definition has more practical implications than might at first appear. On the one side, it distinguishes management as a purposeful process from mutual adjustment characteristic of 'muddling through', where the overall performance is the unintended consequence of interaction among component sub-systems; whether or not it embodies the intelligence of democracy, disjointed incrementalism is not management because there is no locus of responsibility for system performance. On the other side, much discussion of management confuses it with control ... far from being synonymous and interchangeable terms, there is a fundamental distinction between management and control ... predictability is the condition of control. Management comes into play when non-routine responses are needed. Actions are adjusted and responses improvised to take account of changing circumstances and feedback about earlier performance. (Metcalfe and Richards 1990: 37-8)

As Landau and Stout suggest, "There is an inverse relationship between the ability to control and the necessity to manage" (1979: 149). Control is about tighter specifications and greater standardisation, but these can introduce rigidity and prove counter-productive when ends cannot be precisely pre-defined. "Management ... requires discretion to respond to change and stimulate innovation, whereas control procedures quite deliberately programme behaviours and predefine responses. Control techniques presume a greater degree of stability than is frequently found in the politically charged atmosphere of public management. In themselves they offer too narrow a base for making improvements in the performance of public organizations" (Metcalfe and Richards 1990: 38). A matrix which identifies four dimensions to the public managers' role is proposed by Strand (1984) (Figure 11.1), encompassing administrator, producer, integrator, and innovator.

Figure 11.1: The Role of the Public Manager

Change

Procedural Regularity	INTEGRATOR	INNOVATOR	Improved Results
	ADMINISTRATOR	PRODUCER	

Stability

The administrator is the traditional system maintenance role of public managers; the producer is concerned with improving performance; the innovator seeks to achieve existing objectives by more effective means, or achieve strategic changes of direction to meet new objectives; and the integrator negotiates for the support necessary for lasting coordination and cooperation.

Performance indicators established with little sense of the complex demands of public service can often conceal more than they reveal. For example, Michael Bichard, the chief executive of the UK Social Services Benefits Agency, has argued:

> We have a seemingly inexhaustible list of performance indicators: I think at the last count there were 49. However many of them have got much more to do with the internal bureaucratic procedures than with providing a quality service to consumers. Even some which are designed to target customer service, are, to say the least ambivalent. My staff by now are fed up with me pointing to one of them—which is about how quickly you can move someone out of a benefit office—and pointing out that you can do that in two ways, only one of which has got much to do with improving the quality of service. (Bichard 1991: 53)

In this case, a stringent application of a performance indicator may do little more than speed up the completion of an inherently inadequate procedure. As Christine Hancock of the Royal College of Nursing concludes, in the last analysis, "people don't add up like a balance sheet" (1990: 26).

SOCIAL ACCOUNTABILITY

The pace and profound nature of change in the structure and operation of the public sector is now so great, there has been a substantial blurring of the boundaries between the public and private sector, and often the original political principles upon which the public services were erected are forgotten. Kieron Walsh reminds us:

> The development of government in Britain in the post-Second World War period involved the extension of what Marshall called citizenship rights from the legal and political to the social and economic spheres. People were to have a right to those resources and services that were fundamental to living a decent life, notably health, housing, education, social care and protection against unemployment. The welfare state was the expression of the fulfilment of citizenship rights, emphasising equity and equality, and the importance of meeting basic needs if people were fully to be members of society. The relationship between the state and its citizens was not to be one of free exchange, as happens in markets, but one of mutual obligations and duties.... The state expressed the collective nature and the mutuality of obligation of society. (1991b: 9)

Sometimes, it is suggested, the political basis of public enterprise is unfortunate, but this view rather misses the point of the whole endeavour: "Arguably the central justification for local government is nor that it is a good way of providing a wide range of needed services, which it is, but that it enables citizens to participate in decisions affecting their lives and their communities. It is concerned with political freedom and political rights (Hambleton 1992: 11). This may make public sector management difficult, but it is not something which can be avoided, as John Stewart contends:

> Certain writings actually imply that politics is an obstacle to management. Management, it is argued, would be much easier in Local Government if there were no politics. That seems to be almost the equivalent of saying management would be easier in the private sector if you didn't have to make a profit. Politics is the means of achieving the basic purposes of the organisation. The local authority is constituted to make judgments through the political process. The real challenge to management thinking—is how can management both support and express the legitimate political process? What does that actually require from the nature of management? It's a very different question from how can management overcome the problem of politics? Instead, one is treating politics as part of the basic conditions for management. If management starts to deny the political process, it's denying the constitutive basis of the organisation. (1990: 19)

Though public sector managers are now encouraged to assume a more strategic and entrepreneurial role, this must be within an overall framework of democratic accountability, as Bellone and Goerl argue, "Autonomy, a personal vision of the future, secrecy and risk-taking need to be reconciled with the fundamental democratic values of accountability, citizen participation, open policy making processes, and concern for the long term public good (stewardship) ... high risk investment schemes that have gone wrong and resulted in economic losses, failed arbitrage efforts in investing federal grant funds, and short term borrowing to pay operating costs, as in the case of New York City's fiscal crisis of the seventies, are all examples of entrepreneurial risk taking that ignored the prudent concern for the long term public good." In contrast they describe the benefits of a more accountable and responsive entrepreneurship as the accumulation of "civic literacy ... and civil capital," which they define as, "problem solving knowledge possessed by citizens, attitudes that guide civic action, and civic capacity for governance ... the raising of citizen trust in government, the citizen's sense of efficacy, and, hopefully, a shared conception of the common good" (Bellone and Goerl 1992: 131-3).

A dilemma is often posed between accountability and effectiveness—with the implication they may be mutually exclusive—either a protracted political process will be engaged in to secure agreement, sometimes delaying or preventing appropriate action, or a decision will be made quickly and implemented creating a *fait accompli*. As Metcalfe and Richards insist, this is a false choice: "Proper use of power and resources cannot be left to the good intentions and public spiritedness of politicians and officials. In broad terms the function of accountability is to keep organisational performance up to standard. To insure against an abuse of organisational power and yet promote its effective use is one of the classic problems of modern government ... The source of error is a failure to recognise two aspects of accountability; a negative, preventative aspect and a positive, motivating aspect" (Metcalfe and Richards 1990: 43). They call for a recognition of the different dimensions of accountability which apply in the diversity of public organizations or "networks of accountability." The task is to reinforce commitment through developing values which encourage positive motivation, "Excessive reliance on structural accountability constraints leads to poorer performance" (ibid.: 50).

CONTRACTS AND CONSUMERS

New institutional mechanisms for enforcing the accountability of public enterprises to those they are intended to serve include the creation of a contract culture, and the introduction of consumer sovereignty through the operation of quasi-market processes. Michael Geddes has outlined three linked dimensions of a contract approach:

- the extension of contractual relations in the provision of public services *between* the public, private and voluntary-/non—profit sectors, creating new structures of institutional pluralism in what were often situations of public sector monopoly or quasi-monopoly of provision;
- the extension of contractual relationships *within* the public sector, associated with a more decentralised/fragmented organisational structure, and with quasi-market mechanisms within the public sector;
- the development of service/quality contracts *between* public service providers and consumers/users (Geddes 1991).

The emerging consensus around the new contract model for public services ...
is based on new priorities about the role of the public services in the economy.
The primary emphasis is on efficiency and accountability in public service provision, reflecting the political need to rebuild support for public services, and
the recognition of the economic limitations of the tax base ... [T]his involves
both a recognition of the need for new forms of management and performance
within public monitoring to ensure efficiency and quality, and of the need for
flexibility and innovation within public services. This would require, for example, general powers for local authorities to respond actively to both social need
and economic opportunity in their localities, to be flexible, to take risks, and to
be able to compete effectively with private sector providers. (Geddes 1991: 12)

Persuasive arguments have been put that a contract-based model of public services is a progressive means to improve quality, efficiency, and accountability.
However, it is important to question what a "contract" is, and to ask whose rights
will be protected, and what responsibilities will be enforced, by contract relationships in the public services. Contracts will *limit* rights, as well as guarantee them,
particularly in public services which are tightly resource-constrained. A contract
culture may fragment the provision of services, preventing a comprehensive service,
and while contracts formally guarantee rights, it may be difficult, in practice, to
enforce those rights. Contracts will increase the rights of some, but not of others,
and the fear is that they will reinforce the rights of educated middle class users without benefiting the dispossessed. The individualist basis of the traditional contract
model poses the question, "are there possibilities of 'collective contracts' between
the producers and users of services which recognise the social nature of production
and consumption?" (Geddes 1991: 13-14).

Another mechanism of accountability is the attempt to invest a degree of consumer sovereignty in the public services, which has led to the creation of quasi-
markets and experiments with marketing techniques. What is intended is to give
some reality to consumer choice, and to allow the possibility of consumers expressing views which will produce a response. With reference to the private market, these freedoms were conceived by Albert Hirschman as "exit," "voice," and
"loyalty" (1970). "Exit" is the possibility of a dissatisfied customer moving to
another supplier; "voice" when the customer is able to complain in a way that will
lead to some change in the service or product offered; and "loyalty" is where the
consumer stays with the supplier, regardless of the standard of service provided.
In the public sector, traditionally the possibility of "exit" has been minimal, com-
pensated for by an apparent increase in the power of "voice" as citizens with political rights. However, all too often in practice this has been reduced to a silent
acceptance of an unsatisfactory service because of the absence of any alternative,
and resignation about any effective redress—this amounts to a form of enforced
"loyalty." Compared to this, the market often appears a place of remarkable personal freedom and range of choice.

Empowering consumers unsettles the traditional basis of legitimacy, where
both politicians and professionals claim to be acting on behalf of the best inter-

ests of the consumer. Once consumers enter the process of decision-making *as themselves,* interesting changes occur:

> It started off with planners; poor old planners were the first professionals no longer expected to be able to know what sort of houses people wanted to live in. Next came architects; teachers are now having a certain amount of trouble; social workers are no longer treated as speaking on behalf of their clients in the way they used to be; doctors are now being questioned about the extent to which they can speak for their client. And consumers are expressing their own views and using their own knowledge about their own situation. (Goss 1991: 27)

Consumers may have legitimacy when they speak for themselves, but when they speak for others, the questions of who they represent and to whom are they accountable? and what is their knowledge and where does their legitimacy come from? are as relevant as when applied to public officials. Given the cacophony of organized interest groups in modern society, "when resources are limited, it is not just a matter of pleasing consumers, but *which* consumers" (Goss 1991: 28). A question remains as to how far markets empower people, and who gets empowered? As Pamela Gordon, the chief executive of Sheffield City Council argues:

> It is somewhat of a paradox that the canonisation of the consumer as an article of political faith has come at a time when increased limitations on the powers and practices of local authorities have effectively disempowered communities by weakening the local democratic process. The cult of the consumer recognises the right of an individual service user to know what standard of service to expect, and what redress is available if there is a failure to deliver it. At the same time, however, local choices as to that standard are being constrained by externally imposed reductions in resources. More services are being hived off, opted or privatised, within a narrower framework of accountability. (Gordon 1991: 41)

Marketing consists of how transactions are created, stimulated, facilitated, and valued. Walsh makes an important distinction between strategic marketing and customer marketing, and illuminates the relevance of each approach to the public sector. Strategic marketing is concerned with planning the basic direction of a company and the kind of products it will make. Detailed research on product design and customer preferences is required before production commences, which has often been undeveloped in the public sector. In contrast, customer marketing involves a detailed consideration of the basis of commodity exchange. Marketing of services is different from marketing goods, and there are limits to the extent to which it may be commodified since human relationships form the basis of service transactions. The quality of the service may depend as much upon the user as on the producer, as in the case of educational services or health care. In assessing the applicability of marketing techniques, the specific character, conditions, and tasks of the public sector should be considered (Table 11.1).

Table 11.1: The Private and Public Sector Model Compared

Private Sector Model	*Public Sector Model*
Individual choice in the marker	Collective choice in the polity
Demand and price	Need for resources
Closure for private action	Openness for public action
The equity of the market	The equity of need
The search for market satisfaction	The search for justice
Citizenship	Citizenship
Competition as the instrument of the maker	Collective action as the instrument of the polity
'Exit' as the stimulus	'Voice' as the condition

Source: Walsh 1991b: 14.

In the context of these profound differences in character—the techniques of manipulative advertising, marketing as rationing, consumerism and market segmentation—all become more questionable in the public sector than they are in the private market.

> More fundamental objections to the marketing of public services arise from the nature of the services provided and the fact that the public sector is part of the public realm. It can be maintained that the public sector is dealing with the production of what Rawls calls social primary goods, such as liberties, opportunities, income and wealth and the basis of self-respect, and that market principles are not sufficient to ensure fairness of distribution. The nature of the relationship between state and citizen cannot then be based on property rights and exchange, or at least not wholly so. Marketing approaches are unlikely to be either helpful or appropriate in the distribution of basic social goods ... [T]he ethic of commercialism can clearly lead to difficulties when confused with the ethic of service. (Walsh 1991b: 15)

CONCLUSIONS: THE IMPERATIVE OF GOVERNMENT

Whilst the financial and political constraints imposed by central governments, which have lost sympathy with the values and practices of public enterprise, have limited the possibilities for innovation, public organizations have often responded to their newly insecure position with a creative engagement that has seen positive results. Boldness and innovation have been released where before there may have been conformity and tradition. Hambleton projects three possible trends for the public services—a market-, a consumer-, and a community-based approach—each of which involves fundamental changes from the former model of bureaucratic paternalism (1992: 17).

He emphasizes that while there are important political distinctions between the three broad options, which are a subject of ongoing contest, there are three shifts which occur across all of the projections of the future of the public services, in this case local authorities:

> First, the 1990s will be characterised by more pluralistic patterns of public service provision. There can be no going back to the monolithic models of the past. The three broad options point towards different kinds of pluralism—the interesting question is what kind of pluralism will emerge? Second, all three options imply a growth in management by contract, as opposed to management by hierarchy…[T]hird, and related to this, all three scenarios require local authorities to become enabling councils. The key question is not "should councils enable?" It is "who should they enable to do what?" (ibid.:18)

Territorial government will continue to have an important, if more negotiated, part to play in the future of communities (Lewis 1992). The European Charter of Local Self Government for example, promulgated by the Council of Europe and now signed by 19 of the 26 member states, enshrines the principles of local self government, and the ability of local authorities, within the limits of the law, to regulate and manage a substantial sphere of public affairs under their own responsibility and in the interests of the local population. The Charter goes on to deal with questions of the scope of local government, the creation of local administrative structures and resources for local authority functions, and the legal protection of local self government. This is part of reasserting the essentials of local government and good governance.

In pursuing these new objectives, there is no point in simply borrowing from the private sector, "It is all too common for critics of the performance of public companies to jump to the unwarranted conclusion that there are ready made private sector solutions available" (Metcalfe and Richards 1990: ix). Whatever lessons can be learned from private enterprise, the particular ideals and imperatives of the governance of public enterprise will always involve a distinctive approach. As Kate Pinder argues, "There is a need to develop new sorts of management, capable of meshing the requirements of democratic accountability with those of swift response and efficient service delivery, and capable of meeting a range of social objectives without abandoning a concern with value for money" (1993: 412). The awkward and necessary questions of democracy will be as relevant to the future of the public services as they were to the founders of democratic institutions, as Tony Benn insists:

- What power do you have?
- Who gave it to you?

- In whose interests do you exercise it?
- To whom do you account?
- How do we get rid of you? (in Goss 1991: 31)

Critical for the survival of democratic public enterprise will be the capacity to change and respond to new social demands as they arise. "The key issue for the public sector is about learning. Is the public sector capable of sustaining learning adaptive organisations?" (Stewart 1990: 23). New forms of innovative response will be achieved when people in the public services recognise and understand the importance of this in terms of the values they uphold about social results, or, as Susan Weil puts it, "when the energy to reconstruct the world ... becomes self-generating" (1992: 15).

REFERENCES

Argyris, C., and A. Schon. 1974. *Organizational Learning.* Reading, Mass: Addison-Wesley.

Barley, R., and G. Stoker. 1991. *Local Government in Europe—Trends and Developments,* London: Macmillan.

Bellone, C. J., and G. F. Goerl. 1992. "Reconciling public entrepreneurship and democracy," *Public Administration Review.* 52(2) (March/April):130-4.

Bichard, M. 1991. "Experience from the benefits agency," *Managers, Citizens and Consumers,* London: Office for Public Management. 53-58.

Buckland, Y., and H. Joshua. 1992. "Nottingham into the 1990s—Managing change in a district council," *Public Money and Management.* July-September. 21-25.

Caiden, G.E. 1991. *Administrative Reform Comes of Age.* Berlin: Walter de Gruyrer.

Chandler, J. A. 1991. "Public administration and private management: Is there a difference?" *Public Administration.* 69(3):385-91.

Cmnd 1599. 1991. *The Citizen's Charter: Raising the Standard.* Her Majesty's Stationery Office.

Cmnd 2101. 1992. *The Citizen's Charter First Report.* Her Majesty's Stationery Office.

Deakin, N., and A. Wright (1990). *Consuming Public Services,* London: Routledge.

Elcock, H. 1993. "What price citizenship? Public management and the citizen's charter," *Waves of Change in the Public Sector.* Sheffield Business School. 5-6 April: 144-174.

Flynn, M. 1990. *Public Sector Management.* Brighton: Harvester-Wheatsheaf.

Garratt, B. 1990. *Creating a Learning Organization.* Director Books, Simon and Schuster.

Geddes, M. 1991. "Scenarios for the future of public services in the economy," *Warwick Business School Research Papers.* 21 (September): 1-16.

Gordon, P. 1991. "Experience from Sheffield City Council," *Managers, Citizens and Consumers,* Conference Paper 6. London: Office for Public Management. 41-46.

Goss, S. 1991. "The poverty of consumerism," *Managers, Citizens and Consumers,* Conference Paper 6, London: Office for Public Management. 25-32.

Gyford, 1. 1991. *Citizens, Consumers and Councils,* London: Macmillan.

Hadley, R., and K. Young 1990: *Creating a Responsive Public Service,* London: Harvester-Wheatsheaf.

Hambleton, R. 1992. "Decentralisation and democracy in UK local government," *Public Money and Management.* (July-September): 9-20.

Hancock, C. 1990. "What professionals expect from managers," *Managers and Professionals,* Conference Paper 4. London: Office for Public Management. 24-29.

Hanuch, H., ed. 1983. *Anatomy of Government Deficiencies.* Berlin: Springer Verlag. 125-38.

Hayes, R. H., S. C. Wheelwright, and K. B. Clark. 1988. *Dynamic Manufacturing— Creating the Learning Organization.* New York: Free Press.

Hedberg, B., P. Nystrom, and W. H. Starbuck. 1976. "Camping on seesaws: Prescriptions for a self-designing organisation," *Administrative Science Quarterly.* 21:41-65.

Hedberg, B. 1981. "How organizations learn and unlearn," edited by P. C. Nystrom and W.H. Starbuck. 3-27.

Hirschman, A. 0. 1970. *Exit, Voice and Loyalty.* Cambridge, MA: Harvard University Press.

Landau, M. 1973. "On the concept of the self-correcting organization." *Public Administration Review.* 33:533-42.

Landau, M., and R. Stout. 1979. "To manage is not to control," *Public Administration Review.* (March/April):148-56.

Lawton, A., and D. McKevitt. 1993. "Strategic change in local government management," *Waves of Change in the Public Sector.* Sheffield Business School. 5-6 April: 281-293.

Lawton, A., and A. Rose. 1991. *Organization and Management in the Public Sector,* London: Pitman.

Leavitt, H. 1983. "Management and management education in the West," *London Business School Journal.* VIII (I):18-23.

Levine, C. 1984. "Citizenship and service delivery: The promise of coproduction," *Public Administration Review.* 44:178-87.

Lewis, N. 1992. *Inner City Regeneration.* Milton Keynes: Open University Press.

Linblom, C. E. 1965. *The Intelligence of Democracy.* New York: Free Press.

Local Government Training Board (LGTB). 1985. *Good Management in Local Government: Successful Practice and Action.* Luton: LGTB.

Lorenz, C. 1992. "Learning from change." *Managing Fundamental Change,* Conference Paper 7. London: Office for Public Management. 27-32.

March, J. G., and J. P. Olsen. 1983. "Organizing political life: What administrative reorganization tells us about government." *American Political Science Review.* 77:281-296.

Mather, G. 1991. "Serving your right." *Marxism Today.* May.

McGregor, F. B. 1984. "The great paradox of democratic citizenship and public personnel administration." *Public Administration Review.* 44:126-132.

Metcalfe, L., and S. Richards. 1990. *Improving public management.* London: Sage.

Metcalfe, L. 1981. "Designing precarious partnerships," edited by Nystrom and Starbuck. 1.

Mintzberg, H. 1982. "A note on that dirty word 'efficiency,'" *Interfaces.* 12:101-5.

Mulgan, G. 1991. "Power to the public." *Marxism Today.* May.

Murray, R. 1991. "The state after Henry", *Marxism Today.* May: 22-27.

Nystrom, P. C., and W. H. Starbuck. 1981. *Handbook of Organizational Design. Adapting Organisations to Their Environments.* Oxford: Oxford University Press. 1.

Osborne, D., and T. Gabler. 1992. *Reinventing Government.* Reading, MA: Addison-Wesley.

Peacock, A. 1983. "Public X-efficiency: Informational and institutional constraints." *Anatomy of Government Deficiencies,* edited by Haouch, H. Berlin: Springer Verlag. 125-38.

Pedler, M., T. Boydell and J. Burgoyne. 1991. *The Learning Company.* Maidenhead: McGraw-Hill.

Pinder, K. 1993. "Service level agreements and the internal market in local government." *Waves of Change in the Public Sector.* Sheffield Business School. 5-6 April: 411-420.

Pollit, C. 1990. *Managerialism and the Public Services.* Oxford: Blackwell.

PSI. 1990. *Britain in 2010.* London: Policy Studies Institute.

Reed, M., and P. Anthony. 1993. "Between an ideological rock and an organizational hard place: NHS management in the 1980s and 1990s." *The Political Economy of Privatisation,* edited by T. Clarke and C. Pitelis. London: Routledge. 185-204.

Richards, S. 1992. *Who Defines the Public Good? The Consumer Paradigm in Public Management.* London: Public Management Foundation.

Sanderson, I. 1993. *The Management of Quality in Local Government.* London: Longman.

———. 1993b. "Evaluating quality: Principles and issues." *Evaluation and Performance in Local Government.* Leeds Business School. February: 1-l0.

Senge, P. M. 1990. *The Fifth Discipline: The Art and Practice of the Learning Organization.* Doubleday/Currency.

Staw, B. 1977. "The experimenting organization." *Organizational Dynamics.* Summer: 2-18.

Stewart, J. 1986. *The New Management of Local Government.* London: George Allen & Unwin.

———. 1988. *Understanding the Management of Local Government.* Harlow: Longmans.

———. 1990: "Professionalism, politics and public service." *Managers and Professionals,* Conference Paper 4. London: Office for Public Management. 17-23.

Stewart, J. and M. Clarke. 1987. "The public service orientation: issues and dilemmas." *Public Administration.* 65:161-177.

Stewart, J. and G. Stoker. 1989. *The Future of Local Government.* London: Macmillan.

Stewart, J. and K. Walsh. 1992. "Change in the management of the public services." *Public Administration.* 70:499-518.

Stoker, G. 1991. "Introduction: Trends in European local government." *Local Government in Europe,* edited by Barley, R., and G. Stoker. London: Macmillan. 1-16.

Thomson, P. 1992. "Public sector management in a period of radical change: 1979—1992."*Public Money and Management.* July-September: 33-41.

Thomson, W. 1992. "A perspective from local government." *Research and Practice: Shaping the Future of Public Management.* London: Public Management Foundation. 37-40.

Walsh, K. 1991a. "Quality and public services." *Public Administration.* Winter: 503-514.

———. (1991b). "Citizens and consumers: Marketing and public sector management." *Public Money and Management.* Summer: 9-16.

Weick, K. F. 1976. "Educational organizations as loosely coupled systems." *Administrative Science Quarterly.* 21:1-19.

Weil, S. 1992. "Learning to change." *Managing Fundamental Change,* Conference Paper 7. London: Office for Public Management. 9-18.

Wildavsky, A. 1972. "The self-evaluating organization." *Public Administration Review.* September-October: 509-520.

12

Back to the Future: The Twenty-First Century and the Loss of Sensibility

Ralph Hummel

In the twenty-first century, what can public managers expect and not expect from computers?

They can expect greater and greater speed in processing what has already been translated from out of experience into words.

But they cannot expect from computers whatever it takes to get in touch with human experience itself.

Computers are a gift. But they are a gift to logic, not to sensibility.

Sensibility gets us, as humans, in touch with things, where, by things we mean people, objects, states of affairs—our world as it relates to our humanity.

Logic merely defines more precisely what we are in touch with, and it does so not in terms of what makes it possible for us to be in touch with things at all (sensibility), but in terms of categories of pure reason.

To the extent, then, that computers are creations of mere reason, they cannot give us answers to issues and problems that address us in our full humanity. The following deals with the pros and cons of this argument.

In the twenty-first century, will computers run the world? *Can* they run the world?

The two questions are not the same. A world is the totality of significations that comes into being when human beings engage life. Can it be said that computers engage life? that computers interact with life to produce meaning? that computers give birth to worlds?

Computers cannot be adapted to the full range of human knowing and living. Yet we seem to be caught up in a reverse adaptation: human beings are being forced and seduced to conceive of their lives in a way that reduces human potential the more it yields to the functioning of computers. Increasingly, we subject our knowing, judging, feeling, acting, living—our being human—to the limits of what can be punched into and processed by a computer. In doing so, we in effect surrender what it means to *be* and *have* a world. A computer cannot live, act, or feel. Can it make up for these human capabilities by its purported superiority in judging and knowing?

The great strength of computers is that they can engage in logic operations faster than the human brain. It is thus said that computers can think. And in a very specific way, this claim can be held to be true.

For example, in Kantian theory of knowledge to think is to take apart and recombine existing concepts or parts of them (analysis). But knowing is something else. Knowing is not the process by which we combine concepts we already have. Instead, knowing is the process of conceptualizing itself. In coming to know something, we are literally getting a grip on it; the word "concept" itself gives us a clue, coming from the Latin *con-cipere*—that is: taking together, taking hold of, gripping. In making ourselves a concept of what is going on in reality, we do so both in terms of what is there and what our logic can abstract from it (synthesis). Thus, we get a grip on things. Today, there is even an everyday expression for this: What is your take on that?

To grip the new in terms of concepts already established would literally be a mis-take. Having such a take on things would ignore what has not been previously captured in any concept: namely precisely what is new in what newly presents itself. A continuous experience of coming to know and dealing with what has not been conceived before, synthesis in this sense, is essential to human intelligence and existence.

So, if it can be said that computers think, in the limited sense of combining concepts once established, does this mean that—like humans—computers can also synthesize, in the sense of constituting new knowledge by putting a concept together?

Consider a well-known, nearly-the-end-of-the-world experience with computers defending the United States against missile attack during the Cold War.

MAN'S FATE IN THE MOON

On October 5, 1960, the warning system of the North American Defense Command alerted officers that the United States was under massive attack by Soviet missiles. The certainty was calculated at 99.9 percent. Earlier, in the 1950s, a flock of Canadian geese had triggered the same kind of warning; this time, it was something else: no one, in programming the computer, had thought of entering the phases of the moon into the computer system. What the system had detected was the rising moon (Borning 1988: 35; Bracken 1988: 22).

In Kantian terms, we would say that the computer, in both cases, "thinks" and even has the function of "understanding"—that is, is able to combine and arrange the material of knowledge (Kant 1965: 145)—but is incapable of the kind of function that produces that material to begin with. When confronted with a real-world challenge of going beyond its program, the computer does not know how; of itself, it does not know how to know.

For: "To *think* an object and to *know* an object are thus by no means the same thing. Knowledge involves two factors: first, the concept through which an object in general is thought (the category[1]); and secondly, the intuition,[2] through which it is given" (Kant 1965: 146). Thinking can go on in the absence of an object. But knowing involves the synthesis of something taken from reality that is simultaneously grasped within the categories of thought. In computer terms put in Kantian language: thinking is logic processing, knowing is the act of programming (where real-world events are translated in program terms and entered into the machine). Having this view of computers, Kant would have been able to predict the kind of false alarm produced by the computer. The logic machine is simply unable to receive new givens and conceive knowledge anew when a new phenomenon outside its program arises: "For if no intuition could be given corresponding to the concept, the concept would still indeed be a thought, so far as its form is concerned, *and no knowledge of anything would be possible by means of it* (Kant 1965: 146, my emphasis).

The computer, however, does not distinguish thinking (logic processing) from knowing. While, "the thought of an object in general, by means of a pure concept of understanding, can become knowledge *for us* (my emphasis) only in so far as the concept is related to objects of the senses" (ibid.: 146-147), an empty concept is *for a computer,* for all technical purposes, as much "knowledge" as one related to a physical source. Thus, the sensations produced on a radar receptor by the moon can be read as "missiles" as easily as sensations produced by missiles themselves. What is lacking is a judgment rule written into the program that says something like: Every few weeks, along the following phase continuum, you will find "missile" sensations that call for further differentiation because they may also be the moon.

The trick, of course, is to write all possibilities from the real world into the program. But, as the case of the missing moon phases shows, that is exactly the cause of a series of difficulties: the computer is stuck with what humans have programmed. Unlike humans, it cannot go beyond its program and make the kind of judgments that could realistically change the program. But, because we are told again and again by "experts" that computers work pretty much like our brains or that our brains are in fact computers, we tend to treat the results of computer functioning as real. The reason for this being the misunderstanding that computers know, when they really only "think"—and this in the narrow Kantian sense of manipulating empty concepts. Or, in the words of one analyst of the computer role in accidental nuclear war: "The answers to such critical questions as, 'Will the system do what we reasonably expect it to do?' or 'Are there external events that we just didn't think of?' lie inherently outside the realm of formal systems. Computer systems (including current artificial intelligence systems) are notoriously lacking in common sense" (Borning 1988: 37-38).

But, you will say, the moon and the geese are examples of how the computer is pretty much kept under human control. And you are right. So far we have illustrated only the potential for a computer takeover of human judgment. The interesting part of the man/machine development comes when, knowing the potential for computer failure, we nevertheless actually put ourselves in computer-produced situations that cut out any hope for human correction of computer failures.

EXTRUDING MAN FROM SYSTEMS JUDGMENTS

The sociologist Charles Perrow, in his work on normal accidents, describes a normal disjuncture that is necessary in linking production systems to computer control. In a nuclear reactor, when you have almost finished coupling the factory system that makes energy and the computerized control system, you run into one set of linkage where what is positive in one system must be registered as a negative in the other. The trick is to attach a little Post-It note or a little cardboard tag to the computer that reminds you: "When this indicator says the water containment chamber is full, it's really empty." Of course, after several generations of computer controllers' sweat, the mnemonic wears off and the technician on duty the day you have a near-meltdown reads the signal to mean there is actually water to slow the reaction when there isn't. This is what happened at Three-Mile Island (cf., Perrow 1984).

Having a man or woman in the loop to make an intelligent intervening judgment may be pre-empted by the nature of the coupling of systems itself.

To return to nuclear defense: technology has gotten so fast that intercontinental ballistic missiles—and Russia, among others, still has plenty of those—take about 30 minutes to arrive on U.S. targets; submarine launches, less than 10 minutes. The human response to this technological advance has been to move to "launch on warning (LOW)" (a warning being a satellite sighting) or "launch on attack (LUA)" (attack being a sighting by radar), the one being a few minutes earlier than the other. The mathematician Linn Sennott writes that "Consideration of such policies is motivated by fear that, without them, a surprise attack could prove crippling, for example, by a 'decapitation strike'" against national leaders and command centers (Sennott 1988: 43).

The consequence is twofold. First there is the meaninglessness of human beings having only a few minutes to decide on LOW or LUA as retaliation *as if these were real choices: as if, in other words, they could make more than a technical, that is a **human**, difference*. Then there is an increase in false alarms with corresponding decline in time left for resolving them, which further relegates human judgment to the margins (cf., Sennott 1988).

THE THREAT OF FORGETFULNESS IN TECHNOLOGY

The philosopher Martin Heidegger has tried to explore the underlying danger of being so engulfed by technology. Even before the nuclear bombs fall, modern technology poses a fundamental threat to human beings. This threat occurs not so much at the level of error-prone, tightly-coupled systems—a threat that is real—but at the level at which technology interfaces with human potential.

Immanuel Kant's deduction of the limits of human thinking and knowing already served to warn us about the limits of one kind of technology in imitating human intelligence. Heidegger's warning now is a greater one: that we limit not only our thinking and knowing to fit the essence of technology, but our *being*.

And this at the most simple and personal level. As Heidegger once said to a cousin of mine who tried to make him move to the center of his room so a hi-fi system could be installed for the best technical effect: "Dann ist es doch so, dass die Techno-logie den Menschen beherscht, und nicht der Mensch die Techno-logie." [3] (Then things are such that the technology dominates Man, and not Man the technology.) Technology in this case had revealed a way of moving toward "high fidelity" in reproducing the sound of live music. But it also required Heidegger to move away from his accustomed desk near the window and into an uncomfortable position at the apex of a triangulated optimal space to adjust himself and everything else he was and did to the narrow benefit of the hi-fi.

Heidegger (1954/1992) himself puts the warning in this way in his essay "The Question of Technology": technology is a way of unveiling the way things are. As this, technology is not so much merely an instrument of our wants and wishes but is in its essence a way of so approaching reality that we get from it exactly what we want. It is a way of approaching nature and our world, the way a duelist would challenge his opponent.

Heidegger uses the German word for issuing such a challenge—*heraus-fordern*—to describe the essence of technology. In enframing all he knows and does and is, in an approach like that of a challenge, the human being challenges not only nature and the world, but himself—to know, and be nothing else but what can be enframed in such a challenge. *Herausforderung* = literally a calling out; connoting in this case that the human being is called out of its own nature.

Most fully we can think of life as being a way of coming to terms with how things stand and what it is to be human in the interplay with those things—Heidegger refers us to the Greek concept of *poiesis* which discloses this interplay. But, by taking the road of challengeful technology, Man has entered a very narrow way of thinking and knowing himself, others, nature, and the world. On this road, he reduces everything and everybody to serve merely as supplies or resources to be used to satisfy his own will. But in doing so, he is actually shaping not only what he can will for himself, but what he can be. Man himself becomes a mere human resource, an instrumentality, not an end in and of himself. (Heidegger 1982)

The development of this danger has a long history, capable of being traced back to the Platonists'—though not necessarily Plato's—supposition that everything real is a pale imitation of pure ideas, and the rationalists' supposition that all that can be known is determined by the categories of logic. Kant already tried to fight these positions by emphasizing again and again that concepts based on reason alone are mere empty thoughts, and that, for those thoughts to become knowledge, they must be filled with material from direct experience of the world (empirical intuition). With the advent of computers, this problem takes on universal salience. For, once we rely on computer programs, we are easily seduced into slipping from the fact that the computer will not process what it is not programmed to process; into believing that nothing is real if it cannot be programmed into a computer. The enframing that Heidegger warns us against in his essay on technology becomes a fact of daily life. I encounter it every time I turn on my computer and try to operate it in ways it is not programmed. No matter how powerful the urgency of my fleeting thoughts, which can't wait to be put down, the computer, approached in any terms but its own, becomes the immovable object. Solutions to any such stand-off seduce me deeper and deeper into the abyss of programming technique, thus guaranteeing a fatal diversion from creative thought.

But, you will object, that's not the computer's fault; simply render unto experience what belongs to experience and render unto the computer what is the computer's. For reasons already suggested above, including our own wish for a truly orderly world that is completely capable of being comprehended by purely rational rules, this is not what happens in a world dominated by computer thinking. But what further gives impetus to surrendering ordinary human experience to the computer, discarding, in effect, such experience as invalid, if not unreal, is the claim by artificial intelligence advocates that even the products and processes of non-rational experience can be duplicated by the computer.

WHAT ARTIFICIAL INTELLIGENCE CAN'T KNOW

The human/computer interface is even more endangered when, for example, researchers examining the possibility of artificial intelligence (AI) claim that computers can engage in all the thinking and knowing operations of the human brain. In a development co-initiated by a name well-known in public administration, Herbert Simon, but a story untold in these precincts, AI advocates made exactly that kind of claim:

> We have begun to learn how to use computers to solve problems, where we do not have systematic and efficient computational algorithms. And we now know, at least in a limited area, not only how to program computers do perform such problem-solving activities successfully; we know also how to program computers to *learn* to do these things. In short, we now have the elements of a theory of heuristic (as contrasted with algorithmic) problem solving; and we can use this theory both to understand human heuristic processes and to simulate such processes with digital computers. Intuition, insight, and learning are no longer exclusive possessions of human beings: any large high-speed computer can be programmed to exhibit them. (Simon & Newell 1958, cited in Dreyfus & Dreyfus 1988: 6-7)

While admitting that "productive problem-solving"—a kind defined as "constructing new solutions out of more or less 'raw' material"—"depends on both the characteristics of the problem and on the *past experience*...of the problem solver"

(March & Simon 1958: 177), March and Simon nevertheless end up trying to short-circuit the major difficulty: how to get the computer to go beyond the categories of its original program and be sensible to the "raw material" of autonomous things beyond that program to constitute new knowledge.

Under Kantian theory of knowledge, there would be a physical problem, for Kant argues that, for new knowledge to become possible, a sentence's subject must be united with a new predicate from outside that subject. In computer terms, this would mean allowing new data to modify the program even as the program converts the strange new entries into data meaningful to itself. Both the original program and the influx of new givens would run at the same time, making a collision inevitable.

Ultimately, Simon and company [4] try to get around this problem by using the ploy of expert systems. Here, experts in a particular skill, like playing chess or, later, repairing an automobile, reveal their short-cuts to the programmers; these short-cuts are then made part of the program; and eventually a new program is abstracted from the short-cuts. Initially, this procedure was reported to have worked, allowing AI to make progress in having a program play chess. However, as play advanced to more and more difficult levels, the ability of the program declined, and what was originally called the General Problem Solver was given up (Dreyfus 1972/1992: 149ff). Even today, human programmers still have to engage in the function of synthesis on behalf of the machine: making the kind of judgments that would connect old program to data it could not anticipate.

THE LOSS OF SENSIBILITY

But what kind of knowledge is being declared unreal and invalid by thinking the way computers think? What is it that artificial intelligence (AI) programs can't know?

We can understand the answer if we focus on the gambit of getting experts to spell out the short-cuts they use in diagnosing problems—for example, diagnosing the failure of an automobile engine. This gambit involves translation. Knowledge tacitly held—for example, what it feels like when the fingers touch a loose sparkplug connection versus a tight one that allows electricity to flow—has to be translated into words. But words are not the feel. If they were, then anyone could learn how to fix cars from computer instructions *without further fingertip judgment.*

In short, the gambit of getting experts to put their skills into words leaps over what is hidden in the translation from what we apprehend through the senses (the original Greek meaning of the aesthetic) and what we determine or define through logic. Logic processors can neither absorb that part of knowledge which comes from a feel for things, nor can they convey, from out of their language, such a sense for things that anyone following computer instructions would need to connect with reality.

Hubert and Stuart Dreyfus, in their critique of AI, cite an example of having a feel for a non-physical situation. An expert psychiatric nurse, highly regarded for her judgment, says: "When I say to a doctor, 'the patient is psychotic,' I don't always know how to legitimize the statement. But I am never wrong. Because I know psychosis from the inside out. And I feel that, and I know it, and I trust it" (from: Benner 1984: 32, cited in Dreyfus & Dreyfus 1988: 34).

We call such judgments of having "a feel for..." intuition. And, in this context, so would Kant: Before a clear-cut object of knowledge is reasoned out in the mind of the scientist, he or she will have a vague sense for aspects of nature that suggest themselves as potential components and coherences of that yet-to-be-formed object.

The physicist Richard Feynman described this experience in his discussion of fields: "When I start describing the magnetic field moving through space, I speak of the *E*- and the *B*- fields and wave my arms and you may imagine that I can see them. I'll tell you what I see. I see some kind of vague, shadowy, wiggling lines...and perhaps some of the lines have arrows on them—an arrow here or there which disappears when I look too closely.... I have a terrible confusion between the symbols I use to describe the objects and the objects themselves" (Gleick 1993: 245).

Feynman here exemplifies what Kant draws as an essential distinction: between what we have a feel for and what we think about it. Both, though they need to come together to constitute knowledge, must be thought of as distinct mental faculties. Kant: "We therefore distinguish the science of the rules of sensibility in general, that is, aesthetic, from the science of the rules of the understanding in general, that is, logic" (Kant 1965: A52; B76).

This seems to be lost on those who believe they can unproblematically move from having a feel for things, to expressing that feel in terms of an explicit logic system.

Heidegger further develops the idea of a similar pre-judgment operating in everyday life. Such pre-judgment answers the question: What do I have here? It has already operated before we clarify vaguely felt things into mental pictures of objects and symbolic concepts of objects. For example, say I climb on a box in order to reach a light bulb that needs to be replaced in the ceiling for the sake of my further reading and education. Here I do not need to operate with the fully-formed concept "box." I do not employ science or logic to define what I have here in terms of shape, dimensions, or distinction from other things. Nor do I stand apart from it in the detached manner of these approaches. Instead, I am directly involved with the thing at hand and know it only in its outlines relevant to my "in order to" and ultimate "for the sake of." My knowing the box, so to speak, slips and skips and glances over how the box would be fully known in scientific and logical terms so as to *not* give me a detached perspective of it at all. Instead, I know it only in terms of its relevances to my goal. Others who are detached observers may easily label it with the conventional term "box." I experience it as what it serves as: *as*, in fact, a ladder.

Heidegger calls this meaning of what something is to us in use, the "as-structure" of a thing: "Insofar as we address this possibility of taking *something as something* as characteristic of the phenomenon of world, the 'as'-structure is an essential determination of the structure of world" (Heidegger 1995: 311; cf., 1962: section 32).

What operates to constitute things is our care that grasps them in their relation to us as human beings before engaging in rationalistic or objectivizing further definition. Eugene Gendlin, the commentator on Heidegger's (1967) *What Is a Thing?*, brings that ordinary experience we have of that constitutive prejudgment closer to everyday expression by calling it a "felt sense" (Gendlin, 1981: 37ff.; cf. 1967).

Without the felt sense, the as-structure, we have no world.

For computers to process any data from the world so conceived—for example, the measurement of a thing's components or their logical relation—would require the de-worlding of the world as we human beings most directly experience it. Here is where artificial intelligence advocates face a seemingly insuperable hurdle. In contrast to AI advocates viewing all knowing and thinking as a continuum, critics like Hubert Dreyfus consider what Simon calls "nonprogrammed decisions" an "entirely different order" of intelligent activities. This order is separate and distinct from formal reasoning. "This includes all those everyday activities in our human world which are regular but not rule governed." That would include acts such as a perceptive guess, insight, understanding in the context of language use, and the general recognition of varied and distorted patterns (Dreyfus 1972/1992: 294, 292). From a Kantian point of view we would include the pulling together of disparate perceptions into a pattern felt to be useful in formulating, and hence solving, a problem (synthesis of Kantian intuition).

What is disturbing, and an ill omen of the underlying nature of a computer-dominated world, is that some AI experts declare that the distinction between formal and nonformal situations/decisions simply doesn't exist and that its apparent reality can be remedied by bigger and faster machines and "better" programming.

Ultimately what is at stake here is the adoption—or not—of conclusions long disputed in metaphysics. Simon and company believe that both analysis and synthesis, the processing of logic and the constitution of things, are opposite ends of what Simon calls the same "continuum" (from Simon 1969, in Pugh 1985: 206). This reflects an uncritical acceptance of one long train of philosophical thought to the neglect of another. AI adopts the argument of metaphysical idealism that ends in the position that ideas totally determine the object of cognition. This has been put, at the least, in serious question since Kant's great synthesis. By refusing to go back and investigate the arguments that have long danced around this issue of the autonomy of the object, the AI and general computerization advocates project us into a false future. But worse, they pre-empt Man's future altogether: the human being that is unable to fit the world the computer draws out simply must be changed. A logic designed to fit a concept of a human being quite unlike Computer Man is retrofitted and imposed, destroying sense and sensibility.

CONCLUSIONS

Will computers run the world? *Can* computers run the world? We return to these two initial questions. We may conclude that we will dwell in the false belief that they are running the world if we continue to fail to resist the seduction that thinking is knowing. As to the second question: our own computer-dependence may be fatal if we continue to overlook our own function—interpretation of material before it can go into a computer, or come out of it and into action. It has already been demonstrated that such dependence can come close to destroying our world. And it is even more clear that, when confronted with the full understanding of what it means to know, we must admit that computers cannot run the world.

What led to the computer was a train of thought more than two millenia in the making. The computer celebrates the full victory of reason. In our lives, we now face, in the extreme of our dependence on computer logic, the result of that primacy. And yet, we still have the vestigial sense of the gathering activity of experience that brings things together. Constituting each thing, person, and event of a human world must come prior to any translation of that experience into the flat-world representations that can be processed by computer logic. Human beings can imagine more than reason dreams of.

In his exploration of where Kant's *Critique of Pure Reason* leads, namely the uncovering of the buried assumptions on which modern reason rests, Martin Heidegger suggests that imagination is the root of both reason (and its logic) and intuition (and its constituting power). Root and branch, imagination belongs, along with sensibility and understanding, to the tree of knowledge. But imagination is "the root of both stems: sensibility and understanding" (Heidegger 1973: 196ff.).

A specific kind of reason now threatens to imprison us in machine thinking. But this always falls short of a full human knowing: the branch of logic is cut off from the root of imagination. Human beings have known their worlds long before computers came along. The logic that computers force us to adopt is the offspring of a specific moment in history. In the very fact that we are capable of history, in our power to live where future, present, and past meet, we can re-imagine our self. There, in time, is hope also. A self, understood in other than modern terms—not as a thing trying to know other things but as a being capable of opening up worlds—also must produce a different kind of logic. In this hope, in time, rests our imagining of a human future.

NOTES

1. Which brings it to the unity of apperception.

2. Remembering to use "intuition" in the narrow Kantian sense of *Anschauung*, literally a "looking at" appearances stemming from perceptions that constitutes a pre-conceptual, vague sense for what is going on or needs to be constituted before being analyzed.

3. Oral communication from Doris Ruch-Hummel, circa 1991, about her husband's being asked to explore installing a high-fidelity stereo system in Heidegger's cottage in the Black Forest. The spelling of "Techno-logie" (hyphenated) echoes Heidegger's

method of getting to the hidden meaning of words by taking them apart to their origins. In this case, the analytic might be said to reveal Heidegger's position that when we deal with technology, we are engaged in a narrowed dialogue with human potential reduced to a modern version of mere *techne*.

4. The third member of the team was Cliff Shaw.

REFERENCES

Bracken, P. 1988. "Instabilities in the control of nuclear forces." *Breakthrough*, edited by Gromyko and Hellman. New York: Walker & Company. 21-30.

Borning, A. 1988. "Computer system reliability and nuclear war." *Breakthrough*, edited by Gromyko and Hellman. New York: Walker & Company. 31-38.

Dreyfus, H. L. 1972/1992. *What Computers* Still *Can't Do: A Critique of Artificial Reason*. Cambridge, MA.: The MIT Press.

Dreyfus, H. L. and S. E. Dreyfus. 1988. *Mind Over Machine: The Power of Human Intuition and Expertise in the Era of the Computer*. New York: The Free Press.

Gendlin, E. 1967. "Analysis" to Heidegger. 245-296.

———. 1981. *Focusing*. Rev. ed., New York: Bantam Books.

Gleick, J. 1993. *Genius: The Life and Science of Richard Feynman*. New York: Random House—Vintage Books.

Heidegger, M. 1954/1992. The question concerning technology. *Basic Writings*, edited by D. F. Krell. New York: Harper Collins/Harper San Francisco. 307-341.

———. 1962. *Being and Time*. translated by J. Macquarrie and E. Robinson. New York: Harper & Row.

———. 1967. *What is a Thing?* translated by W.B. Barton Jr. and V. Deutsch. South Bend, IN: Regnery/Gateway, Inc.

———. 1973. Kant und das problem der metaphysik. 4th, elaborated ed. Frankfurt am Main: Vittorio Klostermann.

———. 1982. *Die Technik und Die Kehre*. Pfullingen: Verlag Guenther Neske.

———. 1995. *The Fundamental Concepts of Metaphysics: World, Finitude, Solitude*, translated by W. McNeill and N. Walker. Bloomington, IN: University Press.

Kant, I. [1781, 1787] 1965. *Critique of Pure Reason*, translated by N. Kemp Smith. Reprint, New York: St. Martin's Press.

———. (1781=A; 1787=B.) Kritik der reinen vernunft. *Werke*, edited by W. Weischedel. Insel-Verlag. Vol. II.

March, J. G. and H. A. Simon, with H. Guetzkow. 1958. *Organizations*. New York: John Wiley & Sons, Inc.—Carnegie Institute of Technology, Graduate School of Industrial Administration.

Perrow, C. 1984. *Normal Accidents: Living with High Risk Technologies*. New York: Basic Books.

Pugh, D.S., ed. 1985. *Organization Theory: Selected Readings*. 2nd ed. New York: Viking Penguin Inc.—Pelican Books.

Sennott, L. I. 1988. Overlapping false alarms: Reason for concern? *Breakthrough*, edited by Gromyko and Hellman. New York: Walker & Company. 39-44.

Simon, H. L. 1969. Decision making and organizational design. *Organization Theory: Selected Readings*. 2nd ed., edited by D. S. Pugh. New York: Viking Penguin Inc.—Pelican Books. 202-223.

Simon, H. A. and A. Newell. 1958. Heuristic problem-solving: The next advance in computer research. *Operations Research*. 6 (January-February): 6.

PART FOUR

Challenges in Administrative Reform and Policymaking

INTRODUCTION

Shamsul Haque points out that since the emergence of public administration as an academic field, one perennial question in theory building, which has always baffled scholars and experts in the field, has been the issue of administrative ethics. The core of such ethical concern, despite its cross-national and cross-continental variations, has largely revolved around a distinction between the public sphere and the business realm. In the past, the democratic ethical standards associated with the public domain (e.g., representation, equality, justice, impartiality, openness, and accountability) became critical criteria for constructing administrative theory, although the private-sector norms (e.g., utility, efficiency, productivity, competition, and profitability) were not completely ignored either. However, during recent decades, the worldwide movement of the so-called "new public management," based on the principles of neo-managerialism, has altered this public-private configuration in terms of the incorporation of business norms and marginalization of public ethics in government administration. This recent restructuring of ethical standards in practical public governance has critical impacts on the concepts, theories, and domains of academic public administration, and poses a serious challenge to administrative theory building. Haque also explores the major dimensions of recent ethical changes in practical public service professions, and examines how such ethical changes may have critical implications for future theory building in the academic domain of public administration.

David Rosenbloom illustrates that globalization promotes policy diffusion and convergence among nations. This reinforces the traditional assumption of American reformers that administrative practices are freely transferable among different jurisdictional levels and political systems. Rosenbloom argues that the "transferability assumption" promotes failure. It impedes diagnosis and promotes faulty prescription. Reformers should take note of research on comparative administration which indicates that transferability often depends on constitutional arrangements, administrative culture, and the processes used for building and maintaining dominant political coalitions.

Alexander Kouzmin and Alan Jarman discuss that the demise of the "welfare state," in Anglo-Saxon economies, has been a well-documented and much argued process about the parameters of "down-sizing," "de-skilling," and contracting out the Keynesian policy "apparatus." The outer limits of contracting out are heavily contested in the context of globalization, budget surpluses, and emerging avenues for vulnerability and risk for heavily re-engineered public sectors. The authors consider some opportunities for the "smart state" to re-skill itself within parameters of crisis management capabilities, some of the emerging intractable policy problems associated with socio-economic exclusion and the paradoxical requirements of economic sovereignty, much associated with Neo-Liberalism.

13

Reconciling Public Ethics and Business Norms: A Future Challenge to Administrative Theory

—————————————— M. *Shamsul Haque*

INTRODUCTION

In the past, public administration allegedly suffered from various forms of intellectual impasse: the so-called *identity crisis*—caused by the critique of established administrative principles, unresolved controversy over politics-administration dichotomy, and excessive borrowing of fragmented ideas from various fields; the *paradigm crisis*—symbolized by the proliferation of theoretical diversity, lack of a unifying framework, and absence of intellectual consensus; and the *legitimacy crisis*—exacerbated by the field's incapacity to address the diverse needs of academics, practitioners, and citizens (Denhardt 1984; Haque 1996; Ostrom 1974; Ventriss 1987). Although most of these concerns in public administration have not been adequately resolved after decades of intellectual debate and exchange, since the early 1980s a new breed of academic problems has emerged in the field due to the adoption of businesslike reforms in the practical profession public governance. In order to reinforce such a new mode of market-centered governance—often known as "new public management," and adopted under the rhetoric of reinventing or reengineering government—various reform initiatives have been launched in advanced capitalist nations as well as developing countries.[1]

These businesslike reforms in public service practice have considerable impacts on the academic field of public administration, especially in terms of its basic intellectual assumptions, concepts, and theories. As the market norms have come to dominate the public sector and marginalize or replace its established public ethics, the academic domain of public administration has come under increasing pressure to use the principles and criteria of business management in assessing public policies, undertaking research activities, and constructing and reconstructing administrative theories. This newly emerging trend in public administration represents a serious threat to the field, especially to the process of building administrative theory—a theory that represents a body of knowledge related to the public rather than the business domain, and that requires the commitment of scholars interested in generating emancipatory knowledge for the public rather than reproducing instrumental knowledge for the profit-oriented private sector. It has become a formidable challenge to those engaged in theoretical discourse to reconcile public sector ethics and business sector norms without compromising the basic tenets of publicness in administrative theory. In this regard, the paper attempts to address the following issues: the emerging ethical changes in the practical domain of public administration (the public service); the recent ethical transition in the academic sphere of public administration (required and reinforced by changes in the practical domain); the critical implications of these current ethical shifts for the process of building administrative theory (especially for the future theoretical framework); and the exploration of remedial measures or alternatives (needed for overcoming this critical theoretical challenge).

ETHICAL CHANGES IN "PRACTICAL" PUBLIC ADMINISTRATION: RECENT EXPERIENCES

Historically, the basic ethical standards of practical public administration originated from diverse sources. According to Dwight Waldo (1981), some of the major sources of ethical claims in the public service include the constitution, the law, democracy, nation or people, family, friendship, organization, professionalism, race, class, political party, interest group, individual self, religion, humanity, and so on. Among these diverse sources of administrative ethics, however, special attention has often been paid to the regime values, democratic ethos, community ethics, civic virtues, and professional standards (Haque 1996; Jun 1999; Rohr 1989; Van Wart 1998). Emanating from these varying sources of public service norms, the common ethical criteria that emerged in advanced democracies such as the U.K., the U.S., Canada, and France, included standards such as public accountability, citizens' rights, political neutrality, racial representation, public responsiveness, public interest, public disclosure, organizational responsibility, professional integrity, official impartiality, equality and uniformity, public welfare, social commitment, and social justice (see Denhardt 1991; Dobel 1990; Haque 1996; Lewis 1991). These ethical standards also came to shape the official codes of conduct in many newly independent developing nations.

However, in recent years, there has been a widespread movement in Western countries themselves—including the U.S., the U.K., Australia, Canada, and Scandinavian countries—to incorporate the ethos of private sector management into the normative structure of public governance (Peters 1991). It has already been pointed out by some scholars that in many countries, the core administrative values no longer correspond to the values of society at large, especially when the commercial values of the business sector have increasingly become dominant in the public service (Haque 1996; Whitfield 1992). More specifically, the basic ethical standards of the public service—including accountability, representativeness, responsiveness, neutrality, impartiality, equality, citizenship, welfare, justice, and integrity—are rapidly being marginalized by business norms such as efficiency, competition, profit, value-for-money, productivity, cost-effectiveness, and customer satisfaction (Dobel 1990; Haque 1996). This historically significant transition in public service ethics that has taken place in advanced capitalist nations (e.g., Australia, Austria, Belgium, Canada, Denmark, Finland, France, Germany, Italy, Japan, the Netherlands, New Zealand, Norway, Portugal, Spain, Sweden, Switzerland, the U.K., and the U.S.), is also being followed in many developing countries in Asia, Africa, and Latin America, especially under the influence and pressure exerted by international agencies and donor countries (see Dwivedi 1994; Haque 1998a; Llewellyn & Varghese 1997; OECD 1993; 1995). The major features of these businesslike normative shifts in the public service—which have serious implications for the academic sphere of public administration, particularly in terms of constructing and reconstructing administrative theory—are examined below in greater details.

First, there is an emerging shift in the ethical priority of the public service from its social equality to economic efficiency. During the post-war period, the guarantee of social equality—equality between classes, between races, and between genders—became a major ethical concern in both developed and developing nations. This became evident in major public programs, including progressive taxation, anti-poverty programs, affirmative action, gender representation, and so on—undertaken by governments with diverse ideological preferences. Although many of these government policies or strategies might compromise economic efficiency, the question of equality became a crucial public concern in most societies emphasizing a democratic mode of public governance: it became an imperative for the state to ensure equal representation of various classes, races, and genders in the public service and their equal access to public sector organizations and programs. However, under the worldwide triumph of market ideology since the 1980s, the concern for social equality has increasingly been subordinated to the standard of economic efficiency. Although efficiency and productivity are predominantly business-sector norms (Kickert 1997: 28), they have gained ethical dominance in the public sector during the past two decades under the emerging movement known as "new public management."[2] As Lawton mentions, "Critics fear that the public service ethos is being undermined... the concept of a core public service delivering health, welfare, security, transport and education is contested and efficiency and economy are promoted as key virtues" (1998: 55).

Among advanced industrial nations, the public sector's concern for economic efficiency has gained overwhelming priority in countries such as Australia,

Belgium, Canada, France, Germany, Italy, Japan, New Zealand, Spain, Switzerland, the U.K., and the U.S. (see OECD 1995; Wright 1997). In particular, the standards of efficiency and productivity are reflected in the normative orientation of the recently adopted "new public management" that emphasizes the principles and techniques of business management (ILO 1995: 12-13). During the period since the mid-1980s, the significance of efficiency and productivity in public governance has also increased in many developing countries, including Korea, Taiwan, India, Brazil, Bolivia, Uganda, Malaysia, Singapore, Brunei, Indonesia, Thailand, Hong Kong, and the Philippines (Haque 1998a; Salleh 1992; Sobhan 1994; World Bank 1997). In this process of intensifying the normative priority of economic efficiency, the public sector seems to have become relatively indifferent toward one of its established ethical standards, i.e., the question of social equality with regard to class, race, and gender.

Second, there has also been an ethical transition in government administration from its traditional focus on public welfare to criteria such as value-for-money found in the business sector. Prior to the 1980s, the overall performance of a public service used to be judged by the extent of its realization of people's welfare in accordance with the needs and demands of various sections of the population. But one major consideration of the recent public sector reforms, including corporatization, contracting out, and joint venture, has been the guarantee of value-for-money and optimum outcome (ILO 1995; OECD 1993). The increasing concern for this businesslike standard of value-for-money—often paraphrased as "delivering better government"—can not only be found in advanced capitalist nations, it is also becoming a common priority in many developing countries in Asia, Africa, and Latin America, as well as in certain newly emerging post-socialist market economies in Eastern Europe that are reexamining and restructuring the role of the public sector (Dwivedi 1994; Llewellyn & Varghese 1997).

In fact, one of the main components of "new public management," which is rapidly becoming a common global model for public governance, is this criterion of value-for-money (Rhodes 1997: 49). However, although the newly emerging ethical standards, such as value-for-money, may be conducive to the maintenance of quality services provided by the public sector, and thus beneficial to the service recipients, the scope of such beneficiaries is likely to be limited to the affluent sections of the population, because the current provisions of services are increasingly based on market-driven prices and user fees that the low-income households cannot afford. In other words, while the criterion of value-for-money may benefit affluent customers using and paying for high-quality services, it may also constrain the realization of overall public welfare that involves the well-being of all classes and groups of citizens, including the underclass or underprivileged population. In this regard, Sherman mentions that "commercialisation can create ethical tensions particularly between the interests of clients and the [greater] public interest" (1998: 22).

Third, reflecting the above ethical transition in the public service—from public welfare to value-for-money—is its ethical shift from citizenship rights to customers' needs. During the post-war period, the connotation of citizenship expanded to incorporate the civil, political, and social rights of people, and this democratic notion of citizenship became a primary normative benchmark for the public service providing basic services (such as education, health, and housing) to citizens based on their social rights or entitlements. Since the early 1980s, however, this norm of citizenship rights in the public service has come under challenge due to its market-centered transformation under the rubric of "new public management" which redefines citizens as customers or consumers. Such a customer-orientation in public governance—which weakens the principle of a citizen's entitlement to basic services and incorporates the idea of a customer's demand based on one's capacity to pay—has become a common trend in both developed and developing countries following the model of "new public management" (see OECD 1993; Haque 1999; Vanagunas 1997). Countries such as Australia, New Zealand, the U.K., and the U.S. have increasingly moved toward adopting the private-sector norms of consumerism and customer satisfaction in their public services (Arnold, Llewellyn, & Mao 1998; ILO 1995; Varghese & Adams 1997). Various government initiatives and catchphrases have been introduced to reinforce the value of customer-orientation in Asian countries such as the Philippines, Brunei, Malaysia, and Singapore (see Haque 1998a). A similar tendency of market-driven ethical transitions is also occurring in Africa and Latin America, especially under the recent reforms in governance guided by the principles of "new public management." In other words, the primary focus of public governance in many Asian, African, and Latin American countries is being shifted from the general well-being of common citizens to the parochial interests of local businesses and foreign investors representing the privileged customers of the state (see Walton & Seddon 1994).

Although there have been government attempts made recently in advanced industrial countries to introduce some sort of "citizen's charter" to enhance the responsiveness of public officials to customers, such a charter remains relevant to those who use and can pay for various public services (Toonen & Raadschelders 1997). This measure is quite insufficient to ensure the realization of citizenship rights or entitlements—especially the rights of low-income citizens to basic government services such as education, health, housing, and transport. In other words, the adverse impacts of the current normative shift from citizen's right to customer satisfaction, which tends to favor affluent consumers and overlook ordinary citizens, cannot be redressed simply by adopting the so-called citizen's charter in the public service. It has been pointed out by some scholars that although the traditional administrative values are being replaced with the business norms of consumerism and customer orientation, such business norms have allegedly been imposed on citizens, and may not be compatible with the expected public service outlook based on citizenship, representation, and participation (ibid.).

Fourth, in recent years, there has been a proliferation of the norms of public-private partnership, which may have compromised the public service ethics of impartiality based on a public-private distinction. In most democratic societies, there has emerged an ethical standard in public governance stressing the need for maintaining a considerable distance between, or separation of, public officials and the activities of business enterprises in order to avoid any form of corruption or fraud involved in intimate public-private exchanges and deals.[3] But in the current age, which is dominated by market ideology and business ethos, this ethical standard has eroded due to the current emphasis on the norm of business partnership advocated and encouraged by the state in almost all countries. The proliferation of such public-private partnerships has occurred not only in advanced capitalist nations like Australia, Japan, New Zealand, the U.K., and the U.S., but also in developing countries such as Malaysia, India, Singapore, Thailand, the Philippines, Chad, Ghana, Malawi, Senegal, Uganda, Zambia, and Zimbabwe (Haque 1998a; Llewellyn & Varghese 1996; OECD 1990; World Bank 1996, 1997). In the cases of developing countries, however, it is the World Bank that has played a crucial role in influencing governments to undertake initiatives to expand the scope of the private sector and encourage public-private partnership (see World Bank 1996). This normative transition in the public service toward more extensive interaction and partnerships with local and foreign business firms is likely to weaken its ethics of impartiality and integrity, because the partnership norms may influence public policies or decisions in favor of the narrow economic interests of the private sector while overlooking the concerns of common citizens.[4] In short, the extensive use of norms such as public-private partnership may be incompatible with more desirable ethical standards in the public service such as impartiality and integrity.

Finally, although public accountability represents a major ethical standard in the public service, it has come under threat due to the increasing emphasis on norms such as managerialism that stress the operational autonomy of managers as found in the business sector. In line with this principle of businesslike managerial autonomy, especially with regard to finance and personnel, the governments have taken initiatives to create "autonomous agencies," "free agencies," or "executive agencies" in developed nations such as the U.K., New Zealand, Australia, the U.S., Canada, France, Denmark, Finland, the Netherlands, and Spain (Carlos & Pereira 1998; Ingraham 1996; OECD 1993; Toonen & Raadschelders 1997). Similar government efforts have been made in developing countries like Malaysia, the Philippines, Singapore, India, South Korea, and South Africa in order to allow more managerial autonomy in the public sector (Muller et al. 1997; Salleh 1992; World Bank 1995). Although this increasing emphasis on managerialism might encourage innovation in job performance, enhance speed in decision making, and increase operational flexibility, it may pose a challenge to the maintenance of public accountability: under this managerialist approach, the autonomous agencies are often free from essential financial and personnel controls, the contract-based chief executives of these agencies are more likely to be responsive to their respective political heads rather than to democratic institutions such as legislative committees and local communities, and these executives may find more opportunities for private gains in such autonomous public agencies (see Gray & Jenkins 1996; Kernaghan 1992; OECD 1993; Rouban 1993). Even in advanced democratic countries, there is a growing concern that this recent businesslike transition in public governance might have increased the incidence of abuses and scandals, weakened traditional checks and balances, and posed greater challenge to accountability (Arnold, Llewellyn, & Mao 1998). The point, in short, is that the structures and activities associated with the business norm of managerialism—including excessive operational autonomy and opportunity for corruption—are quite incompatible with the democratic ethos and means of accountability in the public service.

However, it should be mentioned that although most countries have undergone business-like ethical changes in public governance toward efficiency, competition, value-for-money, partnership, consumerism, and managerialism, there are considerable variations among nations and among regions in terms of the degree of such a normative transition. For instance, the extent of market-driven administrative ethics may vary between developed and developing nations, and between capitalist and post-socialist countries. Despite these cross-national and inter-regional variations, if one examines the trend within each individual country, it would be observed that during recent decades, the public service has experienced a market-centered ethical transition. In other words, this contemporary ethical shift in public governance largely represents a common global trend, although there are cross-national and inter-regional variations in the degree of such a change.

ETHICS-DRIVEN CHANGES IN "ACADEMIC" PUBLIC ADMINISTRATION: IMPACTS ON THEORY BUILDING

The ethical standards practiced in the practical public service profession largely affect the academic discourse in public administration in terms of its basic assumptions, concepts, and theories. Prior to the emergence of market-driven public governance in recent years, the formation of public service ethics based on democratic values coincided with the corresponding normative benchmarks in the academic public administration, stressing ethical criteria such as democracy, legitimacy, accountability, citizenship, equity, welfare, neutrality, honesty, and integrity, which differed considerably from the market norms in business management (Jann 1997: 95; Lewis 1991: 21). In fact, the democratic ethos in public administration became one of the central intellectual concerns for many early scholars, including Herman Finer, David Levitan, Wayne Leys, L.K. Caldwell, Donald Kingsley, and Paul Appleby (see Nigro & Richardson 1990: 624-627). However, during the last quarter of this century, characterized by the dominance of a market-driven governance known as "new public management," the above mentioned business-like changes in public service ethics—from social equality to economic efficiency, from public welfare to value-for-money, from citizenship right to customer satisfaction, from public-private distinction to public-private partnership, from public accountability to managerial autonomy—have created critical impacts on public administration as an academic field, especially in terms of its intellectual atmosphere, conceptual framework, curriculum structure, and research and publication. As discussed below, such critical impacts of the current ethical changes in public governance on these various dimensions of academic public administration pose a serious challenge to administrative theory building.

First, the business-friendly ethical atmosphere in practical public governance has considerable influence on academic institutions, which have increasingly moved toward an intellectual perspective based on market principles and business ethos. In fact, there has been growing pressure on public administration institutions to restructure their intellectual outlook, course curriculum, and teaching materials in order to maintain adequate student enrollment adversely affected by the anti-public service and pro-business rhetoric of the current age.[5] The recent opinion polls suggest that there is increasing antipathy among university graduates toward the public service as a career, which may account for the declining demand for education in public administration compared to business management (see Haque 1996). This trend of declining educational demand has negative impacts on public administration in terms of the survival of its academic institutions. Thus, in order to keep themselves relevant to the current social context dominated by market ideology, and to maintain a certain level of educational demand, many public administration schools and departments have increasingly moved toward an intellectual outlook normatively based on market criteria or business standards. This overall tendency toward a market-driven framework poses a challenge to the formulation of administrative theory, because this framework may not be compatible with the traditional theoretical focus of public administration on democratic concerns such as public interest, citizenship, representation, and social justice. If the field's intellectual atmosphere is increasingly guided by business or market ethos, it may weaken the established theoretical perspective based on these democratic principles or ideals.

Second, reflecting the above, overall transition in public administration toward a business-like intellectual atmosphere, is the recent emergence of new sub-fields, such as policy sciences or policy studies, that largely emphasize the application of market principles to the public sector (Elhussein 1989). In general, public policy analysis is theoretically based in public choice, which holds neoclassical economic assumptions, and uses individualistic and utilitarian criteria to assess socioeconomic policies undertaken by the public sector (Harmon & Mayer 1986). This public choice perspective —endorsed and used by scholars such as Anthony Downs (1966), Vincent Ostrom (1974), and James Buchanan and Gordon Tullock (1962)—represents a major intellectual framework for the current administrative experts prescribing the market-driven "new public management" that emphasizes disaggregated bureaucracy, interorganizational competition, and consumer choice (Rhodes 1997: 49). Despite such a market-biased, public-choice perspective of policy analysis, it has become a crucial component of public administration programs run by universities in many developed and developing countries (Elhussein 1989; Haque 1996). In fact, during the past two decades, while the scope of policy analysis has expanded, subfields such as comparative administration and development management have been marginalized, if not completely replaced. Due to this shift in educational composition of public administration,[6] there has been a proliferation of administrative theories and models in the domain of policy analysis that borrows heavily from market-biased neoclassical economics. This trend represents the increasing dominance of market principles and quantitative techniques in administrative theory building, and without the use of such principles and techniques, the validity of theoretical research and publications in the field often comes under critical scrutiny.

Third, in line with the previously mentioned rise of business norms in the public service and emergence of market-biased academic subfields, there has been a proliferation of various terms and concepts in public administration that are largely used in business management. As Konig (1997: 218) mentions, the recent trend in public administration is the increasing use of the language of market, competition, customer, and entrepreneurship, which represents a departure from the traditional language of the field. Similarly, Wright (1997: 7) and Lawton (1998: 60) point out that in the current vocabulary of public administration, the main buzz words are *efficiency, effectiveness, economy, contract, competition, customer, market, profit, automization, downsizing,* and *privatization.* This transition has also been reinforced in public administration due to its increasing use of business-sector techniques, including, Strategic Planning, Management by Objectives, and Total Quality Management (Peters 1996). These techniques are conceptually loaded with the language of business. However, the conceptual convergence of public administration with business management tends to diminish the traditional public-private distinction, and raises questions regarding the field's special identity as a body of knowledge related to public interest and concern.

In this regard, there are scholars who have already mentioned that public administration has lost its public identity by using market principles and embracing business languages (see Haque 1996; Ventriss 1987; 1989). Thus, the earlier critique of public administration theory, with regard to its conceptual dependence on business management, may have worsened in recent years due to a more aggressive use of business principles and techniques in the field. In addition, a democratic notion of the "public" and its constitutive ideals such as equality, rights, representation, fairness, and justice—which should constitute the foundation of administrative theory—seem to have become marginalized due to the indiscriminate use of business terms and concepts in public administration in recent years.

Finally, encouraged by the rising market values in public service, and inspired by the business-like intellectual atmosphere in public administration discussed earlier, there has emerged a new breed of scholars and experts who attempt to discredit the established ideas and principles of public administration, and tend to restructure the field by incorporating market principles and business standards. According to Martin (1993: 14), the new genre of authors—including corporate human resource specialists, business school graduates, and management consultants—has made a handsome living by propagating organization theories and models that emphasize the application of business practices and techniques in public administration. Some of the well known works of such authors include, *In Search of Excellence* (Peters & Waterman 1982), *Reinventing Government* (Osborne & Gaebler 1992), *Breaking Through Bureaucracy* (Barzelay & Armanjani 1992), *Banishing Bureaucracy* (Osborne & Plastrik 1997), and so on. These authors not only propagate the strengths of market forces and private corporations, they also prescribe various business ethos—including competition, market incentive, customer orientation, entrepreneurship, and managerial flexibility—for public governance. In addition, there are various regional and international organizations—including the World Bank, the Organization for Economic Co-operation and Development, the Commonwealth Secretariat, and the U.S. Agency for International Development—which have recently begun to publish and disseminate country reports and documents blaming the state-centered public service, and endorsing market-driven administrative reforms undertaken by governments all over the world.

This new breed of authors, experts, and institutions favoring pro-market concepts, standards, and techniques in public administration, pose a serious challenge to scholars who hold a theoretical position based on public-private distinction, critique the intrusion of business principles in public governance, and find the validity of administration theory in its relevance to public concerns. It is because of the current trends toward increasing public-private convergence, the rising dominance of business ethos, and the growing influence of business-minded authors and experts, that the latter group of scholars, those emphasizing the publicness of public administration, may lose intellectual commitment and become marginalized in the academic sphere. This implies a serious loss for the public administration field in terms of its future theory building, because without the intellectual role and commitment of these public-minded scholars, administrative theory may become overwhelmed by the assumptions and principles of business management.

CONCLUDING REMARKS

In the above discussion, it has been pointed out that under the current global atmosphere, which is dominated by market ethos, the public service profession has undergone a considerable ethical transformation, especially in terms of its incorporation of business norms such as managerialism, competition, efficiency, value-for-money, partnership, and customer-orientedness. These market-driven ethical changes in the practical domain of public administration have critical implications for various dimensions of its academic sphere—including its concepts, principles, sub-fields, and publications—and these critical academic conditions, in turn, constitute a challenge to future administrative theory building. This emerging theoretical challenge requires a serious rethinking in the field— e.g., rethinking with regard to the significance of ethics in public administration, the relevance of business ethics to public governance, and the proper interpretation of the term "public" that represents the conceptual foundation of administrative theory in the public domain.

More specifically, it is essential to examine the importance of ethics in both the practical and academic spheres of public administration. With regard to the practical domain, it has been pointed out by Lewis (1991: 18) that a democratic mode of governance depends considerably on public trust, and its credibility to earn such public trust is grounded in its ethical standards. Similarly, Kickert (1997: 34) suggests that in a democracy, public organizations are not commercial business firms, and that a sacrifice of efficiency must be made by the public sector to uphold its values such as liberty, equity, social justice, and legitimacy. Similarly, in relation to the academic sphere, Denhardt suggests that ethical imperatives such as honor, benevolence, and justice, should "make up the moral foundation of public administration, and this foundation should have a central place in education of students of public affairs and administration" (1991: 109). In other words, due to such practical and intellectual significance, ethical discourse must be revived and expanded in public administration, although this ethical question has recently been overshadowed by the rhetoric of structural reengineering in governance under the rubric of "new public management."

In this regard, serious critical studies are needed to reexamine the relevance and applicability of market values or business standards to public administration. It has repeatedly been pointed out by the earlier scholars that business norms are relatively incompatible with public administration,[7] because its foundation needs to be based on democratic principles such as citizens' rights and interests; because the people expect a special set of normative standards from public employees such as accountability, welfare, benevolence, and commitment; and because public governance is supposed to apply criteria such as equality, representation, and justice in serving various social groups and classes (see Coursey & Bozeman 1990; Haque 1998b; 1998c; Ventriss 1987). Since these basic ethical concerns in public administration have increasingly been relegated to a subordinate position under the all-pervasive dominance of market ideology, it has become an intellectual imperative for public administration scholars to deconstruct market-centered assumptions, reexamine the taken-for-granted claims of the strengths or advantages of the business norms, and assess the appropriateness and implication of such assumptions and norms for administrative theory and practice.

In addition, it has become essential for critical thinkers in the field to articulate and reinforce a comprehensive interpretation of the *public*, an interpretation which has remained relatively ambiguous, and is increasingly being identified as an aggregation of consumers. Because a well constructed concept of publicness is essential for understanding the nature of public-private distinction, so is assessing the feasibility and implication of incorporating private sector norms and principles into public affairs, thereby facilitating the process of building a sound public administration theory.[8] In the existing literature of the field, there is a dominant, but problematic tendency to characterize the public domain in terms of the sphere of the state or government, because in many instances (especially developing countries), the state may not represent the general public in terms of its composition, and does not serve the public in terms of policies and programs.[9] A similar problem lies with the utilitarian interpretation offered by the public choice perspective, which tends to view the public in terms of an aggregate of atomistic individual choices, and fails to take into account issues such as citizenship right, power structure, and exchange and interaction involving various classes and groups of people constituting the public. The point, in short, is that since the existing notion of the public is quite inadequate (as discussed above), since the debate on the issue appears to have weakened (due to the diminishing emphasis on public-private distinction), and since the prevalent interpretation is increasingly based on market-driven consumerism (evident in the redefinition of citizen as customer), there is an immediate need for rethinking and reviving a genuine concept of the public that is so central to the process of building an administrative theory for public governance.

NOTES

1. Examples of such reforms include the Next Steps in the U.K., Public Service 2000 in Canada, Financial Management Improvement Programme in Australia, Modernization Program for the Public Sector in Denmark, Renewal of the Public Service in France, Major Options Plan in Portugal, Administrative Management Project in Austria, and Fundamental Policy of Administrative Reform in Japan (OECD 1993). Similar business-like reforms in the public sector have been undertaken in Belgium, Finland, Germany, Italy, the Netherlands, New Zealand, Norway, Spain, Sweden, Switzerland, Turkey, the Philippines, Singapore, Jamaica, Malaysia, Mexico, Brazil, and Zambia (see Haque 1998; Nunberg 1997; OECD 1995).

2. In this regard, Whitfield (1992) mentions that since the 1980s, there has been diminishing priority of equality, social needs, and public interest in the public service.

3. In the case of the U.S., it has been observed that an increase in the number of government contracts with private enterprises has led to public concern regarding the potential problems emerging from government-contractor relationships, including ambiguity in the performance of contractors, use of illegal tactics, and opportunities for kickbacks (Frederickson & Frederickson 1995; Rubin 1993; Wise 1990).

4. In fact, a closer alliance between the public and private sectors may be confusing to the common public, because due to joint management based on public-private partnership, the people may not know whether it is public agencies or private firms that are responsible for delivering services (Peters 1993).

5. In both developed and developing countries, the public service has come under attack from various sources—including business elites, political leaders, and international agencies—for its alleged inefficiency and mismanagement (Haque 1996).

6. In this regard, it is pointed out that public administration has become so close to business management that "in many graduate programs the training of MPAs has become nearly identical to the training of MBAs" (Hart & Wasden 1990: 770).

7. As Rhodes (1997: 56) mentions, "The civil service culture is a blend of values including honesty, loyalty, impartiality, propriety and a respect for intelligence....

Managerialism, open competition, impropriety and macho-ministers add up to a dilution of this culture and ethos."

8. It has been pointed out by some scholars that a proper conceptualization of the term *public* is crucial for formulating administrative theory, evaluating public policies, and overcoming intellectual vulnerability that exists in public administration (Coursey & Bozeman 1990; Ventriss 1987; 1989).

9. Mathews (1985: 123) suggests that "the root words for public are not the same as the root words for the polity, the state, the government."

REFERENCES

Arnold, G., J. Llewellyn and Q. Mao. 1998. International trends in public administration—notes. *Canberra Bulletin of Public Administration.* May, No.88.

Barzelay, M. and B. J. Armanjani. 1992. *Breaking Through Bureaucracy: A New Vision for Managing in Government.* Berkeley, CA: University of California Press.

Buchanan, J. M. and G. Tullock. 1962. *The Calculus of Consent: Logical Foundations of Constitutional Democracy.* Ann Arbor, MI: University of Michigan Press.

Carlos, L. and B. Pereira. 1998. Managerial public administration: Strategy and structure for a new state. *Journal of Post Keynesian Economics.* 20(1):7-24.

Coursey, D. and B. Bozeman. 1990. Decision making in public and private organizations: A test of alternative concepts of "publicness." *Public Administration Review.* 50(5):525-535.

Denhardt, K. G. 1991. Unearthing the moral foundations of public administration: Honor, benevolence, and justice. *Ethical Frontiers in Public Management,* edited by J. S. Bowman. San Francisco, CA: Jossey-Bass Publishers. 91-109.

Denhardt, R. B. 1984. *Theories of Public Organization.* Pacific Grove, CA: Brooks/Cole Publishing Company.

Dobel, J. P. 1990. Integrity in the public service. *Public Administration Review.* 50(3): 354-66.

Downs, A. 1966. *Inside Bureaucracy.* Boston, MA: Little, Brown.

Dwivedi, O. P. 1994. Structural adjustment programmes and administrative reforms in Third World. *Structural Adjustment, Public Policy and Bureaucracy in Developing Societies,* edited by R.B. Jain and H. Bongartz. New Delhi: Har-Anand Publications. 351-367.

Elhussein, A. M. 1989. Policy analysis and public administration: A theoretical review. *Indian Journal of Public Administration.* 35(2):220-232.

Frederickson, G. and D. G. Frederickson. 1995. Public perceptions of ethics in government. *Annals of the American Academy of Political and Social Science.* 537 (January):163-172.

Gray, A. and B. Jenkins. 1996. Public administration and government 1994-95. *Parliamentary Affairs.* 49(2):235-255.

Haque, M. S. 1996. The intellectual crisis in public administration in the current epoch of privatization. *Administration & Society.* 27(4):510-536.

———. 1998a. New directions in bureaucratic change in Southeast Asia: Selected experiences. *Journal of Political and Military Sociology.* 26(1):6-114.

———. 1998b. Legitimation crisis: A challenge for public service in the next century. *International Review of Administrative Sciences.* 64(1):13-26.

————. 1998c. Paradox of bureaucratic accountability in developing nations under a pro-market state. *International Political Science Review*. 19(4):357-372.

————. 1999. Relationship between citizenship and public administration: A reconfiguration. *International Review of Administrative Sciences*. 65(3):309-325.

Harmon, M. M. and R. T. Mayer. 1986. *Organization Theory for Public Administration*. Boston: Little, Brown and Company.

Hart, D. K. and C. D. Wasden, C. D. 1990. Two roads diverged in a yellow wood: Public administration, the management orthodoxy, and civic humanism. *International Journal of Public Administration*. 13(6):747-775.

ILO International Labor Organization. 1995. *Impact of Structural Adjustment in the Public Services*. Geneva: International Labor Office.

Ingraham, P. W. 1996. The reform agenda for national civil service systems: External stress and internal strains. *Civil Service Systems in Comparative Perspective*, edited by H. A. G. M. Bekke, J. L. Perry, and T. A. J. Toonen. Bloomington, IN: Indiana University Press. 247-267.

Jann, W. 1997. Public management reform in Germany: A revolution without a theory? *Public Management and Administrative Reform in Western Europe*, edited by W. J. M. Kickert. Cheltenham, UK: Edward Elgar Publishing. 83-102.

Jun, J. S. 1999. The need for autonomy and virtues: Civic-minded administrators in a civil society. *Administrative Theory & Praxis*. 21(2):218-226.

Kernaghan, K. 1992. Empowerment and public administration: Revolutionary advance or passing fancy? *Canadian Public Administration*. 35(2):194-214.

Kickert, W. 1997. Public management in the United States and Europe. *Public Management and Administrative Reform in Western Europe,* edited by W. J. M. Kickert. Cheltenham, UK: Edward Elgar Publishing Ltd. 15-39.

Konig, K. 1997. Entrepreneurial management or executive administration: The perspective of classical public administration. *Public Management and Administrative Reform in Western Europe,* edited by W. J. M. Kickert. Cheltenham, UK: Edward Elgar Publishing Ltd. 217-236.

Lawton, A. 1998. Business practices and the public service ethos. *Public Sector Ethics: Finding and Implementing Values,* edited by C. Sampford, N. Preston, & C. A. Bois. London: Routledge. 53-67.

Lewis, C. W. 1991. *The Ethics Challenge in Public Service*. San Francisco, CA: Jossey-Bass Publishers.

Llewellyn, J. and M. Varghese. 1996. International trends in public administration—notes. *Canberra Bulletin of Public Administration*, November, No.82.

————. 1997. International trends in public administration—notes. *Canberra Bulletin of Public Administration*, December, No.86.

Martin, B. 1993. *In the Public Interest: Privatization and Public Sector Reform*. London: Zed Books Ltd.

Mathews, D. 1985. The public in practice and theory. *Public Administration Review*. 44:120-125.

Muller, J. J. et al. 1997. Civil service systems in comparative perspective: South Africa—A country study. The Conference on Civil Service Systems in Comparative Perspective, School of Public and Environmental Affairs, Indiana University, Indiana. 5-8 April.

Nigro, L. G. and W. D. Richardson. 1990. Between citizen and administrator: Administrative ethics and PAR. *Public Administration Review*. 50(6):623-635.

Nunberg, B. 1997. Leading the horse to water: Transnational inducements to administrative reform. The Conference on Civil Service Systems in Comparative Perspective, School of Public and Environmental Affairs, Indiana University, Indiana. 5-8 April.

OECD Organization for Economic Co-operation and Development. 1990. *Public Management Development Survey 1990*. Paris: OECD.

————. 1993. *Public Management Development Survey 1993*. Paris: OECD.

————. 1995. *Public Management Developments Update 1995*. Paris: OECD.

Osborne, D. and T. Gaebler. 1992. *Reinventing Government: How the Entrepreneurial Spirit is Transforming the Public Sector*. Reading, MA: Addison-Wesley Publishing Company.

Osborne, D. and P. Plastrik. 1997. *Banishing Bureaucracy: The Five Strategies for Reinventing Government*. Reading, MA: Addison-Wesley Publishing Co.

Ostrom, V. 1974. *The Intellectual Crisis in American Public Administration,* rev. ed. Tuscaloosa, AL: The University of Alabama Press.

Peters, G. B. 1991. Government reform and reorganization in an era of retrenchment and conviction politics. *Handbook of Comparative and Development Public Administration,* edited by A. Farazm. New York: Marcel Dekker. 381-403.

Peters, B. G. 1993. Searching for a role: The civil service in American democracy. *International Political Science Review*. 14(4):373-386.

Peters, B. G. 1996. *The Future of Governing: Four Emerging Models*. Lawrence, KA: University Press of Kansas.

Peters, T. J. and R. H. Waterman. 1982. *In Search of Excellence: Lessons From America's Best-Run Companies*. New York: Harper & Row.

Rhodes, R. 1997. Reinventing Whitehall, 1979-1995. *Public Management and Administrative Reform in Western Europe*, edited by W. J. M. Kickert. Cheltenham, UK: Edward Elgar Publishing Ltd. 43-60.

Rohr, J. A. 1989. *Ethics for Bureaucrats: An Essay on Law and Values*. New York: Marcel-Dekker.

Rouban, L. 1993. France in search of a new administrative order. *International Political Science Review*, 14(4):403-418.

Rubin, I. S. 1993. The politics of expenditures: Managing competition, accountability, and acceptability. *The Political Environment of Public Management,* edited by P. Kobrak. New York: HarperCollins Publishers. 221-253.

Salleh, S. H. 1992. A glance at the civil service reforms in the Asean countries. *Civil Service in the South Asian Region,* edited by S.H. Salleh. Kuala Lumpur: Asian and Pacific Development Centre. 27-53.

Sherman, T. 1998. Public sector ethics: Prospects and challenges. *Public Sector Ethics: Finding and Implementing Values,* edited by C. Sampford, N. Preston, and C. A. Bois. London: Routledge. 13-25.

Sobhan, R. 1994. The public sector: Review of role, trends, constraints; conclusion. *The Role of the Public Sector in Promoting the Economic Development of Developing Countries,* edited by United Nations. New York: United Nations. 1-50.

Toonen, T. A. J. and J. C. N. Raadschelders. 1997. Public sector reform in Western Europe. The Conference on Civil Service Systems in Comparative Perspective, School of Public and Environmental Affairs, Indiana University. 5-8 April.

Van Wart, M. 1998. *Changing Public Sector Values*. New York: Garland Publishing.

Vanagunas, S. 1997. Civil service reform in the Baltics. The Conference on Civil Service Systems in Comparative Perspective, School of Public and Environmental Affairs, Indiana University, Indiana. 5-8 April.

Varghese, M. and J. Adams. 1997. International trends in public administration—notes. *Canberra Bulletin of Public Administration*, February, No.83.

Ventriss, C. 1987. Two critical issues of American public administration: Reflections of a sympathetic participant. *Administration & Society*. 19(1):25-47.

———. 1989. Toward a public philosophy of public administration: A civic perspective of the public. *Public Administration Review*. 49(2):173-179.

Waldo, D. 1981. *The Enterprise of Public Administration*. Novato, CA: Chandler and Sharp.

Walton, J. and D. Seddon. 1994. *Free Markets & Food Riots: The Politics of Global Adjustment*. Cambridge, MA: Blackwell Publishers.

Whitfield, D. 1992. *The Welfare State: Privatization, Deregulation, Commercialization of Public Services: Alternative Strategies for the 1990s*. London: Pluto Press.

Wise, C. R. 1990. Public service configurations and public organizations: Public organization design in the post-privatization era. *Public Administration Review*. 50(2):141-155.

World Bank. 1995. *Bureaucrats in Business: The Economics and Politics of Government Ownership*. New York: Oxford University Press.

———. 1996. *World Bank Annual Report 1996*. Washington, DC: International Bank for Reconstruction and Development.

———. 1997. *World Development Report 1997: The State in a Changing World*. New York: Oxford University Press.

Wright, V. 1997. The paradoxes of administrative reform. *Public Management and Administrative Reform in Western Europe*, edited by W. J. M. Kickert. Cheltenham, UK: Edward Elgar Publishing Ltd. 7-13.

14

Administrative Reformers in a Global World: Diagnosis, Prescription, and the Limits of Transferability

—————————— David H. Rosenbloom

Sometime in 1997, I received a phone call from a researcher on contract with a major international development organization. He asked whether I might be interested in helping to design a comprehensive administrative reform package for a Latin American nation. I averred that my knowledge of the country was confined to its location, the fact that it is Spanish-speaking (which I am not), and that it exports fine baseball players to the U.S. major leagues. I also admitted that I did not even know whether it had a parliamentary or presidentialist political system. No matter, I was told, my expertise could help, and if I needed to speak with the nation's president, I could do so in English as he grew up in the same area of the U.S. as I did and had pretty much the same accent. I joined the project, but never stopped wondering whether this was any way to go about reforming a national bureaucracy. (David H. Rosenbloom.)

INTRODUCTION

It is now broadly accepted that American public administration was "misfounded" at its inception in the 1870s-1920s (Wamsley and Wolf 1996; McSwite 1997). The civil service reformers and Progressives of that era built the field on at least two mistaken assumptions: first, that public administration does not involve politics; and second, that administrative practices are freely transferable from one jurisdiction or political system to another. The failures of the "politics-administration dichotomy" are, of course, now well understood (Rabin and Bowman 1984). However, the "transferability assumption" continues to impede the diagnosis of administrative problems, the prescription of remedies, and, as a result, the viability of many attempts at reform.

As globalization promises to be a major force at the outset of the new millennium, it is imperative that the diffusion of administrative reforms be far more successful than was the case in the twentieth century. This article draws on the accumulated observations of comparative administration researchers in arguing that constitutional arrangements, and administrative culture, as well as the processes used for building and maintaining dominant political coalitions, should be considered central to the potential transferability of substantial, system reorienting reforms.

THE RISE AND PERSISTENCE OF THE "TRANSFERABILITY ASSUMPTION"

In the United States, both the creation of the administrative state and the self-conscious study of public administration were informed by the transferability assumption. The merit system, instituted by the Civil Service Act of 1883 (Pendleton Act), is usually viewed as the cornerstone on which much of the next century of federal administrative development rested. It was "a foreign invention" imported by the U.S. civil service reform movement from Great Britain, though partly "Americanized" by a Congress wary of copying specific features derived from the British social class system (Van Riper 1958: 96-112).

The transferability assumption was also central to Woodrow Wilson's foundational call, in 1887, for the scientific study of public administration. In Wilson's famous words:

> If I see a murderous fellow sharpening a knife cleverly, I can borrow his way of sharpening the knife without borrowing his probable intention to commit murder with it; and so, if I see a monarchist dyed in the wool managing a public bureau well, I can learn his business methods without changing one of my republican spots. He may serve his king; I will continue to serve the people; but I should like to serve my sovereign as well as he serves his. (Wilson 1887: 23)

Leonard White followed suit in his *Introduction to the Study of Public Administration*—the first American textbook on the subject—with the assumption that "...administration is a single process, substantially uniform in its essential characteristics wherever observed, and therefore avoids the study of municipal administration, state administration, or federal administration as such" (White 1926: 57).

Stated so starkly, the transferability assumption might appear preposterous on its face. After all, will Wilson's monarchist afford procedural due process, equal protection, and whistleblowing rights to his employees? Will there be open meetings, freedom of information, and public participation in rulemaking? Will White's municipal government have a bicameral legislature or an elaborate separation of powers system? Will his states have only two elected executive branch officials? Will their legislatures take as much interest as Congress in specifying appropriate administrative procedures through administrative law?

Yet despite massive logical and practical problems inherent in the transferability assumption, many reformers cling to it. As a design science, public administration has long been oriented toward techniques for delivering and managing public services. No doubt there is much knowledge and experience—a good deal of it technical—that is transferrable. However, reformers have a history of overestimating the limits of transferrability, as Gerald Caiden explains:

> Given the tremendous strides that had been made in organization, administration and management since the beginning of the [twentieth] century and the great successes of post-war reconstruction, there was cause for optimism that the well-tried models of the past and the new models of the (then) present would work. If they were not working out as expected—and already in the 1960s there was mounting evidence to suggest that this was the case—it was not the models so much at fault as the people employing the models. They had not been properly prepared or they lacked the proper skills or they held the wrong attitudes. In time, given sufficient education, training, and experience, they would come around. Changing administrative systems needed patience and understanding but change they would; managerial engineering worked. (1991:15-16)

David Osborne and Ted Gaebler's prescriptions for thoroughgoing administrative reform provide a contemporary example. Their phenomenally successful and influential book, *Reinventing Government* (1992), assumes that what works in a relatively small, homogenous city manager form of government will work for a sprawling federal department. No matter that Sunnyvale, California faces nothing like the fragmented legislative and interest group involvement in administration that is the hallmark of bureaucratic politics at the national level, or that federal agencies now have layers upon layers of political appointees (Light 1994).

Globalization, with its pressures for the convergence of public policies across nations, reinforces the tendency to believe that fundamental reforms, like very limited ones, are readily transferrable. As regional and inter-regional economies become more substantially linked, and the world begins to develop meaningful international human rights and labor law, why should administrative systems resist standardization? For instance, former Vice President Al Gore's National Performance Review (NPR; renamed National Partnership for Reinventing Government in 1998) borrows ideas from reformers in parliamentary systems in the hope that Congress will voluntarily stop "micromanaging" federal agencies in favor of merely reviewing their "results" on an after-the-fact basis (Gore 1993:34). But ever since 1946, when it enacted the Administrative Procedure Act and reorganized itself to exercise "continuous watchfulness" of the agencies, Congress has been deepening its direct involvement in federal administration (Rosenbloom 1998; 2000). Its micromanagement is connected to the members' incumbency (Fiorina 1989; Rosenbloom 2000) and is not very likely to change based on the putative success of reforms in Great Britain,

Australia, and New Zealand, in which the parliamentary role in administration is quite different.

Perhaps Alasdair Roberts most precisely hits the correct cautionary note regarding transferability:

> Of course it would be foolish to suggest that we should ignore the experience of other public services or overlook innovative practices that may well produce benefits at home. On the other hand, it is important to remember that public services are not interchangeable: each is shaped by distinctive political and social conditions and is the product of a unique series of historical events. We would be well advised, when looking over our borders for models for reform, to question whether these models were designed to accommodate circumstances very different from our own. (1996: 76-77)

Such an assessment is crucial because, as Caiden notes, contemporary administrative reform "...rarely succeeds as expected and usually fails through faulty implementation" (1991: 296).

THE TRANSFERABILITY ASSUMPTION AND DIAGNOSIS

The transferability assumption impedes diagnosis (Dx) or its utility in at least two ways. First, it subtly diminishes the effort devoted to Dx. The availability of a reform, and its legitimation through implementation in an important setting, leads reformers to define administrative problems in terms of what that reform may be able to fix. In other words, the malady tends to be defined in terms of the prescription (Rx) available.

B. Guy Peters and Donald J. Savoie provide an excellent analysis of this problem. In an article entitled, "Civil Service Reform: Misdiagnosing the Patient," they explain how Great Britain, Canada, and the United States applied a similar reform package to problems which, although superficially alike, were actually quite distinct because they were embedded in dissimilar administrative systems and cultures (Peters and Savoie 1994). Relying on the broad assumption that private managerial practices are superior to those used in public administration, reforms in all three nations sought to bring private sector expertise, technique, and customer orientation to the civil service.

According to Peters and Savoie, the "assumption that all organizations are the same" fostered a dysfunctional "...tendency to aggregate public and private organizations..., as well as for a tendency to treat all public sector organizations as the same" (ibid.: 422). The price of inadequate attention to Dx was steep: "The result has been that government departments that were well managed in the 1970s are still well managed but the reforms have had limited impact on those that traditionally were not well managed (i.e., departments and agencies having a high policy content as opposed to carrying out routine tasks)." Among the casualties in all three nations was a relative decline in administrators' capacities to provide much needed policy advice (ibid.: 418).

A second problem the transferability assumption creates for diagnosis is the mirror image of the first. Rather than giving short-shrift to Dx in favor of a leading reform of the day, the Dx is strong. However, an accurate Dx does not automatically yield an appropriate Rx. If it did, no diagnosed disease would be without a cure. The transferability assumption promotes a tendency to try something already available as opposed to developing a *cure de novo*, especially when the Dx creates intense pressure for reform. This "off-the-shelf" approach is bolstered by the proclivity of reformers to overrate and oversell their models, perhaps at the price of gaining serious consideration by policymakers. Moreover, as noted earlier, the tendency in a design science like public administration is to assume that problems can be fixed. The disconnect between the Dx and the Rx is disregarded in favor of action.

According to Caiden, this tendency can run very deep in among reformers:

> it has been largely theorists who have warned the practitioners in administrative reform not to fall too much in love with their models to forget what was wrong with them where they were culture-bound (and not universal) and how they had to be reshaped to meet specific circumstances. These theorists, virtually all academics, were dubbed the doubters, the spoilers, the troublemakers, who always could find fault and cast gloom on any party. (1991: 15)

However, if the nay sayers could not fix the problems, neither could the wrong prescriptions.

The U.S. federal government's adoption of merit pay for managers as part of the Civil Service Reform Act of 1978 provides a good illustration. The Dx was that federal agencies were inefficient and ineffective partly because managers' were not held personally accountable for organizational performance. There was broad agreement that managers had little incentive to make difficult decisions, innovate, deal effectively with poorly performing employees, or push for results. Much less thought was given to the Rx of merit pay, which did not work as intended at first, or even after a variety of modifications were tried (Ingraham 1993).

Alan Campbell, who played a major role in shaping and implementing the reform legislation as the last Chair of the Civil Service Commission and first Director of the Office of Personnel Management, subsequently admitted that he "saw no need" to experiment with pay-for-performance *before installing it government-wide*. It had been his "perception that it worked fine in the private sector" (Ingraham 1993: 349). However, any number of academic experts and reflective practitioners could have warned him that merit pay was an inadequate Rx for improving federal administrative performance through better management. Merit pay may motivate federal managers, but it does not provide them with the tools and flexibility they need to manage for greater cost-effectiveness. Although Gore's NPR focuses on empowering employees rather than managers, it recognizes that cost-effectiveness is impaired by unclear missions, legislative involvement, and layers of procedural regulations intended to promote other values (such as due process and transparency).

In the worst case when diagnosis either receives inadequate attention or is too loosely connected to the Rx, it fails to guide reform at all. Alasdair Roberts (1996) provides a startling example. In 1918-1919, an unwieldy, complex, and rigid personnel system designed for Chicago was adopted by the Canadian national government *without benefit of serious Dx*. Roberts observes,

> The system that had been installed in the Canadian service was designed for a different kind of government: most notably, one in which senior line officials were partisans and very often corrupt too. The Canadian deputies were not politicized in the same way as were their Chicagoan counterparts, and they were generally not corrupt. The Canadian system, unlike the Chicago system, did not need to be made "burglar proof." (1996: 62)

SYSTEMIC BARRIERS TO THE TRANSFERABILITY OF REFORMS

There are at least three main systemic barriers to the transferability of substantial administrative reforms: constitutional scheme, administrative culture, and the means of building dominant political coalitions.

Constitutional Scheme

Woodrow Wilson claimed that public administration "…at most points stands apart even from the debatable ground of constitutional study" (1887: 18). He was dead wrong, though it took comparativists a relatively long time to say so. Writing in 1994, Fred Riggs, concluded that:

> Acceptance of Woodrow Wilson's myth that governance in a presidentialist regime should and could be "centralized" in the parliamentary sense. . . has led to the view that, somehow, the President is or should be the exclusive "manager" of the public bureaucracy according to norms of "efficiency" and "effectiveness." Yet, without a fundamental revision of the Constitution, the Congress and the courts will also shape American public administration, in competition with the president. We cannot, therefore, ignore or discount the competing values of responsiveness and representativeness, legality and individual human rights, which often clash with those of efficiency and effectiveness in our administrative system. (Riggs 1994: 475)

Elsewhere Riggs went to the heart of a constitutional scheme's potential impact on bureaucratic politics in observing that a powerful bureaucracy could "overwhelm" a presidentialist system with separated executive and legislative powers, whereas it might be well managed in a parliamentary system in which they are fused (Riggs 1991: 65).

Parliamentary and Presidentialist Logics: Two Examples

ISRAEL, 1996

A remarkable opportunity to observe the effects of constitutional arrangements on the design and implementation of administrative reforms occurred in Israel in 1996. From its birth in 1948 until the elections in 1996, Israel was a classic parliamentary system. The legislature, known as the Knesset, consisted of 120 members. Elections were by proportional representation from party lists, with the entire nation serving as a single constituency. No significant threshold for gaining a seat existed, and no single party had ever been a majority of the Knesset.

During the 1970s, a pattern of electoral competition emerged in which two major parties of roughly equal size had to compete for the support of smaller parties in order to form governments. Dominant coalitions became hostage to the continuing participation of smaller and sometimes narrowly-focused parties. In the 1980s, the major parties, Likud and Labor/Alignment, formed national unity governments in response to the growing influence of the smaller parties.

The national unity governments had a significant impact on the executive. The prime minister and cabinet members were no longer able to dominate the Knesset. Security concerns and economic problems continued to fill the political agenda. However, in the absence of consensus, decisive executive leadership was generally difficult, if not impossible.

The political system fell into crisis in the early 1990s, when the Labor Party brought down a Likud dominated coalition in the first successful "no confidence" vote in the nation's history. But Labor was then unable to form its own majority coalition. As Reuven Hazan explains, the nation was soon treated to "...coalition horse trading; political blackmail and extortion by small extremist parties; shamelessly open political bribery; blatant and obsessive partisanship by the nation's top policymakers; complete disregard for matters of national interest..." (1996: 22).

In response, Israel fundamentally changed its political structure by moving it toward presidentialism. In 1992, it enacted a new electoral law providing for the direct popular election of the prime minister along with parallel elections for members of the Knesset. The candidate successfully running for prime minister must receive an absolute majority of the votes cast. If no candidate receives a majority on the first ballot, a run-off between the top two contenders is held within two weeks. The prime minister's term of office is four years. Only he or she is empowered to form a government. This prevents bidding wars among the larger parties for coalition partners. The elected prime minister creates a cabinet of not more than eighteen members, half of which must be drawn from the Knesset. Knesset approval of the cabinet is required before the new government can function. A Knesset vote of no confidence by an absolute majority of 61 votes topples both the prime minister *and* the legislature, triggering the need for new national elections. (A provision also exists for removing the prime minister, presumably for cause such as incapacity, by an extraordinary majority of 80 votes while leaving the legislature in place.) With the consent of the nation's president (a largely symbolic official elected by the Knesset), the prime minister can dissolve the Knesset. This would also cause new elections to be held for both the prime ministership and the entire Knesset. The system creates a "balance of terror" in which a successful vote of no confidence or dissolution of the legislature puts both the prime minister and the members of the Knesset out of office (see Rosenbloom and Segal 1998: 440-444).

This structural change was put into effect in 1996. Benyamin Netanyahu was elected prime minister, however, his Knesset alignment parties won only 32 seats. After forming a government, Netanyahu took several steps to modify the implementation of a major administrative reform that had been underway since 1994 (Galnoor, Rosenbloom, and Yaroni 1998; Rosenbloom and Segal 1998: 450-452). The Civil Service Commission, which had been housed in the Ministry of Finance, was transferred to the Prime Minister's Office. This move was explicitly explained as a response to the new "semi-presidentialist" governmental structure. It was claimed that once the prime minister became more directly responsible to the voters for the quality of public management, he or she needed greater influence over the personnel system.

The Netanyahu government's rationale was similar to that put forth by the United States by the Supreme Court in *Myers v. United States* (1926) and the U.S. President's Committee on Administrative Management in 1937. Presidents need control of personnel in order to meet the executive mandate for faithful execution of the laws. *Myers* reasoned that the president's constitutional responsibility to execute the laws could not be fettered by Senate participation in the removal of presidentially appointed executive officers. The U.S. President's Committee on Administrative Management rationalized its proposal for centralizing federal administration under the president on the basis that "The President is indeed the one and only national officer representative of the entire Nation" (1937: 1). The U.S. Civil Service Reform Act of 1978 also reflects this same presidentialist logic. Among other features, it abolished the independent bi-partisan Civil Service Commission and established the Office of Personnel Management as an arm of the president for personnel policy development and implementation.

Netanyahu also halted the process of decentralizing personnel administration to the agencies, which had begun in 1994. Again, the rationale was essentially presidentialist. Netanyahu's Civil Service Commissioner argued that, rather than continue to improvise with the hodgepodge of personnel laws and regulations that had developed since the nation's birth in 1948, the entire personnel system should be placed on a new legal basis that reflected the structural change in the government (Rosenbloom and Segal, 1998: 451). Decentralization was viewed as compromising unity of command and accountability to the prime minister.

In addition, Netanyahu decided to permit the political appointment of the deputy directors general in the various ministries, positions previously selected through merit procedures. This move provided the prime minister with potentially greater reach into administrative decision-making and operations. It follows Riggs' prescriptions for successful presidentialism. When the executive and legislature are not fully fused, the chief executive needs greater leeway in making top administrative appointments and greater reach into administrative operations as means of defending his or her independence.

THE U.S. FEDERAL GOVERNMENT PERFORMANCE AND RESULTS ACT OF 1993

The Israeli experience since 1996 exemplifies some impacts of presidentialism on the logic of administrative arrangements. By contrast, the U.S. Government Performance and Results Act of 1993 (GPRA) illustrates some problems that reforms originating in parliamentary systems may face when being transferred to presidentialist ones. The act is a New Public Management (NPM) style reform. It requires federal agencies to formulate strategic plans with concrete objectives and measures, preferably quantitative, for gauging outputs and/or outcomes. The overall purpose is to hold agencies accountable for results through a system of performance budgeting. A congressional initiative, the act enjoyed the Clinton-Gore Administration's strong support because it dovetailed with the NPR's NPM emphasis on managing for results (see Gore 1993: 7; Radin 1998).

Little-discussed when passed, the act requires the agencies to develop their strategic plans in consultation with Congress, interested parties, and the executive branch Office of Management and Budget (OMB). Apparently, the NPR reformers thought that congressional participation would be pro forma, but the Republican majority has made it substantial (Barr 1997a; 1997b; 1998). In practice, congressional committees and subcommittees will now be able to write specific goals into agency strategic plans—even goals to which the president and his political appointees may be opposed. This can go a long way toward enabling Congress, through its committees, to steer the agencies' use of delegated legislative authority.

Viewed in a historical context, GPRA is an extension of the design Congress consciously developed in 1946 for realigning itself vis-à-vis the agencies (Rosenbloom 1998; 2000). In a presidentialist system, where legislative and executive power are separated, a strong legislature will seek means of monitoring, directing, and checking the use of the legislative power it delegates to administrative agencies. Contrary to the executive perspective, administration is viewed as involving legislative functions, such as rulemaking, and therefore not considered off-limits to legislative structuring of administrative procedures and processes (Rosenbloom 1998; 2000).

Ironically, when transferred to a presidentialist system, a results-oriented measure like GPRA may promote *less* accountability rather than more. By clarifying missions and performance measures, it exacerbates conflicts over appropriate goals within the legislature, and between the legislature and the political executive. Inevitably, agencies and programs are engulfed in such conflicts and are forced to respond to confusing cross-pressures. Congress has already criticized the agencies' strategic plans for lacking specificity (Barr 1998). Reforms requiring explicit executive-legislative coordination simply may not travel well in presidentialist systems.

Rights

As Riggs suggests, the extent to which a constitution makes public administration rights-oriented by virtue of judicial decisions is another factor that can affect the transferability of reforms. For instance, by the mid-1990s in the U.S., the Supreme Court brought privatization under the ambit of constitutional law (Rosenbloom, 1999). Contractors now have essentially the same substantial free speech rights, in the context of their relationship with government, as do public employees (*Board of County Commissioners, Wabaunsee County v. Umbehr* 1996; *O'Hare Truck, Inc. v. City of Northlake* 1996). Race or ethnicity can be taken into account in letting contracts only when it serves a compelling governmental interest in a narrowly tailored fashion (*Adarand Constructors, Inc. v. Pena* 1995). Private organizations and public-private hybrids are subject to constitutional constraints in dealing with the public when they become "state actors" (e.g., engage in a public function such as incarceration) (Rosenbloom 1999; Gilmour and Jensen 1998). Private employees engaged in state action face greater liability for constitutional torts than do ordinary civil servants (*Richardson v. McKnight* 1997). Rights and liabilities protect individuals from abuse, of course. Nevertheless, when viewed through the lens of administration, such decisions can impair flexibility, potentially raise the cost of contracting out, and, in various contexts, make outsourcing less attractive for both government and private firms.

Administrative Culture

Administrative culture can also be a substantial barrier to the portability of administrative reforms (Nachmias and Rosenbloom 1978). The transferability assumption is in keeping with Max Weber's (1958) acultural abstraction of the ideal type bureaucracy. However, in the real world, administrative capacity, status, image, support, trust, standards, impersonality, formalism, representativeness, openness, and honesty are among the key determinants of how administrative systems function. They vary widely, even among nations at the same levels of economic development. What is standard operating procedure in one administrative system may be considered corrupt in another (Heidenheimer 1989).

Contemporary reforms involving deregulation of the public service and empowerment of public employees illustrate how administrative culture can impede transferability. Deregulation and empowerment depend on honesty, trust, professionalism, sense of duty, and agreement on appropriate behavior. Vice President Gore supports such reform strategies on the theory that "...people—in government or out—are, for the most part, neither crooked nor stupid. Most people want to do the right thing, so long as the right thing makes sense" (1995: 33).

But nobody would suggest such reforms in a regime with a "culture of corruption" (LeVine 1989).

Most nations are somewhere in between Gore's idealization, and thorough corruption. But there is apt to be a broad range of views on what "the right thing" is. This is especially true in multi-cultural and socially diverse societies in which uniform social controls are relatively weak. Should an administrator bend the rules for members of his or her family? Social group? Region or town? Political party? Personal sense of justice? "Yes," in some systems; "No," in others. What if street-level functionaries apply the law more harshly to one social group than another, as in the case of the "driving while black" phenomenon (Larrabee 1997). Administrative reformers such as Gore might be taken aback by a line of American constitutional law cases that views street-level discretion as a "grave danger" that can promote "evil" law enforcement (*Terry v. Ohio*, 1968; *Delaware v. Prouse*, 1979; *Kolender v. Lawson*, 1983).

Additionally, the success of deregulation and empowerment is likely to depend partly on just what "most people" means. Is it 99.9 percent or 50.1 percent?

Political Coalitions

In democratic nations, the formation of political coalitions is voluntary and consensual. They are based on a mix of ideology, policy preferences, social and regional ties, as well as specific inducements and other factors. Their basis may directly affect administrative practices and, therefore, the transferability of reforms.

For example, in the U.S., winning legislative coalitions are often formed on the ad hoc basis of vague legislation that delegates the task of formulating clear standards to administrative agencies. As a matter of formality, constitutional law requires that delegated legislative authority be accompanied by an "intelligible principle" to guide administrative discretion (*J.W. Hampton, Jr., and Co. v. United States*, 1928). In practice, however, delegations are frequently so broad as to turn administrative agencies into supplementary legislatures. For instance, Chief Justice William Rehnquist once called a vacuous, but key standard in a delegation "...a legislative mirage, appearing to some Members [of Congress] but not to others, and assuming any form desired by the beholder..." (*Industrial Union Department, AFL-CIO v. American Petroleum Institute*, 1980: 681).

Broad delegations have a profound effect on bureaucratic politics. As Norton Long explained in 1949:

> the American system of politics does not generate enough power at any focal point of leadership to provide the conditions for an even partially successful divorce of politics from administration. Subordinates cannot depend on the formal chain of command to deliver enough political power to permit them to do their jobs. Accordingly they must supplement the resources available through the hierarchy with those they can muster on their own, or accept the consequences in frustration.... (Long 1949: 180)

The fact that agencies act as supplementary law-makers also explains a great deal about U.S. administrative law, organization, and leadership (Rosenbloom 1998 ; 1999; 2000; Seidman 1970; Riggs 1994).

Coalition formation along U.S. lines creates a serious impediment to administrative reforms requiring agreement on policy means and ends. The definition of results is endogenous to the administrative process, rather than exogenously mandated by the legislature. GPRA can help change this by enabling congressional committees to define legislative goals for Congress as a whole through their participation in agency strategic planning. But the executive will nevertheless continue to exercise some discretion and have a major impact on the pace and quality of implementation. In one way or another, unspecific legislative goals contributed to a long list of failed budget reforms at the federal level, including the much heralded Planning Programming Budget System and Zero Based Budgeting approaches (Wildavsky 1961; Schick 1973; Pyhrr 1977). Thus far, it has also frustrated efforts to establish performance budgeting at federal level.

In parliamentary systems, by contrast, partisan coalitions are often formed after elections. Administrative appointments may be used as an inducement or payoff to encourage parties to join in the formation of post-election majority legislative coalitions. For example, as noted earlier, well into the 1970s in Israel, it was common for the dominant Labor Party to offer administrative leadership positions to its smaller coalition partners. In time, the National Religious Party, which was small and focused on resisting secularization, was able to gain influence far disproportionate to its strength in the electorate (Nachmias 1974; Nachmias and Rosenbloom 1978: 52).

The "colonization" of ministries, departments, or agencies by political parties can present several barriers to the transferability of reforms. For instance, budgetary and personnel decentralization may strengthen the tendency toward policy autonomy on the part of lesser coalition partners. Deregulation and empowerment may do the same. Centralizing reforms may be difficult or impossible to install because they undercut the value of joining majority coalitions.

CONCLUSION: BEYOND THE TRANSFERABILITY ASSUMPTION

As globalization proceeds, it may be difficult to part with the transferability assumption. "Convergence" is a common contemporary theme as economic competitiveness and international organizations promote standardization across nations. But there is still more than enough variation in constitutional structure, administrative culture, and coalition building to frustrate the interchangeability of administrative reforms. *Failure has been the norm.* What is an alternative?

The best available approach is a medical model (Caiden 1991: 296-298). It requires individualized diagnosis of each organization, bureaupathology, and administrative system. Attention to history, culture, and overall condition is important. Hubris is out; "humility in the face of reality" is in (Caiden 1991: 297). The short-term costs may be greater, but so may the long-term success rate. The immediate learning curve will be steep. Caiden warns us that "[a]dministrative reform today is well behind where medicine used to be even a hundred years ago" (ibid.: 298). But the transferability assumption has been a significant part of the problem. It leaves us with more ideology than systematic knowledge or science (ibid.: 15). It hampers learning by locking reformers into inappropriate claims and general models (Roberts 1996: 77-78). It undercuts Dx, encourages faulty Rx, and frustrates experimentation.

The medical model can be operationalized in a number of ways. The key is to avoid one-size-fits-all prescriptions and trying to treat everything at once. One approach, used with mixed results in Israel, is to implement reforms one ministry at a time, or in limited numbers (Galnoor, Rosenbloom, Yaroni 1998). "Model ministries" can serve as examples, and can be reformed according to separate framework agreements. If one or two can be successfully reformed, it may create a snowballing effect. The medical model is inherently incremental, and some nations may be tempted to speed up their reforms, as did Israel, but it also avoids broad, across-the-board catastrophic failures (see Farazmand 1998).

The medical model could also improve applied research and education in public administration. It goes against the current grain by emphasizing idiographic approaches and diagnostic skills, rather than social scientific theory building and hypothesis testing. But it holds great promise. Medicine is both art and science. It is taught as such. In view of twentieth century administrative reform's checkered record, perhaps it is time for the reformers to reform their own method and thinking. Although globalism may make the transferability assumption all the more alluring, a great deal of evidence indicates that discarding it in favor of individualized Dx and Rx is certainly worth careful consideration.

REFERENCES

Adarand Constructors v. Pena. 1995. 515 U.S. 200.
Barr, S. 1997a. Congress seeks seat at the table. *Washington Post.* 7 March: A19.
———. 1997b. Congress pushes agencies on results act deadline. *Washington Post.* 5 June: A19.
———. 1998. GOP sees no results in results act. *Washington Post.* 9 June: A4.
Board of County Commissioners, Wabaunsee County v. Umbehr (1996). 116 S.Ct. 2342.
Caiden, G. 1991. *Administrative Reform Comes of Age.* New York: Walter de Gruyter.
Delaware v. Prouse. 1979. 440 U.S. 648.
Farazmand, A. 1998. Failure of administrative reform and the revolution of 1978-79 in Iran: A contextual and comparative analysis. *Korean Review of Public Administration.* 3:93-123.
Fiorina, M. 1989. *Congress: Keystone of the Washington Establishment*, 2nd ed. New Haven, CT: Yale University Press.
Galnoor, I., D. Rosenbloom, and A. Yaroni. (1998). Creating new public management reforms: Lessons from Israel. *Administration & Society.* 30:393-420.

Gilmour, R., and L. Jensen. 1998. Reinventing government accountability: Public functions, privatization and the meaning of 'state action.' *Public Administration Review.* 58:247-257.

Gore, A. 1993. *From Red Tape to Results: Creating a Government That Works Better & Costs Less.* Washington, DC: U.S. Government Printing Office.

———. 1995. *Common Sense Government Works Better & Costs Less.* Washington, DC: U.S. Government Printing Office.

Hazan, R. 1996. Presidential parliamentarism: Direct popular election of the Prime Minister, Israel's new electoral and political system. *Electoral Studies.* 15:21-37.

Heidenheimer, A. 1989. Perspectives on the perception of corruption. *Political Corruption,* edited by A. Heidenheimer, M. Johnston, and V. LeVine. New Brunswick, NJ: Transaction. 149-163.

Ingraham, P. 1993. Of pigs in pokes and policy diffusion: Another look at pay for performance. *Public Administration Review.* 53:348-356.

Industrial Union Department, AFL-CIO v. American Petroleum Institute. 1980. 448 U.S. 607.

J.W. Hampton, Jr., and Co. v. United States. 1928. 276 U.S. 394.

Kolender v. Lawson. 1983. 461 U.S. 352.

Larrabee, J. 1997. "DWB (Driving While Black)" and equal protection. *Journal of Law and Policy.* 6:291.

LeVine, V. 1989. Supportive values of the culture of corruption. *Political Corruption,* edited by A. Heidenheimer, M. Johnston, and V. LeVine. New Brunswick, NJ: Transaction. 363-373.

Light, P. 1994. *Thickening Government.* Washington, DC: Brookings Institution.

Long, N. 1949. Power and administration. *Classics of Public Administration.* 3rd edition, 1992, edited by J. Shafritz and A. Hyde. Pacific Grove, CA: Brooks/Cole. 179-187.

McSwite, O. 1997. *Legitimacy in Public Administration.* Thousand Oaks, CA: Sage.

Myers v. United States. 1926. 272 U.S. 52.

Nachmias, D. 1974. Coalition politics in Israel. *Comparative Political Studies.* 7:316-333.

Nachmias, D. and D. Rosenbloom. 1978. *Bureaucratic Culture: Citizens and Administrators in Israel.* New York: St. Martin's Press.

Osborne, D. and T. Gaebler. 1992. *Reinventing Government.* Reading, MA: Addison-Wesley.

O'Hare Truck, Inc. v. City of Northlake. 1996. 116 S.Ct. 2353.

Peters, B. and D. Savoie. 1994. Civil service reform: Misdiagnosing the patient. *Public Administration Review.* 54:418-425.

Pyhrr, P. 1977. The zero-base approach to government budgeting. *Public Administration Review.* 37:1-8.

Rabin, J. and J. Bowman., (eds.) 1984. *Politics and Administration.* New York: Marcel Dekker.

Radin, B. 1998. The Government Performance and Results Act (GPRA): Hydra-headed monster or flexible management tool? *Public Administration Review.* 58:307-316.

Richardson v. McKnight. 1997. 138 L.Ed. 2d. 540.

Riggs, F. 1991. Public administration: A comparataivist framework. *Public Administration Review.* 51:473-475.

Riggs, F. 1994. Bureaucracy and the Constitution. *Public Administration Review.* 54: 65-72.

Roberts, A. 1996. *So-Called Experts*. Toronto, Ontario, Canada: Institute of Public Administration of Canada.

Rosenbloom, D. 1998. 1946: Framing a lasting congressional response to the administrative state. *Administrative Law Review*. 50:173-197.

————. 1999. Constitutional problems for the new public management in the United States. *Current Public Policy Issues*, edited by R. Carter and K. Thai. Philadelphia, PA: PrAcademics Press. 143-174.

————. 2000. *Building a Legislative-Centered Public Administration: Congress and the Administrative State, 1946-1999*. Tuscaloosa, AL: University of Alabama Press.

Rosenbloom, D. and Z. Segal. 1998. Presidential political systems and contemporary administrative reform: Israel's "semi-presidentialism" as a natural experiment. *International Journal of Organization Theory & Behavior*. 1:437-458.

Schick, A. 1973. A death in the bureaucracy: The demise of Federal PPB. *Public Administration Review*. 33:146-156.

Seidman, H. 1970. *Politics, Position, and Power*. New York: Oxford University Press.

Terry v. Ohio. 1968. 392 U.S. 1.

U.S. President's Committee on Administrative Management. 1937. *Report of the Committee*. Washington, DC: U.S. Government Printing Office.

Van Riper, P. 1958. *History of the United States Civil Service*. Evanston, IL: Row, Peterson.

Wamsley, G. and J. Wolf., (eds.) 1996. *Refounding Democratic Public Administration*. Thousand Oaks, CA: Sage.

Weber, M. 1958. Bureaucracy. *From Max Weber: Essays in Sociology*, edited by C. Mills and H. Gerth. New York: Oxford University Press. Chap. 8.

White, L. 1926. Introduction to the Study of Public Administration. *Classics of Public Administration* (3rd edition, 1992,) edited by J. Shafritz and A. Hyde. Pacific Grove, CA: Brooks/Cole. 57-65.

Wildavsky, A. 1961. Political implications of budgetary reform. *Public Administration Review*. 21:183-190.

Wilson, W. 1887. The Study of Administration. *Classics of Public Administration* (3rd edition, 1992), edited by J. Shafritz and A. Hyde. Pacific Grove, CA: Brooks/Cole. 11-24.

15

From Welfare and Contract States: Towards "Smart State" Policy Capacities

Alexander Kouzmin and Alan Jarman

INTRODUCTION

Post-war governments in Liberal-Democratic economies have performed many functions, including economic management and provision of infrastructure. Contrary to conservative opinion, in particular, such governments have not functioned to the detriment of the private sector (Simms 1983: 49). However, a functionalist perspective is less appropriate in accounting for the crisis-driven decades in welfare economies since 1972. Political conflict over the allocation of resources and the size of the national budget, for example, suggests the need for a more *complex* analysis of government activity within a corporatist and globalizing context. Conditions of economic crisis and political strain lead to a renewed interest in the policy connections between politics and economics, especially in the form of observing empirical linkages within a political-business cycle (McFarlane 1978: 53).

Economists, with their propensity to "externalize" much of social and political, let alone economic, complexities, have one saving grace in that they, at least, have attempted to situate the state, albeit inadequately, and, at times, ideologically. In contrast, political scientists have tended to assume the state's existence; giving it no history and no functions (Simms 1983: 44) and, one might add, giving the state no organizational or policy sophistication, let alone, complexity.

For Kaufmann, theories of governance do not account enough for complexities and problems (1991: 7). Failures in markets and hierarchies are well-documented (Hirschman 1970; Lindblom 1977) but, more importantly, these two

institutional forms of coordination and policy formation do not exhaust typologi-
cal possibilities or current empirical developments in patterns of governance that
emerge when questions are raised regarding the coordinating capabilities and
institutional arrangements in modern industrial society (Kaufmann 1991: 12).

At a time when the Bretton Woods Institutions are increasingly concerned about
"re-inventing" governance and building institutional capacities, the new millennium is an appropriate moment to re-focus public discourse and policy-making
debates about the complexities of market-state dependencies and emerging public-
private partnerships. Building social solidarity, trust, and political legitimacy is a
new priority in many developed and transitional polities (World Bank 1997). The
emerging willingness to re-assess the instruments and practices of economic
liberalism, in different political *milieus*, also raises many significant questions
about the limits and enhanced capabilities of the state to be an effective manager
of the "public interest" (Schultze 1977; Kettle 1994).

The last twenty years have seen the fundamental re-structuring of many public
sectors (World Bank 1997). Policy-makers have increasingly looked to markets to
overcome political conflicts triggered by the perceived increase in the scarcity of
resources. The "hollowing out" of the Keynesian welfare state and the widespread
acceptance of the idea of "less state and less taxes" raises serious policy questions
of social resilience and the governance capacities in these diverse jurisdictions
(Boyer and Drache 1996). Conventional wisdom about the convergent effects of
economic globalization gives further weight to these questions, especially in light
of the fact that significant differences in public policy responses tend to be
ignored. This neglect of apparent divergence in policy-outcomes and expenditure
practices—especially in labor market strategies—underscores the need to audit
critically, in comparative and sectoral ways, systematic differences in the management of market failure and the social distortions flowing from enlarged markets (Berger and Dore 1996).

FRAMING ISSUES AND POLICY CONTEXTS

Speculation about futures needs to be guided and informed by a double hypothesis: the first is the emergence of a markedly smaller state, but one with more complex functions for the twenty-first century. The possibility for the emergence of
new policy capabilities for different market economies is a primary research focus.
The thesis, here, is that this important re-positioning can only occur with strategic
changes in the functioning of the state—the need to become a "smart state"; consisting of institutions that learn, that effect long-term and strategic change, and that
create high quality and crisis sensitive modes of policy reasoning.

A second and closely-related issue that bears directly on policy making is the
future role of the public domain in different market economies. No state should
underestimate the importance of the social dimension to economic growth and
development. The reason is that it is one of the resources relied on by government
to minimize social dislocation when markets expand beyond the moral and polit-

ical boundaries within which they are necessarily constrained to operate (Dertouzos et al. 1989; Boyer and Drache 1996). In optimal conditions, public domains define the institutional capacity to bring about consensus, achieve equity and protection and create opportunities for entrepreneurship. They refer to those assets held in common but unable to be bought and sold in the open market. They cover a range of economic activities that the private sector cannot deliver, or can only partially effect. A main thrust of future research would be to build on this cornerstone concept in order to audit putatively shrinking public domains and policy capacities in an age of globalization and strategically-downsized governments. Since public domains and spending practices of national and regional authorities differ markedly, both within Western European countries and between these countries and their Anglo-Saxon counterparts (Kouzmin and Scott 1990), because this diversity necessarily frames public policy debate in significantly important ways, these domains and practices need to be empirically tracked (Johnston and Kouzmin 1998).

For most scholars of administrative history, the founding "giants" of the discipline are usually represented by a multi-national list of "greats": Max Weber, Frederick Taylor, and Henri Fayol et al. (Harmon and Mayer, 1986). To this list one should add the eclectic array of British Fabians who were politically active and astute, shared the social backgrounds of the other administrative "reformers" and were very "bullish" on the idea that the "entrepreneurial" spirit, at least in the United Kingdom, was not confined only to the private sector. They could be regarded as the political progenitors of the concept of the *Public Good*—Bentham was British.

There is little specific evidence that these people were aware of each other's ideas and contribution to the growing field (in nineteenth century terms) of "progressive" managerialism. In this context, Weber had more in common with the Fabians: G.B. Shaw, H.G. Wells, The Webbs, and others well known in London's intellectual circles (later congregating in Bloomsbury, in London). This connection was an important early element of socialist thinking in Australia (Graycar 1979). As the new Commonwealth developed into today's confederation, so the overseas intellectual influences were translated into the partisan ideas so dominant in Australia during the past one hundred years.

Historically, the big, global trends of change have never been too distant from the Antipodes. Such internationalist trends are stated as a summary of public policy changes during this century: a brief "snapshot" of state (as distinct from private) welfarism since the end of the previous century. Fifteen-year time "spaces" are used, suggestively, to label a short era of definitive social, economic, cultural, and political change. The list is arranged as follows:

1890-1915:   Getting organized: the second communications' revolution toward personalized forms of transportation.

1915-1930:   Industrial War, growth, and "capitalist" prosperity.

1930-1945:   Depression and the emergence of state welfarism as a "public good."

1945-1960:   Butter and Guns: the Cold War and the global spread of the "American Dream."

1890-1915:   Getting organized: the second communications' revolution toward person-alized forms of transporation.

1960-1975:   Institutionalizing the Cold War: The Military-Industrial-University arrange-ments become more complex whilst funding the "Great Society."

1975-1990:   Less Butter, more Guns: Carter leads into Star Wars followed by the Sorcerer's Apprentices (Thatcher and Reagan). Welfarism's *denouement* and the emergence of the more "frugal" managerialist state.

1990-2005:   Global "managerialism" rampant: public choice versus public goods—the fading Fabian dream in a rapidly Balkanizing World. The third communi-cations' revolution and toward personalizing the networked computer.

THE DECLINING WELFARIST STATE IN THE COMPUTER AGE

In summary, the idea and practice of state "welfarism" has waxed and is now waning at the end of this century (Kerin 1999a; 1999b). Today, Lyndon Johnson's notion of the "Great Society" is rarely, if ever, mentioned by U.S. Democrats: Former Vice-President Al Gore, Jr. is much more comfortable behind a computer than "glad-handing" the homeless across urban America. Indeed, the Clinton Administration had sought to raise (at least, prospectively) "alternate (sources of) revenue" by using public funds to speculate in the booming stock market.

Netizens are those who, for the past fifty years, have built large welfare bureaus. In doing so, especially in the era of incremental budgeting, such policy actors have institutionalized "dependence." Cyber-netizenship is a direct threat to those managing dependence. With the eventual development of real-time, on-line, and mobile communication systems, the means of client control, through face to face communication, become less relevant, especially in situations of financial entitlement payments. The paperless society is likely to be a quicker development than the long-promised paperless office.

This essay does not discuss policies in detail. On the other hand, it does seek to consolidate these themes into a relatively comprehensive melange of concepts using a reconstructive decision-making schema begun in earlier papers (Kouzmin and Jarman 1989; Jarman and Kouzmin 1990; 1994a; 1994b). These papers pre-sented a concept of "creeping crises," whereby a crisis-related continuum was posited concerning the established concepts of Allison's (1971) Model III, Garbage Canning, Disjointed Incrementalism and, finally, Group Think.

Three major eras can be discerned from these fifteen-year "snapshots;" from 1900 to 1945, from 1945 to 1975, and from that date until today and into the twenty-first century. The years 1900 to 1945 constitute the growth of state wel-farism, especially in the United States. The U.S., Europe, and Australia represent early initiatives in establishing governmental welfarism, whereby overseas ideas concerning this topic were both accepted and practiced. In Australia, the uniformity of such welfarism was, indeed, enhanced by a referendum action in 1944.

Like other nations, Australia also adopted the notion that in the post-war era, both central planning of large scale infrastructure and Keynesian "full employment" goals were to become priorities of national policy-making. Labor parties, including the American Democrats, proselytized these ideals and, in most cases, passed legislation to that effect.

The Cold war dominated foreign policy-making until the early 1990s. From 1945 until President Carter's last two years (1978-80), the Guns and Butter policy "culture," funded by taxation revenue "bracket creep," was regarded as "affordable." In 1978, however, two seemingly disconnected events merged: President Carter's interest in "Alternate Services Delivery" was transferred across the Atlantic—where Mrs. Thatcher "institutionalized" such reforms, especially as they related to profligate local authorities—then to Whitehall. Thatcher brought US advisers to the UK so that her advice was not sanitized by the incumbent "grandees" and their friendly "Sir Humphreys."

Coincidental, and barely recognized in governmental "mainframe IT" circles, was the emergence of the personal computer (PC). Apple led the way as a globalizing company in the early 1980s—IBM followed. The deregulation of "Ma Bell" heralded President Reagan's move toward Thatcherism—the deregulation, if not sale, of major public utility assets. The Alternate Services' Delivery agenda begun by Carter became "mantra." The Sorcerer's Apprentices were generally ruthless toward the "downsizing" of non-defense assets, including the very profligate (a favorite word of both apprentices) state welfare system. Today, as is true in other Anglo countries, the new and novel task of allocating governmental budget surpluses is causing considerable political debate.

DECISION MODES TO CRISIS

It has been stated above that this paper represents an extension of an earlier schema prepared, for the most part, to conceptualize different aspects of crisis management "modeling." The topic of deinstitutionalizing "group think" constitutes the first such enhancement. The overall objective is to operationalize the various schema for general policy-making purposes. Specifically, two key assumptions inform this conceptual modification. First, the contemporary state welfarist system prefers to make its policy more as a form of "bounded rationality" than what is labeled, crudely, as (welfare) "economic rationality." Second, the presumption is that the policy shift away from "profligate" welfarism is, in practice, continuous, if not irreversible. Such trends are important globally if such change is bi-partisan.

Four possible policy-making process states—Allison's, (1971); Cohen, March, and Olsen's (1972); Hirschman and Lindblom's (1969); and, finally, Janis and Mann's (1977) Group Think schema—are germane to this overview. All four policy types are both logically and empirically possible in any neo-satisficing context.

The assumption here is that Group Think, probability, is highest in importance (t 'Hart 1990).

Each of the four possible policy types need to be discussed in order. Two main interactive factors will be considered: Real or Contrived crisis circumstances and, secondly, Short or Protracted crisis circumstances. Propositions concerning these four permutations are briefly discussed below. For the moment, the nature of the ascending line from any current status quo situation towards crisis may be considered as follows:

1. **Allison's Model III (1971)**: This model represents a real crisis situation which occurred over a relatively short period of time (in Cuba). The time span to crisis along this crisis path is short. The reason for this is that it represents a real crisis which the US government responded to quickly and decisively to meet the contemporary Soviet danger. Critical to all four discussions concerning contingent type of slides into crisis is the nature of the "early warning systems" available. In the case of the Cuban Missile Crisis, both forward and back channels of communications with the Soviets were instigated, and proved, ultimately, to be effective. The environment was "turbulent," so the system could have spun "out of control"; this did not happen, in part because the back channels were both important and used to the mutual benefit of both sides of the confrontation. Human intelligence, as opposed to the technical, was important in this regard.

2. **March and Olson's Garbage Canning (1972)**: In this second schema (of slides into crisis), it is important to show that unrevealed, but desired, goal-status dominates the key player's interests. As distinct from the Allison (1971) construct, the player's arena is highly pluralist, the environment more benign, and there exists a power symmetry, even though information-sharing may be a-symmetrical (by the design of a key player). The important characteristic of Garbage Canning is the degree of deception used between the players. In essence, each is seeking to be a more effective "horse trader" than the other. This desired process state can be achieved by the use of skillful "crisis contrivance," perhaps over protracted periods of time (Polsby 1984). For serious players, committees, public relations and mass media channels, the recurrent budget game is critical. Large-scale capital expenditures are less important than the stable and growing relevance of budget growth.

3. **Hirschman and Lindblom's Disjointed Incrementalism (1969)**: Unlike the Garbage Canners who are pro-active concerning their "environmental" relationship, the slide into crisis environments is more sanguine. Disjointed Incrementalists are, nevertheless, concerned about their chosen process efficacy: disjointed incrementalism is predicated on the belief that efficient pluralism will fine-tune internal decision-making problems—in a word, the real meaning of the term "the Hidden Hand." Such optimism may relate to crisis states which are real rather than contrived, but such are usually protracted. Time is the healer given good faith by the respective players who are also willing to compromise. As they state, "problems are not solved, they are repeatedly attacked." Such crises are, therefore, rarely terminal, but they can become chronic. Welfare systems display these characteristics to a large degree. Paradoxically, it is tempting to hypothesize that the less chronic the problem, the less likely Garbage Canning proves to be the more effective strategy.

4. **Janis and Mann's Group Think (1977)**: In this final, possible, even probabilistic state, welfarists can become enamoured with the infallibility of their own logic, rarely rationality. As one should expect in the most Neo-Satisficing of states, "means" decidedly dominate "ends" (if they are ever considered rationally at all, and if they are, they will almost certainly be wholly self-serving). This state may be considered as the *reductio ad adsurdum* of garbage canning. Worse, whereas Garbage Canning may be a little interested in moral issues, the Group Thinkers are self-deceptive to the point of dismissal of others' values altogether. The list of characteristics presented by Janis and Mann (1977: 132) is instructive in this regard:

- illusion of invulnerability;
- collective rationalization;
- belief in inherent morality of the group;
- stereotyping of out-groups;
- direct pressure on dissenters;
- self-censorship;
- illusion of unanimity; and
- self-appointed mind-guards.

TOWARD THE "SMART" STATE: CONTEXT, CONTINGENCY, AND CRISIS MANAGEMENT STRATEGIES

In the case of the "de-institutionalization of group think," there exists the implication that the "Smart" state is one which actually seeks to avoid the pathologies of group think, as analyzed by Janis and Mann (1977). Group thinkers might show how their "rationalizing" assumptions can be operationalized (as they would wish) but, at the same time, only on rare occasions are they prepared to develop strategies to reduce pathologies should they arise.

The crisis schema (Kouzmin and Jarman 1989; Jarman and Kouzmin 1990; 1994a; 1994b) provides a richer heuristic base than mere classification and description. It is used to define four possible policy states: the *Steady* State; the *Crazy* State; the *Cyber* State; and the *Smart* State.

Such a contingency-based schema can allow policy-makers to consider trends, goals, and options for establishing different social and economic polities. This is now being considered in Australia so as to reduce perceived protracted and chronic welfare "dependency" (AAP 1999). To summarize briefly: the Steady State is where one is now; the Crazy State is one which is heading toward the full crisis situation; the Cyber State uses information technology (IT) to be more rationalist in its service provision capability; and the Smart State seeks to be very sensitive to environmental feedback and to have amelioration strategies in place. In general terms, the Smart State will be like the Steady State except much more "cybernetic," both in terms of information processing and inevitable crisis management strategies.

The contingency modeling concerning the four possible states begins with the plausible assumption that contemporary Australia, like other (Neo) Liberal

Democracies, displays the general characteristics of the Steady State. On balance (a much-favored bureaucratic phrase), the nation is "doing well." To many in the welfare "industry," this viewpoint will be regarded as sanguine, if not completely wrong-headed (Martin 1999: 10). But, importantly, as is sometimes the case with neo-satisficing states of affairs, pluralist-based cybernetics are generally in place and working. The recent 1999 shock defeat for the coalition government in Victoria demonstrates the robust nature of a democracy resistant to over-weening Executive rule, as practiced recently in that state (Jackson 1999). Too many critical social service cuts and too little public accountability have both contributed to the extent of this serious political reversal (Ignatius Centre 1999; McGann 1999: 19).

Surprises at the polls are increasingly frequent. Governments at all levels now receive unexpected "wake up calls," not always to their liking. In state politics, in Australia, the electorate is becoming less predictable in this regard—the pollsters were quite wrong in Victoria. Two consequences follow from these trends confirmed at the polls after election day. First, the extant "marginal" seats can become the focus of an inordinate amount of Executive attention, which can easily skew resource allocations. Second, and related, such skewing can raise many equity issues, especially where in increasingly "bi-polar" labor markets it is really the needy who are not part of the marginal groupings in conservatively-governed states (McCorny 1999: 5).

Again, in a confederal system of government, interjurisdictional differences, say between state and local governments, might be able to redress such iniquitous imbalances. Such "checks and balances" are well known in the "federalist" literature which readily acknowledges the *potential* balancing aspects within the Steady States as defined above. Finally, what would be too sanguine is to presume that such "potentiality" necessarily becomes manifest: that is just not so. Nevertheless, the Steady State presupposes such a possibility, which is not entirely without justification in the real world of federal politics.

THE CRAZY STATE: CRISES BOTH REAL AND CONTRIVED

Dror's interesting analysis of 1971 informs the development of the contingent types. It should be noted, at the outset, that a Crazy State is rarely one sought deliberately by those holding power. On the other hand, it should also be obvious that when states are chronically mismanaged, the Crazy State can become manifest from any of the antecedent neo-satisficing process conditions: Allison's (1971) Model III or Garbage Canning (Cohen, March and Olsen 1972) or Disjointed Incrementalism (Hirschman and Lindblom 1969). Group Think (Janis and Mann 1977), however, would seem to constitute, *a priori*, the shortest and most probable route toward this undesirable state of affairs.

According to Dror (1971: 62f), the symptoms of a Crazy State may be listed as follows:

- deception;
- take-over from within;
- conversion to new ideology;

- erosion by incremental takeover;
- isolation of adversaries;
- alliances with external others;
- provocation seeking over-reaction;
- blackmail;
- occupation of authority roles;
- destruction of target groups or areas; and
- timing of sub-strategies' mix.

Any organization operating for a protracted period of time in a manner related to a mix of the above sub-strategies is almost, certainly, heading toward the full "crisis state" (Kouzmin and Jarman 1989). Nevertheless, such tactical battles are fought within many organizations, both public and private. But, as noted above, such a norm would usually become either quickly or slowly counter-productive.

In this context, once detected, the discernible movement toward the Crazy State can rarely be protracted. Therefore, detection and amelioration are commonly required aspects of systems in crisis: hence the earlier the detection the better. Yet, this statement is clearly too sanguine and optimistic. In the crisis literature, in case study after case study, often "middle management" defaults by not passing the "bad news" upward. Hierarchical miscommunication appears in most of the better textbooks. Two factors intersect, both well-known as aphorisms (if not injunctions): "if it ain't broke; don't fix it;" and, "carry up the bad news: they'll shoot the messenger, not me."

To return to Dror (1971), one way of destabilizing opponents is to contrive a "crisis." Polsby (1984) is quite insistent on this point. In summary, the Crazy State is rarely avoidable should such deliberate sub-strategies "go wrong." This is a risky way to run the State, but, then, some can be "crazy like a fox."

THE CYBER STATE: ENHANCING "LEARNING" CAPABILITIES IN RAPIDLY ACCELERATING ENVIRONMENTS

Whereas the Crazy State normally constitutes a strategic condition of avoidance, the self-proclaimed rationalist, (new Managerialist, since the late 1970s), seems to evoke admiration if not adulation by many academics (for decades) and practitioners (Sutherland 1977; Micklethwait and Woolridge 1996). Such an assertion is highly contentious, but the debates concerning the pros and cons of such managerialism seem to be endless (Kouzmin, Leivesley, and Korac-Kakabadse 1997; Kouzmin and Korac-Kakabadse 1999). Concern, here, is much more prosaic: to attempt, within the limitations of the contingency schema, to seek to avoid the Crazy State and, if possible, define the end limits of the Cyber State so that it, too, does not become, at the least, Orwellian. Pathological avoidance is an important attribute of "good-governance."

Using today's literature in this regard represents a tall order; it can be as mixed and muddled as the former concerns about the "integrity" of Organization Theory during the early systems analysis' literature (Checkland 1981). To add to such ambiguity, the empirical world is shifting at historically accelerating rates, especially concerning technological change (in hardware, software, communications, and, indeed, user applications). So, as to distinguish this contemporary situation from the earlier literature, one would assert that one no longer operates in High-Velocity Environments; rather, the present rate of change involves Rapidly Accelerating Environments (RAEs).

The Cyber State represents, therefore, the public aspect of policy change within RAEs. Conceptually, this "drag" affect toward the "turbulence/crisis" phase is challenging to Cyber State policy makers (Shaw 1999: 8). To counteract such drag effects in RAEs, two "correcting" factors must be permitted. First, the environmental feedback mechanisms must be designed and not be fortuitous. Second, and even more important, it is the negative (error correcting) aspects of the dynamic feedback systems which must be effectively operational. Chance must be preceded by trial and error where error is not necessarily (as the optimists would have it) "self-correcting" (Churchman 1971).

The Cyber State, more positively speaking, will be aware of most of these issues. It is the "learning state" by implication when it is operating at its best (although is rarely "optimal"). However, it would be extremely optimistic to believe that personal or interest group gain is not both a political and technological possibility. The recent high-level and global debates concerning encryption, domain naming, export licensing, world trade liberalization, and anti-hacking strategies immediately come to mind (Garten 1999: 12). In this context, the public-to-private data "mining" relationships (both informal and contractual), are likely to become particularly problematic. Finally, the Cyber State must become more accountable than present trends would suggest (Uren 1999: 48). In Australia, State-level scandals are far too commonplace to permit complaisance with regard to this serious matter (Summers 1999: C3). Invariably, the large scale multi-nationals are party to such practices (Wheatley 1999: 4).

THE NEW WORLD ORDER: DIVERGENCE OR CONVERGENCE?

Modern states have long recognized the social-binding importance of maintaining strong public domains (Esping-Andersen 1990). The emergence of the welfare state, especially in post-Second-World-War Europe, is the most well-known expression of this. However, the intention to improve people's lives significantly required specific adaptations of social policy to meet the unique needs of individual countries. From Beveridge and Keynes in the United Kingdom, the conspicuous involvement of the Nordic states in their economies, the social markets of France and Germany, and the American adaptation of Keynesianism in President Johnson's "Great Society," to the strategic involvement of government in the "Tiger" economies of Asia, public domains have underpinned social and economic development (Fallows 1994).

For many experts, the public domain is not seen in these terms and is confused with the drive to reduce, in stark ways, the public sector—specifically, the demand to reduce public expenditure and to limit perceived increased government regulation of the economy. Public policy is, thus, driven by the view that if one reduces rent-seeking behavior within government bureaucracies, then competitive advantage will accrue to industries and, consequently, the economy. Within a globalized economy, it is argued that such advantages will be further enhanced by a dramatically smaller state presence (Rosenscranz 1996; Bergsten 1996). Such a policy position, within a globalized world, ignores important evidence that the public domain is becoming more significant, and is, in fact, being re-defined by forces over which public authority has little control (DiIulio 1994; Ruigrok and van Tulder 1995). In the "new world order," public domains need to be empirically studied because this diversity necessarily frames public policy debate in four critical areas.

Area 1: The Constituent Elements of Public Domains in Contrasting Jurisdictions

The decline of civic capital has been a growing concern in many societies— a concern not readily addressed in economics-dominated public policy circles (Putnam 1993; Dahrendorf 1995; Kouzmin, Leivesley, and Korac-Kakabadse 1997). The first order of policy capability would be to establish a methodology for empirically tracking institutions and core competencies remaining within the public sector. In this case, re-structured public sectors are seen to be the most direct and empirically sensitive index for measuring the scope of public domains.

One hypothesis is that the public sector, as commonly understood, comprises, among other elements, government program expenditures and transfer payments and, thus, the number of public employees remains an effective measure of the on-going existence of the public domain. Yet, much administrative reform is *ad hoc*, incremental, or a mixture of both. Governments often do not have a comprehensive sense of what has been changed, privatized, and outsourced, or what core, residual functions of government should be. Still, many public policy experts have little sense of whether administrative reform has gone far enough, too far, or about right in establishing new benchmarks of public policy undertakings (Peters and Savoie 1995). Taking stock of what *remains* is a priority to clarify, both empirically and conceptually. Finally, auditing the "residual" public space and domains in the North-South polarization of a globalizing world will require looking at the emergence of public domains in economically-developing jurisdictions. The principal aim would be to determine the extent of the "shrinking" or "expanding" state during a time of declining sovereignty—a form of learning capacity.

Area 2: Optimal Sizes for Governments and the Issue of Divergence

Monetarism, in its many different forms, has been adopted as the policy fundamental for governments in surprisingly diverse political contexts (Williamson 1994). Economic globalization under-scores the importance of deregulation and the alleged costs of compliance attributed to government intervention. Arguably, these shifts have gone too far (Hutton 1996).

Strategies of administrative reform have been used to bring about the commercialization of many government services in *laissez-faire* economies. Public enterprises have been put on a private sector footing or have been fully privatized. This has occurred in European social market economies as well. Also, there has been considerable outsourcing of some government functions. Much rhetoric prevails with these controversial initiatives (Kelsey 1995). The extent that privatization and outsourcing have shaped current public domains is an unresolved issue (Egon and Streeck 1991).

A second, but related, area is to investigate what public policy officials have learned about the functionality and dysfunctionality of cutting back government services and state functions (DiIulio 1994). For example, in the information technology domain in Australia, whole-of-government-approaches to outsourcing IT requirements for the national government are being hotly debated in terms of the capacity and vulnerability of state functions rendered *dependent* on external provisions of IT capability. While this may be an extreme example, it raises the significant and larger issue of defining and measuring appropriate *core functions* of the state in social market economies, in the *laissez-faire* Anglo-American model, *and* the "Tiger" economies, including Japan.

Outsourcing can be construed as a form of "de-skilling" the public sector (Johnston and Kouzmin 1998). The question is, is this the case? or does it presage the redesign of a smaller but "smarter" state? Finally, the strategic question to address is optima issues for the restructuring of state capabilities with regard to learning and innovation. One aim would be to identify institutions appropriate for the "smart" state.

The divergency issue raises some very interesting questions about the speed with which monetarist policies were adopted in the cases of Australia, New Zealand, and Canada. Special research, which is overdue, needs to be commissioned to explain the mechanisms of policy transfer and ideas to these jurisdictions (Williamson 1994; Kelsey 1995).

Area 3: The New Architecture of the State—The Economic Sovereign and the Political Local

This policy area would explore the capacity and confidence of national policy to decentralize and devolve policy-making authority and resources to the local level at a time of large-scale adjustment pressures. It would also track and give further evidence of the opportunities and challenges these changes afford for devolution and subsidiaries (Santos 1995).

One measure of decentralized decision-making is to identify divergent practices in state policy, market behavior, and public domains in the face of convergent economic fiscal pressures to reduce state spending. One needs to determine whether significant differences in the way markets, states, or other institutions operate has a significant impact on economic outcomes and public policy at the regional or local levels (Streeck 1991).

Regarding devolution in a global context, the degree of devolution, the forms such devolution takes, and the limits of devolution remain unexamined questions in many jurisdictions (World Bank 1997). Policy research would try to answer the question as to which of these decentralized arrangements, if any, help to create new institutional capacities for macro-economic policy and the micro-management of change. For example, is the European social market, which underpins effective social welfare provisions, more effective in utilizing its public domains towards decentralization than the *laissez-faire*, liberal, U.S. market that is more aligned to regional job-creation policies?

Policy research here would explore comparative experiences in macro-economic management with the opportunities for policy learning in mitigating, local impacts of globalization. A reliance on sectoral analysis and case material in such areas as the information economy, social policy, labor market, and job creation would be prominent aspects of research.

Area 4: Risk and Citizenship—Policy "Wickedness" in a Global Age—The Impact of Trade Blocs on Public Accountability

Globalization exposes public domains to new sources and levels of risk, especially in the environment-and-standards-setting. It also creates expectations and capacities for regulation and monitoring of such risks in the context of integration (Anderson and Blackhurst 1993). The globalized risk-society discounts futures in significant ways, and part of an effective public domain is a growing expectation of active citizens being involved in the determination of intergenerational costs and benefits. Policy research needs to map the impact of globalized trade blocs and agreements, such as NAFTA, EU, and the WTO, on regulatory functions of the state in very specific domains relevant to risk management and citizenship expectations regarding the environment, health standards, and government accountability (Appleton 1994).

The task is to identify whether, and to what degree, new trade arrangements impact on key policy areas of risk management and citizens' rights. The second is to develop a cost-benefit analysis of investors' rights juxtaposed against citizens' expectations and rights. Thirdly, states will be increasingly subject to a double-regime of accountability; on the one hand, supranational agencies or trade agreements, and, on the other, domestic electorates. This capacity to be transparent and accountable is, arguably, an integral part of the public domain. The question is, how will these conflicting requirements be met and accommodated, if at all, by governments in a divergent world? Changes in the policy process and, possibly, changes to electoral processes that will flow as a result of double-regimes of accountability are issues largely ignored by conventional paradigms. Special policy analysis needs to focus on these new theoretical, as well as practical, problems.

THE SMART STATE: LEARNING TO BALANCE THE LIMITS OF THE CYBER AND CRAZY STATES IN RAEs

In part, the role of the Smart State is similar to that of the Steady State discussed above. This means that some form of a "balancing" role must be acknowledged and, where necessary, implemented as strategy actions within the polity. Brewer and deLeon (1983) represent one conceptual approach to this issue. However, they go further than Deutsch (1966) in that they present both a static and dynamic representation of troubled states.

Essentially, Brewer and deLeon (1983) modify La Porte's (1975) collected work on the "complexity" literature. They do this by inter-relating (from La Porte, (1975)) the Simplicity-Complexity nexus with the cybernetic (from Weaver 1948) and the Organized-Disorganized nexus resulting in four contingent possibilities. These may be summarized as follows: Organized Simplicity (OS); Organized Complexity (OC); Disorganized Complexity (DC); and Disorganized Simplicity (DS).

As static categories, when used as problem-solving processes, these four types would approximate the following policy-related situations; all of which now apply to La Porte's recent work (1996) on High-Reliability Organization Systems (HROs). For example:

- **OS** is a complicated piece of machinery;
- **OC** is a system where the knowledge of the parts is greater than the knowledge of the properties of the whole ("a polity");
- **DC** is more actuarial in that it is possible to calculate statistically how the whole may operate without being able to determine the behavior of any single individual part (the basis of "normal accident theory"); and
- **DS** is, rarely, a state where any calculations can be made at all. In a RAE, value "congruence" can be more important than "calculability"—in a word, consensus can constitute the *sine qua non* of DS (especially in the turbulent state).

The implications of the pathologies of both Crazy and Cyber-Statism will be considered elsewhere—a consideration which will analyze, in more detail, the issues associated with state welfarism as one relevant example of Cyber-netizenship. The immediate conceptual concern here, is with the topic of defining the limits and boundaries of the *Smart State* (Hellaby 1999: 59; Summers 1999: C3).

Minimizing such pathologies is obviously not an easy task when RAEs become highly probable. Certainly, Brewer and deLeon's (1983) static and dynamic formulations help as meta-policy strategies in this regard. However, they are not necessarily the sufficient conditions to prescribe fully the character-istics of the Smart State. One additional factor relating to this difficult but com-pelling task concerns the use of other schema, most notably the work of those authors beginning to operationalize the ideas associated with Chaos Theory (Stacey 1996).

Their specific intellectual role is to convert, to policy analysis situations, a mixture of Quantum Mechanics and Chaos Theory. Stacey's (1996) under-standing of both topics is apposite and useful as he has sought to "modernize" the earlier work concerning General Systems Theory (GST) begun in the 1960s and enhanced, later, by Sutherland's (1977) thought provoking deductivism. Mindful of these earlier contributions, one would wish to conclude that RAEs do not nec-essarily lead to chaos (Hardy and Schwartz 1996).

To pursue this point further; earlier work on crisis management shows that "Creeping Crises" can be every bit as catastrophic as those of direct immediacy (Jarman and Kouzmin 1994a; 1994b). If the Smart State is to have any chance of survival and growth in the next century, then public policy and administration research must address the issues raised above. As argued, excesses of either Crazy or Cyber-Statism can lead to crisis situations (quickly or slowly). Therefore, the Smart State needs to be robust and resilient (both terms which Wildavsky uses in his discussion of this topic (Douglas and Wildavsky 1982)). For him, "richer was safer" (Wildavsky 1988); for the authors, "inequitable is riskier," and this is what the global debate about the future of the welfare-state is largely about (Horin 1999).

CONCLUSION

States are having to confront a range of *intractable* issues; the result of the social consequences of globalization. Public authority will be increasingly under pres-sure to exercise its supervisory role "when there are no other strong social values to compete with that of money and wealth" (Albert 1993: 104). If Albert's prin-cipal assumption is valid, public authority will be hesitant about transferring many of its prerogatives to the private sector. Indeed, there are many pressures forcing states to re-think the balance that society must strike with the market. Among these are:

- The local significance of globalization will require devolution of decision-making and the delivery of services. The degree of devolution, the forms such devolution takes, and the limits of devolution remain unexamined questions (Putnam 1993).
- The accommodation of the information revolution, and associated problems of access, has raised the expectation that information flows will be readily accessible for the gen-

eral public. Complex regulatory practices will need to be developed in the provision of utilities, communications, and food standards (OECD 1997).

- Environmental degradation and pressing issues of sustainable economic growth are creating political tensions of some proportion. The public increasingly looks to government to exercise its fiduciary responsibilities and protect the environment from the risks and needs of short-term wealth creation (Santos 1995).
- The magnitude of the job-creation crisis and growing income disparities are threatening the legitimacy of many governments. In light of volatile financial markets, flexible and mobile manufacturing strategies, and "social dumping" by corporations, states will have to develop pro-active policy responses to manpower planning and labour market practices (OECD 1994).
- The politically-vulnerable issue of maintaining sovereignty over cultural and identity issues in a "borderless" world has hardly been addressed (Held 1995). Transparency in government activity needs to coincide with redefinitions of active citizenship. The redefinition of citizenship in many domains to that of passive, consuming clients of state services, distorts democratic expectations and obligations in serious ways. Increasingly, electorates are critical of government's failure to reform its practices and address the costs of social exclusion (Dahrendorf 1995; Hutton 1996).

In the struggle between states and markets, it is not, therefore, a foregone conclusion that markets have regained the upper hand. Indeed, it appears that the public domain—the non-tradable, social-goods sector that exists in every society—is ready to make a comeback. Still, there is much that needs clarification and empirical verification regarding the relationship between the public domain, state practices, and markets (Cable 1995; Strange 1995). For this additional reason, in the "new world order," public domains need to be empirically studied because this diversity inevitably, and necessarily, frames public policy debate in critical ways.

There is now considerable bi-partisan *confusion* in liberal democracies about the forthcoming shape and resourcing of the post-cold war welfare state. Internationally, governments are using their newlyfound surpluses erratically, marginally, disjointedly, and not always incrementally.

President Clinton has been labelled the "last of the new dealers," and Prime Minister Blair has declared the "end of the welfare state as we know it." However, two factors should be noted. First, President Clinton's most likely Democratic Party successor is a Vice-President wholly familiar with the concepts and language of "The Information Superhighway." Second, and less personal, the U.S. Administration is forecasting continuing federal budget surpluses into the next millennium. How such money might be spent, however, also includes the role of appropriations in future Republican-dominated Congresses. The basic idea of this paper is that such seemingly "bi-partisan" reform will herald a shift from conventional welfarist "netizenship" toward a new style of government, titled here "cyber-netizenship" and a "smart" state. This change in title and concept is both radical and profound, especially in an era where governmental surpluses actually exist.

Policy advice within this rapidly changing socio-political milieu could become yet another form of electronic commerce. It is now well established that conventional "think tank" roles have changed toward the more ideological during the 1990s: instant "guru-ism" often became an instant form of "faddish" television expression—in a word "info-tainment." Media critiques abound on this topic alone. More fundamental, however, is that cyber-netizens will use the internet as a payment or protest medium of communication—informing politicians of "attitude" to "salient" issues.

Nationally, in a "digital" era where the laptop screen, home HDTV, and workstation can be technically as one, it is argued that the further commercialization of E-mail and TV will probably lead political leaders and senior bureaucrats to bombard the airwaves with essentially instant, self-serving, ideologically "correct" messages, often presented as an up-market form of info-tainment. At the local level, the situation could be otherwise; salient, serious, and sensible within the context of small-scale advocacy democracy: "localism," so defined, is possible as never before. This is already happening with regard to welfare reform which will constitute, where appropriate, advanced forms of cyber-netizenship. The *Smart State* agenda is compelling, as it is pressing.

REFERENCES

AAP. 1999, "Newman Locks Up Welfare Documents," *The Canberra Times*. 13 November: 3.

Albert, M. 1993. *Capitalisme Contre Capitalisme*. Paris: Seuil.

Allison, G.T. 1971. *Essence of Decision: Explaining the Cuban Missile Crisis*. Boston: Little Brown.

Anderson, K. and R. Blackhurst, eds. 1993. *Regional Integration and the Global Trading System*. New York: Harvester Wheatsheaf.

Appleton, B. 1994. *Navigating NAFTA*. Toronto: Carswell.

Berger, S. and R. Dore, eds. 1996. *National Diversity and Global Capitalism*. Ithaca: Cornell University Press.

Bergsten, F. 1996. "Globalizing free trade." *Foreign Affairs*, Vol. 75, No. 3, May/June: 105-120.

Boyer, R. and D. Drache, eds. 1996. *States Against Markets: The Limits of Globalization*. London: Routledge.

Brewer, G. D. and P. deLeon. 1983. *The Foundations of Policy Analysis*. Homewood: Dorsey Press.

Cable, V. 1995. "The diminished nation-state: A study in the loss of economic power," *Daedalus*, Vol. 124, No. 2, Spring: 23-53.

Checkland, P. 1981. *Systems Thinking, Systems Practice*. Chichester: Wiley.

Churchman, C. W. 1971. *The Design of Inquiring Systems*. New York: Basic Books.

Cohen, M. D., J. G. March, and J. P. Olson. 1972. "A garbage-can model of organizational choice." *Administrative Science Quarterly*, Vol. 17, No. 1, March: 1-20.

Dahrendorf, R. 1995. "A precarious balance: Economic opportunity, civil society and political liberty." *The Responsive Community*, Vol. 5, No. 3, Summer: 13-38.

Dertouzos, M. L., R. K. Lester, and R. M. Solow. 1989. *Made in America*. Cambridge: MIT Press.

Deutsch, K. W. 1966. *The Nerves of Government*. Free Press, New York.

DiIulio, J. J., ed. 1994. *De-Regulating the Public Sector*. Washington: Brookings Institution.

Douglas, M. and A. Wildavsky. 1982. *Risk and Culture: An Essay on the Selection of Technical and Environmental Dangers.* Berkeley: University of California Press.

Dror, Y. 1971. *Crazy States: A Counter-Conventional Strategic Problem.* Lexington: DC Heath.

Egon, M. and W. Streeck, ed. 1991. *Beyond Keynesianism.* Aldershot: Edward Elgar.

Esping-Andersen, G. 1990. *The Three Worlds of Welfare Capitalism.* Princeton: Princeton University Press.

Fallows, J. 1994. *Looking at the Sun: The Rise of the New East Asian Economic and Political System.* New York: Pantheon.

Garten, J. E. 1999. "A sophisticated assault on global capitalism." *Business Week.* 8 November: 12.

Graycar, A. 1979. *Welfare Politics in Australia: A Study in Policy Analysis.* South Melbourne: Macmillan.

Hardy, R. E. and R. Schwartz. 1996. *The Self-Defeating Organization: How Smart Companies Can Stop Out-Smarting Themselves.* Sydney: Harper Business.

Harmon, M. M. and Meyer, R. T. 1986. *Organization Theory for Public Administration.* Boston: Little, Brown.

Held, D. 1995. *Democracy and the Global Order: From the Modern State to Cosmopolitan Governance.* Stanford: Stanford University Press.

Hellaby, D. 1999. "Smart state gets $A1 billion." *The Australian.* 7 September: 59.

Hirschman, A. O. 1970. *Exit, Voice and Loyalty: Responses to Decline in Firms, Organizations and States.* Cambridge: Harvard University Press.

Hirschman, A. O. and C. E. Lindblom. 1969, "Economic development, research and development, policy-making: Some converging views." *A Sociological Reader on Complex Organizations,* edited by A. Etzioni. New York: Holt, Reinhart and Winston. 87-103.

Horin, A. 1999. "Reforms imperil charities: ACOSS." *The Sydney Morning Herald.* 10 November: 10.

Hutton, W., ed. 1996. *The Stakeholder Society: The Ideas That Shaped Postwar Britain.* London: Fontana.

Ignatius Centre. 1999. *Unequal in Life: The Distribution of Social Disadvantage in Victoria and NSW.* Melbourne.

Jackson, C. 1999. "Too late for leopard to become pussycat." *The Canberra Times.* 25 September: C2.

Janis, I. and L. Mann. 1977. *Victims of Groupthink: A Psychological Analysis of Conflict.* New York: Free Press.

Jarman, A. M. G. and A. Kouzmin. 1990. Creeping crisis: A contingency-theory simulation heuristic for the Challenger shuttle disaster 1983-1989. *Contemporary Crises,* Vol. 14, No. 4: 399-433.

———. 1994a, "Creeping crises, environmental agendas and expert systems: A research note." *International Review of Administrative Sciences,* Vol. 60, No. 3, September: 399-422.

———. 1994b "Disaster management as contingent meta-policy analysis: Water resource planning." *Technological Forecasting and Social Change,* Vol. 45, No. 3, May: 119-130.

Johnston, J. and A. Kouzmin. 1998, "From the ideological attack on public officials to the 'Pork Barrell' *Par Excellence*—Privatization and out-sourcing as oligarchic corruption." *Administrative Theory and Praxis,* Vol. 20, No. 4, December: 478-507.

Kaufmann, F-X. 1991. "Introduction: Issues and context." *The Public Sector: Challenge for Coordination and Learning,* edited by F-X Kaufmann. Berlin: Walter de Gruyter. 3-28.

Kelsey, J. 1995. *The New Zealand Experiment: A World Model for Structural Adjustment?* Auckland: Auckland University Press.

Kettle, D. 1994. "De-regulating the boundaries of government." *De-Regulating the Public Service,* edited by J. J. DiIulio. Washington: Brookings Institution. 223-247.

Kerin, J. 1999a. "Welfare-dependent feel heat of reform." *The Australian.* 10 November: 4.

————. 1999b, "Senate Block Challenged." *The Australian.* 11 November: 7.

Kouzmin, A. and A. M. G. Jarman. 1989. "Crisis decision-making: Towards a contingent decision path perspective." *Coping With Crises: The Management of Disasters, Riots and Terrorism,* edited by U. Rosenthal, M. T. Charles, and P. t' Hart. Springfield: Charles C. Thomas. 397-435.

Kouzmin, A. and N. Korac-Kakabadse. 1999. "From efficiency to risk sensitivity: Reconstructing management capabilities after economic rationalism." *The Australian Journal of Emergency Management.* Vol. 14, No. 1, Autumn: 8-19.

Kouzmin, A., R. Leivesley, and N. Korac-Kakabadse. 1997. "From managerialism and economic rationalism: Towards re-inventing economic ideology and administrative diversity." *Administrative Theory and Praxis.* Vol. 19, No. 1, April: 19-42.

Kouzmin, A. and N. Scott, eds. 1990. *Dynamics in Australian Public Management: Selective Essays.* Melbourne: Macmillan.

La Porte, T.R., ed. 1975. *Organized Social Complexity: Challenge to Politics and Policy.* Princeton: Princeton University Press.

La Porte, T. R. 1996. "High-reliability organizations: Unlikely, demanding and at risk." *Journal of Contingencies and Crisis Management.* Vol. 4, No. 2, June: 60-71.

Lindblom, C. E. 1977. *Politics and Markets: The World's Political-Economic Systems.* New York: Basic Books.

Martin, L. 1999. "Cabinet approves reigning in welfare." *The Sydney Morning Herald.* 10 November: 10.

McCorny, P. 1999. "Australians don't all get a fair go." *The Australian Financial Review.* 13 November: 5.

McFarlane, B. J. 1978. "Political economy and futurology: Responses to economic crisis." *Politics,* Vol. 13, No. 1: 53-64.

McGann, T. 1999. "We are all Losers." Melbourne *The Melbourne Herald-Sun.* 20 September: 19.

Micklethwait, J. and A. Wooldridge. 1996. *The Witch Doctors: What the Management Gurus are Saying, Why it Matters and How to Make Sense of It?* London: Heinemann.

OECD 1994. *OECD Jobs Study: Facts, Analysis, Strategies.* Paris: OECD.

————. 1997. *Global Information Society.* Paris: OECD.

Peters, G. and D. Savoie, eds. 1995. *Governance in a Changing Environment.* Montreal: McGill-Queen's University Press.

Polsby, N. 1984. *Political Innovation in America: The Politics of Policy Innovation.* New Haven: Yale University Press.

Putnam, R. 1993. *Making Democracy Work.* Princeton: Princeton University Press.

Rosenscranz R. 1996. "The rise of the virtual state." *Foreign Affairs,* Vol. 75, No. 4, July/August: 45-61.

Ruigrok, W. and R. van Tulder. 1995. *The Logic of International Re-Structuring.* London: Routledge.

Santos, de S. B. 1995. *Towards a New Common Sense: Law, Science and Politics in the Paradigmatic Transition.* London: Routledge.

Schultze, C. 1977. *The Public Use of Private Interest.* Washington: Brookings Institution.

Shaw, M. 1999. "Shredders bring threats by bracks." *The Melbourne Age.* 22 September: 8.

Simms, M. 1983. "The political economy of the state in Australia." *Public Sector Administration: New Perspectives,* edited by A. Kouzmin. Melbourne: Longman Cheshire. 37-56.

Stacey, R. D. 1996. *Strategic Management and Organizational Dynamics* 2nd Edition. London: Pitmans Publishing.

Strange, S. 1995. "The defective state." *Daedalus.* Vol. 124, No. 2, Spring: 55-73.

Streeck, W. 1991. "On the institutional conditions of diversified quality production." *Beyond Keynesianism,* edited by E. Matzner and W. Streeck. Aldershot: Edward Elgar. 21-61.

Summers, K. 1999. "Rituals behind a secret state." *The Canberra Times.* 4 September: C3.

Sutherland, J. W. 1977. *Administrative Decision-Making: Extending the Bounds of Rationality.* New York: Van Nostrand, Reinhold.

t'Hart, P. 1990. *Groupthink in Government: A Study of Small Groups and Policy Failure.* Amsterdam: Swets and Zetlinger.

Uren, D. 1999. "Responsible leaders need ability to account." *The Australian.* 20 November: 48.

Weaver, W. 1948. "Science and Complexity." *The American Scientist.* 36: 536-544.

Wheatley, A. 1999. "Pressure groups tighten screws over world trade." *Business Times.* Malaysia. 6 October: 4.

Wildavsky, A. 1988. *Searching for Safety.* New Brunswick: Transaction Books.

Williamson, J., ed. 1994. *The Political Economy of Policy Reform,* IIE. Washington.

World Bank. 1997. *The State in a Changing World.* New York: Oxford University Press.

PART FIVE

Deliberative Democracy, Discourse, and New Governance

INTRODUCTION

The article by John Forester sets out a critical and pragmatic approach to the study of planning practice that can integrate analyses of power, structure, and "communicative" action in planning settings. Forester rejects three myths elaborated by critics of "communicative planning": that it ignores power, that it ignores space, and that it obscures value questions by reducing critique to good intentions. Building upon the author's recent book *The Deliberative Practitioner* (Forester 1999a), he explores an account of an Italian planning consultant's work to illuminate issues of power, structure, and ethics, as revealed by a critical-pragmatic communicative analysis of professional practice.

David Farmer recapitulates and extends discussions on anti-administration from the perspective of discourse theory. First, it discusses discourse theory, explaining that the discourses of anti-administration aim toward the inclusion of marginalized or excluded perspectives. Second, it outlines some anti-administration theory. Parallel to the action of anti-matter and matter, the interaction of freshly demarginalized discourse perspectives and traditional discourse can yield anti-administrative resultants. Used in describing these resultants is Herbert Marcuse's notion of one-dimensional man. Third, Farmer's paper offers macro and micro examples of anti-administration gains in terms of problem definition and response resources. It underscores that anti-administration can recognize its affinity not only to the post-modern, but also to critical theory perspectives.

Most discussions of the relationship between public administration and society emphasize the governing process between citizens, groups, and non-governmental organizations. The essay by Jong Jun is to explore ways of enhancing governance in the context of a civil society. One of the challenges of the new century is to emphasize the governance approach as an alternative way of strengthening democracy and civil society that can work side by side with pluralistic politics in a liberal democracy. Governance is no substitute for the governing responsibility of public institutions, but it can strengthen local governments in, and through, civil society.

16

Deliberative Practice and the Myths of Communicative Planning: The Distinctive Approach of the Deliberative Practitioner

John Forester

This article sets out a critical and pragmatic approach to the study of planning that can integrate analyses of power, structure, and "communicative" action in planning settings. In doing so, the article rejects three myths elaborated by critics of "communicative planning": that it ignores power, that it ignores space, and that it obscures value questions by reducing critique to good intentions. As developed here, such a "critical-pragmatic" analysis of planning can strengthen the dialogue between practice and theory, for example the dialogue between practitioners' insightful accounts of their work and theorists' careful interpretations of those accounts. Taking practice seriously, and actually listening to accounts of skillful practitioners, we can assess, politically and practically, planners' day to day work involving diverse meetings, negotiations, and briefings. Insightful analysis of planning encounters can encourage still better practice—not by producing abstract lessons or decision-rules, but by suggesting what planners might better do through practitioners' vivid, instructive, and even moving accounts of their successes and failures alike.

"Communicative planning" seems to be alive and well in the planning literature (Innes 1995; Healey 1996;1997; Healey & Hillier 1996; Hoch 1994), and it has spawned a series of reactions or critiques (Yiftachel & Huxley 2000; Flyvbjerg 1996; 1997) which only partially hit their targets. In particular, three objections to "communicative planning" seem particularly problematic—that accounts of communicative planning are (1) inherently blind to questions of power; (2) inherently silent about spatial relationships or consequences; and (3) inherently idealized, reducing critique and ethics to matters of good intentions or utterly unattainable idealized conditions. But not one of these criticisms, however, seems inherent in a communicative analysis of planning, even if these qualifications may be more or less true of particular authors.

To show the promise of a critical-pragmatic, communicative analysis of planning practice, I will analyze a practitioner's story of a participatory planning case in Italy to show how we can not only understand planning practice as significantly communicative, but understand issues of power, spatiality, and ethical critique as well. I begin by characterizing the distinctive approach I have set out in *The Deliberative Practitioner* (Forester 1999a), then turn to an account by Professor Allesandro Balducci of the Politechnic of Milan, and I then assess Balducci's story in political, spatial, and ethical terms. Finally, I present a conceptual chart, Table 16.1, that shows how a critical-pragmatic analysis of planning might attend both to daily practice and institutional structure, as shaped by relations of power that not only constrain, but enable action and change as well.

THE DISTINCTIVE APPROACH OF THE DELIBERATIVE PRACTITIONER

By examining practitioners' "practice stories" as windows into the world of planning, *The Deliberative Practitioner* radically extends and deepens the communicative analysis of *Planning in the Face of Power* (Forester 1989), both practically and theoretically. Probing planners' stories rests on an assumption not widely shared in the fields of planning and public policy: astute practice in messy, highly politicized settings provides important intellectual challenges to planning theory, and, more generally, to social and political theory. Tacit practice can lead written theory. Skillful practice can help us to identify problems and to refocus practice-oriented theory, whether those problems involve political power or cultural difference, popular mobilization or social justice. Accordingly, *The Deliberative Practitioner* presents a plea for academic "theorists" to take practice more seriously, to recognize sensitively and to analyze powerfully what insightful practitioners do well in the most challenging moments of their work. Put a bit moralistically: criticism is too often cheap, and planning-bashing is a national pastime. The point here is not to celebrate planning, but to encourage its more politically astute and ethically critical practice.

This approach complements, but also differs from, related work concerned with urban governance, policy analysis, and planning practice. For the sake of contrast—but at the risk of exaggerating differences, rather than assessing similarities—with authors with whom this approach shares a great deal, we can consider, in turn, three groups of distinctive research questions that relate to: (1) the institutional and political staging of planning practice; (2) the character of planners' day to day interactions; and (3) the normative character or value-dimensions of what planners do.[1]

1.   The Institutional-Political Approach

- Where some focus on power as structuring and limiting (Yiftachel 1995), we can take power to be enabling as well, a politically shifting relationship rather than a fixed position or possession.
- Where some take the analysis of planning to center upon the local state, we can take it to focus on political agency, staged by political-economic structure and culture as well (cf. Clavel 1985; Healey 1996; Krumholz & Forester 1990).
- Where some see citizens' participation in planning processes as matters of advocacy and legal rights (Checkoway 1994); we can take participation not only to present well-known dangers of manipulation (Arnstein 1969), but also to present real political opportunities for deliberative, even transformative, learning and participatory action research. In a world in which rights are not self-implementing, advocacy planning in many forms is essential, to be sure.
- Where some see deliberative, consensus-building processes as relatively insulated from ideology, imbalances of power, and structural political-economic forces (Innes 1996); we can see such deliberative processes as precarious and vulnerable achievements created on existing political stages.
- Where some see planning as having a dark side (Flyvbjerg 1996); we can see planning as having many sides, some controlling and others empowering, some more strategic and others more deliberative—with the structure and politics of planning always shaping, rather than pre-determining, the character and consequences of planners' work in any real case.

2.   The Interactive Approach

- Where some authors focus on psychological aspects of planning, for example, we can focus upon planners' more social and political interactions (cf. Baum 1990; Healey 1992; Moore 1995).
- Where some focus on meaning, we can focus on the deliberate or even strategic production of meaning, along with its daily interpretation in the political and ethical work of "listening critically" and developing practical judgment (cf. Healey 1993a; Marris 1996; Yankelovich 1991).
- Where some take mediated-negotiations and consensus-building processes to be stand-alone procedures, we can take them to be directly related to the ongoing staff duties of planners and policy advisors who must work with task-forces, special committees, working groups, and formal and informal advisory boards every week (Susskind & Cruickshank 1987, but cf. the seminal Rivkin 1977).
- Where some see practitioners' reflection-in-action as a largely psychological process of reframing problems, a process of changing one's mind (Schön 1983); we can see such recognition as integral to deliberation in which parties, together, learn about fact, value, and strategy all together.

3.   The Normative (or "Values-Matter") Approach

- Where some focus upon ethics as a system of rules or codes, we can take ethics to encompass the allocation and recognition of value; so, we can understand ethics not as standards to follow, but as pragmatic action always done well or poorly, always potentially assessable via standards, consequences, and qualities of action (virtues) (cf. Hendler 1995; Rorty 1988; Nussbaum 1990).
- Where some see pragmatism loosely connected to ethics, more a process of learning from experience (Schön 1983), with Hilary Putnam (1990), we can take pragmatism and our pragmatic action to be integrally connected to ethics, for we learn in action not only about what "works," but about what matters as well.
- Where some focus on rationality in planning as a mental process of decision-making (Alexander 1996); we can take rationality to be an interactive and argumentative process of marshaling evidence and giving reasons, a process which, in principle, minimizes excluding relevant information and which encourages the testing of conjectures, a process that welcomes rather than punishes value inquiry (Fischer & Forester 1993; Gutmann & Thompson 1996; Healey 1993b).
- Where some take planning theory to be about intellectual history (Friedmann 1987) or decision-making (Faludi 1996); we can take it to assess planning as deliberative action that shapes others' understandings of their cities, theirselves, and, crucially, their possibilities of action, for better or worse. As importantly, we can take planning theory to finish the sentence that begins, "When I am planning...."

Now, these distinctive avenues of inquiry complement one another. How they are explored depends on the insights of researchers and the tools of theory and insight they bring to the task. I would like to illustrate these themes through an excerpt of a story of participatory planning recounted by Allessandro Balducci about his work in Pesaro, a city of 90,000 inhabitants on the eastern coast of Italy.

FOCUS GROUPS IN A PARTICIPATORY PLANNING CASE

In an interview conducted by this author and Judy Innes in the summer of 1998, Balducci recounted several participatory planning experiences, including this summary of the first focus-group stage of the participatory planning process he facilitated in Pesaro:

Balducci begins with an overview and describes the process:

> The first level took four months for everything. All the phases lasted, comprising the interviews and everything, six months. One phase was the interviews, the work on the documents and the newspapers, then we identified themes, then we did the focus groups, and then we drew from these focus groups guidelines for the new master plan. We presented these guidelines to all the participants in a general assembly of all the participants. These guidelines came out from the focus group work.
>
> What I want to stress here is that the group of people that participated in the focus groups, at a certain moment of time, gained trust in the project that was not gained at the beginning. They had been curious, but they didn't trust it.

After the focus groups, we prepared a report of the proceedings of the groups, and they were very happy to see how we organized and presented their ideas. So they were able to be part of the process from the first meeting to the presentation of the guidelines.

Balducci emphasizes his facilitating role:

I want to stress that at a certain point something happened, so we changed course. And this change was something that had to do with building an event, a collective event in the group process. It was not something that I did. After the previous experiences I waited for that. I felt that at a certain point working seriously with them we would see a change. What I want to underline is that many new ideas came out, and that was the indicator that this happened. These new ideas were put together by very different people: the representatives of the small shops, small industries, very small industries, and the representatives of architects, and so on. They discussed together, for example, a new path of linking together the museums and the historical center. They discussed the idea of enlarging the historical center with policies that could add to the traditional paths, some new centers of interest. We were able to put very concrete things in the guidelines that went, in some way, into the master plan.

What happened at first was that everyone gave his or her contribution to the discussion, but in a bilateral way; so giving it to us, the leader. Then a kind of trust developed both among them and in the work. So at a certain time this happened and this was a very important element in generating new ideas. It wasn't so much that I made it happen, but I knew to wait for it to happen. I refer to this as a process of sense-making: at a certain point people make sense of what is happening and people understand where we began and where we are going.

What I did was always try to let this discussion be generative. They had this opening paper, and they arrived having read it. We started with interventions where everyone in the group said what they thought about the topic and then we recorded that on the wall. I always had three pieces of paper: one with questions, another one with proposals, and another one with problems to be dealt with later. So at the end of this first turn, we read what we had recorded on the wall, and then I proposed to them questions, problems to be dealt with later, and proposals. Then we started to discuss these *together*, which was quite an important function for me—not only to facilitate the process—because from my experience of urban policy and town planning I could also suggest some things in order to make better use of what people said during the process.

But his facilitation required judgments of its own, as Balducci explains:

In the first place I did this by asking each one to make an intervention at the beginning and then trying to manage it. I had the responsibility of keeping quiet people who were too exuberant, and trying to have everybody make a contribution. I tried to reassure each one of them that they had the opportunity to give their position and make it clear, even if they could not speak very well.

That was very important in my previous experience with ordinary citizens, even with very uneducated people. So the main objective was to allow everyone to participate, but *not only to allow it, but to encourage everyone to participate* in the process. They were not political representatives of anything; they were there as people who knew the city from different perspectives and had relevant information. It was very important for me, too, not just to allow the local expert politicians to give their very well-known positions.

For each focus group we came out with an agreement—what kind of recommendation to give to the master plan. We did the work of putting all these results together and presenting them [as part of] the standard recommendations. There were many, many ideas, but during the focus groups we used a process of grouping, putting things together, showing that a long list of problems could be expressed in the master plan as one.

For example, the process of abandonment of the smaller commercial shops from the city center, the process of old people who couldn't find places to meet, and the problem of people who couldn't find housing within the center, were all part of the same kind of city center development problem. The idea that came out was an integrated policy to deal with all these different kinds of problems. We were able to tell the public administration that you can have this kind of integrated policy to deal with all these different problems.

Balducci distinguishes his role from more common notions of expertise:

I could contribute my professional knowledge at many different points. My idea of expertise in this context is that it is *experience*, not expert advice. So I expressed it as, "In *that* city, this problem has been dealt with in this way…," reporting experiences of other towns and even what's normally said in town planning about that kind of problem. For example, to deal with the problem of housing or the difficulties of young people opening new shops in the city center, I know about experiences of making small business incubators, financed by the public administration to try to start a new process of opening new shops by younger people. I showed them that was a good proposal. So I never said, "This is what planning proves."

He summarizes,

You have to argue in many ways in this context. The contract with people was that it was their contribution to the master plan, so my help to make this kind of work more effective was to help them work together; keeping all the ideas, helping to find ways of solving problems in a more effective way, or putting together the elements that they raised—not hiding what I was, or my knowledge.

The end phase that we were working toward was the presentation of all the guidelines to the planners and to the public administration. That was done in an open city council meeting, open to all the city, with all the groups of citizens who had done this second phase of work.

So after the focus groups, we started the second level of activity, and that was within the neighborhoods. We went to the neighborhoods and we said,

"Here we are, we've already done this kind of work in focus groups with the associations and now we want to gather all the proposals for projects that you want to bring to the planner who will design the master plan—any kind of proposals. We can help you make them technically acceptable and reasonable."

POWER, SPACE, AND VALUE—EVEN IN AN ACCOUNT OF FOCUS GROUPS

What are we to make of this practitioner's account? Although this vignette only suggests a great deal of prior work, still it tells us a good deal *about the kinds of problems planners face*, problems we can explore further *if we listen closely*. Following the approach of *The Deliberative Practitioner* sketched above, then, we can explore three categories of questions—three distinct, yet related, lines of theoretical inquiry. First, we can ask not only about the participants' "talk," but about the institutional and political structuring of their process. Second, we can ask not only about the *intentions* or goals of the participants, but about what they actually did together, their actions and interactions. Third, we can ask not only about these institutionally staged actions, but about how these have made the world a better or worse place: how they have allocated value, squandered opportunities or created value, damaged spaces or relationships or creatively enhanced them. We want to know, then, about qualities of (1) power, (2) interaction, and (3) value. These three lines of *questions provide windows into the world* of planning practice, as good theories do, and they do not reduce, at all, to any one theorist's perspective. Indeed, to study power, interaction, and value, we need the theoretical insights of several lines of theory, hardly exhausted by Habermas or Foucault, Weber or Nietzsche, Giddens or Goffman. (Not only is fact richer than diction, but cases are richer than single theories!)

POWER AND STRUCTURE

Consider the questions about institutional staging and structure first. We can ask how Balducci's account addresses issues of power and how it does not, and then how we, as critical readers, can explore questions of power *beyond* Balducci's own account. We should remember, of course, that this account comes from a directed interview, and that while the interviewee has discretion, certainly, about what he wishes and does not wish to say, still we have no reason to think that any given account is an interviewee's last word on a subject. This means, too, that whatever a practitioner says, suggests, or implies about power, they may, in addition, have a good deal more to say about the subject. We should take their account as first words, perhaps, about their experiences and situations, but surely not as their last words.

Now Balducci tells us a bit about the political structuring of this planning process. He mentions the potential power built into his role as planning expert, and he distinguishes his role of sharing experience from one invoking a more scientific authority to "prove" the efficacy of a given strategy. He tells us of his facilitator's work to counteract the power that dominant (exuberant, voluble) speakers exert in participatory processes. He warns us of another form of power when he tells us of the power of elected politicians to dominate a discussion: "It was very important for me, too, not to allow just the local expert politicians to give a very well-known position."

Balducci tells us also of the power of relevant information—local knowledge ("people who know the city from different perspectives and had relevant information"), the power of more-and less-organized and prepared parties, the power of the emergent group discovering it could address options no one had considered before, and the power of a facilitator to encourage the voice of people who previously "could not speak very well." Having referred earlier to the city council, the power of the politicians who would ultimately decide upon options after the planning group proposed it's guidelines, Balducci also tells us about the possibility of influencing the implementers: "we were able to tell the public administration that you can have this kind of integrated policy to deal with all these different problems (of the city center)." So if we listen closely, we see that this account notes issues of potential power plays again and again; it is hardly *silent* about power at all. But we should not confuse the account itself—the practitioner's story—with the broader analysis of power in the case or analysis of the practitioner's intervention, strategy, or experience, any more than we should confuse an analysis of good parenting with any given parent's story. Practitioners' stories give us examples of practice to study, but we must *study* them; *we must bring further questions to their stories*, to their cases, so that we learn about strategies and skills and challenges and responses that are not only possible, but desirable.

So far, then, we can see that Balducci's story begins to detail issues of power and inequality in several ways, and we ignore these structuring questions at our own risk. We can easily imagine following up and asking questions like the following: What, if any, of the guidelines proposed by this process did the city council actually adopt? Which newly devised options, previously unthought of before this process, were implemented? Which voices apparently included in this process felt afterwards that they were really (not) included or listened to? and which felt that they were used or manipulated in the process? Which issues historically raised in this community were relatively "untouchable" (if any)? What powers of persuasion or incentive or negotiation were used to formulate the guidelines as they emerged in the planning process? If we do not ask such questions, we can hardly understand what really happened here, much as we certainly should take Balducci's account as the opening of the door to the process.

When he tells us that the group built trust and emerged with new ideas, we should ask what powers of disorganization and history discouraged such ideas previously, and how those same ideas might be implemented with various degrees of support or coalition-backing now. None of these questions should lead us away from an interest in participation, since we will be able to develop stronger processes of participation only when we are attentive to the ways these processes are vulnerable to being corrupted—to make politicians, or dominant interests, or well-established citizens groups more firmly entrenched than they already are.

But these questions of the play of power and influence—for better or worse—also lead us to ask how new groups like Balducci's may propose new options that lead to new actions and actually transform the cities and environments in which we live. In this way, we remain open not only to the dark side of planning (I participate, you participate, we participate, they profit, as Sherry Arnstein (1969) warned and Flyvbjerg (1996) reminds us), but to the progressive and public-serving side in which new voices come forward, participate, and learn from and teach one another; and a diverse public transforms itself and the space—the environment—in which it lives.

Space and the Physical City

Balducci's comments about the focus group process tell us something not only about the qualities of interaction in the planning process, but the qualities of the physical space in which these participants live and meet one another. Balducci tells us that he worked to distinguish questions, proposals, and problems as a facilitator, which means, in effect, distinguishing uncertainties about the city, future possibilities in the city, and difficulties needing yet to be addressed about the physical well-being of the city. He stresses the "very different people" involved in some way, and his indication of these differences, "the representatives of small shops, very small industries, architects," and "old people who couldn't find places to meet, ...people who couldn't find housing within the center," suggests a plurality and diversity in the physical city that needed to be addressed, respected, and honored. But more than that, when Balducci tells us of the "trust" that developed in this diverse group, he is also telling us of a potential spatially-diverse coalition of actors who then made it possible for "many new ideas" to come out to fuel proposals for master plan guidelines.

When Balducci tells us that the process generated new ideas to deal with the "city center development problem," he is telling us not just about an effective and creative group process, but about the reimagination of the city center itself, the reimagination of the physical city. Similarly, when Balducci tells us of the participants deliberating about "enlarging the city historical center with policies that could add to the traditional paths, some new centers of interest," he is telling us not just about the generation of new possibilities in public deliberations, but he is telling us how this process encouraged the reimagination of the historical center, its re-evaluation with "new centers of interest" of that historical, physical city, and a revisioning of the traditional physical center with new elements of value and significance formulated. Thus, even though we need more information if we wish to learn any more about Pesaro, the communicative analysis of Balducci's work easily points us toward several distinct ways that this planning process led to the reformulation and reimagination of the spatial, physical city. If we looked, now, at the actual guidelines generated, and traced their potential implementation, we could map the spatial and physical consequences of this deliberative planning process (its efficacy, its contributions to alleviate problems or to control specific populations and their access to particular spaces). If we look just at the deliberative process itself, we see both the character of physical and historical diversity of the spaces involved, and the emergent rethinking of those spaces on the parts of the planning participants. Just as the communicative approach opens several avenues of inquiry related to power, so too, then, does it lead to questions about the spatio-physical world at stake in any given planning deliberation we may study. An analysis of planning practice that is attentive to its communicative dimensions—the ways the planning process structures voice and participation, shapes agendas, formulates proposals selectively, and involves the rethinking of space and the built environment—need not be silent at all about issues of power and space (Yiftachel and Huxley 2000).

Value and Ethics

Balducci tells us a good deal about value, about significance, and about the desirable as well, and we should listen closely. He tells us the group came to change itself—to form new relations, to encourage everybody to participate, to develop trust, to recognize that it could actually address issues and gain a hearing by the local planners and politicians—so that diverse participants who did not know one another or appreciate one another's views now came to see one another, and themselves, in new and valued, trusted ways. He tells us of the value of facilitation too—the skillful work with a group to define problems, present proposals, keep track of future issues to be dealt with—relative to groups that are more free form, hit and miss, poorly managed. He tells us that the group was able to build upon "the traditional paths" to the historic center of Pesaro to add "new centers of interest," which reflects a re-valuing, or new valuing, of the city itself. Here, spatiality and ethics come together, for "new centers of interest" are immediately geographically diverse, linked and located with respect to the center, but they are "of interest," of value in terms of the tourism dollars potentially spent by visitors to Pesaro, for the benefit of shopkeepers and the citizens of Pesaro too. He tells us that the group was able to link issues now that had previously been disconnected so that the city council could develop "an integrated policy," a newly viable strategy with a promise of effectiveness and efficiency that nobody had devised before. Efficiency gains are, quite simply, value added, and here they have come as the result of a participatory planning process, as Balducci suggests.

Balducci identifies several other values at stake in his process. He notes the trust emerging from a background of distrust, and thus, the value of improved relationships among diverse community members of Pesaro. He notes the deliberative creativity of the process, the "many new ideas" that grew out of this planning exercise. He notes the value of participants' ownership of the process: the value of everyone giving his or her contribution, encouraging "everyone to participate in the process." He notes the value of agreement, actual proposals for master plan guidelines, which he illustrates with the "integrated policy."

We have no hint of Balducci's orchestrating an idealized dialogical process here. We have no suggestion that this deliberative process suffered because its participants did not adopt attitudes seeking undistorted communication with each other. Instead, we see Balducci working as a practical facilitator to pay attention to both more- and less-dominant voices; to the emergent trust and generative qualities of the group; and to a critical, but pragmatic focus on shaping practical proposals to take to the city council for implementation. A communicative analysis of Balducci's work begins to show us how he actually convened and facilitated these focus groups in Pesaro; it does not criticize either the planners or the participants for failing to achieve some idealized dialogic situation, even if this analysis would indeed lead us to look carefully at whose voices are included and whose voices are excluded.

A critical-pragmatic communicative analysis, then, tries to finish the sentence that begins, "When Balducci was planning,..." with (an assessment of) "what did he do?" By accounting for the rich diversity of his actions, these brief remarks suggest, this line of planning theory and analysis can open up questions of power, space, and value(ethics)—the critics of "communicative planning" notwithstanding! But consider now how a critical-pragmatic communicative analysis can help us to assess both the constraining and enabling faces of power, just as it helps us to assess issues of structure and action together.

POWER, STRUCTURE, AND ACTION IN COMMUNICATIVE PLANNING

Notice that Balducci's story tells us not only about problems, but about possibilities too; not only about inequalities of power and access, but about a "generative process"—the creation of new policy ideas—as well. Power constrains, but it also enables (as a long history of analysts of power have always known, e.g. Marx, Weber, and not least of all, Foucault). His story tells us, too, not only about elements of political structure, but about challenges of practical action. We learn, for example, that within a structure of elected, organized politicians and a city council, who presumably were to make decisions about the master plan and its implementation, the focus groups brought together diverse stakeholders who began to build trust among one another.

Once we realize that power may constrain or enable day to day planning actions, as well as longer-term structures of planning, we can map a field of critical but pragmatic possibilities, as in Table 16.1.

Table 16.1. Power, Structure, and Action in Communicative Planning

Planning assessed as/	*Power that Constrains*	*Power that Enables*
Action	cooptation (Arnstein) manipulation of participation deliberate exclusion (*danger*: cynicism)	consensus-building (Susskind) advocacy planning/organizing inclusive participation (blindness to constraint)
Structure	systemic exclusion class domination (Marx) ethnocracy ideology (complaint vs critique)	systemic reform empowerment (Freire) politics of recognition critique (utopianism)

We can see here that communicative planning operates in each of these four quadrants, and we have important literatures in planning, political science, and public administration to help us understand the institutional behavior and problems of action that link these quadrants in real life, at the center of the Table. Consider each quadrant in turn:

First, we see in Balducci's short vignette that social actions may not all be "enabling" or generative; indeed, Balducci tells us that he has to work hard as a facilitator to ensure that many voices are heard, that the "professional politicians" do not dominate the discussions, that the inherited distrust of the group does not poison all future deliberations. The classic analysis of the "dark side" of participatory processes, the manipulatory possibilities of the "good intentions" of encouraging citizen participation, appears in Sherry Arnstein's "Ladder of Citizen Participation" (Arnstein 1969)

Second, we see that even in the background of the constraints of the first quadrant, some "generative" action is possible. Facilitation can help a diverse group generate new ideas; distinguish problems, proposals, and future issues; and build trust in ways that generate new policy measures to bring forward as guidelines for the city council to adopt. This is no panacea, but here we have a the co-generative learning that participatory action researchers describe (Levin in Forester, 1999a)—learning that helps educate citizens, and fuel planning and political action as well. A great deal of work addresses these possibilities, much of it collected and referenced in Susskind and others' new *Consensus Building Handbook* (1999). It is also reflected in the literature on collaborative problem-solving processes (Gray 1989; Healey 1997) and deliberative learning (Hoch 1994), and anticipated in a quite political way by Paulo Freire's seminar *Pedagogy of the Oppressed* (1970)—a politically sensitive communicative analysis if there ever was one!

Third, Balducci tells us clearly, if we listen, that the political structure of the situation is not one of some ideal world, but one of inequality, distrust, differential power and access, skepticism, and public need. Some groups are organized and others are not; some have wealth and resources and others do not; some have housing and transportation and others do not; some are political system insiders and others are not, and so on. Balducci's story suggests as much in even this brief vignette, and no "communicative analysis" of his work could miss this. All of the literature on the political economy of planning becomes relevant here, from analyses of planning and the role of the state, to regime theories and less systematic analyses of the politics of development in capitalist economies (Campbell & Fainstein 1996; Luria 1997).

Fourth, Balducci suggests also, however, that the political structure of the situation raises certain possibilities. Certainly he holds out the promise that the focus groups might generate useful guidelines and that these might be, in turn, adopted by the city council. This is the least surprising and most conventional reading of the political process: not that it is particularly functional, not that it is free of (quadrant three's) structural inequalities, but that once in a while it might function to adopt, and eventually implement, good policy. Further, though, Balducci suggests that a participatory planning process can be structured to be "generative," structured so that citizens deliberate together and, in learning from one another, come to generate new design and policy ideas which can then gather sufficient political support to be implemented to change their physical and spatial reality. In this case, the change at hand may be physical, spatial, social, or economic: with new resources invested in the historic center of Pesaro, the spatial configuration of residents' and tourists' routes and uses may shift, the physical structure itself may be preserved better or transformed, and socio-economic policies that support a combination of housing and job creation may be implemented by the city council. Extensive literature in political science and public administration addresses these possibilities of administrative and political restructuring and reform, even if the planning literature is decidedly thinner here (Moore 1995).

In any given case of course, local and national politics might place most of a case in any or all of the quadrants of Table 16.1. Oren Yiftachel's work (1995) on social control of space, the "dark side of planning," and Flyvbjerg's (1997) story of Aalborg suggest that a great deal of the politics of planning falls on the left hand side of Table 16.1: that again and again the strategic bargaining of actors leads to misrepresentations of benefits and gains, that the structure of the planning in capitalist economies leads to differential access and information for affected citizens, that the operation of business as usual among the business people and politicians leads to spatial exclusion and economic appropriation—the effective inequality of power, access, and action that we see in quadrants I and III. Yiftachel demonstrates spatial inequality and control even if he does not suggest what countermeasures might effectively resist such patterns (1995). Flyvbjerg raises issues that are crucial to any understanding of city politics—as cases before Aalborg's have shown us—even if it's not clear how appeals to Foucault and Nietzche help us to understand how *different uses of power (or different planning interventions) might lead to any better or worse public outcomes (or more or less domination, more or less democratic politics, etc.)* (Forester 1999b).

My point here, illuminated by Table 16.1, is simply that *communicative plan-ning analyses need to take into account not just a light side or a dark side of planning, but the full range of political influences that stage planners' actions.*

So analyses that only address the "dark side" will leave us in the dark. They will not suggest answers to Lenin's famous question in the face of domination, "What is to be done?" Similarly, analyses of planning that only address the light side of well-intentioned, collaborative conversations will leave us light-headed, blind to the political inequalities that any real planner in any real situation has to anticipate and face. An analysis of planning that ignores power risks being will-fully blind to the real world, but an analysis that ignores possibilities of real action risks a cynical complicity with the forces it purports to "expose,"—I say com-plicity because it tells us nothing about what we can do to resist the power that now seems all the more deeply untouchable, or unchangeable. If a planning analy-sis that ignores power or ignores "what can be done" has nothing to do with the "communicative" character of the analysis, this is a matter of the intentions and motivations of the analysts.

But if we are to understand how planning processes can exclude some people and questions while including others, and if we are to understand how planning processes are constituted by shifting relations of political power (relationships in which human beings remake their physical, spatial, political, and socio-economic worlds) we need to understand both political structure and practical action. To do that, we will need an analysis that pays as much attention to the "communicative" aspects of planning practice as it pays to the structural shaping of who is able to "communicate" or "understand" what, or better yet, who is able do DO what, together, or to one another.

NOTE

1. This opening section discusses material from the introduction to *The Deliberative Practitioner* (Forester, 1999a).

REFERENCES

Alexander, Ernest. 1996. After rationality: Towards a contingency theory for planning. *Explorations in Planning Theory*, edited by S. Mandelbaum, L. Mazza, and R. Burchell. New Brunswick: Center for Urban Policy Research.

Arnstein, Sherry. 1969. A ladder of citizen participation. *Journal of the American Institute of Planners*. 35((4)):216-224.

Baum, Howell. 1987. *The Invisible Bureaucracy: The Unconscious in Organizational Problem Solving*. New York: Oxford University Press.

———. 1990. *Organizational Membership*. Albany: State University of New York Press.

Campbell, Scott and S. Fainstein, (eds). 1996. *Readings in Planning Theory*. Cambridge: Blackwell.

Checkoway, Barry. 1994. Symposium: Paul Davidoff and advocacy planning in retrospect. *Journal of the American Planning Association*. 60:139-161.

Clavel, Pierre. 1985. *The Progressive City*. New Brunswick: Rutgers.

Faludi, Andreas. 1985. The return of rationality. *Rationality in Planning*, edited by M. Breheny and A. Hooper. London: Pion.

Fischer, Frank and J. Forester. 1993. *The Argumentative Turn in Planning and Policy Analysis*. Durham: Duke University Press.

Flyvbjerg, Bent. 1996. The dark side of planning: Rationality and realrationalitat. *Explorations in Planning Theory*, edited by S. Mandelbaum, L. Mazza, and R. Burchell. New Brunswick: Center for Urban Policy Research.

Flyvbjerg, Bent. 1997. *Rationality and Power*. Chicago: University of Chicago Press.

Forester, John. 1989. *Planning in the Face of Power*. Berkeley, CA: University of California Press.

———. 1999a. *The Deliberative Practitioner: Encouraging Participatory Planning Processes*. MIT Press.

———. 1999b. An instructive case hampered by theoretical puzzles: Critical comments on Bent Flyvbjerg's *Rationality and Power*.

Friedmann, John. 1987. *Planning in the Public Domain*. Princeton, NJ: Princeton University Press.

Freire, Paulo. 1970. *Pedagogy of the Oppressed*. New York: Herder & Herder.

Gray, Barbara. 1989. *Collaborating: Finding Common Ground for Multiparty Problems*. San Francisco: Jossey Bass.

Gutmann, A. and D. Thompson. 1996. *Democracy and Disagreement*. Cambridge, MA: Harvard University Press.

Healey, Patsy. 1992. A day's work: Knowledge and action in communicative practice. *Journal of the American Planning Association*. 58:9-20.

———. 1993a. The communicative work of development plans. *Environment and Planning B: Planning and Design*. 20:83-104.

———. 1993b. Planning through debate: The communicative turn in planning theory. *The Argumentative Turn in Policy Analysis and Planning*, edited by F. Fischer and J. Forester. Durham: Duke University Press. 233-253.

———. 1996. The communicative turn in planning theory and its implications for spatial strategy formation. *Environment and Planning B: Planning and Design*. 23:217-234.

———. 1997. *Collaborative Planning: Making Frameworks in Fragmented Societies*. London: Macmillan.

Healey, Patsy and J. Hillier. 1996. Communicative micropolitics. *International Planning Studies*. 1:2.

Hendler, Sue. 1995. *Planning Ethics*. New Brunswick: Center for Urban Policy Research.

Hoch, Charles. 1994. *What Do Planners Do?* Chicago: APA Planners Press.

Innes, Judith. 1995. Planning theory's emerging paradigm. *Journal of Planning Education and Research*. 14(3) (Spring):183-189.

Innes, Judith. 1996. Planning through consensus building: A new view of the comprehensive ideal. *Journal of the American Planning Association*. 460-472.

Krumholz, Norman and J. Forester. 1990. *Making Equity Planning Work*. Philadelphia: Temple University Press.

Luria, M., (ed). 1997. *Reconstructing Urban Regime Theory*. Thousand Oaks, CA: Sage.

Marris, Peter. 1996. *The Politics of Uncertainty*. London: Routledge.

Moore, Mark. 1995. *Creating Public Value*. Cambridge: Harvard University Press.

Nussbaum, Martha. 1990. *Love's Knowledge*. New York: Oxford University Press.

Putnam, Hilary. 1990. *Realism With a Human Face*. Cambridge: Harvard University Press.

Rivkin, Malcolm. 1977. *Negotiated Development: A Breakthrough in Environmental Controversies*. Washington, DC: Conservation Foundation.

Rorty, Amelie. 1988. *Mind in Action: Essays in the Philosophy of Mind*. Boston: Beacon Press.

Schön, Donald. 1983. *The Reflective Practitioner: How Professionals Think in Action*. New York: Basic Books.

Susskind, Lawrence and J. Cruickshank. 1987. *Breaking the Impasse*. New York: Basic Books.

Susskind, Lawrence, J. Cruickshank, J. T. Larmer, and S. McKearnan, (eds). 1999. *The Consensus Building Handbook*. Los Angeles: Sage.

Yankelovich, Daniel. 1991. *Coming to Public Judgment*. Syracuse: Syracuse University Press.

Yiftachel, Oren. 1995. Planning as control: Policy and resistance in a deeply divided society. *Progress in Planning*. 44:116-187.

Yiftachel, Oren and M. Huxley. 2000. Debating dominance and relevance; The "communicative turn" in planning theory. *Journal of Urban and Regional Research*. 24(3).

17

The Discourses of Anti-Administration[1]

———————————— David John Farmer

The discourses of anti-administration aim toward the inclusion of perspectives (lenses, frames, even people) marginalized or excluded by the constraints of traditional public administration (P.A.) discourse. This inclusion, bringing together elements of anti-administrative and administrative discourses, is designed to yield resultants which are of critical significance for P.A. thinking and practice. The metaphor of anti-administration is borrowed from anti-matter in physics. Anti-matter refers to the noncommonsensical notion of antiparticles (antineutrons, antiprotons, positrons, etc.) corresponding to nuclear particles (neutrons, protons, electrons, and so on). Antiprotons have the same mass and spin as protons but have the opposite electric charge and magnetic moment. For example, an antihydrogen atom consists of a negatively charged antiproton with an orbital positron. "Normal matter and anti-matter would mutually annihilate each other upon contact, being converted totally into energy" (U.S. Atomic Energy Commission 1967). In a similar way, anti-administration is administration which is directed at negating administrative-bureaucratic power. The suggestion here is that the encounter can give rise to fresh P.A. energy, which P.A. thinkers and practitioners should seek to understand.

This essay focuses on anti-administration from the perspective of discourse theory. First, it discusses some discourse theory in order to explain what it means to claim that the discourses of anti-administration aim toward the inclusion of marginalized or excluded perspectives. Second, it outlines some anti-administration theory. It suggests that, parallel to the action of anti-matter and matter, the interaction of freshly demarginalized discourse perspectives and traditional discourse can yield anti-administrative resultants. Used in describing these resultants is the Marcusian notion of multi-dimensionality, where perspectives in "another" dimension are "critical" in standing against "uncritical" acceptance of the existing system, structures, norms, and behaviors. The chapter describes a spirit of administering anti-administratively that includes a self-conscious discourse approach consistent not only with openness to the marginalized and the excluded, but also with the view that not all perspectives are equally good (or bad). Third, the chapter offers macro- and microexamples of anti-administration gains in terms of problem definition and response resources—gains denied by the marginalizations and exclusions of traditional P.A. discourse.

This article recapitulates what I have described in other publications (e.g., Farmer 1995; 1998). There is some extension of that work, e.g., the present account of anti-administration indeed owes much to Herbert Marcuse's analysis of one-dimensional man (1991). The recapitulation is designed to emphasize that neither anti-administration nor discourse theory are "wedded 'til death they do part" with postmodernism. It is true that there is an affinity, and postmodern insights have added significantly. Anti-administration has been described more than once in postmodern terms. Earlier, an account was given of anti-administration as a shift away from rationalism and technocratic expertise in an emerging postist context (Farmer 1998a). Yet, the postmodern v. modern debate can be sidestepped in thinking about both terms. An intent of this paper is to underscore that anti-administration, no less than discourse theory, can recognize its affinity not only to the postmodern, but also to critical theory perspectives. This is possible because the discourses of anti-administration are understood as basically plural. There is no "one right way" in discourse reform; hope for a single answer is misguided. The differing accounts are understood as complementary, looking at the "same" entity from different discourse perspectives.

SOME DISCOURSE THEORY

The reader is invited to engage in the first of two thought games (or experiments) as we consider three ideas prominent in discourse theory. Proceeding through these three features, the first game invites the reader to concretize the points by considering in his/her own mind how they could be applied to certain surface discourses or work subcultures—say, the discourse of administering, the discourse of a program-area like policing, and the discourse of another program-area like social work. All that the paper-and-pencil game requires is completing a three-by-three grid. As headings for the three columns, the three discourses can be listed—administering, policing, and social-working. As side-headings for the rows, the three discourse features can be noted. In the matrix, the reader can enter her own concrete examples, as in Table 17.1 below. In doing so, we can bear in mind two preliminary points. People often operate in more than one surface discourse, e.g., a police commissioner operates in the discourses of administering, policing, and some others. Also, the hardest discourse (like an accent) to identify is our own, because our own seems exceptionally "natural." As the reader concretizes these three points, it should become clearer what it means to claim that the discourses of anti-administration aim toward the inclusion of perspectives (lenses, frames, even people) marginalized or excluded by the constraints of traditional P.A.

Table 17.1: Discourse Differences

Overlapping Aspects	Administering	Policing	Social-Working
Discourse as a perspective on our context.	e.g., world tends to consist of my agency (or program), similar agencies (or programs), and others.	e.g., world tends to consist of good guys and bad guys.	e.g., world tends to consist of needy clients and others.
Discourse as involving constraints that marginalize and/or exclude.	e.g., true administrator directs, coordinates and controls.	e.g., true cop is a crime-fighter.	e.g., true social worker is a helping professional.
Discourse as situated in a practice of a time and place.	e.g., common expectation for manager in some agencies to "fit in" with existing agency and/or local mores.	e.g., macho and para-military values now privileged in some agencies.	e.g., requirement now for MSW degree in some agencies

"Discourse" has been interpreted variously as discourse theory has developed and achieved important results in non-P.A. disciplines such as philosophy, sociology, linguistics, psychology, critical theory, post-colonial studies, and postmodern feminisms; and discourse theory arrived later in P.A. The account used in *The Language of Public Administration* (Farmer 1995) relies on thinkers like Michel Foucault and Ludwig Wittgenstein, for example. But there are others, e.g., Mikhail Bakhtin's notion of a voice within a text. Most discourse theorists would agree that all claims, all ascriptions of meanings, all actions and events to which meanings are attached—that is, all discourses—are situated within constraints which are largely unconscious. What we can claim as true or relevant is shaped by such constraints, which include the social, the institutional, and other larger contexts within which we do our thinking. Most would agree that discourse should not be understood as limited to mere words. For example, discourse can be nonverbal, and, as is noted later, we all have "right sides" to our brains (e.g. see Farmer, R. 1998). From among these various understandings, we are electing to focus on three features in the forefront of Foucauldian and most other versions of discourse theory (e.g., see Mills 1997).

First of the three ideas about discourse theory is that the categories, beliefs, and values implicit in discourse constitute a way of looking at the world—or a "perspective on our context." Could it not be said that administrators (of course, there are deviations from the mean) tend to look at their context in a specifiable

way? So do street police officers; so do front-line social workers. To give a trivial example from this surface level, an NYPD police inspector, in 1972, faced
with a secretary who was habitually late for work, threatened that he would "lock
her up for theft of services;" an administrator or a social worker is unlikely to see
the world in such terms. The constraints of our discursive practices structure our
sense of reality. As Foucault puts it, discourse is not simply a group of signs or a
text, but rather the "practices that systematically form the objects of which they
speak" (Foucault 1972). This does not imply that the world is not real. Real
though the world surely is, discursive practices can limit us to perceiving as real
only certain features of that reality. Discourse involves a narrowing of the "observational" field. It also involves the establishment of patterns of admissible connections between one set of statements and others, blocking yet other claims. So
we are not surprised to read that acts of vision are not merely mindless responses
by the brain and retina to light beams; rather vision is an active process shaped by
a meaning-hungry mind (Hoffman 1999). The NYPD example above was correctly described as trivial, and as surface-level in the sense that the discourses of
the modern American administrator, police officer, and social worker jointly share
deeper and conditioning discourses like that of the enlightenment project (of
which the U.S.A. has been described as an outstanding example). Similar to the
Russian *matryoshka* doll (the doll within a doll within a doll...), there are interrelated discourses within discourses within yet other discourses. Yet that image is
too neat for the complexity of the reality.

A second idea is that discourses are mainly formed around practices involving
marginalization and/or exclusion. Discursive mechanisms both limit "and"
encourage what statements can be made, shaping what is considered to be worth
knowing, for example there are no departments of astrology, alchemy, or even
psychoanalysis in American universities; once, there were no departments of
women's or African-American studies. Administrator discourse (yes, there are
deviants from the mean) privileges recipes for action that serve administrative
needs, for example, as Chester Barnard pointed out, the work of the C.E.O. is not
"of" the organization (Barnard 1938). Police officer discourse tends to see a
world of bad guys and good guys (illustrated by the fact that all major American
police departments set up internal affairs units); social workers typically do not
speak in terms of internal affairs units. On truth, for example, Foucault observed
that truth is produced "only by varieties of multiple forms of constraint. And it
induces regular effects of power" (Foucault 1980: 131). On the related topic of
relevance, the penchant for practicality in American P.A. discourse tends to privilege efficiency of a certain type. This efficiency is where the solutions are micro,
commonsensical, and open to immediate acceptance and implementation—easy-
to-cook recipes ready for popping "this" food into "this" oven "now" for "my"
dinner. Practicality is constrained within specified narrow limits, and the constraints of this discourse tend to marginalize problematics and solutions that do
not fit. None of this is to imply that discourse constraints (like the practices of
academic disciplines) do not have benefits, as Foucault explains when describing

how constraints aid in the production of knowledge, but a cost is the marginalization and the exclusion of facts which may be important. Increasing the cost is that the exclusions have an arbitrary nature. The exclusions are not "natural," even though—from within a particular discourse—they seem natural.

The senses in which discourse constraints are arbitrary differ between the modernist and postmodernist perspectives. As suggested earlier, discourse theory is indeed an emphasis both of some modernists and postmodernists. On the modernist side, for example, critical theorists like Jurgen Habermas can place discourse at the forefront of their concerns, laying bare what they see to be the structure of discourse constraints. On the post-structuralist side, the postmodernists are also concerned with discourse, but they are skeptical of anyone's capability of delineating fixed structures. They attach more importance to the Dionysian, rather than the Apollonian, aspects of life. They recognize that our human condition is ungrounded and beyond our complete understanding; we deceive ourselves with "rational" illusions. Some suppose that the "Dionysian life positively celebrates human capacity by looking absurd existence in the eye" (Chamberlain 1999: 104).

Third is the idea that discourse is situated in the practice of a time and place, or, in other words, in a way of thinking and doing. For the most part, discourse is not an unconstrained individual choice. In the same way that most persons do not choose their own mother tongues, we tend to join a pre-existing discourse of public administration. When people become either social workers or police officers, they join a pre-existing discourse. The form of the discourse is shaped by constraints on the demand side (like public and political expectations for the respective groups, e.g., social workers and police officers) and on the supply side (e.g, differences resulting from differentials in entry-level educational requirements for the median police officer and social worker). While the administrator (or police officer, or social worker) may struggle to create individual and new texts, it is largely the case that the text of which they are a part tends to speak through them. So it is for you—and me.

SOME ANTI-ADMINISTRATION THEORY

The discourses of anti-administration, in the present account, focus on the effect of including the perspectives marginalized or excluded by the set of traditional P.A. discourses. For convenience, we can use the singular—"the" traditional P.A. discourse—when writing of the set of traditional P.A. discourses. Parallel to the action of anti-matter and matter, the excluded discourse perspectives and the traditional discourse can be viewed as interacting and yielding resultants, or, as we can say, anti-administrative resultants. That is, the discourse perspectives "previously marginalized (or excluded) but now demarginalized (or included)" interact with the traditional discourse.

This account of anti-administration borrows from Herbert Marcuse's analysis of one-dimensional man. It is modernist in the sense, for example, that it is consistent with the view that modernity is an incomplete or improvable project (Habermas 1983). Earlier accounts have been given in terms of the postmodern perspective. So, the earliest version wrote in terms of the postmodern anti-administration that would stress imaginization, rather than rationalization (Farmer 1995). It is in the spirit and letter of the reflexive language paradigm, described at that time and noted below, that this account attempts to look at the "same" entity from a different perspective.

Anti-administration looks to a change away from the one-dimensionality of traditional P.A. discourse toward multi-dimensionality. An interaction between a freshly-demarginalized or freshly-included discourse perspective (freshly demarginalized or included in the sense that it was previously marginalized or excluded) and traditional P.A. discourse is of significance in anti-administrative terms insofar as it yields multi-dimensionality. Marcuse explains the one-dimensional thinking which he considered to be pervasive in contemporary society in terms of the uncritical acceptance of existing structures, norms, and behaviors: "The most advanced areas of industrial society exhibit throughout these two features: a trend toward consummation of technological rationality, and intensive efforts to contain this trend within the established institutions" (1991: 17). It is thinking that accepts that, under conditions of a rising standard of living, non-conformity with the overall system is "socially useless" (ibid.: 2). "The Happy Consciousness—the belief that the real is rational and that the system delivers the goods—reflects the new conformism which is a facet of technological rationality translated into social behavior" (ibid.: 84). Among his illustrations of such one-dimensional thinking is his interpretation of how the study of labor relations in the Hawthorne Works of the Western Electric Company (ibid.: 108ff.), in service of the system, uses a repressive reduction of thought from the universal, to the operational, concept. Against all this, Marcuse recommended the "great refusal."

What are of interest are anti-administrative results that contribute toward a dimension beyond that of the existing system. It is thinking that is able to transform by "standing against." What "standing against" means can be approached by considering Marcuse's account of the flattening out of the antagonism between culture and social reality in the rationalizing context that accompanies capitalism (Marcuse 1991: 56ff.). He claims that this flattening out has obliterated the "oppositional, alien, and transcendent elements in the higher culture by virtue of which it constituted another dimension of reality" (ibid: 57). As an example, we may think of the "losing" battle of musicians like Anton Webern, who wanted to liberate music from the hierarchical structures placed on it by tonality. Webern's music "stands against" the existing musical system in seeing each individual tone as having its own expressive possibilities, independent of the traditional discourse of harmony. Marcuse goes on to explain that the "liquidation of two-dimensional culture takes place not through the denial and rejection of the 'cultural values,' but through their wholesale incorporation into the established order, through their reproduction and display on a massive scale" (ibid.: 57).

The anti-matter/anti-administration metaphor is not intended to imply that anti-administration is slated simply as excluding administration. Rather, it is a matter of "opening" P.A. to multi-dimensional thinking, not exchanging one set of discourse blinders for another. The in-between between administration and anti-administration is, indeed, the conceptual space that is the site of interactive meaning generation over time.

The anti-matter/anti-administration metaphor is intended to urge a more open attitude, for example, toward the unfashionable and toward less powerful voices. For this reason, a helpful rule-of-thumb may well be to provide for admission to the dialog of the marginalized (or excluded) perspectives in a maximally-feasible non-marginalizing (or non-exclusive) way. The term "unfashionable" is used here to point to the relative powerlessness connected with some ideas. The Foucauldian insight about the connection of power and what counts as truth was noted earlier. There is a tendency to confuse the "power speaking" and "speaking to power" elements in P.A. thinking, and it is a reasonable confusion when mainstream political discourses emphasize the Civics 101 half-truth about democratic government being owned by the people. Foucault's claim about power and truth should alert us that a general direction of P.A. theory should be toward fully recognizing theory's "speaking to power" component. The term "less powerful voices" includes the disadvantaged (e.g., women) and also those whose voices cannot be heard, like the future generation and the mentally ill.

How should a person determine which non-traditional P.A. discourse perspectives should be demarginalized (or included)? In administering anti-administratively, are all "other" perspectives equally bad (or good), or are some (to various degrees) good and others bad? Such questions lose much of their import, even if it is recognized (as it should be) that the administrative decision-making is a person-centered "art" rather than a science. To the extent that "I" am able, "I" make "my" decisions about changing "my" discourse from within the discourse in which "I" think and speak. "I" must make decisions for me about what discourse constraints "I" will admit. "I" decide which perspectives "I" consider to be more or less acceptable.

That is not the end of the story, however. In the course of exercising the "art" of making "my" decisions, "I" can aim for the more or less "multi-dimensional;" "I" can be more or less "open to the other." It has been argued, for instance, that it is better if "my" decisions have a self-conscious style (Farmer 1999). The claim was made that P.A. discourse privileges an inflexibly narrow style. On the other hand, a style including greater self-consciousness can contribute to the dimensionality of "my" disciplinary thinking. Yes, my decisions are better if I recognize realistically "my" epistemological situation (my capacity to know); "I" can hold that a realistic position calls for moral concern in a context where "I" should be skeptical about—and hesitant about—my own moral claims. Yes, my decisions are better if "I" am alert to the P.A. context, what is taking place on the P.A. ground. The self-consciousness in "my" P.A. discourse that is emphasized here concerns the importance for multi-dimensionality of consciousness of the relationship between "my" discourse constraints and what public administration facts "I" see.

This understanding is reflected in the reflexive (or reflexive language) approach which is so natural in a discipline like P.A. That approach does not suppose that humans have available a God's-eye view of the world, a view from nowhere—like that purported to occur in traditional Economics theorizing. Rather, it considers that our views are always partial—even this view—in that they are from a particular perspective. Following this, it has been suggested that bureaucracy can be best studied from a variety of perspectives or dimensions, where the student is conscious of the co-shaping of the perspective used. A multi-perspectival, or reflexive, approach typically involves looking at P.A. "facts" and theories (first-order data) from various second-order perspectives, where second-order is used idiosyncratically to mean perspectives outside the discipline. Looking at a problem, for instance, the sociologist sees a sociological problem, the economist an economic problem, and so on; the idea is that different perspectives will offer fresh interpretations and that we can recognize how the interpretations are co-shaped by the perspective or lens chosen. Consciousness about this relationship between constraints in the perspectives (frames, lenses, blinders) and the public administration item described is advantageous. It is even more advantageous if some of these perspectives contribute to multi-dimensionality in the sense borrowed from Marcuse. Anti-administration resultants should be "critical" perspectives in supporting a dimension that stands against "uncritical" acceptance of existing structures, norms, and behaviors.

MACRO AND MICRO P.A. APPLICATIONS

The reader is invited to participate in a second thought game (or experiment) to emphasize the claim that practical utility for discourses of anti-administration can be identified at the macro and micro levels. This utility starts from the fact that traditional P.A. discourse(s) does tend to marginalize and/or exclude. P.A. understandings and action are unduly narrowed in such overlapping terms as problem formulation (selection, delineation) and the spectrum of response resources considered available in responding to such problems as are identified. Utility lies in going beyond the one-dimensional.

The reader is invited to name and describe the anti-administrative resultants that can be expected at the macro and micro levels from four examples of the interaction of selected administrative discourse elements with marginalized and/or excluded perspectives. Table 17.2 provides the four examples. All that the game requires is that the reader write in the third column a name that attempts to capture the character of the anti-administrative resultant, and that he/she add notes describing this character. A key recognition is that the anti-administrative resultant should be "other" dimensional in the Marcusian sense; it should be a "critical" perspective that is in a dimension that stands against "uncritical" acceptance of existing structures, norms, and behaviors. Involved in this recognition is

Table 17.2: Some (Overlapping) Interactions

ADMINISTRATIVE DISCOURSE	+	*PREVIOUSLY MARGINALIZED*	=	*ANTI-ADMINISTRATIVE ENERGY*
MICRO-ORIENTED Micro practicality. Organization focus.	+	MACRO-ORIENTED Macro practicality. Refusal of limitations in focus.	=	RESULTANT (?)
HIERARCHY Citizen-state interrelationships. Technical expertise. Bureaucratizing.	+	LATERALITY Citizen-citizen interrelationships. Anarchizing	=	RESULTANT (?)
MARKETIZATION Market efficiency. Grounded ethics.	+	ALTERITY "Ungrounded" ethic	=	RESULTANT (?)
RATIONALIZATION Work through procedure. Bureaucratic rationalism. Left-braining. Patriarchal.	+	IMAGINIZATION Play. Creativity. Right-braining. Feminine.	=	RESULTANT (?)
etc.	+	etc.	=	etc.

that part of the system which the resultant "stands against" is the circumscribing of energies within descriptive boxes, within definitions. Attempting to circumscribe (seeking, striving) is valuable; supposing that one has succeeded in circumscribing may be a failure.

The game can begin by considering the interaction (noted in the table) of the micro and macro orientation, and asking about the anti-administrative resultant of that bringing together of a traditional discourse perspective and a perspective which is now marginalized. The beginning point is the contention that, compared against the privileging of the micro, macro problematics have been marginalized. The second interaction is represented on the chart by the alignment of hierarchy and laterality. Compared against a privileging of hierarchy issues, the problems and response resources of laterality have been marginalized in P.A. The third interaction is between marketization and alterity. Compared against a privileging of marketization, the problems and response resources of alterity—the moral relation with the other—have been marginalized. The fourth interaction is between rationalization and imaginization. Compared against the privileging of rationalization, the problems and response resources of imaginization have also been marginalized.

Comments are offered, in turn, on each of the four interactions—as well as suggestions about identifying the anti-administrative resultants. They are intended to supplement the brief notes provided on the chart of items covered by these headings. While each is relevant to both micro and macro issues, the comments on the first two interactions focus mainly on the macro, and the remaining two on the micro. There is a literature on micro concerns and discourse (e.g., Grant et al. 1998), and examples are available of the effectiveness of discourse theory (e.g., Miller 1998). Yet, such are the constraints of traditional P.A. discourse that there is liable to be less satisfaction at the micro level about the relevance of either anti-administrative or discourse theory until more book-length studies have been conducted in particular program areas, e.g., such as on the relevance of discourse theory for social work (in Hutchinson, pending). More studies are needed, e.g. in police, fire, taxation, etc.; recipes are especially valued.

Macro and Micro

"Problem selection" in P.A. discourse has tended to privilege the problematics of the micro effectiveness and efficiency of the bureaucratic machine; the macro problems of the bureaucratization of society, while not excluded, remain marginalized. Testimony to the "marginalized macro" in P.A. discourse is the absence of a robust Macro Public Administration. A Macro P.A. would analyze the society-wide character of public administration (in the same sense that Macro Economics examines the society-wide character in the economic sphere), as contrasted with a micro analysis which concerns the individual government (e.g., the Federal Government) or the individual firm (e.g., General Motors).

The macro or society-wide problematics of bureaucracy are symbolized in Max Weber's metaphor of the "iron cage" and "cage." They are problematics that cannot be addressed by limiting our thinking to goals like upgrading the efficiency of aspects of the bureaucratic machine. Weber's metaphor refers to the suffocating "side-effects" of modern society's increasing rationalization—capitalism's privileging of economic technical efficiency or instrumental rationality. He speaks of the pervasiveness and the dehumanizing character of bureaucratization. Weber explains that care for external goods should be worn like a light cloak; but fate decreed that the cloak should become "an iron cage" (1978).

Against this Weberian specification of macro and longer-term problematics of bureaucratization, contrast the micro, or one-dimensional, character of traditional P.A. discourse. The micro thrust of traditional P.A. discourse reflects, in part, the character of P.A.'s origin and the shape of its later development. This original character, in the United States for instance, included confidence that the important macro answers were known; it was a matter of implementing them, and the role of research was to find out "facts" to facilitate the doing. The principal needs were to rationalize the personnel, the financial, the organizational, and the managerial situations. The direction of P.A. was toward fixing the bureaucratic machine, leaving the theorist with the role of mechanic's helper. The macro issues are marginalized as outside the scope of real practicality. The shape of the later development of P.A.—in academe and in the general run of professional journals and in organizations—has not broken this original pattern.

In assessing the P.A. anti-administrative resultant of this interaction, we can perhaps learn from the burst of energy experienced by the economics discipline following the virtual creation of Macroeconomics by John Maynard Keynes (Keynes 1936). Economics was transformed in character and influence. Clearly, an extra dimension is added to P.A.—a robust Macro P.A. So in the naming game, some readers may want to include a word like "multi-dimensional." Benefit also occurs to the micro, however. As in the Economics case, micro activity is now pursued and understood in its macro context—suggesting candidate words for the P.A. naming like "critical awareness" or "contextual holism." Issues like the theory-practice nexus, a perennial for P.A. conferences, are now transformed. The fulcrum of theorizing shifts.

Hierarchy and Laterality

The second interaction is between hierarchy and laterality, and the game is to identify the anti-administrative resultant. "Problem selection" in P.A. discourse has tended to marginalize issues of laterality. Fredrick Thayer's book, *An End to Hierarchy and Competition: Administration in the Post Affluent Society*, aptly points out this issue (Thayer 1981). Compared against the problematics that accept the inevitability of hierarchy, however, laterality remains marginalized. The seriousness of laterality issues is illustrated here by recalling what it means to claim that citizen-citizen interrelationships have been marginalized in contrast to citizen-state relationships.

A shift toward anti-administration, an earlier account argued, involves a move toward radically non-deferential politics (toward authority, hierarchy, and the established) that seek psychic energy not in the state-citizen relationship, but in the citizen-citizen interrelationship (Farmer 1998a). It was claimed that the context of a shift toward anti-administration should include conceptualizing the citizen-citizen interrelationship as irreducibly primary and as providing vitalizing and liberating energies. It was suggested that a P.A. discourse of anti-administration would embrace the opportunities and paradoxes of this emergent feature. It could be expected to privilege anarchism in the sense of seeking to favor using the skills and full potential of discourse and citizen-citizen dialogue rather than relying so much on hierarchical structure.

Citizen spirit and interrelationships, it was added, have interested thinkers throughout western history—and throughout American history and today. "Where is our republicanism to be found?" asked the author of the Declaration of Independence. Thomas Jefferson's answer was, "Not in the constitution certainly, but merely in the spirit of our people" (Brudney 1992). The concern was reflected in the debates between the Federalists and the Antifederalists. Today, communitarians seek a renewal of civic virtue. The concern has not been limited to a focus on republican or civic virtue, however. An example is the important literature and interest in civil society. Concern with citizen spirit and relations has been the subject of important empirical and other study, often under overlapping headings such as civil society, volunteerism, trust, or citizen engagement (e.g., Pew Research Center 1996). An example is Robert Putnam's essay "Bowling Alone" (Putnam 1995). The concern has been reflected in the works of some contemporary philosophers, sociologists, and others. It has been reflected in some statements and actions of Republican and Democratic politicians, like the two most recent presidents.

Such attention to the citizen-citizen relationship accents the turn away from the hierarchical and toward discourse in democratic politics. On the opportunities side, we see that a move toward discursiveness has been welcomed by a variety of thinkers. Benjamin Barber, for example, emphasizes strong participatory democratic discourse (Barber 1984: 177). Then there is Jürgen Habermas, whose critical theory perhaps best symbolizes this turn toward discourse. He has continued his thinking, a work in progress, by rejecting what he calls "liberal" (grounded in Hobbes) and "civic republican" (rooted in Aristotle and Rousseau) democracies (Habermas 1996). He favors "deliberative democracy," with an emphasis on activities like mutual consultative discourse and shared meanings, rather than on implementing summed preferences.

There are difficulties, contraries, and aporia in such a shift toward discourse. At one level, our long history of hierarchical arrangements leaves us with a steep learning curve; there are relatively few on-the-ground examples (like Quaker meetings or some Athenian practices) of operating through dialogue and not through a hierarchical structure. At another level, we might doubt the viability of government by discourse as a general matter. We might despair about the difficulties in gaining consensus over large numbers. It is well established that the choice of aggregation function can lead to different results, e.g., using the Borda, the Condorcet, or other decision rules. Kenneth Arrow's possibility theorem speaks to the gigantic problems in the mere summing of citizen preferences (Arrow 1963). At yet another level, we might doubt the desirability of the sovereignty of the crowd. Our world contains divergent kinds of people, both the capable and the incapable.

In considering the anti-administrative resultants of the interaction between hierarchy and laterality for the naming game, the reader can turn to what O.C. McSwite calls the "discourse movement" in American P.A. (1998a). That movement is concerned with the opposition between hierarchy and laterality and related terms—wanting to demarginalize authentic dialogue in contrast with technocratic expertise, to demarginalize anarchism in contrast with bureaucratizing. McSwite's characterization includes the view of the discourse movement as including a wide range of positions committed to authentic dialogue, recognizing the boundedness of human consciousness. (1998a) (The discourse movement also points to other resultants discussed here. As White (1998) explains, it also encompasses the array of arguments seeking to advance the P.A. field beyond its identification with rationalism, economic efficiency, and technocratic expertise.) This may suggest candidate names for the anti-administrative resulting energy like "critical dialogue," or "deep dialogue," or even "dynamic laterality." Such terms have the advantage of reflecting recognition that the issues of laterality and hierarchy are not merely administrative. Rather, they are surrogates for competing manifest and latent nonbureaucratic perspectives. For example, hierarchy is described as a surrogate not only for a rational order of justice, but also for the feasibility of epistemological certainty (Farmer & Farmer, R. 1997). Recognizing this surrogate character of the hierarchy-laterality interaction, and appreciating the interaction's involvement with dialogue, the resultant anti-administrative energy is seen as implicating another dimension.

Marketization and Alterity

The interaction between marketization and alterity is not limited to issues of market efficiency v. justice (or ethics). The word "alterity" (moral relationship to the other) is used because the ungroundedness of ethics is significant. It is true that contemporary society is torn between two competing organizing principles. One can be described in such terms as self, efficiency, production, and the market; the other involves terms like the other, justice, fairness, and the public interest. It is true that there has been a revival during the past 25 or so years recognizing the role of the ethical in P.A. That revival followed the parent revival in Social Philosophy; the parent revival, in turn, followed the publication of John Rawls' *A Theory of Justice* (Rawls 1971).

The element that has been marginalized in the P.A. revival is ungroundedness. "Ungroundedness" is exemplified in Georgia Warnke's discussion of what she calls a "hermeneutic or interpretive turn" in justice philosophizing. Warnke explains the hermeneutic or interpretive turn (away from groundedness) by explaining that "many important political theorists no longer try to justify principles of justice or norms of action on what might be called Kantian grounds; by appealing to formal reason, to the character of human action or to the neutral procedures of rational choice" (Warnke 1993: vii). Rather, justifying social and political principles turns simply to showing the suitability of the principles for that society, or to showing that the principles express the "meanings of the society's goods and practices, history and traditions" (Warnke 1993: vii). Even John Rawls has switched from offering Kantian or objective prescriptions. Instead, he now restates what a society thinks is justice—the "settled convictions" of a society (Rawls 1980: 518).

The energy involved in the anti-administrative resultant lies in working out the implications of moral concern, which recognizes the significance of morality's lack of compelling intersubjective grounding. There is a practical distinction between the assertiveness of traditional P.A. discourse and authentic hesitation (e.g., see Farmer 1995), and between the views of the manager who directs, coordinates, and controls all of the activities and personnel of the assigned unit and of the manager as less Napoleonically-challenged. It is reflected in the context of bureaucracy in our cultural preference for debate and confrontation rather than dialogue and shared exploratory discourse (e.g., Tannen 1998). For the present naming game, terms like "authentic hesitation" and "morally concerned skepticism" are candidates. The ungroundedness of ethical prescriptions and a movement toward alterity raise the prospect of a Marcusian dimension.

Rationalization and Imaginization

Rationalization, expressed in the narrowness of administrative rationality in our traditional discourse, aligned with imaginization can yield significant micro (and macro) resultants. Consider the micro practicality of less managerial narrowness in terms of "experimentalism," perhaps a component of the resultant of this interaction. The discourse of rational administration does not include, routinely, the systematic and natural experimental work described long ago by Alice Rivlin (1972). What Rivlin had in mind was similar to the medical model, where promising drugs are rigorously tested to find out what works and what does not work; some patients might receive the wonder drug and others a placebo. By contrast, a city administrator or a police chief does not consider experimentalism to be a routine part of her administrative work. Perhaps Rivlin did not suppose that such experimentalism would be a routine ingredient of managing, as opposed to Federal leadership, in such local government studies (ibid.: 86). Federal-supported evaluations do continue in some local-level program areas, e.g., drug enforcement, but the experiment-friendly management in mind would not depend on Federal dollars; it would be part of the warp and woof of more imaginative managing.

Imaginization is a term used to suggest that the role of imagination in the emerging context could parallel that described for rationalization in modernity. As Habermas describes Max Weber's characterization of this, a leading feature of modernity is the development of substantive reason in three autonomous spheres: objective science, morality and law, and art (1983). In our intellectual and societal context, the autonomies could collapse. The dominance of imagination in the context of justification need no longer be confined merely to the aesthetic. At the micro level, managers would extend responsibility for imagining to subordinates. Individuals would give imagination the central role in their work lives.

Imaginization is consistent with a shift in P.A. discourse toward activities like "play." Playing with the rules for P.A. thinking and practice can yield significant insights. Practical programmatic benefits for gaming have been recognized in a number of agencies, e.g., military war games, and Federal Reserve stock market games. Practical opportunities exist in radical play with the game rules of bureaucracy, e.g., such "rules" as that "every employee must show loyalty to the organization," or that "every employee must work X hours per week whether needed or not."

This does raise the question of mismatches between surface discourses. On the issue of imagination, for example, it may be wondered whether street-level operatives are more or less likely to be "playful" about their work than their governing administrative discourses wish to permit them. Part of the administrative discourse is the need for control (the "direct, coordinate and control" noted earlier and found in the typical job specification) In agencies like the N.Y.P.D., the volume of rules "directing, coordinating and controlling" officer discretion is quite substantial; this may or may not match the discourse of street-level policing. On a general level, there are significant opportunities in thinking through the mutual interrelationships of administrative and programmatic discourses. To indicate the complexity of the interplay between rationalization and imaginization, consider the demarginalization at the micro level of the unconscious as opposed to the merely rational. The case for considering a shift toward the unconscious has been made (e.g., by Farmer, R. 1998). She is not suggesting that important work has not been done on the unconscious in organizations. Rather, it is a matter of gross imbalance. "In looking at organizations, the scene needs to shift, in part, to the unconscious..." (Farmer, R. 1998: 72). She points out that the right hemisphere (the "non-linear and non-rational part of the brain") is often taken as the seat of the unconscious. She argues that, in understanding and administering organizations, we should not be half-brained. The managerial task should be adjusted more thoroughly to recognize the therapeutic. Some micro-relevant messages of Mary Parker Follett could be rediscovered.

Naming the profound energy release that results from the interaction of rationalization and imaginization is difficult. Candidate words include "experimentalism," "critical playwork," "openness to the poetic," "multi-linear," and "reflexive thinking." But each seems sub-optimal.

There has been an excessive reliance in traditional P.A. discourse on rational expectations—its scientism and its technologism. The discourse has relied too much on the notion of human beings as rational desirers. It has ignored the fact that humans are more impulse rationalizers (e.g., Russell 1997). But it is more than that; P.A. facts tend to be conceptualized largely as rational entities (McSwite 1998). Should organizations be understood as basically rational phenomena—organization charts, job specifications, and rules and regulations—spiced with a little knowledge about informal organizations? The answer was "yes" for the discourse of thinkers like Luther Gulick and Herbert Simon, if they wanted to develop a "science" of Public Administration. For the rest us, the "reality" of organizations looks more like an id than a rationalizing ego.

SUMMARY

This essay recapitulated and extended discussions on anti-administration from the perspective of discourse theory. First, it discussed discourse theory to explain the claim that the discourses of anti-administration aim toward the inclusion of marginalized or excluded perspectives. Second, it outlined some anti-administration theory. It suggested that, parallel to the action of anti-matter and matter, the inter-action of freshly demarginalized discourse perspectives and traditional discourse can yield anti-matter resultants. Used in describing these resultants is Herbert Marcuse's notion of one-dimensional man, leading to the view that perspectives in "another" dimension are "critical" in standing against "uncritical" acceptance of the existing system, structures, norms, and behaviors. The essay described a spirit of administering anti-administratively that includes a self-conscious discourse approach is consistent not only with openness to the marginalized and the excluded, but also to the view that not all perspectives are equally good (or bad). Third, the essay offered macro and micro examples of anti-administration gains in terms of problem definition and response resources. The essay's account under-scored that the discourses of anti-administration can recognize their affinity not only to the postmodern, but also to critical theory perspectives.

NOTE

1. An earlier version of this article was presented at the sixtieth national conference of the American Society for Public Administration, Orlando, Florida, April 1999.

REFERENCES

Arrow, K. J. 1963. *Social Choice and Individual Values*. New York: John Wiley.
Barber, B. 1984. *Strong Democracy*. Berkeley, CA: University of California Press.
Barnard, C. I. 1938. *Functions of the Executive*. Cambridge, MA: Harvard University Press.
Brudney, K. 1992. Machiavellian lessons in America: Republican findings, original prin-ciples, and political empowerment. *The Federalists, The Antifederalists, and the American Political Tradition*, edited by W. C. McWilliams and M. T. Gibbons. pp. 13-26. Westport, CT: Greenwood Press, p. 17, citing Thomas Jefferson, *The Writings of Thomas Jefferson, Vol. 15*, Albert Ellery Bergh, Ed., Washington, DC: Thomas Jefferson Memorial Association.
Chamberlain, L. 1999. *Nietzsche in Turin: An Intimate Biography*. New York: Picador.
Farmer, D. J. 1995. *The Language of Public Administration: Bureaucracy, Modernity, and Postmodernity*. Tuscaloosa, AL: University of Alabama Press.
———. ed. 1998. *Papers on the Art of Anti-Administration*. Burke, Virginia: Chatelaine.
———. 1998a. Schopenhauer's Porcupines: Hegemonic change in context. *Administrative Theory and Praxis*. 20(7):422-433.
———. 1999. Public administration discourse: A matter of style? *Administration and Society*. 31(3):299-320.
Farmer, D. J. and R. L. Farmer. 1997. Leopards in the temple: Bureaucracy and the Limits of the in-between. *Administration and Society*. 29(5):507-528.1
Farmer, R. L. 1998. Recognizing the right brain in organizations. *Papers on the Art of Anti-Administration*, edited by D. J. Farmer. Burke, VA: Chatelaine.
Foucault, M. 1972. The archaeology of knowledge, translated by S. Smith. London: Tavistock.

————. 1980. *Power/Knowledge: Selected Interviews and Other Writings 1972-1977.* Brighton, England: The Harvester Press.

Grant, D., T. W. Keenoy, and C. Oswick, eds. 1998. *Discourse and Organization.* Thousand Oaks, CA: Sage.

Habermas, J. 1983. Modernity: An incomplete project. *The Anti-Aesthetic: Essays on Postmodern Culture,* edited by H. Foster. Port Townsend, WA: Bay Press.

Habermas, J. 1996. Between facts and norms: Contributions to a discourse theory of law and democracy. Cambridge, MA: MIT Press.

Hoffman, D. 1999. *Visual Intelligence: How We Create What We See.* New York: W.W. Norton & Company.

Hutchinson, J. pending. *The Orphaning of Child Welfare: A Discourse Analysis.*

Keynes, J. M. 1936. *The General Theory of Employment, Interest, and Money.* New York: Harcourt Brace.

Marcuse, H. 1991. *One Dimensional Man: Studies in the Ideology of Advanced Industrial Society.* Boston, MA: Beacon Press.

McSwite, O. C. 1998. Stories from the real world: Administering anti-administratively. *Papers on the Art of Anti-Administration,* edited by D. J. Farmer. Burke, VA: Chatelaine. 17-36.

————. 1998a. The new normativism and the discourse movement: A meditation. *Administrative Theory and Praxis.* 20(3):377-381.

Miller, H. T. 1998. Method: The tail that wants to wag the dog. *Administration and Society.* 30(4):462-470.

Mills, S. 1997. *Discourse: The New Critical Idiom.* New York: Routledge.

Pew Research Center. 1996. *Trust and Citizen Engagement in Metropolitan Philadelphia.* Washington, DC: The Pew Research Center for the People and the Press.

Putnam, R. D. 1995. Bowling alone. *Journal of Democracy.* 6(1):65-68.

Rawls, J. 1971. A Theory of Justice. Cambridge, MA: Harvard University Press.

Rivlin, A. M. 1972. *Systematic Thinking for Social Action.* Washington, DC: The Brookings Institution.

Russell, B. 1997. *Principles of Social Reconstruction.* London: Routledge.

Tannen, D. 1998. *The Argument Culture: Moving from Debate to Dialogue.* New York: Random House.

Thayer, F. C. 1981. *An End to Hierarchy and Competition: Administration in the Post-Affluent World.* New York: Franklin Watts.

U.S. Atomic Energy Commission. 1967. *Nuclear Terms: A Brief Glossary.* Washington, D.C.: A.E.C.

Warnke, G. 1993. *Justice and Interpretation.* Cambridge, MA: MIT Press.

Weber, M. 1978. *The Protestant Ethic and the Spirit of Capitalism,* translated by Talcott Parsons. New York: Scribner.

White, O. 1998. The ideology of technocratic empiricism and the discourse movement in contemporary public administration: A clarification. *Administration and Society.* 30(5).

18

New Governance in Civil Society: Changing Responsibility of Public Administration

Jong S. Jun

With the new millennium at hand, the nature of government in both new and established democracies is undergoing a great transformation. Public administrators are encouraging citizens to participate in the governance of their communities, and promote policies that hold much promise for enhancing a strong democracy as well as allowing those who govern to develop a broader view of community issues and potential solutions. The strengthening of local governance is particularly important as a balancing force in representative democracy. In an era of economic globalization, strong democratic governance (in the context of a civil society) educates and empowers individuals, and "tames the marketplace" (Barber 1999: 9-10). Furthermore, a democratic local government, supported by shared networks of citizens, groups, and organizations, can overcome the shortcomings of a pluralistic democracy ("democracy's deficiency") and is more representative than the hierarchical governing practiced by the national government.

Citizens in Western and non-Western countries now find themselves questioning whether the pluralistic politics of representative democracy are a desirable means for protecting democratic values and promoting sustainable development (Norris 1999). Citizens increasingly distrust politicians and high-level government officials who prevent citizens from developing the ability to participate in governance. Since representative democracy cannot be replaced, an alternative perspective is to build a new sense of community that promotes shared social networks, social capital, and social collaboration among people. To do this, a governance process that facilitates the development of networking and the participation of citizens, groups, and community organizations, without the government being the center of power or the authority for coordinating activities, must be developed.

This chapter explores ways of enhancing the governance process in the context of a civil society. First, I will illustrate the meaning of *governance,* contrasting it with the governing aspect of government institutions. Throughout the essay, I will emphasize the new governance approach as an alternative way of strengthening democracy that can work side by side with pluralistic politics in a liberal democracy. Governance is no substitute for the governing responsibility of public institutions, but it can strengthen the governmental process in, and through, civil society. Because civil society takes on the attributes of a wide range of public activities, the effect of governance would be to reduce the role of hierarchical control of public organizations and to promote accountability through the democratic self-governance of citizens, groups, and organizations.

THE MEANING OF GOVERNANCE

In recent years there has been a growing interest in governance as it concerns the effects of social networks, social capital, trust and mutuality, and the participation of local citizens in the strengthening of democracy. Some recent writings argue that, because of the flaws inherent in interest-group politics in the community, the idea of governance should be emphasized by local communities, along with promoting dialogue and discourse through public deliberation. The literature of the new public management approach, on the other hand, stresses a contrary argument, which is that the role of management, particularly the governing responsibility of public institutions, is essential to optimal organizational performance. Still others limit the argument to joint partnership between public and private organizations in order to bring about more efficiency in the implementation of public programs, as well as to infuse governments with an entrepreneurial spirit.

The argument for effective governance in civil society stems from the belief that pluralistic politics limit the development of a strong democracy (Barber 1984; Rawls 1996; Sandel 1996; Bohman & Rehg 1997). There are a number of reasons why the governing of public organizations in a liberal democracy is ineffective in dealing with complex social problems. First, as governmental interventions in managing public programs and regulating society become complex, large bureaucracies are less and less efficient and responsive to the needs of citizens and the community. They are more concerned with legitimizing a centralized and bureaucratic government at a time when the need for decentralization and a devolution of authority is increasing. This phenomenon is particularly conspicuous in governmental efforts to achieve administrative reform. Another common problem is that decision-making in a liberal democracy is heavily influenced by interest-group politics. Those groups with few resources have little influence on decisions that affect their interests. Disadvantaged groups and citizens are particularly unable to participate in the policy-making process, except in elections. Lastly, the world is becoming more multicultural in terms of political, social, economic, and cultural interactions among people, social groups, and organizations. Because of fragmentation and decentralized growth in society, government agencies are no longer the centers of decision-making.

The concept of governance is explored in various fields, including political science, public administration, and sociology (Rosenau & Czempiel 1992; Kooiman 1993; March & Olsen 1995; Peters 1996; Rhodes 1997). Although there is no common definition of *governance*, Rosenau provides the most qualified description of the concept of governance that distinguishes it from the term *government*. According to Rosenau, *governance* is not synonymous with *government*. Although both are goal-oriented activities, government generally involves activities that are backed by formal authority and policing power in implementing duly constituted policies. Governance, on the other hand, refers to activities backed by shared goals among citizens and organizations that may or may not derive from legal and formally prescribed responsibilities, and that do not necessarily rely on policing powers to overcome defiance and attain compliance (Rosenau 1992: 4).

As opposed to the hierarchical and authoritative nature of government, the concept of governance is grounded in the constructivist view that reality is socially constructed by citizens in the community and, specifically, by the stakeholders, in the social situation. Thus, the concept of local governance is an outgrowth of an increasing awareness on the part of citizens that, currently, they have very little to say about the political processes that determine the interests and shape the decisions that are a product of the community in which they live. The governance approach essentially focuses on the process of concerned citizens, groups, and organizations, constructing an intersubjective reality by sharing their experience and concerns.

The central aims of governance, as opposed to governing by local government, are as follows: (1) to share the power in community decision-making and (2) to encourage not only autonomy and independence in local citizens, but also to provide the process for developing the common good through civic engagement. Governance is based on the assumption that by enhancing the ability of citizens to participate in local decision-making, people can learn to manage their community and their future. Governance stands in contrast to hierarchical governing, which is often characterized as a depersonalizing bureaucracy. Governance is a way of enhancing civil society not just through the participation of individuals, but through the broad participation of groups, associations, and institutions. It is a process that transforms the power structure of local government. Depending on the issue, public administrators can facilitate governance or they can help citizens and groups form grass-roots organizations by providing the necessary support of local government. The local governance approach cannot replace governing by local governments; instead, this approach seeks to complement and transform local government. As the participation of citizens and groups increases, local government can democratize the distribution of power. Thus, the emerging form of governance is one that has no single authoritative power center. Governance is a form of argumentative politics in deliberative democracy involving multiple actors in the public sphere, as advocated by Habermas and others (Habermas 1984: 18-42; 1996: chapters 7 & 8; Bohman 1996; Elster 1998; Macedo 1999; Gutmann & Thompson 1996). The governance approach aims to create opportunities for people to participate in public life through the process of articulating issues and setting agendas, that is, through open dialogue and discourse that deal with both agreements and disagreements. Through the argumentative and participatory process, participants may be able to formulate a public reason for collective action, as well as a reason for supporting or opposing a particular public policy or a planning agenda (Bohman 1996; Forester 1999).

Local governments operate under the considerable constraints of most public agencies: they have limited resources, jurisdiction, imagination, entrepreneurial spirit, courage, time, and so on. For local governments to fulfill their potential in developing viable communities, they need citizen organizations as their partners. Communities need to strengthen their social capacity in order to develop shared knowledge and understandings, and to develop mutually satisfactory patterns of interactions so that they can undertake productive activity. Japan, with its high degree of social capital, has a strong potential for increasing effective local problem solving, as well as local productivity, if the national government actively promotes decentralization and local autonomy. On the other hand, the United States faces a different challenge because of the multicultural nature of its urban communities. In recent years, the acceleration of globalization and migration of people has created culturally diverse and fragmented urban cities, of which Los Angeles, New York, Chicago, Cleveland, and San Francisco are examples (Wilson 1997; Clarke & Gaile 1998; Shuman 1998). At the end of the twentieth century, the trends in these cities clearly suggest the growth of smaller communities around the large city, as well as diverse subcommunities consisting of different ethnic groups within the city. Unlike the strong city hall politics of the past, the lack of a power center has become the strength of urban cities. The solution to many U.S. urban problems is the development of a new politics that promotes social networks and civic capacity in order to deal with local issues, such as growth limitation, environmental protection, crime, traffic congestion, homelessness, education, and so on. In other words, one of the smartest strategies that local governments can adopt to enhance citizens' governance capacity, along with developing a civil society, is to support autonomous communities. This will work to create self-governance capacity ("governance without government") or in some areas, governance with government, the latter acting as grantor and facilitator.

SUCCESSFUL GOVERNANCE INITIATIVES

The nature of governance in civil society is deeply political and social in that social interactions among citizens, associations, government, and the market continuously occur, with civil society as an intermediate sphere between government and market (O'Connell 1999; Ehrenberg 1999; Janoski 1998; Keane 1998; Seligman 1992). The identification of public administration in civil society is psychologically important in promoting citizen participation and public solidarity, as Box (1998) and King and Stivers (1998) emphasize. They oppose a dualistic vision of the "government is them" in the eyes of citizens. Thus, deliberative democracy, emphasizing the democratic political process of facilitating dialogue and discourse as well as creating an intersubjective reality, is a way of reducing the dualistic phenomenon of "us versus them," and working to build "we-relations." This is the most important theoretical contribution made by many social theorists, such as Schutz (1967), Merleau-Ponty (1973), Habermas (1984; 1990), Winter (1971), Buber (1958), and many others.

Political and administrative institutions play an important role in governance by facilitating and supporting voluntary activity, equality, plurality, fairness, and the inclusion of nongovernmental and civic organizations. The following two case studies illustrate the interactions among citizens, associations, and community organizations that provide social services.[1]

A Nonprofit Coalition for Community Vision

Napa County, located about twenty miles north of the San Francisco Bay area, is famous for its wine industry. The county administers a varied geographical area of 794 square miles. Public roads, public safety, health care, and social services are but four of more than one hundred major services and hundreds of individual programs provided to county residents and administered by county government. The county receives money from three sources: 42 percent from Federal and State subsidies and grants; 28 percent from local sales, property, and other taxes; and 30 percent from fees, fines, service charges, and prior year fund balance. Most of the Federal and State money received by the county is allocated to County Health and Human Services and Criminal Justice Programs. County property taxes pay for such services as the sheriff, libraries, and public health activities.

The county is known as one of the most innovative regions in California in terms of improving social and health services, particularly in providing integrated services for the poor, and is frequently selected as a location for pilot state programs. Previously, numerous nonprofit organizations in the county had competed for funding in order to meet the needs for social services. This had caused a high degree of mistrust between county agencies and community organizations. In 1994, the County Department of Health and Human Services recruited Don Cosello, a retired director of the agency, as a consultant for promoting community capacity-building. He has been successful in developing a coalition among fifty nonprofit organizations that provide social services to the poor. Since most nonprofit organizations expressed a feeling of repugnance toward politics, people who had attended the earlier meetings elected Don Cosello as Executive Director of the newly formed coalition. The purpose of the coalition is to identify community needs and explore ways of meeting them. The coalition now consists of the Board of Directors and six committees that deal with issues of housing, safety-net food programs, mental health, drug and alcohol, community development block grants, parenting, and senior services, including Alzheimer's disease.

The coalition is a collaboration of fifty nonprofit social services organizations, such as Aldea (a mental health program), the Red Cross, Boys and Girls Clubs, Clinic Olé (a community health clinic), Child or Parent Emergency, Community Counseling, Community Resources for Children, Community Resources for Independence, and Family Services of the North Bay. The coalition also includes nonvoting members representing government agencies. The formation of the coalition has thus far produced a reduction in the fragmentation of the nonprofit sector and in the duplication of services. The Executive Director has played a major role in sustaining the participation of citizens and representatives of community organizations. With the volunteer leadership effort provided by him and others, the coalition has eliminated much of the in-fighting which had occurred among the various groups. Now these groups work collectively, even preparing grant proposals together and sharing their resources. Since its inception in 1994, the coalition has received adequate funds in grants. The coalition members (nonprofit organizations) are more concerned with how to innovate programs with additional funds. This was not possible in the past, due to the lack of funding for personnel.

The coalition has allowed members to share resources for training volunteers who can work in community-based services. The various members participate in the process of developing a curriculum and locating skilled facilitators to conduct various phases of the training. So far, there have been numerous training sessions. The coalition has also developed an intensive internship program for college graduates in psychology, social work, and other fields. Instead of working at one county agency, the interns are given the opportunity to work in several different agencies. Furthermore, one staff member at the county Health and Human Services agency acts as a clearinghouse for all of the interns, and makes sure that they receive the supervision they need to obtain their clinical hours. Having the interns has increased the service delivery capacity of all of the members of the coalition. Also, the coalition members have shared staff time, moving people from agencies that were overstaffed to those that were understaffed.

In late 1996, the County Department of Social Services initiated a two-part conference entitled "Future Search," inviting the staff from fifty-seven community-based nonprofit organizations and the staff from several social service agencies including Mental Health, Alcohol and Drug, and Health and Social Welfare Services. The purpose of the conference was to discuss the new federal welfare reform policy and explore ways of developing joint collaboration between the county and nonprofit organizations that are involved in the delivery of social services to clients. In each phase of the conference, the participants were engaged in a series of dialogues to review the problems, explore possibilities for common ground, and make action plans. Those involved in the "Future Search" conference say that it was an unqualified success; most important, they say, is the fact that the county staff members have developed a better relationship with the staff members of the nonprofit organizations.

The prospect for the coalition is bright in terms of its effort in obtaining the federal, state, and foundation grants. The Board of Directors is moving toward the possibility of hiring a permanent executive director of the coalition in order to sustain its success. The coalition has also become a significant political force in the community by strengthening a governance process between the public, private, and nonprofit organizations that is collaborative and open. The effective governance of the coalition has largely been attributed to the regular meetings among the representatives of the members, including the weekend retreats that involve open dialogue and active strategic planning not only to review problems and anticipated issues, but also to develop community-based social services, resource sharing, and new grant proposals.

Resolving the Soup Kitchen Controversy

The city of San Rafael is located in the center of Marin County's eastern corridor, about seventeen miles north of San Francisco. It is an affluent community nestled in valleys surrounded by wooded, grassy hillsides. The business district has a mixture of Victorian buildings, ethnic restaurants, retail stores, and financial institutions which sustain the city's hometown flavor. Representatives of the St. Vincent de Paul Society and the city have been working for years to try to resolve issues regarding the soup kitchen being located in the downtown business district, ie., to minimize the soup kitchen's negative impact in terms of the sight of food lines and homeless people in a commercial district. The limitations of the existing facility, combined with escalating operational and criminal problems, were such that the city and St. Vincent's jointly resolved to move the soup kitchen to a different location in the city. Throughout the years, numerous discussions have been held and limited cooperative agreements have been reached on several issues, yet significant operational problems remain at the soup kitchen, and the relocation issue has not been resolved. Since 1982, the soup kitchen has made a positive impact on the plight of hungry people, but its operation has been an eyesore. Downtown businesses, shoppers, and nearby residents complain about diners' panhandling, public drunkenness, reported drug dealing, verbal abuse, litter, and public urination.

On February 23, 1998, the issue of relocation came to a head. An emergency meeting of the city council was called after a rancorous city council meeting had been held the week before. The room, built for two hundred, was packed with double that number spilling out into the hallways and outdoors from the side-door exits. Three well-organized groups representing different sides of the issue had come two hours early to ensure that they would get on the public speakers' list, and to secure clustered seating for group cheerleading and booing. In a military manner, they set up numerous boards displaying statistics, facts, and photos, showing sacred turf lines not to be crossed and the opposition's positions and targets (lines of threatened advance). The atmosphere inside the city council chamber was that of war; the mindset of many was to hold ground at all costs and to take no prisoners.

There were two major groups opposing each other in this issue. The opposition group was made up of the Downtown Business Improvement group, the city's Redevelopment Agency, the Chamber of Commerce, the residents of the surrounding neighborhoods, and the employees and parents at nearby public and private schools. The group in support of the "soup kitchen" in the core of the downtown retail shopping district run by the St. Vincent de Paul religious charity, included the kitchen's board of advisors, its director, and the not-so-huddled masses of the unkempt, disabled, mentally-ill, homeless and elderly. This latter group filled the city council chamber seats, put up poster board displays, and briefed the members of the newspaper and TV media. They were under direct attack with nowhere to go and nothing to lose by standing and fighting back for their place of refuge. Joining them, in a surprise stroke of political and symbolic genius, were the priests, rabbis, and ministers of virtually every church and temple in the community. This alliance between a stubborn and independent soup kitchen and the local religious community, which tended to be mostly upper-class clients, suddenly shifted the balance of power in the struggle for the soup kitchen to stay in its downtown location. Until now, the downtown business community and most voters had encouraged the city council to wage a fight against the drug dealers, child molesters, the crazies, litters, doorway "pissers," and other homeless and suspicious characters of the streets, who were drawn to the downtown shopping area by the "kitchen."

The public debate lasted for five hours, from 7 P.M. to 2 A.M., and involved mostly disagreements about relocation. The city manager, Rod Gould, was caught in a bind. He had acted aggressively and made minimum concessions in negotiations, as per the city council's strongly worded public and private direction. Now he could be the head offered up to quiet the uproar if he did not act quickly but carefully. His available options seemed nonviable. If the soup kitchen were to stay at its current site, it would infuriate the business community and embarrass the city council. If he were to force the soup kitchen to move, he would face the wrath of the soup kitchen, the neighborhood to which he moved it, and the entire religious community—and still leave the city council with a politically awkward situation. The city manager had to act quickly to buy time to find a new approach. He suggested that soup kitchen discussion be tabled and dealt with at a special joint city council/Redevelopment Agency meeting. This would buy him a few days to find a new solution.

At the next city council meeting, the city council members had no choice but to back away from their insistence that the soup kitchen for poor and homeless residents move out of downtown. The city council decided instead, that the soup kitchen could move to the Ritter Street area, a downtown neighborhood that, ironically, the soup kitchen's operators had wanted to explore a year earlier, but at the time, the city council had rejected this location. So the city council compromised, and the soup kitchen agreed to operate under a use permit in an attempt to move beyond this conflict. The city council appointed a 17-member committee, consisting of business leaders, residents, diners, religious leaders, neighborhood associations, community charity organizations, and officials from the St. Vincent de Paul Society, and the city staff. This Ad Hoc Dinning Room Committee was responsible for locating an acceptable site in the Ritter street area, as well as for establishing conditions of operation. The committee spent hours in meetings and consulted many people, designing a survey and plans for improving the Dining Room's operation. On June 4th 1998, after researching and reviewing eight sites for relocation and conducting numerous public dialogues, the Ad Hoc Committee was informed that Pacific Gas and Electric company (PG&E) had offered to sell the city a piece of a property located in the Ritter street area, and was also interested in redeveloping the entire three acre block in conjunction with the city. In late August, 1999, PG&E announced that Marriott International had been selected as the hotel developer of the new site, and the city of San Rafael, the St. Vincent de Paul, and Marriott will soon commence negotiations regarding the development of the new dining facility on 16,000 square feet of the three-acre Third Street parcel. A conditional use permit will govern the operation of the new facility when it opens some time in the year 2002.

The anticipated result will be a new, improved facility for St. Vincent's to enable it to continue its mission to feed and serve the needy in the community. The Neighborhood Advisory Committee is convinced that services to the poor should be better coordinated through the coordination among the twenty-one nonprofit social services organizations in the community, such as the Ritter House, Goodwill Industries, Marin Jobs Connection, and St. Vincent de Paul. Finally, this case demonstrates that a constructive resolution can emerge as a result of the people's sense of purpose in building a community-based dining room, one supported by, and accepted by, its surrounding businesses and neighborhood. The process was conducted outside the conventional city politics controlled by the government and the powerful interest groups.

Implications

Due to space limitations, the preceding cases were not presented in detail, but they suggest some important implications about the responsibility of public officials and administrators in working with local citizens, groups, and organizations. First, in order to explore unknown possibilities in dealing with complex community problems, the democratic process must be continuously exercised through public participation, dialogue, discourse, and deliberation. The first case demonstrates that unlike a rational community planning process, a capacity-building process involving the nonhierarchical relationships among the coalition members, as well as a future search conference focusing on value-based action planning by the participants, stresses a learning process "toward a desired future for a community, organizations, or issue" (Weisboard & Janoff 1995: 5). As people engage in public debate, they develop a sense of community, trust, and a better understanding of the experiences of others. They can then move toward a socially grounded agreement. Even if they are unable to reach a consensus due to irreconcilable differences, they are likely to go away with a better understanding of the issues. When the issues surface again, citizens' past experience will guide them. The case of the soup kitchen reflects a major shift in people's understanding of one another. The soup kitchen had a weak organization with no political influence in the community, no rules, and constant problems with its clients, fighting, panhandling, drinking in public, and committing petty crime. Even so, the case illustrates that the poor and needy residents have as much voice in the city's future as merchants and officials with grand visions for the city's urban renewal. The change came about when it became clear that many believed no one should be denied food regardless of his or her behavior. After long public deliberation, the city council was persuaded by the religious community.

Another important lesson of these case studies is that the community can be governed without hierarchical intervention by government authority. In both cases, political and administrative authority played a significant role in the process by providing a public forum so that citizens could disclose their views on the issues at hand. The government agencies in the first case worked as facilitators and grantors of funding. In civil society, nonhierarchical networking is most effective when citizens, politicians, and administrators volunteer to promote the public good, and are willing to be facilitative leaders: to work with citizens' values, listen to citizens' voices, learn from others, and question their own assumptions in a reflexive manner.

Other numerous applications of the governance approach in civil society can be found in the areas of sustainable economic development, environmental protection, community policing, human rights, and community-based social programs such as those involving education, health, and social welfare. The surge of nongovernmental organizations (NGOs) throughout the world is an example of a governance movement working through networking by citizens, groups, and organizations dealing with various issues, both domestically and internationally.

THE SUSTAINABILITY OF LOCAL GOVERNANCE

A strong democratic governance stems from the psychological commitment of citizens and stakeholders in the community to meet their collective needs, participate in politics, and develop expectations for the future. March and Olsen explain this phenomenon of community social interaction using an exchange theory perspective; they say that "self-interested exchange as the basis for interpersonal relations" will lead to citizens' developing "coalitions and policies" (1995:

7-26). Their second theoretical perspective is an institutional concept of democratic governance that helps to develop "identities of citizens and groups in the political environment," as well as "capabilities for appropriate political action" (ibid.: 44-47). Their theoretical perspectives explain how citizens and groups work in the instrumental and rationalistic contexts of pluralistic democracy. They describe how political coalitions and policy decisions are made in terms of the micro and macro perspectives. They do not, however, offer any possibilities for improving the flow of pluralistic politics. They underestimate the possibilities of exploring a governance alternative of dialogue and discourse among concerned citizens, groups, and organizations without governmental intervention, or of a voluntary group of citizens working to create the public good.

It may be argued that the process of governance is unlikely to be effective or sustainable unless the community builds a true communal spirit that is compassionate and knowledgeable, has a concern for justice and fairness, draws on shared experience, and has a shared conception of the common good. This is the argument of Habermas (1984), Rawls (1996), and Sandel (1996). Furthermore, the civic virtues of citizens and administrators—such as a concern for others, autonomy, compassion, self-reflexivity, the pursuit of fairness and justice, and mutuality—make the community viable and civilized (Jun 1999). To nurture these qualities in the community, I suggest in the text that follows, strategies for developing a democratic process that facilitate the participation of citizens, groups, associations, and institutions, and encourage them to join the networking process. These strategies include a wide range of possibilities for facilitating social interaction. Innovative strategies can emerge as people come together and engage in dialogue and discourse concerning the improvement of process, agenda-setting, continuous interaction, communication, and the social design of projects. However, based on the common arguments for, and practical examples of community-based services and problem solving, the strategies that follow can assist the public administrators and community leaders as they work to promote governance capacity and the effective participation of citizens, largely relying on process-building. Strategies for local governance should take into account the political, social, institutional, psychological, and cultural dimensions of any issue, and participants should work towards building a democratic community, decentralization and power-sharing, and social capital and trust.

Building Democratic Community

To build a democratic community, the social reality of a community, which shapes social relations, must be understood. Furthermore, the reality of a lack of community must be understood before beginning to build a community. The development of a community and the responsibility of individual citizens are the backgrounds of an ongoing debate about individualism versus communitarianism. During the 1960s and 1970s in the United States, many young people were involved in self-discovery and questioning authority (Reich 1970). This individualism is characterized as freedom of choice, justice, competition, and individual success, and seems to be the hub of American culture (Bellah et al. 1985; Gross & Osterman 1971). Beginning in the 1980s, there have been numerous inquiries about the responsibility that each individual has as a citizen, as well as how to reconcile individualism with communitarian ideas.

Liberal democratic theorists argue that communitarian ideas put too much emphasis on building community, and not enough on individualism. Critics also argue that communitarianism demands too much conformity from individuals to collective needs and sensitivity to problems of others, rather than a respect for individual difference; communitarianism calls for a readiness to participate in collective tasks as opposed to tenacious independence.

The expectation of communitarianism is that, within a participatory democracy, people have the responsibility to carry out their civic duties by engaging in social obligations and community activities (Etzioni 1993; 1995; 1996). Ideally, this would mean that people would be involved in the governance of community in which they live. According to Etzioni, liberal individualism has a widespread disregard for personal responsibility, an overemphasis on individual differences and disagreements, and an inability to discuss and embrace the values we share. He argues that we have disconnected from one another; and we need to reconnect. What is lacking in the argument made by Etzioni and other communitarian scholars is the sense of ethics in the autonomous individual within the community. MacIntyre (1984) stresses the individual's ability to critique communal demands and pressure. Although Habermas's position is close to liberal communitarianism, he argues that ethics of an individual emerge from the relational context within which people engage in communicative action within the public sphere (Habermas 1984; 1990; 1996). Both MacIntyre and Habermas suggest a major implication for governance in a democratic polity; that is, the individual's reflexive role toward communal responsibility.

In summary, the communitarian approach to democratic governance makes demands on individuals, and on individuals acting together in the public interest. Human activity is always and everywhere norm-driven, and involves the acts of individuals who work together with full seriousness and shared experience. Civil society, however, needs to promote the practice of civic virtues without sacrificing the autonomy of the individual. Accordingly, democratic governance can work only when citizens not only have a reasonable and trustworthy commitment to their community, but also demonstrate a substantial responsibility to themselves. In this way, liberal individualism will evolve into republican liberalism (Dagger 1997). Since communitarians often overemphasize the importance of political community and governing institutions, its theoretical tendency is to endanger liberty and autonomy. Thus, the recent theoretical arguments for civic reciprocity offer a cooperative possibility in which citizens would enjoy autonomous life as well as concern with civic duties (Rawls 1996; Sandel 1996; Dagger 1997; Taylor 1989; Kymlicka 1995; Galston 1991; Jun 1999; Kass 1999: 23-38).

Decentralization and Power-Sharing

The development of new governance means little if the distribution of governmental power remains undisturbed. This means that government agencies must find ways to share their decision-making power with the public. Japan's first step, as well as Korea's, is an ongoing effort to decentralize local governments. The next logical step would be for local government to concern themselves with the way in which decentralized authority granted by the central government can be applied to local conditions, and how local people can be involved in the democratic process. As the professionalization of local administration increases, there is a tendency to rely on technical skills and rational analysis to solve complex social problems. If this solution is to have public support, then public deliberation is essential so that citizens are empowered to argue the rational justification of administrative initiatives and decisions, resulting in a common understanding of the limits of instrumental and rational solutions.

The political and institutional arrangements practiced in Western countries are not readily applicable to other countries, particularly to non-Western countries, where politics and administration are highly centralized and democracy is relatively new. In those countries, governmental reforms must first take into consideration ways of developing citizens' capacity for self-governance, as well as improving management capability of local public institutions, before experimenting with political and administrative decentralization. For example, in many African countries where decentralization programs were introduced, the outcomes were corruption and a waste of resources. This was largely due to the lack of local government capability and civic culture.

Decentralization without power-sharing between the higher and lower levels of institutions is simply a structural rearrangement: the central authority delegates functions to the local authority. It does not empower the people at the lower echelon of the institution. Democratic governance calls for a weak hierarchical or nonhierarchical organization. Those with administrative responsibilities should act as the facilitators, coordinators, or representatives of citizens. Members should play an active and deliberative role in the governance process.

Development of Social Capital and Trust

Social capital is a concept often stressed by economists and other social scientists in order to explain and understand various human relationships, as well as people's connections to associations and community affairs (Coleman 1990; Putnam 1993; 1995; Fukuyama 1995). It is used as a framework for bridging theory and practice as local citizens (or local stakeholders) develop a vision for collective action through mutual trust and cooperation in society and community. Social capital develops through social networks, dialogue, understanding, and mutual learning among diverse individuals, groups, and organizations. Thus, social capital links the individual to the group, to the organization, and to the community, not the other way around. Particularly in the social sphere, social capital can foster the social action and community spirit that are essential for collective problem solving. It is a dialectical frame that can be used to help make cooperative relationships among community stakeholders, groups, and organizations work better.

The notion of social capital is being applied to the process of collaborative problem solving, such as public-private partnerships, the distribution of community resources, neighborhood associations, citizen participation, civic infrastructure and community building, and sustainable development and environmental protection (Kass 1999). The findings of various domestic and cross-cultural case studies regarding social capital have begun to emerge. Social capital works better in comparatively homogeneous countries, such as in the Italian regions discussed in Putnam's work (1993) as well as in Japan and Germany, where citizens traditionally share a high level of trust and social responsibility (Fukuyama 1995). Because of the consensus characteristic of the concept of social capital, it could have both positive and negative effects on community members; the negative effect would occur when an individual did not conform to the norms of the community. When it is applied to a multicultural and less communitarian society, such as the United States, the individual's commitment to neighbors and community cooperation tends to be weaker, particularly when issues do not affect him or her directly. Furthermore, an imbalance of power and in participation among different racial and ethnic groups in the community make cooperation difficult. In a multiracial democracy, because social norms vary among groups, different social and policy strategies should be designed in order to foster social capital and build citizens' capacity for governance.

In order to utilize and cultivate social capital across diverse groups, the community needs to develop various strategies, such as processes for improving participation, the inclusion of different people and groups, meetings, the public deliberation of issues, and dialogue and communication. As Ostrom states, if social capital is unused or not recognized, its significance declines rapidly (Ostrom 1993).

LOOKING BACKWARD, MOVING FORWARD

The twentieth century was a time of enormous progress in science and technology, the growth of nation-states, and industrialization. There were, however, many undesirable consequences of development and progress, such as inequality and injustice, environmental disasters, holocaust, wars, and hunger. Among many gains that politics and administration were made in the last century, perhaps two things were most relevant to the growth of public administration: the strengthening of the role of the nation-state, and the professionalization of public service. In the United States, since the 1930s, the Federal government has played the major role in the development of the economy, the management of defense, and the development of social welfare policies. State and local governments have cooperated in the implementation of national policies and programs. Since the 1980s, the ideology of governing from Washington has gradually shifted; the policy orientation has moved toward decentralization, deregulation, and the devolution of authority. This transition is directly linked to the conservative politics that began with the Reagan administration, and that brought about a crisis in public organizations regarding managing them properly and serving the public well.

Policymakers and administrators at every level of government have begun to accept the conservative movement in society and have adopted more conservative policies in approaching various crises. After 1993, the Clinton administration was relatively successful in its socioeconomic policies by moving toward the center of American politics, away from the liberal policies of the past. Two conclusions can be drawn about the changing nature of public administration. Many perplexing problems facing society, such as environment, social, and economic problems, cannot be solved exclusively at the national level. First, I think that the national, state, and local governments are unable to sustain local prosperity and democracy without promoting civic capacity at the community level. Furthermore, the ability of government to solve complex societal problems is inevitably limited due to the changing conditions of local communities, as well as the forces of economic globalization. The policy of governing from the top down should be reexamined because of the transformations that have occurred in development ideology. In many countries, socioeconomic development has changed from the industrial development led by the state to participatory development that is self-critical, fragmented, and differentiated (Beck 1994). Development has to be reoriented toward more egalitarian, democratic, sustainable, cooperative, and people-oriented projects (Korten 1990; Pirages 1996; Stead & Stead 1992; Panitch 1996).

Second, the professionalization of public service has contributed to the internal management of public institutions and, at the same time, has produced a governing process that is hierarchical, impersonal, and rationalistic. In the decades to come, the emphasis on a professional public service will continue, and will be necessary, as long as public administration takes the responsibility of managing and governing. It is also obvious that the current practice of the new management approach will continue to generate excessive rationalism. At the same time, rationalism, and technical rationalism in particular, will be less efficient as the changing conditions of the community, the society, and the world require more qualitative and creative solutions. The technical skills of professional administrators must be complemented by other action skills and a broader knowledge of the public aspect (or the publicness) of public administration, such as the skills in dialogue, reflexivity, social learning, self-governance, and community civic-mindedness.

Sandel's critique of "the loss of self-government and the erosion of community" suggests a guide for restoring the governance aspect of civil society. He emphasizes the need for developing political institutions capable of governing the global economy, as well as cultivating "the civic identities necessary to sustain those institutions, to supply them with the moral authority they require" (Sandel 1996: 338). To strengthen civil society, liberal communitarians, such as Sandel (1996), Rawls (1996), Waltzer (1983), and Taylor (1989), see the restoration of a voluntary and self-governing community as the fundamental cure. Government authority at the national level would continue to play the major role in large issues, such as global trade issues, defense, and foreign policy. As I have argued throughout this essay, political and administrative authority should be decentralized. With this approach, the national government would no longer play the major role in guiding society. Power would be fragmented and shared by citizens, groups, associations, and institutions through overlapping social networks. They would have a significant say in local governance, and would contribute to the enhancement of civil society.

To recapitulate my argument in this essay, I do not believe that the local governance approach can replace representative democracy in local communities, or that the public service role of public administration can simply be transferred to the civil society movement. New governance in a civil society can, however, create the context for dialogue and discourse that involve vigorous argument, agenda-setting, and the exploration of alternatives. Strengthening governance at the local level can encourage politics and social interactions that emphasize openness to new ideas. Because citizens (or stakeholders) are empowered and are opposed to the hierarchical and bureaucratic tendencies of governing by national and local governments, the governance process discloses people's agreements and disagreements, and explores possibilities for collaboration and mutual learning. The new governance approach is an important democratic alternative for sustaining public solidarity and participation in the community, using the politics of deliberative democracy. Some common ground needs to be articulated that genuinely merges public deliberation into representative democracy, governance along with governing, with each being challenged to transcend itself in a way to build a strong democratic community. A helpful starting point might be the concept of building self-governing communities with networks of social interactions and participation. Participatory politics in local governance can bring people out of isolation and into community, as well as create the context for enhancing individual autonomy and citizenship. This is the challenge to local governance as we enter a new millennium.

NOTE

1. I am greatly indebted to Karl Porter, a manager of the NAPA County Department of Health and Human Services, for providing the source material for the first case, and Paul Golden, a consultant, for the second case. They hold an MPA degree from California State University, Hayward.

REFERENCES

Barber, B. R. 1984. *Strong Democracy: Participatory Politics for a New Age.* Berkeley, CA: University of California Press.
———. 1999. Clansmen, consumers, and citizens: Three takes on civil society. *Civil society, Democracy, and Civic Renewal,* edited by R. K. Fullinwider. Oxford: Rowman & Littlefield Publishers.

Beck, U. 1994. The reinvention of politics: Towards a theory of reflexive modernization. *Reflexive Modernization: Politics, Tradition and Aesthetics in the Modern Social Order,* edited by U. Beck, A. Giddens, and S. Lash. Stanford, CA.: Stanford University Press. 1-55.

Bellah, R., R. Madsen, W. Sullivan, A. Swidler, and S. M. Tipton. 1985. *Habits of the Heart.* Berkeley, CA: The University of California Press.

Bohman, J. 1996. *Public Deliberation: Pluralism, Complexity, and Democracy.* Cambridge, MA: The MIT Press.

Bohman, J. and W. Rehg, eds. 1997. *Deliberative Democracy.* Cambridge, MA: The MIT Press.

Box, R. C. 1998. *Citizen Governance: Leading American Communities into the 21st Century.* Thousand Oaks, CA: Sage Publications.

Buber, M. 1958. *I and Thou,* translated by R.G. Smith. New York: Scribner.

Clarke, S. E. and G. L. Gaile. 1998. *The Work of Cities.* Minneapolis, MN: University of Minnesota Press.

Coleman, J. 1990. *Foundations of Social Theory.* Cambridge, MA: Belknap.

Dagger, R. 1997. *Civic Virtues: Rights, Citizenship, and Republican Liberalism.* Oxford: Oxford University Press.

Elster, J., ed. 1998. *Deliberative Democracy.* Cambridge, U.K.: Cambridge University Press.

Ehrenberg, J. 1999. *Civil Society: The Critical History of an Idea.* New York: The New York University Press.

Etzioni, A. 1993. *The Spirit of Community: Rights, Responsibilities, and the Communitarian Agenda.* New York: Crown Publishers.

———. 1995. *New Communication Thinking: Persons, Virtues, Institutions and Communities.* Charlottesville, VA: University Press of Virginia.

———. 1996. *The New Golden Rule: Community and Morality in a Democratic Society.* New York: Basic Books.

Forester, J. 1999. *The Deliberative Practitioner: Encouraging Participatory Planning Processes.* Cambridge, MA: MIT Press.

Fukuyama, F. 1995. *Trust: The Social Virtues and the Creation of Prosperity.* New York: Free Press.

Galston, W. 1991. *Liberal Purposes: Goods, Virtues, and Duties in the Liberal State.* Cambridge: Cambridge University Press.

Gross, R. and P. Osterman, eds. 1971. *Individualism: Man in Modern Society.* New York: Dell Publishing.

Gutmann, A. and D. Thompson. 1996. *Democracy and Disagreement.* Cambridge, MA: Harvard University Press.

Habermas, J. 1984. *The Theory of Communicative Action: Reason and the Rationalization of Society.* Vol. I. Boston: Beacon Press.

———. 1990. *Moral Consciousness and Communicative Action,* translated by C. Lenhardt and S. W. Nicholsen. Cambridge, MA: MIT Press.

———. 1996. *Between Facts and Norms: Contributions to a Discourse Theory of Law and Democracy,* translated by W. Rehg. Cambridge, MA: MIT Press.

Janoski, T. 1998. *Citizenship and Civil Society.* Cambridge, U.K.: Cambridge University Press.

Jun, J. S. 1999. The need for autonomy and virtues: Civic-minded administrators in a civil society. *Administrative Theory and Praxis.* 21(2):218-223.

Kass, H., ed. 1999. Community capacity, social trust and public administration. *Administrative Theory and Praxis.* 21(1):10-119.

Keane, J. 1998. *Civil Society: Old Images, New Visions.* Stanford, CA: Stanford University Press.

King, C. and C. Stivers. 1998. *Government Is Us.* Thousand Oaks, CA: Sage Publications.

Kooiman, J., ed. 1993. *Modern Governance: New Government-Society Interactions.* Thousand Oaks, CA: Sage.

Korten, D. 1990. *Getting to the 21st Century: Voluntary Action and the Global Agenda.* West Harford, CT: Kumarian.

Kymlicka, W. 1995. *Multicultural Citizenship.* Oxford: Oxford University Press.

March, J. G. and J. P. Olsen. 1995. *Democratic Governance.* New York: The Free Press.

MacIntyre, A. 1984. *After Virtue: A Study in Moral Theory.* 2nd ed.. Notre Dame, IN: Notre Dame University Press.

Macedo, S., ed. 1999. *Deliberative Politics: Essays on Democracy and Disagreement.* Oxford: Oxford University Press.

Merleau-Ponty, M. 1973. *Adventures of the Dialectic.* Evanston, IL: Northwestern University Press.

Norris, P., ed. 1999. *Critical Citizens: Global Support for Democratic Governance.* Oxford: Oxford University Press.

O'Connell, B. 1999. *Civil Society: The Underpinnings of American Democracy.* Hanover, NH: Tufts University Press.

Ostrom, E. 1993. *Social Capital and Development Projects.* Prepared for social capital and economic development, American Academy of Arts and Sciences. Cambridge, MA. 30-31 July.

Panitch, L. 1996. Rethinking the role of the state. *Globalization: Critical Reflections,* edited by J. H. Mittelman. London: Lynne Rienner.

Peters, B. G. 1996. *The Future of Governing: Four Emerging Models.* Lawrence, KS: The University Press of Kansas.

Pirages, D.C., ed. 1996. *Building Sustainable Societies: A Blueprint for a Post-Industrial World.* New York: M. E. Sharp.

Putnam, R. 1993. *Making Democracy Work: Civic Traditions in Modern Italy.* Princeton, NJ: Princeton University Press.

———. 1995. Bowling alone: America's declining social capital. *Journal of Democracy.* 6(1):65-78.

Rawls, J. 1996. *Political Liberalism.* New York: Columbia University Press.

Reich, C. 1970. *The Greening of America.* New York: Random House.

Rhodes, R. A. W. 1997. *Understanding Governance.* Buckingham, U.K.: Open University Press.

Rosenau, J. N. 1992. Governance, order, and change in world politics. *Governance Without Government: Order and Change in World Politics,* edited by J. N. Rosenau and E. Czempiel. Cambridge, U.K.: Cambridge University Press. 1-29.

Sandel, M. 1996. *Democracy's Discontent.* Cambridge, MA: Harvard University Press.

Seligman, A. B. 1992. *The Idea of Civil Society.* New York: The Free Press

Shuman, M. H. 1998. *Going Local: Creating Self-Reliant Communities in a Global Age.* New York: The Free Press.

Schutz, A. 1967. *The Phenomenology of the Social World,* translated by G. Walsh. Evanston, IL: Northwestern University Press.

Stead, W. E. and J. G. Stead. 1992. *Management for a Small Planet: Strategic Decision Making and the Environment.* Newbury Park, CA: Sage.

Taylor, C. 1989. *Sources of the Self.* Cambridge, MA: Harvard University Press.

Walzer, M. 1983. *Spheres of Justice: A Defense of Pluralism and Equality.* New York: Basic Books.

Weisboard, M. R. and S. Janoff. 1995. *Future Search: An Action Guide to Finding Common Ground in Organizations and Communities.* San Francisco: Berrett-Koehler Publishers.

Wilson, D., ed. 1997. Globalization and the changing U.S. City. *The Annals of the American Academy of Political and Social Science.* Vol. 551.

Winter, G. 1971. *Elements for a Social Ethic.* New York: Macmillan.

Index

About the Editor and Contributors

Peter Bogason, has a Ph.D. in political science from the University of Copenhagen and is a professor in public administration at Roskilde University, Denmark. Until 1991, he taught at the Department of Political Science, University of Copenhagen, 1990-91 as head of the department. He is a deputy editor of the journal of Public Administration (Oxford). He has published nationally and internationally within the realm of public policy and public administration. A recently edited book is *New Modes of Local Political Organizing: Local Government Fragmentation in Scandinavia* (1996). His next book is *Public Policy and Local Governance: Institutions in Postmodern Society*, scheduled for publication in July 2000.

Francesco P. Cerase is professor of sociology at the University of Naples Federico II (Italy). His present primary research interests concern organizational analysis in public administration. His most recent publications on this subject include: *Pubblica amministrazione. Un'analisi sociologica* (1998) and *La nuova dirigenza pubblica* (ed.) (1999).

Thomas Clarke was awarded his doctorate from the University of Warwick Business School, UK and is Professor of Management at the University of Technology, Sydney. He was previously DBM Professor of Corporate Governance at the Leeds Business School, UK, and Visiting Professor at the China Europe International Business School, Shanghai; FGV Business School, Sao Paulo, Brazil and UAM Business School, Mexico City. He has published five books, including *Rethinking the Company* (1994), which has been translated into five languages, and with Stewart Clegg *Changing Paradigms: The Transformation of Management Knowledge for the 21st Century* (1998), which examines the transformation of business enterprises in the new global competitive environment and the sources of sustainable business.

Stewart Clegg is Professor of Management at the University of Technology, Sydney. He has worked at leading Business Schools around the world, including Honk Kong University Business School, and St Andrews University in Scotland. He has published over 20 books and two hundred research articles in international academic and professional journals. With Cynthia Hardy and Walter Nord he edited *The Handbook of Organization Studies* (1997), which won the George R. Terry award for the best business book of the American Academy of Management. With Thomas Clarke he wrote *Changing Paradigms: The Transformation of Management Knowledge* which was nominated for the best management consultancy book of the UK management consultants association.

Michael A. Diamond is the Stephen Furbacher Professor of Organizational Change and Director of the Center for the Study of Organizational Change at the University of Missouri-Columbia. He is also professor of public affairs in the new Graduate School of Public Affairs at the University of Missouri-Columbia, where he writes, teaches, and consults on organizational analysis and change. He is author of *The Unconscious Life of Organizations* (1993) and co-author of *The Human Costs of a Management Failure* (1996) and *Managing People During Stressful Times* (1997), Quorum Books, Greenwood Publishing. He has published widely in scholarly journals and was co-editor-in-chief of the *American Review of Public Administration* from 1987-to-1995. He earned his doctoral degree in 1981 from the University of Maryland at College Park. In 1994 he was awarded the Harry Levinson Award for Excellence in Consulting Psychology from the American Psychological Association and in 1999 he was awarded the prestigious William T. Kemper Award for Teaching Excellence from the University of Missouri-Columbia.

David John Farmer is Professor of Political Science and Public Administration at Virginia Commonwealth University. His experience includes employment by the U.S. Government and the City of New York. His publications include "The Language of Public Administration: Bureaucracy, Modernity, and Postmodernity" and, as editor, "Papers on the Art of Anti-Administration." He has a Ph.D. in Economics (University of London) and a Ph.D. in Philosophy (University of Virginia).

John Forester is Professor and Department Chair of City and Regional Planning at Cornell University. A long standing member of the Public Administration Theory Network, his interests include the politics and ethics of planning and administrative practice, the negotiation and mediation of public disputes, and the collection of oral historical materials presenting "profiles" of planning and administrative practitioners. He has recently published *The Deliberative Practitioner* (1999). His best known work is *Planning in the Face of Power* (1989)

Yiannis Gabriel is Reader in Organizational Studies, School of Management, University of Bath. He has a degree in Mechanical Engineering from Imperial College London, where he also carried out post-graduate studies in industrial sociology. He has a Ph.D. in Sociology from the University of California, Berkeley. His main research interests are in organizational and psychoanalytic theories, consumer studies, labor process, organizational symbolism and culture. Dr Gabriel is author of *Freud and Society, Working Lives in Catering* and *Organizations in Depth*, co-author of *Organizing and Organizations*, *The Unmanageable Consumer: Contemporary Consumption and Its Fragmentation and Experiencing Organizations*. His book, *Storytelling in Organizations,* will be published in February 2000. Other publications include recent articles on computer folklore, organizational nostalgia, chaos and complexity in organizations, fantasies of organizational members about their leaders, organizational insults and research methodology using stories and narratives. He is Joint Editor of *Management Learning*.

Louis C. Gawthrop is currently an Eminent Scholar and Professor of Government and Public Administration at the University of Baltimore. He was the 1998 recipient of the American Political Science Association's John Gaus award for a lifetime of exemplary scholarship in the tradition of political science and public administration. He has contributed to numerous volumes on public administration and has written numerous articles on ethics and the administrative implementation of public policy. He is the author of five books. He was editor-in-chief of *Public Administration Review* from 1978 to 1984.

M. Shamsul Haque is with the Department of Political Science, National University of Singapore. His recent articles have appeared in journals such as *Administration & Society, Governance, International Political Science Review, International Review of Administrative Sciences, Peace & Change, Administrative Theory & Praxis,* and *Journal of Political and Military Sociology.* He is the author of *Restructuring Development Theories and Policies: A Critical Study* (1999).

Ralph Hummel is best known in public administration for his *The Bureaucratic Experience*, still in print in its fourth edition at the turn toward the twenty-first century. He is working on a philosophy of work and management in the Department of Public Administration and Urban Studies at The University of Akron and at the Institute of Applied Phenomenology, Spruce Head Island, Maine.

Alan Jarman is a Senior Lecturer in Management in the School of Administrative Studies, Faculty of Management, University of Canberra, Australia. He was educated in Industrial Engineering, Economics and Politics and did his doctoral work in Administration. Prior to the University of Canberra he taught at the University of Queensland and, on secondment, at the University of South Pacific. At the

University of Canberra (1974–1991) he was the former Academic Director (1979–1983) of the Australian Center for Local Government Studies. He has advised, consulted and researched policy issues dealing with regional economic planning; high technology location; financial and strategic planning and satellite-based technological development. More recently, he has published widely on crisis management issues. He has been a visitor to the University College, London; University of California (Berkeley) and (Irvine); Yale University and the Brookings Institution.

Jong S. Jun is professor of public administration at California State University, Hayward. He was editor of *Administrative Theory and Praxis* and coordinator of the Public Administration Theory Network between 1993 and 1999. He has published books and articles on a wide range of topics, such as people-oriented development, democratic governance and civil society, globalization, critique of administrative reform, reflexive understanding, social design in public problem solving, the public good, and philosophy of administration. He has served on the editorial boards of a number of journals. He received his Ph.D. from University of Southern California.

Alexander Kouzmin holds the Foundation Chair in Management in the Graduate School of Management at the University of Western Sydney, Nepean, Australia. His research interests include organizational design, technological change, project management, comparative management, administrative reform, and crisis management. He has published eight volumes of commissioned work. Among these are his edited *Public Sector Administration: Newer Perspectives* (1983); his co-edited (with N. Scott) *Dynamics in Australian Public Management: Selected Essays* (1990); (with L. Still and P. Clarke) *New Directions in Management* (1994); (with J. Garnett) *Handbook of Administrative Communication* (1997); and (with A. Hayne) *Essays in Economic Globalization, Transnational Policies and Vulnerability* (1999). He has contributed articles to many national and international volumes and has published some 160 papers, including scholarly and review articles in more than 45 leading international refereed journals.

O.C. McSwite is the pseudonym of Orion F. White, Professor of Public Administration at the Center for Public Administration and Policy at Virginia Polytechnic Institute and State University, and Cynthia McSwain, Professor of Public Administration at the George Washington University. They have published widely on the topics of organization development and change, the application of psychological theory to public administration, and the connection of public administration to broader issues of social process. Their recent book includes *Legitimacy in Public Administration: A Discourse Analysis*.

Martin Parker is Reader in social and organizational theory at the University of Keele. He holds degrees in anthropology and sociology from the Universities of

Sussex, London and Staffordshire and previously taught sociology at Staffordshire. His writing is usually concerned with organizational theory and the sociology of culture. His most recent books are *Ethics and Organization* (1998), *The New Higher Education* (with David Jary, 1998) and *Organizational Culture and Identity* (1999).

David H. Rosenbloom is Distinguished Professor of Public Administration at American University in Washington, DC. He is the 1999 recipient of the American Society for Public Administration's Dwight Waldo Award for distinguished contributions to the professional literature of public administration. Rosenbloom writes extensively on public administration and democratic constitutionalism.

Curtis Ventriss is a Professor of Political Science and Natural Resources Policy at the University of Vermont. He was the former Associate Editor of *Public Administration Review* and has taught at Johns Hopkins University and Oxford University. He has published numerous articles in public administration journals.

Hendrik Wagenaar is associate professor of public administration, Leiden University, the Netherlands, with a specialization in public policy. He received a Ph.D. in Urban Studies from the Massachusetts Institute of Technology in 1987. Publishes on practice and discourse in public administration, and on the unintended consequences of public policy. In preparation: *Administrative Practice: Practice and Narrative in Public Administration* (monograph; working title), to be published in 2000.

Hugh Willmott is Professor of Organizational Analysis in the Manchester School of Management. He is currently working on a number of projects whose common theme is the changing organization and management of work, including projects in the Economic and Social Research Council Virtual Society and Future of Work programs and an Institute of Chartered Accountants in England and Wales funded study of strategic reorientation. His most recent books are *Critical Management Studies* (1992, co-edited), *Making Quality Critical* (1995, co-edited), *Managing Change, Changing Managers* (1995, co-authored), *Making Sense of Management: A Critical Introduction* (1996, co-authored) and *Management Lives* (1999, co-authored). *The Re-engineering Revolution* (co-edited), *The Body and Organizations* (Sage, co-edited) and *Managing Knowledge; Critical Investigations of Work and Learning* (co-edited) are due to appear in 2000. He has served on the editorial boards of a number of journals including *Administrative Science Quarterly*, *Organization, Organization Studies* and *Accounting, Organizations and Society*.

Dvora Yanow is professor in the Department of Public Administration at California State University, Hayward. She received her Ph.D. in Planning, Policy and Organizational Studies from the Massachusetts Institute of Technology's Department of Urban Studies and Planning. Her research interests focus on interpretive analyses of organizations, including organizational learning, and of public policies, including race-ethnic related ones. Her teaching areas include organizational studies, public policy studies, philosophy of social science, and interpretive research methods. Her articles appear in several journals, among them *Administration & Society*, *Policy Sciences*, *Policy Studies Journal*, *Organization Science*, the *Journal of Management Inquiry*, *Journal of Architectural and Planning Research*, and public administration journals. She has published two books and is completing a manuscript on race-ethnicity in policy and administrative practices.